D1878939

Right to Education in India

Right to Education in India

Vol. I

History Since 1813

Dr Ajit Mondal
Dr Jayanta Mete

GYAN

ISBN : 978-81-212-1336-3

Price : ₹ 2000 (set of 2 Vols)
₹ 990 (Vol–I)

First Published, 2016

Published by

Gyan Publishing House
5, Ansari Road
Daryaganj, New Delhi-110002
Phones: 9811692060
E-mail: books@gyanbooks.com

Printed at: G. Print Process, Delhi.

Cataloging in Publication Data—DK
Courtesy: D.K. Agencies (P) Ltd. <docinfo@dkagencies.com>

Mondal, Ajit, author.
Right to education in India / Dr Ajit Mondal, Dr Jayanta Mete.
volumes cm
Includes bibliographical references.
Contents: vol. I. History since 1813 — vol. II. Act, 2009.
ISBN 9788121213363 (v. 1)
ISBN 9788121213370 (v. 2)

1. Right to education—India—History. 2. Educational law and legislation—India. 3. India. Right of Children to Free and Compulsory Education Act, 2009. I. Mete, Jayanta, author. II. Title.

KNS1610.M66 2016 DDC 344.54079 23

Contents

Foreword

Education is globally recognised as a fundamental human right, and considered as the bed-rock of all socio-economic development of the nation. Just as food, clothing and shelter are basic necessities for survival, education is equally essential for self-sustenance and growth. It is also an established fact that basic education improves the level of human well-being especially, with regard to life expectancy, infant mortality and nutritional status of children. Education is the fundamental requirement not only for the individual but also for the success of democratic system of government. But sadly, education especially elementary education has remained inaccessible to many and education system at this level is being run in many places all over India like factories where the primary intention of owners is self-interest and profiteering. The failure of the Indian state more than six decades after independence to provide free and compulsory quality education to all children irrespective of all caste, creed, colour and other social discriminations must surely rank among the most dismal and significant failures of the development project in the country. After a continual demand of making the education a fundamental right from all corners, the government made the 86th Amendment of the Constitution of India (2002). This Amendment Act has added a new Article 21-A after Article 21 which makes the right of education of children for the age group of 6-14 years as Fundamental Right. The Right to Education commonly known as RTE (the Right to Free and Compulsory Education Act, 2009) was finally passed by the Parliament on 26th August 2009. This Act came in force with effect from the 1st April, 2010. It is now a matter of satisfaction that RTE is the first legislation in the world that puts the responsibility of enrollment, attendance and competition of education on the government.

The Present book – '*Right to Education in India History since 1813*' has analysed the chequered history of right to education legislation in India as a fundamental right. The book can also be of value for all the stakeholders of education by offering opportunity to delve into the history of the enactment of the RTE Act. I convey my thanks to Dr Ajit Mondal and Dr Jayanta Mete for writing a documentary history on the Right to Education in Indian History since, 1813 context.

Professor (Dr) Mita Banerjee
Vice-Chancellor
The West Bengal University of Teachers' Training, Education Planning and Administration
Kolkata, West Bengal

Preface

"Our progress as a nation can be no swifter than our progress in education. The human mind is our fundamental resource."

– John F. Kennedy

Justice B. P. Jeevan Reddy, chairman of the Law Commission of India at the outset of the 265th Report on "Free and Compulsory Education for Children", 1998 stated magnificently the necessity of education in human life. According to him, "Education is essential for all." This is fundamental to our all-round development material as well as spiritual. Education is quintessential for economic, social and human development. It also leads to better healthcare, smaller family norms, greater community and political participation, less income inequality and a greater reduction of absolute poverty. The importance of education in nation building is not a new concern. Post-independence, the Kothari Commission, 1964-66 perceptively highlighted the crucial importance of education in shaping the future of our country. It acknowledged education as a "powerful instrument of social, economic and political change" (Chapter 1, Para 1.04). Thus, there can be no doubt that it is education that will determine our nation's future.

Education is globally recognised as a fundamental human right, and people with access to education can develop the skills, capacity and confidence to secure other rights. The right to education thus acts as an enabling right that functions as the voice through which rights can be claimed and protected. It is therefore considered as the bed-rock of all socio-economic development of the nation. Education is a basic human right and has been recognised since the adaptation of the Universal Declaration of Human Rights (1948, UNO). The Article 26 of the UDHR states that "everyone has the right to education".

Since then numerous international treaties have reaffirmed this right and have supported entitlement to free, compulsory and universal elementary education for all children, irrespective of caste, creed, colour, gender, religion and all other social stratifications across the globe.

Universalisation of elementary education has been one of the most important goals of educational development in India since independence. Universalisation of elementary education in India involves three conditions i.e. Universalisation of Provision, Universalisation of Enrollment and Universalisation of Retention. As per MHRD (2000), Universalisation of elementary education means "100 per cent enrollment and retention of children with schooling facilities in all habitations". India's commitment to universal elementary education dates backs to 1950.

The Right to Education legislation in India has seen a chequered history in evolving from a directive principle to a fundamental right. Attempts to make the right to free and compulsory education available to the Indian child began a little more than a century ago. The Act has its long history and starts from pre-constitutional era. Attempts to make the right to free and compulsory education available to the Indian child began a little more than a century ago. When in the years 1870, 1876 and 1880 Compulsory Education acts were passed in Britain, a demand was raised in India to provide similar facilities in its colonies. From this time onwards began the struggle for making elementary as a right of all children in India and as a duty on the state. After Independence, the national and international policy in general and the Directive Principles of the Indian Constitution in particular bound to provide free and compulsory elementary education to all the children. But despite the constitutional and international commitments, the number of out of school children, particularly from the disadvantaged groups and those engaged in labour, and those receiving poor quality education has continued to remain very large. Even in such a situation it took more six decades for the Indian state to frame and implement the Right to Education Act, 2009 so that the mandate of the Constitution could become an enforceable right. The RTE Act and its notification are rightly hailed by many as a landmark in the history of education in post-independence India. Had the directive principle been implemented in letter and spirit, the need for the 86th Amendment and the RTE Act would not have arisen. The RTE Act is the first Central Act in the domain of elementary education in post-independence India.

The role of Universal Elementary Education (UEE) for strengthening the social fabric of democracy through provision of equal opportunities to all has been accepted since the inception of our Republic. The original Article 45 in the Directive Principles of State Policy in the Constitution mandated the State to endeavour to provide free and compulsory education to all children up to age fourteen in a period of ten years. The National Policy on Education (NPE), 1986 / 92, states "*In our national perception, education is essentially for all. Education has an acculturating role. It refines sensitivities and perceptions that contribute to national cohesion, a scientific temper and independence of mind and spirit – thus furthering the goals of socialism, secularism and democracy enshrined in our Constitution*".

With the formulation of NPE, India initiated a wide range of programmes for achieving the goal of UEE. These efforts were intensified in the 1980s and 1990s through several schematic and programme interventions, such as Operation Black Board (OBB), Shiksha Karmi Project (SKP), Andhra Pradesh Primary Education Project (APPEP), Bihar Education Project (BEP), U.P. Basic Education Project (UPBEP), Mahila Samakhya (MS), Lok Jumbish Project (UP), and Teacher Education which put in place a decentralised system of teacher support through District Institutes of Education and Training (DIET), District Primary Education Programme (DPEP). Currently, the Sarva Shiksha Abhiyan (SSA) is implemented as a Centrally Sponsored Scheme in partnership with State Governments for universalising elementary education across the country.

Over the years there has been significant spatial and numerical expansion of elementary schools in the country. Access and enrollment at the primary stage of education have reached near universal levels. The number of out-of-school children has reduced significantly. The gender gap in elementary education has narrowed and the percentage of children belonging to scheduled castes and tribes enrolled is proportionate to their population. However, quality of learning achievement is not always entirely satisfactory even in the case of children who complete elementary education.

The Constitution (Eighty-sixth Amendment) Act, 2002 inserted Article 21-A in the Constitution of India to provide free and compulsory education of all children in the age group of six to fourteen years as a Fundamental Right in such a manner as the State may, by law, determine. The Right of Children to Free and Compulsory Education (RTE) Act, 2009, which represents the consequential legislation envisaged under Article 21-A, means that every child has a right to full time elementary education of satisfactory and equitable quality in a formal school which satisfies certain essential norms and standards. The need to address inadequacies in retention, residual access, particularly of un-reached children, and the questions of quality are the most compelling reasons for the insertion of Article 21-A in the Constitution of India and the passage of the RTE Act, 2009 in the Parliament. Article 21-A and the RTE Act came into effect on 1 April 2010. The new law provides a justifiable legal framework that entitles all children between the ages of 6–14 years free and compulsory admission, attendance and completion of elementary education. It provides for children's right to an education of equitable quality, based on principles of equity and non-discrimination. Most importantly, it provides for children's right to an education that is free from fear, stress and anxiety. SSA has been operational since 2000–2001. With the passage of the RTE Act, changes need to be incorporated into the SSA approach, strategies and norms. With the recommendation of the Committee on Implementation of RTE Act and the Resultant Revamp of SSA (2010) under the chairperson of Sri Anil Bordia, former Union Education Secretary, the SSA's Framework of implementation has been revised and its norms have been modified to align them with the requirement of RTE Act, 2009. Now let us discuss about the long up-hill journey from 1813 to 2009 of the RTE Act, 2009 and the problems of its effective implementation in detail.

In the wake of the growing awareness about the invaluable right, the authors have made a humble endeavour to explore the journey of right to education from the pre-Constitutional era to the enactment of the RTE Act, 2009. It is necessary to analyse the major events at constitutional level and at policy level after post-independence leading to the 86th Constitution Amendment Act, 2002 to make free and compulsory elementary education a Fundamental Right in India in order to understand some of the problems that one can encounter in attempting to provide education for all children. In this Book the educational policies during the British Period; and the programmes taken after the independence to achieve the goal of UEE have also been critically analysed for building a sound background for the present Book.

It is expected that this book will be able to enlighten all types of stakeholders of education about RTE Act, 2009. The present book is designed to serve a reference book under the ambit of RTE Act, 2009. We express our deep gratitude and indebtedness to Professor Vinod Raina, Professor Anil Sadgopal, Professor Nalini Juneja, Professor R. Gobinda and Professor Arun C. Meheta whose valuable articles on RTE Act, 2009 have helped us in incorporating some chapters in this book. Reports and publications from West Bengal Board of Secondary Education, (Sarvasiksha Abhiyan Cell), UNICEF-India, ASER, MHRD, NUEPA, NCERT, NCTE, Bharat Gyan Vigyan Samiti (BGVS), NCPCR have also helped us with invaluable information on the RTE Act. We shall feel rewarded if our dear stakeholders of education find this helpful. We seek any suggestion from all corners for improving the book in future.

Kalyani, West Bengal **Dr Ajit Mondal and Dr Jayanta Mete**
2016

Abbreviations

ABL	: Activity Based Learning
AIE	: Alternative and Innovative Education
BAS	: Baseline Achievement Survey
BE	: Budget Estimate
BPL	: Below Poverty Line
BRC	: Block Resource Centre
BTEC	: Basic Teacher Education Centre
CABE	Central Advisory Board of Education
CBGA	: Centre for Budget and Governance Accountability
CRC	: Cluster Resource Centre
CTE	: College of Teacher Education
CWSN	: Children with Special Needs
DIET	: District Institute of Education and Training
DISE	: District Information System for Education
DPEP	: District Primary Education Programme
EBB	: Educationally Backward Block
ECCE	: Early Childhood Care and Education
ECE	: Early Childhood Education
EDI	: Educational Development Index
EFA	: Education for All
EGS	: Education Guarantee Scheme
GDP	: Gross Domestic Product
GOI	: Government of India
GP	: Gram Panchayat
IASE	: Institute of Advanced Studies in Education

ICDS	: Integrated Child Development Services
KGBV	: Kasturba Gandhi Balika Vidyalaya
KV	: Kendriya Vidyalaya
LJP	: Lok Jumbish Project
MDM	: Mid-day Meal
MGNREGA	: Mahatma Gandhi National Rural Employment Guarantee Act
MHRD	: Ministry of Human Resource Development
MLL	: Minimum Levels of Learning
MS	: Mahila Samakhya
MTA	: Mother Teacher Association
NCE	: National Commission of Education
NCERT	: National Council of Educational Research and Training
NCF	: National Curriculum Framework
NCPCR	: National Commission for Protection of Child Rights
NCTE	: National Council of Teacher Education
NDC	: National Development Council
NFHS	: National Family Health Survey
NGO	: Non-Government Organisation
NIEPA	: National Institute of Educational Planning and Administration
NLM	: National Literacy Mission
NPE	: National Policy on Education
NPEGEL	: National Programme for Education of Girls at Elementary Level
NRHM	: National Rural Health Mission
NUEPA	: National University of Educational Planning and Administration
OBB	: Operation Black Board
OBC	: Other Backward Community
POA	: Programme of Action
PRI	: Panchayati Raj Institution

PROBE	: Public Report on Basic Education
PTA	: Parent Teacher Association
RE	: Revised Estimate
REPA	: Right to Education Protection Authority
RTE	: Right to Education
SC	: Scheduled Caste
SCERT	: State Council of Educational Research and Training
SCPCR	: State Commission for Protect of Children Rights
SES	: Selected Educational Statistics
SIEMAT	: State Institute of Educational Management and Training
SKP	: Shiksha Karmi Project
SMC	: School Management Committee
SRC	: State Resource Centre
SSA	: Sarva Shiksha Abhiyan
ST	: Scheduled Tribe
TET	: Teacher Eligibility Test
TLM	: Teaching Learning Material
UEE	: Universalisation of Elementary Education
UN	: United Nations
UNDP	: United Nations Development Programme
UNESCO	: United Nations Education Scientific and Cultural Organisation
UNICEF	: United Nations International Children's Emergency Fund
URC	: Urban Resource Centre
UT	: Union Territory
VEC	: Village Education Committee

Chapter - 1

Introduction to the Concept of the Key Words

Education is the most important and powerful instrument to shape and mould the individual and society in a desirable manner. The history of the world proves that education has been at the base for any change encompassing the social, cultural, spiritual, political and economic aspects of human life. In fact, education has become one of the basic necessities of human life like food, clothing and shelter. Today, life is education and education is life. Hence, no differentiation can be made between life and education and the Right to Education, therefore, is looked upon as Right to Life. Thus, the Right to Education which is characterised as a Fundamental Right can also be considered as the 'Right of Higher Order' that it determines whether other rights can actually be exercised or not. None of our civil, political, economic and social rights can be exercised unless they receive a certain minimum education, without which their access to such right will remain illusory and theoretical. No one will deny that education is the basis for development and an important instrument to combat all forms of discrimination with regard to women, minorities, other deprived sections and children. It provides valuable developmental opportunities to children. That is why the Right to Education is high on the agenda of the international community. It is also affirmed in numerous human rights treatise, recognised by governments as a pivotal instrument in the pursuit of development and social transformation.

The Indian education system is the second largest in the world and is perhaps the most complex in terms of its spatial outreach and profile of students and teachers in terms of their linguistic, social, cultural and economic background. Education is one of the fundamental necessities of man. It is also one of the essential instruments for satisfying other needs. Especially, elementary education is the most crucial stage of education as it is the foundation of a child's formal education and plays a pivotal role in personal, social and national development. The basic skills of reading, writing and arithmetic are acquired at this stage. It also lays foundation for the personality, attitude, learning skills and communicative capabilities of pupils. In any nation, elementary education has been given highest priority and importance because the success of any developmental programme such as economic, social or political, elementary education is the pre-requisite. Education is a basic human right and has been recognised since the adaptation of the Universal Declaration of Human Rights (1948, UNO). The Article 26 of the UDHR states that "everyone has the right to education". Since then numerous international treaties have reaffirmed this right and have supported entitlement to free, compulsory and universal elementary education for all children, irrespective of caste, creed, colour, gender, religion and all other social stratifications across the globe.

Universalisation of elementary education has been one of the most important goals of educational development in India since independence. On 26th January 1950 when Indian Constitution came in force, it had in its Article 45 a directive principle promising free and compulsory education for all children until they complete the age of 14 years. This was to be attained within 10 years. But the state could not do so for next five decades. In order to enforce the Unnikrishnan judgement, several public interest litigation petitions were filed in different High Courts. On the other hand, at global level International conventions like Jomtein Declaration Dakar Declaration and UNCRC have directed to provide free and compulsory education to all children. As a whole, this created tremendous pressure on the parliament for a constitutional amendment to include the right to education as a fundamental right. The Indian State adopted the Eighty Six Amendment Act, 2002 to the Constitution, thereby conferring on education the status of a fundamental right. Through 86th Constitutional Amendment, Article 21-a (part III) was inserted in the fundamental right section of constitution under which, "The State shall provide free and compulsory education to all children of the age of 6 to 14 years in such manner as the state may, by law, determine. On the 27th day of August 2009, Right of Children to Free and Compulsory Education Act 2009 was notified. The path to the most sought 'Right to Education' was an uphill journey. For understanding it in a better way, the present paper tries to analyse the movement discourse on the right to free and compulsory education from directive principle to fundamental right.

Universalisation of elementary education in India involves three conditions i.e. Universalisation of Provision, Universalisation of Enrollment and Universalisation of Retention. As per MHRD (2000), Universalisation of elementary education means "100 per cent enrollment and retention of children with schooling facilities in all habitations". India's commitment to universal elementary education dates backs to 1950. The directive principles of Indian constitution stipulated that the state would endeavour to provide free and compulsory education to all children up to the age of 14. Since then many steps have been taken and different commissions and committees have given suggestions to universalise elementary education. In 2002, the 86th constitutional amendment made education a fundamental right for children in the age group of 6-14 years. The RTE Act came into force on 1st April 2010. The right to education legislation has been chequered history in evolving from directive principle to fundamental right.

Education is the most potent tool for socio-economic mobility and a key instrument for building an equitable and just society. Attempts to make the right to free and compulsory education available to the Indian child began a little more than a century ago. When in the years 1870, 1876 and 1880 Compulsory Education acts were passed in Britain, a demand was raised in India to provide similar facilities in its colonies. From this time onwards began the struggle for making elementary as a right of all children in India and as a duty on the state. After Independence, the national and international policy in general and the Directive Principles of the Indian Constitution in particular bound to provide free and compulsory elementary education to all the children. Even post-constitutional era the movement discourse on the right to free and compulsory education from directive principle to fundamental right has seen a chequered history. But despite the constitutional and international commitments, the Government of India failed to provide free and compulsory education to all children. Had the directive principle been implemented in letter and spirit, the need for the 86th Amendment to the constitution and the RTE Act would not have arisen. It was the first central legislation in the landscape of elementary education in India which was brought in force by a speech by the Prime Minister of India. The present book will make us aware more and more of the movement discourse on right to education in Indian territory from directive principle to fundamental right so that we may evaluate the significance of the 86th Amendment to Indian Constitution. The RTE Act, 2009 encouraged the authors to explore the uphill journey of compulsory education in India since the British rule in order to understand the previous attempts in detail in this direction and to analyse the present Act. The history of development of the Act will function as backdrop for building awareness about the RTE Act, 2009 among the stakeholders of education. This Book will also be effective in raising awareness about India's legislative progress since the Patel Act in 1916 towards ensuring the right of free and compulsory education as a fundamental right. Thus, the historical analysis of UEE with reference to RTE Act, 2009 has been emerged as a subject of study.

A strong consciousness for the need of compulsory Primary Education in India was affected by enactment of the Compulsory Education Act in 1870 in England. A number of Indian leaders began to stress the need for compulsory primary education. Ultimately Universalisation of elementary education has been one of the most important goals of educational development in India since independence. In 1950, the provision of Universal Primary Education was incorporated in the Article 45 of the Constitution of India. The provision of Universalisation of Primary Education was scheduled to be achieved by 1960. But the state could not do so for next five decades. Had the directive principle been implemented in letter and spirit, the need for the 86th Amendment and the RTE Act would not have arisen. On the other hand, education has been formally recognised as a human right since the adoption of the Universal Declaration of Human Rights in 1948. This has since been affirmed in numerous global human rights treaties. The Right of Children to Free and Compulsory Education Act (RTE Act), 2009 came into force from 1st April 2010, pursuant to the 86th Amendment to the Constitution (2002) which guarantees elementary education as a fundamental right and in compliance with the international obligations to fulfilling the constitutional mandate for free and compulsory education.

In the wake of the growing awareness about this invaluable right, the authors have found it necessary to analyse the chequered history of right to education legislation in India in evolving from a directive principle to a fundamental right. The book can also be of value for all the stakeholders of education by offering opportunity to delve into the history of the enactment of the RTE Act. The book is also expected to facilitate the authors to comprehend in what extent the RTE Act is in compliance with the dreams of our national leaders towards universalisation of elementary education in India. Finally, it is hoped that it would be useful for foreign educationists and authors interested in studying the history of universal elementary education in India. The book will also contribute to the building sound awareness among the stakeholders about the first central legislation in the history of elementary education in India. The book will be very helpful in evolving a holistic picture of the history of the development of the free and compulsory Education in India in detail and in evaluating the present Act in the light of previous efforts of 200 years. It hence, was thought worthwhile to undertake the matter for shaping into a book. Before dealing with the key aspects of the book, we should build a comprehensible understanding about the basic concept of some key terms. They have been explained here in Indian context.

Concept of Elementary Education in Indian Context

Elementary education constitutes a very important stage of the entire structure of education. It is at this stage that the formal education of the child starts. It is the foundation of the entire educational ladder. It is universally acknowledged fact that an educated and enlightened citizenry is an essential condition for the successful functioning of democracy. Education, at least up to elementary level, is considered essential for every individual in a democratic country. Elementary education provides the necessary foundation for strengthening human resources because the quality and efficacy of human resources assume special significance for our personal, social and national development. The entire edifice of our national development is based on the availability and quality of Elementary Education. It was with this objective that the framers of our Constitution pledged to provide free and compulsory Elementary Education to each and every child. After becoming independent, India, as a democratic welfare state, announced Universalisation of Elementary Education (UEE) and equal opportunity for all as its basic principle. Universalisation of education refers to any system of education that extends opportunities to concerned population regardless of an extraneous consideration like race, colour, caste, religion, sex and ability. According to Professor Saima Siddiqui "Elementary education constitutes a very important part of entire structure of education system. It is the backbone of the educational pattern of a country. No pattern of education can ever be successful as long as it does not have a sound primary educational system. Elementary education is crucial for spreading mass literacy which is the basic requirement for the effective functioning of democratic institutions, economic development and modernisation of social structure. It also represents an indispensable first step towards the provision of equality of opportunity to all the citizens" (Siddiqui, 2008: 4-5).

Now the authors have cited the statements of the National Policies on Education and Planning Commission of India about it before conclusion. The **National Policy on Education 1986** at the time of pointing out the common educational structure (10+2+3) in terms of the National System of Education, prescribed the further break-up of the first 10 years by moving "towards an elementary system comprising five years of primary education and three years of upper primary, followed by two years of High School" (Para 3.3.). According to the **11th Five Year Plan (2007-2012)**, Elementary education, that is, classes I–VIII consisting of primary (I–V) and upper primary (VI–VIII) is the foundation of the pyramid in the education system (Para 1.1.2).

Hence, Elementary Education in India is defined as the education from Class I to VIII, and roughly covers, children from the age of 6 to 14 years. Elementary education is further divided into two stages: primary and upper primary education. Primary education lasts up to Class V and covers children in the 6-11 age group. Upper primary covers Class VI to VIII, and includes children in the age group of 11-14 years. However, while this is the national picture, there are minor variations in some states. Some have primary schooling upto Class IV only, while a few have upper primary upto Class VII only. Elementary education forms the foundation for all levels of learning and development. It empowers and equips individuals with analytical capabilities, instils and fortifies them with determination to achieve goal-setting competencies.

Universalisation of Elementary Education (UEE)

Universalisation of Elementary Education (UEE) is an educational term refers to make education available to all children in the age of group of 6-14 or in Class I-VII. It means the education for every child to complete the stage of Elementary or Primary Education either formal or non-formal means of education. Here all children covered the children of every community, castes, creed, religions, handicapped, orphans or destitute and disadvantaged groups. It signifies that education is for all and not for a selected few. This concept accepts that education is the birth right of every child. Universalisation of elementary education also means free and compulsory elementary education for all children till they complete 14 years of age. Universalisation of Elementary Education involved the three years stages or steps, which are Universalisation of Provision, Universalisation of Enrollment, and Universalisation of Retention (Sharma, 2013:14).

Universalisation of Elementary Education (UEE) in that country means making education available to all children in the age group of six to fourteen (6 – 14) years or in the Classes (I – VIII) and to provide opportunities for this education through formal and non-formal means of education. It signifies that education is for all and not for a select few. This concept of UEE accepts that education is the birthright of every child irrespective of one's religion, caste, colour, and creed or sex etc. This also means that all children of the country belonging to the rich and poor, living in towns and in rural areas and in places which are accessible with difficulty have to be provided with the facilities of elementary education (Rani, 2012, p. 6).

Universalisation of Elementary Education (UEE) has been accepted as a national goal since 1950. The Directive Principles of the Constitution of India envisage provision of free and compulsory elementary education to all children upto the age of 14 years.

The Constitution was amended in December 2002 to include free and compulsory education for all children in the age group 6 - 14 years as a fundamental right, while expanding the provision for children upto the age of six, to include early childhood care and education within the Directive Principles. The overall goal in this regard is to provide free and compulsory education of satisfactory quality to all children. It is significant to note that the National Policy on Education defines universal elementary education in a broad framework, changing the emphasis from enrollment to participation, retention and achievement (MHRD, 2003, p. 21).

The **Eighth Five Year Plan** envisaged Universalisation of Elementary Education (UEE) to mean Universalising access, universal retention and universal achievement (GoI, 1998:1). The **Tenth Five Year Plan** laid emphasis on Universalisation of Elementary Education (UEE) guided by five parameters: (i) Universal Access, (ii) Universal Enrollment, (iii) Universal Retention, (iv) Universal Achievement, and (v) Equity (Para 1.1.6). According to the Report of the Saikia Committee (1997), the thrust of the Central and State Government in Universalisation of Elementary Education (UEE) has been on three aspects: (i) Universal access and enrollment, (ii) Universal retention and children upto 14 years of age; and (iii) To bring about substantial improvement in the quality of education to enable all children to achieve essential levels of learning. Professor J. S. Rajput (2010) stated that in India the term used for compulsory education for all is Universal Elementary Education (UEE). It fits in the MDG2 (Achieving universal primary education) (p. 112).

Hence, conclusion can be dawn that Universalisation of Elementary Education (UEE) has been a national goal since Independence. The original Article 45 in the Directive Principles of State Policy in the Indian Constitution had mandated the State to endeavour to provide free and compulsory education to all children until they complete the age of fourteen years within a period of ten years from the commencement of the Constitution. The national resolve to achieve universal elementary education gained further momentum with the adoption of the Constitution (Eighty-sixth Amendment) Act, 2002 which inserted Article 21-A in the Constitution of India to provide free and compulsory education for all children in the age group of six to fourteen years as a Fundamental Right in such a manner as the State may, by law, determine. The Constitution (Eighty-sixth Amendment) Act, 2002 also enjoins the State "to provide early childhood care and education to all children until they complete the age of six years". Universalisation of Elementary Education (UEE) in India implies universal access and enrollment, universal retention, bridging gender and social category gaps in primary and upper primary education, and elementary education of satisfactory quality.

Understanding Human Rights

Human rights are rights inherent to all human beings, whatever our nationality, place of residence, sex, national or ethnic origin, colour, religion, language, or any other status. We are all equally entitled to our human rights without discrimination. These rights are all interrelated, interdependent and indivisible (United Nations Human Rights, Retrieved from:http://www.ohchr.org/EN/Issues/Pages/WhatareHumanRights.aspx). Justice Durga Das Basu has defined human rights: "those minimal rights which every individual must have against the state or other public authority by virtue of his being a member of the human family, irrespective of any other consideration…(Basu, 1994:5)." Katerina Tomasevski, former United Nations Special Rapporteur on the Right to Education opined that "a large number of problems cannot be solved unless the right to education is addressed as the key to unlock other human rights. From the human rights' viewpoint, education is an end in itself rather than merely a means for achieving other ends" (Katarina, 2003, pp. 32-33).

So the authors can summarise that human beings are born equal in dignity and rights. These are moral claims which are inalienable and inherent in all individuals by virtue of their humanity alone, irrespective of caste, colour, creed, and place of birth, sex, cultural difference or any other consideration. These claims are articulated and formulated in what is today known as human rights. Education is a fundamental human right and essential for the exercise of all other human rights. It promotes individual freedom and empowerment and yields important development benefits.

Education as a Human Right – Why?

Education is both a human right in itself and a means for realising and promoting other human rights. Education can be defined in a broad sense to imply "the entire process of social life by means of which individuals and social groups learn to develop consciously within, and for the benefit of, the national and international communities, the whole of their personal capacities, attitudes, aptitudes and knowledge" (Hodgson, 1998, p. 3).

Education has been formally recognised as a human right since the adoption of the Universal Declaration of Human Rights in 1948. This has since been affirmed in numerous global human rights treaties, including the United Nations Educational, Scientific and Cultural Organisation (UNESCO) Convention against Discrimination in Education (1960), the International Covenant on Economic, Social and Cultural Rights (1966) and the Convention on the Elimination of All Forms of Discrimination against Women (1981). These treaties establish an entitlement to free, compulsory primary education for all children; an obligation to develop secondary education, supported by measures to render it accessible to all children, as well as equitable access to higher education; and a responsibility to provide basic education for individuals who have not completed primary education. Furthermore, they affirm that the aim of education is to promote personal development, strengthen respect for human rights and freedoms, enable individuals to participate effectively in a free society, and promote understanding, friendship and tolerance. The right to education has long been recognised as encompassing not only access to educational provision, but also the obligation to eliminate discrimination at all levels of the educational system, to set minimum standards and to improve quality. In addition, education is necessary for the fulfilment of any other civil, political, economic or social right. The United Nations Convention on the Rights of the Child (1989) further strengthens and broadens the concept of the right to education; in particular through the obligation to consider in its implementation the Convention's four core principles: non-discrimination; the best interests of the child; the right to life, survival and development of the child to the maximum extent possible; and the right of children to express their views in all matters affecting them and for their views to be given due weight in accordance with their age and maturity. These underlying principles make clear a strong commitment to ensuring that children are recognised as active agents in their own learning and that education is designed to promote and respect their rights and needs. The Convention elaborates an understanding of the right to education in terms of universality, participation, respect and inclusion.

Human rights are rights that are basic in nature and entitled to every human being, irrespective of his nationality, place of residence, sex, national or ethnic origin, colour, religion, language, or any other status. Such rights would include right to life, equality before the law, freedom of expression, the right to work, right to social security, right to education, collective rights, such as the rights to development and self-determination, etc. Therefore, as is evident human rights are inseparable, interrelated and interdependent. The improvement of one right makes the progress of the others possible. Correspondingly, the denial of one right has negating affects on the others. The right to education is marked priority on the agenda of the international community since right to education is not only a human right in itself but also is quintessential for the exercise of all other human rights. A number of human rights treaties accepted and recognised internationally, identifies right to education as a fundamental aspect for development and social transformation.

Human rights are widely recognised and accepted by the international community as ideals to be defended and entitlements to be guaranteed to all people, and by all people. The list of matters which are considered as human rights is broad and keeps growing since human rights are understood as tools for enabling people to live in dignity, equity and freedom (Gupta, 2009, p. 7). All human rights are hierarchically equal and cannot be implemented separately as they are interdependent and affect each other throughout their realisation. There are so many human rights such as civil and political rights, economic, social and cultural rights and community or solidarity rights. The **right to education** is among the listed human rights whose status affects the realisation of all other rights. The right to education however defies classification either as a civil and political right or an economic, social and cultural one. It forms, indeed, all core human rights treaties.

The right to education represents an interface between civil and political rights and economic, social and cultural rights.

There are a large number of human rights problems, which cannot be solved unless the right to education is addressed as the key to unlock other human rights. The right to education is clearly acknowledged in the United Nations' Universal Declaration of Human Rights (UDHR), adopted in 1948, which states:

> "Everyone has the right to education. Education shall be free, at least in the elementary and fundamental stages. Elementary education shall be compulsory. Technical and professional education shall be made generally available and higher education shall be equally accessible to all on the basis of merit. ..." (Article 26)

Apart from UDHR, right to education is affirmed, protected and promoted in numerous international human rights treaties, such as the following:

- Convention concerning Discrimination in Respect of Employment and Occupation (1958) - Article 3.
- Convention against Discrimination in Education (1960).
- International Covenant on Economic, Social and Cultural Rights (1966) - Article 13.
- Convention on the Elimination of All Forms of Discrimination against Women (CEDAW) (1981) –Article 10.
- The United Nations Convention on the Rights of the Child (1989) – Articles 28 and 29.

The right to education has therefore long been recognised by these international treaties as encompassing not only access to educational provision, but also the obligation to eliminate discrimination at all levels of the educational system, to set minimum standards and to improve quality. The prominent organisations around the world striving for promotion of Right to Education are:

- United Nations Educational, Scientific and Cultural Organisation (UNESCO)
- United Nations Children's Fund (UNICEF)

- World Bank
- International Labour Organisation (ILO)

The RTE Act, 2009 is not an imperative for realising rights but it a useful tool, which can assist on the claiming of a right. It is not a determinant of whether or not people have their right to education realised but it can be used as a mobilisation tool to transform rights and policies into reality.

Fundamental Rights and Directive Principles under Indian Constitution

Fundamental Rights are essential human rights that are offered to every citizen irrespective of caste, creed, race, place of birth, religion, gender and other social stratifications. These are equal to freedoms and these rights are essential for personal good and the society at large. The Constitution of India provides for two types of rights: (a) civic and political rights and (b) social and economic rights. Articles 12 to 35 of the Constitution constitute the fundamental rights which are justiciable. Article 32 of the Constitution guarantees remedies for enforcement of civic and political rights. The ninety-third constitutional amendment has transformed education from its status as a social and economic right to that of a civic and political right. Till now only Articles 28, 29 and 30 among the fundamental rights addressed issues in education relating to religion and non-discrimination. Articles 36 to 51 of the Constitution of India constitute the social and economic rights. They fall under directive principles of state policy (Seetharamu, 2002). The Supreme Court in Unnikrishnan's case (AIR 1993 SC 2178) went to the extent of observing that the Directive Principles constitute "Conscience of the Constitution".

Differences between the Fundamental Rights and DPSP: Interpretation of Part III and Part IV of the Constitution by the Supreme Court in number of cases has now crystallised the differences that exist between the Directive Principles of State Policy and the Fundamental Rights. The Directive Principles of State Policy are not enforceable in the Courts and they do not create any justiciable rights in favour of individuals. The Directives require to be implemented by Legislation, but, at the same time no existing Law or Legal Right can be violated under the colour of following a Directive. The Courts can declare any law as void on the ground that it contravenes any of the Fundamental Rights. The Courts are not competent to compel the government to carry out any Directive or to make any law for that purpose. The Directives per se do not confer upon or take away any Legislative Power from the appropriate Legislature. Although it is the duty of the State to implement the Directives, yet the State can do so only subject to the limitation imposed by the Constitution itself i.e., Article 13(2) prohibits the State from making any law which takes away or abridges the Fundamental Rights conferred by Part III and the Directive Principles therefore cannot override this categorical limitation.

The Part IV of the Constitution comprises the Directive Principles of State Policy that are not "enforceable by any court" but are "nevertheless fundamental in the governance of the country" and the State is duty bound to "apply these principles in making laws" (Article 37). In contrast, the Part III comprises Fundamental Rights that are enforceable in the courts. However, underlining the criticality of Part IV, the Supreme Court ruled in its Unnikrishnan Judgment (1993) that whereas the Part IV provides the goals of the Constitution, the Part III provides the means to achieve these goals (Sadgopal, 2010: 48).

The Constitution of India provides for two types of rights: (a) civic and political rights and (b) social and economic rights. Articles 12 to 35 of the Constitution constitute the fundamental rights which are justiciable, Part – II [Right to Equality, Right to Freedom, Right against Exploitation, Right to Freedom of Religion, Right to Constitutional Remedies]. Article 32 of the Constitution guarantees remedies for enforcement of civic and political rights – 32.(1) The right to move the Supreme Court by appropriate proceedings for the enforcement of the rights conferred by this Part is guaranteed. Thus, the 86th Constitutional Amendment Act has transformed education from its status as a social and economic right to that of a civic and political right. Till now only Articles 28, 29 and 30 among the fundamental rights address issues in education relating to religion and non-discrimination. Articles 36 to 51 of the Constitution of India constitute the social and economic rights. They fall under directive principles of state policy. Article 36 – 51 Part – III, Directive Principles of State Policy.

Free Education under the RTE Act

The Constitution (Eighty-sixth Amendment) Act, 2002 inserted Article 21-A in the Constitution of India to provide free and compulsory education of all children in the age group of six to fourteen years as a Fundamental Right in such a manner as the State may, by law, determine. The Right of Children to Free and Compulsory Education (RTE) Act, 2009, which represents the consequential legislation envisaged under Article 21-A, means that every child has a right to full time elementary education of satisfactory and equitable quality in a formal school which satisfies certain essential norms and standards. The RTE Act came into effect on 1 April 2010. The title of the RTE Act incorporates the words 'free and compulsory'. 'Free education' means that no child, other than a child who has been admitted by his or her parents to a school which is not supported by the appropriate government, shall be liable to pay any kind of fee or charges or expenses which may prevent him or her from pursuing and completing elementary education.

Compulsory Education under the RTE Act

The term 'compulsory education' tends to bring forth different meanings and interpretations from different people. Most often, compulsory education is interpreted in terms of mandatory attendance requirements or it is considered as the first stage of education. Even we think that compulsory education is connected with the right to education. That's why, to most of the people compulsory education and right to education mean, more or less, the same. However, there is a slight but important difference. The right to education can be applied to adults. Adult education is not, as a rule, compulsory since adult can choose whether they will take advantage of the facilities provided to them for education or not. On the hand, system in a country forces parents to send their children to school compulsorily.

Compulsory education is also used synonymously and interchangeably with the first stage with formal education and that's why in most of the countries, the years in which education is compulsory are harmonious with the first stage of formal education. Compulsory education refers to the number of years or the age-span during which children and youth are legally obliged to attend school for a specified number of years (EFA 2000 Assessment-Technical Guidelines,

UNESCO 1998). That which must be attended or undertaken by the law of a particular country or state. The legal requirement may be education from a certain starting age to a certain school-leaving age or it may be education to a certain standard (International Dictionary of Education, by G. Terry Page and G. B. Thomas, Kogan Page, London (1997)].

According to Professor Nalini Juneja (2003), the meaning of the term, compulsory education tends to refer to the requirements on the parts of both children and governments in relation to this stage. The requirement implies that the children must attend school and that government must provide these schools.

When compulsory education is perceived as a right the focus shifts to 'self-assertion'. This meaning implies a vehicle for safeguarding a human right for people under age, propagated by liberal and socialist philosophers, politicians and educationists. UNESCO Year Book of Education (1986) viewed compulsory education as a right – "The compulsory nature of education refers not only to the child's obligations to receive it but also the state's obligation to provide" (UNESCO, International Year Book of Education, Vol. XXXVIII, 1986).

However, in the context of the present book, compulsory education refers to what the RTE Act, 2009 mandates. According to the Act, 'Compulsory education' casts an obligation on the appropriate government and local authorities to provide and ensure admission, attendance and completion of elementary education by all children in the 6–14 age groups. It casts a legal obligation on the Central and State Governments to implement this fundamental child right as enshrined in the Article 21A of the Constitution, in accordance with the provisions of the RTE Act.

Epitomising Free and Compulsory Education under the RTE Act

Free and Compulsory Education for Children Bill, 1998 proposed by the Law Commission of India defined compulsory education as: "compulsory education means and implies an obligation on government to take all steps to ensure that every child is enrolled and retained till the prescribed level of education in a school imparting the prescribed courses of study and the steps taken in that behalf" [Sec. 2(g), pp. 87-88].

Law Commission of India, 1998 defines 'free education' means "exemption from the obligation to pay tuition fee or other charges which schools usually collect from pupils in a school. It extends to provision of free supply of text-books, note-books and other study materials and may also include healthcare nutrition where the appropriate government so declares by rules under the Act" [Sec. 2(h), pp. 88]. Right to Education Bill, 2005 defines these terms as - "Compulsory Education" means an obligation on the State to take all necessary steps in terms of this Act to ensure that:

(1) Every child of the age of six years enrols in a school, participates in it, and completes elementary education.

(2) Every child over six years, but less than 14 years, who was not enrolled in a school at the commencement of this Act, is enrolled in a school, participates in it, and completes elementary education [Sec. 2(i)].

According to the Right to Education Bill, 2005, "Free Education" means freedom for the child and her parent/guardian from liability to:

(1) Pay any fee or charges to the school where his child/ ward is studying, or to any other external body providing any service through the school.

(2) Incur such other expenses, as may be prescribed, which are likely to prevent the child from participating in and completing elementary education.

provided that if textbooks and any other teaching learning material are supplied free to a non-disabled child under this clause, they shall be supplied free to a disabled child in such modified form as would meet her learning needs [Sec. 2(o)].

The Right of Children to Free and Compulsory Education Act, 2009 defines 'compulsory education' as obligation of the appropriate government to - (i) provide free elementary education to every child of the age of six to fourteen years; and (ii) Ensure compulsory admission, attendance and completion of elementary education by every child of the age of six to fourteen years [Sec. 8(a)].

The RTE Act, 2009 defines 'free' as "no child shall be liable to pay any kind of fee or charges or expenses which may prevent him or her from pursuing and completing the elementary education" [Sec. 3(2)]. Thus, free and compulsory education implies State's obligation to have all children of 6-14 years and retain in schools up to completion of elementary education.

Organisation and Structure of School Education in India

There are broadly four stages of school education in India, namely, primary, upper primary, secondary and higher secondary. In pursuance of the National Policy on Education of 1968 and 1986, there have been attempts to evolve a uniform pattern of school education with 12 years of schooling, commonly known as 10 + 2 pattern. The 'plus two' stage refers to classes XI and XII, which constitute higher secondary stage in all 35 States/UTs. (In some States, higher secondary stage is part of collegiate education, known as junior colleges.)

However, within the States and the UTs, there remain variations in the number of classes constituting the Primary, Upper Primary, High and Higher Secondary school stages. It may be observed that the structure of primary stage covers Classes I to IV in some States/UTs whereas in the majority of the States/UTs, the primary stage includes Classes I to V. In this context, it may be pointed out that the NPE - 1986, Curriculum for Ten Years Schooling (1975), National Curriculum for Elementary and Secondary Education-1988, National Curriculum Framework for School Education (NCFSE)-2000 and National Curriculum Framework (2005) had recommended primary stage of five years from Classes I to V. The upper primary stage includes Classes VI to VIII/ V to VII in most of States and UTs. Only in Andhra Pradesh Classes VI and VII and in West Bengal Classes V to VIII constitute the upper primary stage. The 1975 Curriculum for Ten Years Schooling, the NPE 1986, the 1988 National Curriculum for Elementary and Secondary Education, and the NCFSE 2000 and NCF 2005 recommended Classes VI to VIII under the upper primary stage of school education (Yadav, 2011 and Babu, 2009).

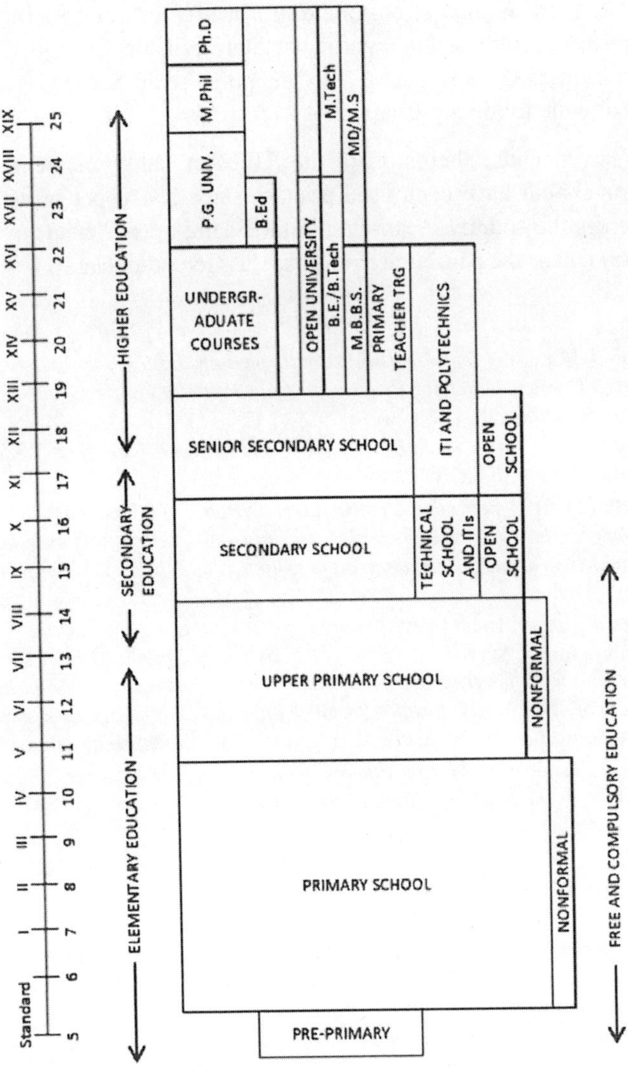

Source: Development of Education: 1986-1988. National Report of India NIEPA, 1988.

Diagram – 1.1: Structure of Education in India.

Within the overall framework of the national policy on education, each State/UT has been independently determining the educational structure to be adopted. This is particularly true of the school stage. However, there is almost complete uniformity in the pattern of educational structure within a particular State or Union Territory. A broad consensus has also emerged for adoption by all States/UTs, as indicated in the following **Diagram – 1.1:**

However, under the ambit of the RTE Act, 2009, elementary education should have comprised primary stage and upper primary stage across the country. According to the Section 2(f), "elementary education means the education from first class to eighth class".

References

- Babu, J. R. (2009). *Universalisation of Elementary Education: A Study of District Primary Education Programme from South India*. UK: Cambridge Scholars Publishing.
- Basu, B. B. (1994). *Human Rights in Constitutional Law.* New Delhi: Prentice Hall of India Pvt. Ltd.
- CABE (2005). *Report of the Central Advisory Board of Education (CABE) Committee on Free and Compulsory Education Bill and Other Issues Related to Elementary Education (Right to Education Bill 2005).* New Delhi: CABE, GOI.
- Government of India (1998). *Report of the Steering Committee for Formulation of Ninth Plan (1997-2002) on Early Childhood Education Elementary Education (Formal) Non-Formal Education Secondary Education Vocational Education Distance Education Adult Education.* New Delhi: Education Division, Planning Commission, Government of India.
- Gupta, S. (2009). *What are the different strategies and approaches to realize Right to Education (RTE) in India?* Sussex: Institute of Development Studies (IDS), University of Sussex.
- Hodgson, Douglas (1998). *The Human Right to Education*. Aldershot: Dart-mouth Publishing Company Limited.
- Juneja, N. (2003). *Constitutional Amendment to make Education a Fundamental Right – Issues for a Follow-Up Legislation*. New Delhi: NIEPA.
- Law Commission of India (1998). *One Hundred Sixty Fifth Report on Free and Compulsory Education for Children*. New Delhi: Law Commission of India.
- MHRD (2003). *Education for All – National Plan of Action*. New Delhi: Department of Elementary Education and Literacy, MHRD. GOI.

- Planning Commission, GOI. (2008). *Eleventh Five Year Plan (2007-2012), Social Sector,* Volume II. New Delhi: Oxford University Press.
- Rajput, J. S. (2010). Millennium Development Goals of Achieving Universal Primary Education-The Road Travelled by India So Far. *Journal of the Human Rights Commission*, Vol. 9, 2010.
- Rani, S. (2012). *An Objective Based Evaluation of Rehbar-E-Taleem Scheme in Kashmir Division* (Unpublished Doctoral Thesis). University of Kashmir, Faculty of Education, Srinagar, Kashmir.
- Sadgopal, A. (2010). Right to Education vs. Right to Education Act. *Social Scientist.* 38(9-12) September–December 2010, pp. 17-50.
- Seetharamu, A.S. (2002, February 9). Fundamental Right Status for Education: Opportunity or eyewash? Retrieved from http://www.deccanherald.com.
- Sharma, H. I. (2013). Universalisation of Elementary Education under Sarva Shiksha Abhiyan in Manipur. *Voice of Research*. L (4): 14-17.
- Siddiqui, S. (2008). Universalisation of Elementary Education in India. *Journal of Educational Research*. 11(1): 4-12.
- Tomasevshki, Katerina (2003). *Education Denied: Costs and Remedies*. New York: Zed Books Ltd.
- Yadav, S.K. (2011). *National Study on Ten Year School Curriculum Implementation*. New Delhi: Department of Teacher Education and Extension, National Council of Educational Research and Training (NCERT).

Chapter - 2

Educational Policies in India under the British Rule

India has a long tradition of education both through formally organised institutions (such as Institutes of Higher Learning at Takshashila and Nalanda) as well as less formal ones like hermitages or 'ashrams' where pupils were under the complete custodial care of their Gurus. A mass education movement, however, began during the age of Jainism and Buddhism when a widespread attempt was made to use the people's spoken language to impart education related to the needs of people.

Right from the beginning of their relationship with India, the British, who had come as traders and had become rulers and administrators, had influenced the economic, political and educational systems of the country. Their impact on the cultural and social life of India was, however, gradual. It is essential to review the educational policies under the British rule to understand the present and visualise the future. In the light of the very backdrop, the history of the development of free and compulsory education in India has been analysed later. Hence the present Chapter aims to briefly look at educational policies adopted by the British rulers in India from the Charter Act of 1813 to the attainment of Independence in 1947.

Development of education system during the British period was determined by the needs of the colonial powers. If we analyse the development, we will find that the colonial interests of the British always shaped the then educational policies of India. European trading companies began their commercial activities in India from 1600 A.D. Gradually the Portuguese, the French, the Dutch and the English settled in some parts and commercial centres of India. Among them the English East India Company was ultimately able to establish their rule in India. Till the nineteenth century, they did not evolve any definite educational policy (Ramana, 2012, p. 81).

One should not suppose that there had been no educational system before the coming of the East India Company. When the British came to India and were gradually establishing themselves in Bengal, they met such a system (Ghosh, 1989: 2). F. W. Thomas was of the opinion that "Education is no exotic in India. There is no country where the love of learning had so early an origin or has exercised so lasting and powerful an influence" (Thomas, 1891, p. 1).

The modern system of education came to be established in India during the British period at the cost of the traditional indigenous system. Before the British established a new system of education in India both the Hindus and the Muslims had their own systems of education. Both the systems went into oblivion gradually and suffered a set back because of political turmoil and lack of a strong centralised political authority and want of suitable patronage (Purkait, 1992, p.1). Indian education had always been of a classical and spiritual rather of a practical nature. It was communicated through the sacred classical languages of the Hindus and the Muslims, namely Sanskrit, Arabic and Persian (Ghosh, 1989, p. 2). The Tols and Madrassas were the highest seminaries of learning meant for the specialists. These institutions were not meant for education of an elementary kind. For primary education, there were in the villages, Patsalas and Maktabs where the Gurus and Maulavis imparted knowledge of the three "R"s to the boys of the locality. There was no school for the education of the girls though the Zamindars often had their daughters educated at home (Ghosh, 1989, p. 3). The indigenous Indian Education started with the advent of the British. The colonial interests of the British shaped the then educational policies of India. In his book, '*Education in British India*' Arthur Howell says, "Education in India under the British Government was first ignored, then violently and successfully opposed, then conducted on a system now universally admitted to be erroneous and finally placed on its present footing" (1872:3).

The development of education system during the British period was determined by the needs of the colonial powers. However, the attitude of the British to education when they came to Bengal was one of the differences, and this was naturally so since India was yet to be a British colony and they were not yet the representatives of the British Crown. They were the employees of a great commercial concern called the East India Company. The Head- quarter of the Company were located at London and consisted of twenty four Directors, who used to manage the affairs of the Company abroad. For each of the British establishments in Calcutta, Bombay and Madras, they appointed a Governor. After Regulating Act of 1773, the Governor of Calcutta was called the Governor-General and was given supervisory power over the Governors at Bombay and Madras.

The East India Company became a ruling power in Bengal in 1765. Following the example of the contemporary English Government, the Court of Directors refused to take on itself the responsibility for the education of the people of India and decided to leave education to private effort. However, the Indian officers of the East India Company urged the Court of Directors to do something for the oriental learning. Some half-hearted efforts were made by the Company's Government to foster oriental learning. Warren Hastings, himself an intellectual, set up the Calcutta Madrasa in 1781 for the study and learning of Persian and Arabic. In 1791, the efforts of Jonathan Duncan, the British Resident at Benares, bore fruit and a Sanskrit College was opened at Benares for the cultivation of laws, literature and religion of the Hindus. These early attempts for the education of the people in oriental languages met with little success. The historians Grover and Alka (2014) explained the hidden policy of the British East India Company in their attempts of the people in oriental languages that administrative needs of the Company required Indians well-versed in the classic and vernacular languages. In the Judicial Department Indians conversant with Sanskrit, Arabic or Persian were required to sit as assessors with English judges and expound Hindu or Muslim law from Sanskrit or Persian or Arabic books. Besides, the knowledge of Persian and vernaculars was valued in the political department for correspondence with rulers of Indian states. The clerical staff in the revenue and commercial departments had contacts with uneducated masses and for them knowledge of vernaculars was a must (p. 257).

Although the East India Company was established in 1600 A.D., it took no educational activities for nearly one hundred years of its existence (Narullah and Naik, 1943, p. xiv). The development of modern system of education in India...may be said to have begun with the Charter Act of 1813 which provided through the Section 43 that "a sum of not less than one lakh of rupees in each year shall be set apart and applied to the revival and improvement of literature and the encouragement of the learned natives of India, and for the introduction and promotion of a knowledge of the sciences among the inhabitants of the British territories in India; and that any schools, public lectures, or other institutions, for the purposes aforesaid, which shall be founded at the Fort William, Fort St. George, or Bombay, or any other part of the British territories in India, in virtue of this Act shall be governed by such regulations as may from time to time be made by the said Governor-General in Council;" (Sharp, 1920, p. 22).

The Charter Act of 1813, therefore, forms a turning point in the history of Indian education. With it...the education of the Indian people was definitely included within the duties of the Company; comparatively large amount was annually secured for educational activities;...thereby lying the foundation of the modern educational system" (Narullah and Naik, 1943, p. 67). The Clause 43 of the Charter Act of 1813 assumed more importance when one remembers that in those days education was not a State responsibility in England, and except Scotland, no public money was spent on elementary education, which was left mostly to charity schools, village dames, to private Sunday schools movement started by Robert Raikes and private efforts of individual like Hannah More (Ghosh, 1989, p. 26).

The Charter Act of 1813 constitutes a landmark in the educational history of British India. Its Clause 43 contained the first legislative admission of the right of education in India in the public revenues (Misra, 1989, p. 189). This Act was the first legislative recognition of the right for education (Jayapalan, 2000, p. 81). However, The Charter Act made it obligatory on the part of the East India Company to spread education in India; it laid the foundation of State System of Education in India. For the first time, the British Parliament included in 1813 Charter, a clause under which the Governor-General-in-Council was bound to keep a sum not less than one lakh rupees, for education. This Act renewing the East India Company's Charter for a twenty year period produced two major changes in Britain's relationship with her colony: one was the assumption of a new responsibility towards native education, and the other was a relaxation of controls over missionary activity in India.

Section 43 of the Charter Act 1813 had only defined the objects of the educational policy, viz. **'the revival and improvement of literature'**, **'the encouragement of learned natives of India'** and **'the introduction and promotion of a knowledge of sciences among the inhabitants of the British territories in India'**; but it had no directions regarding the methods to be employed to secure these objects (Nurullah and Naik, 1943, p. 68). Actually the Company had not been given any specific instruction on this issue. Consequently, the direction of education remained uncertain during the next 22 years on the following issues:

1. **The Medium of Instruction:** It could not be decided whether the medium of instruction should be English or Indian Languages.
2. **Aim of Education of the British Policy:** Whether education should be available to all or should be given to only a selected few.
3. **Type of Knowledge:** Whether to preserve and promote Oriental learning or to introduce Western knowledge, culture and science.
4. **Agency of Education:** Whether the government should assume direct responsibility of educating the Indians or the Indigenous system of education of the country to continue.
5. **Role of Missionaries:** Whether the missionaries should be given a free hand in their educational practices or should the Company itself shoulder the total responsibility.

The vagueness of the Clause 43 of the Charter Act of 1813 intensified the Oriental and Occidental educational controversy in India.

One group was of the Orientalists who wanted the promotion of Indian education through the medium of Sanskrit, Arabic, and Persian where as the other group was of Anglicists who were in favour of developing western education in India through the medium of English. Thus fund was kept unspent till 1823 due to the controversy.

That's why the recommendations of the Charter Act of 1813 were delayed until 1823 when the Governor General in Council appointed a General Committee of Public Instruction (G.C.P.I.) for the Bengal Presidency to look after the development of education in India. The Committee consisted of ten members and the grant of one lakh of rupees provided by the Charter Act of 1813 was also placed at the disposal of the Committee. A decade before Lord Macaulay arrived in India; the General Committee of Public Instruction was formed in 1823, which was to guide the company on the matter of education. The Orientalists dominated the committee and advocated the promotion of Oriental learning rather than the Anglican one. The Committee of Public Instructions consisted of members with Orientalist attitude till 1824. However, when new members, imbued with the growing liberal influences were recruited, the committee lost its homogeneous character and in 1835 the differences of opinion over the competing aims of oriental and occidental learning began to come to surface. As a result of the Orientalist-Anglicist controversy, the spread of education in India was halted until 1835, when Macaulay's Resolution provided a somewhat clear picture of the British education policy.

In the words of Kochhar (1982), the General Committee of Public Instruction was guided by two principles:

(a) It wanted to win the confidence of the educated and influential classes, by encouraging the learning and literature that they respected.

(b) As the funds at the disposal of the Committee were quite inadequate, it would be best to apply the funds to the higher education of the upper classes as distinguished from the general elementary education of the masses. These people were of the opinion that if leaders were educated, their education would naturally 'filter down' to the masses (pp. 6-7).

The Charter was eventually renewed in 1833 for another term of 20 years. It did not contain any direct educational clauses but added a Law Member to the Executive Council of the Governor General of Bengal which had hitherto consisted of three members only. The first Law Member to be appointed was Macaulay who came to India in 1834 and turned a new page in the history of educational policy in India (Nurullah and Naik, 1943, p. 97).

The controversy between the Anglicists and the Orientalists did not lend itself to any solution. The differences, which were present almost from the inception of the Committee in 1823, came to a head by about 1834.The Secretary to the General Committee of Public Instruction in his two letters dated the 21st and the 22nd January, 1835 referred the issue to the Governor-General of India in Council. The result was the famous Minute of Lord Macaulay, which attempted to provide a solution to the dilemma posed by the educational clause in the Charter Act of 1813. In his Minute dated the 2nd of February, 1835 Macaulay wrote:

> This lakh of rupees is set apart not only for 'reviving literature in India', but also 'for the introduction and promotion of the knowledge of the Sciences among the inhabitants of the British territories' — words which are alone sufficient to authorise all the changes for which I contend (Sharp and Richey, 1920, Vol.1, pp.107-08).

Macaulay argued that the word "literature" occurring in the Section of 43 of the Charter Act of 1823 could be interpreted to mean English literature, that the epithet of a "learned native of India" could also be applied to a person versed in the philosophy of Locke or the poetry of Milton, and the object of promoting a knowledge of sciences could only be accomplished by the adoption of English as the medium of instruction (Nurullah and Naik, 1943, p. 103).

Macaulay wrote in his Minute, "We must at present do our best to form a class of persons, Indian in blood and colour, but English in taste, in opinions, in morals and in intellect" (Chand, 2007, p. 5). Macaulay rejected the claims of Arabic and Sanskrit as against English because he considered that English is the key to modern knowledge and English is the language sponsored by the ruling class. It is likely to become the language of commerce throughout the seas of the East.

In support of English, Lord Macaulay said, "It stands pre-eminent even among the languages of the West... whoever knows that already access to all the vast intellectual wealth which all the wisest nations of the earth have created and hoarded in the course of ninety generations. It may also be said that the literature now extent in that language is of greater value than all the literature which three hundred years ago was extent in all languages of the world" (Sharma and Sharma, 2012:81). This Minute also stated that British government's main aim was to spread European literature and science among Indians and so all the money granted for education would be spent for that purpose through English medium. His Minute ultimately decided the policy, medium, means and aims of education in India as the then Governor-in-General himself was admirer of English language.

Ultimately Macaulay in his Minutes of 1835 instituted an education policy in support of the British Raj which denigrated Indian languages and knowledge, established the hegemonic influence of English as medium of colonial 'instruction' (not education) and used the ploy of limitation of resources to "form a class who may be interpreters between us and the millions whom we govern - a class of persons Indian in blood and colour, but English in tastes, in opinions, in morals and in intellect..." (Chennai Declaration, 2012).

English education was also seen as an important basis for expanding the British market in India by harnessing English values and tastes. Anglicised Indians would be potential customers of British goods. Acquainted with them by means of their literature and medium of English, the Indian youth would almost cease to regard them as foreigners.

Spreading English education provided a positive bond between the rulers and the ruled. In 1833, when the Charter Act was passed, the East India Company was in acute financial crisis. The 1833 Charter opened the lower order Civil Service jobs to English educated Indians. By adopting Downward Filtration Theory, the British Government wanted to make higher classes blind followers of the government. The educated people educated on British lines through English medium would get higher post in government services and in return they would use their influence in controlling the masses from going against the government rule.

The Macaulayian system was a systematic effort on the part of the British Government to educate the upper classes of India through the medium of English language. Education of the masses was not the aim of Macaulay. He believed that the English education Indians would act as "a class who may be interpreters between us and the millions whom we govern. Thus, a natural consequence of Macaulay's theory was the development of vernacular languages as secondary to the teaching of English.

British Educational Policies till 1835 – An Appraisal

The modern system of education came to be established in India during the British period at the cost of the traditional indigenous system. Before the British established a new system of education in India both the Hindus and the Muslims had their own systems of education. The Tols and Madrassas were the highest institutes of learning meant for the specialists. These institutions were not meant for education of an elementary kind. For primary education, there were in the villages, Patsalas and Maktabs where the Gurus and Maulavis imparted knowledge of the three "R"s to the boys of the locality.

Development of education system during the British period was determined by the needs of the colonial powers. The colonial interests of the British always shaped the then educational policies of India.

The East India Company became a ruling power in Bengal in 1765. The Court of Directors refused to take on itself the responsibility for the education of the people of India and decided to leave education to private effort. However, some half-hearted efforts were made by the Company's Government to foster oriental learning. The early attempts for the education of the people were the establishment of Calcutta Madrasa in 1781 and Sanskrit College (1791) at Benares. The hidden policy of the British East India Company in their attempts of the people in oriental languages was administrative needs. The Company required Indians well-versed in the classic and vernacular languages for administration.

- In the Judicial Department Indians conversant with Sanskrit, Arabic or Persian were required to sit as assessors with English judges and expound Hindu or Muslim law from Sanskrit or Persian or Arabic books.
- The knowledge of Persian and vernaculars was valued in the political department for correspondence with rulers of Indian states.
- The clerical staff in the revenue and commercial departments had contacts with uneducated masses and for them knowledge of vernaculars was a must.

The development of modern system of education in India begun with the Charter Act of 1813 which provided through the Section 43 that "a sum of not less than one lakh of rupees in each year shall be set apart and applied to the revival and improvement of literature and the encouragement of the learned natives of India, and for the introduction and promotion of a knowledge of the sciences among the inhabitants of the British territories in India" (Sharp, 1920, p. 22). Its Clause 43 contained the first legislative admission of the right of education in India in the public revenues. However, The Charter Act made it obligatory on the part of the East India Company to spread education in India; it laid the foundation of State System of Education in India.

The vagueness of the Clause 43 of the Charter Act of 1813 intensified the Oriental and Occidental educational controversy in India. This fund was kept unspent till 1823 due to the controversy. That's why the recommendations of the Charter Act of 1813 were delayed until 1823 when the Governor General in Council appointed a G.C.P.I. for the Bengal Presidency to look after the development of education in India. As a result of the Orientalist-Anglicist controversy, the spread of education in India was halted until 1835, when Macaulay's Resolution provided a somewhat clear picture of the British education policy.

Macaulay was appointed as the first Law Member to the Executive Council of the Governor-General of Bengal. Lord Macaulay attempted to provide a solution to the dilemma posed by the educational clause in the Charter Act of 1813. In his Minute dated the 2nd February, 1835 Macaulay wrote: *This lakh of rupees is set apart not only for 'reviving literature in India', but also 'for the introduction and promotion of the knowledge of the Sciences among the inhabitants of the British territories' — words which are alone sufficient to authorize all the changes for which I contend* (Sharp and Richey, 1920, Vol.1, pp.107-08). Macaulay also wrote in his Minute, *"We must at present do our best to form a class of persons, Indian in blood and colour, but English in taste, in opinions, in morals and in intellect"* His Minute ultimately decided the policy, medium, means and aims of education in India.

British Educational Policy in the Context of the Macaulay's Minute

The colonial interests of the British always shaped the then educational policies of India.The Charter was eventually renewed in 1833 for another term of 20 years. It added a Law Member to the Executive Council of the Governor General of Bengal which had hitherto consisted of three members only. The first Law Member to be appointed was Macaulay who came to India in 1834 and turned a new page in the history of educational policy in India.

Lord Macaulay in his Minute dated the 2nd of February, 1835 Macaulay wrote: **"We must at present do our best to form a class of persons, Indian in blood and colour, but English in taste, in opinions, in morals and in intellect".** So Lord Bentinck resolved that "the great object of the British Government ought to be the promotion of European literature and science among the natives of India; and that all the funds appropriated for the purpose of education would be best employed on English education alone".

(1) Ultimately Macaulay in his Minutes of 1835 instituted an education policy in support of the British Raj which denigrated Indian languages and knowledge, established the hegemonic influence of English as medium of colonial 'instruction' (not education) in order to **"form a class who may be interpreters between us and the millions whom we govern."**

(2) English education was also seen as an important basis for expanding the British market in India by harnessing English values and tastes. Anglicised Indians would be potential customers of British goods.

(3) Acquainted with them by means of their literature and medium of English, the Indian youth would almost cease to regard them as foreigners.

(4) Spreading English education provided a positive bond between the rulers and the ruled.

(5) In 1833, when the Charter Act was passed, the East India Company was in acute financial crisis. The 1833 Charter opened the lower order Civil Service jobs to English educated Indians.

(6) By adopting Downward Filtration Theory, the British Government wanted to make higher classes blind followers of the government. The educated people educated on British lines through English medium would get higher post in government services and in return they would use their influence in controlling the masses from going against the government rule.

(7) The Macaulayian system was a systematic effort on the part of the British Government to educate the upper classes of India through the medium of English language. Education of the masses was not the aim of Macaulay. He believed that the English education Indians would act as "a class who may be interpreters between us and the millions whom we govern". Thus, a natural consequence of Macaulay's theory was the development of vernacular languages as secondary to the teaching of English.

Lord William Bentinck (1828-1838) endorsed the Minute on the 7th March 1835 by writing one line beneath it, "I give entire concurrence to the sentiments expressed in the Minute."

Lord Bentinck's Resolution of the 7th March 1835

Lord William Bentinck (1828-1838) endorsed the Minute by writing one line beneath it, "I give entire concurrence to the sentiments expressed in the Minute" He passed the Resolution of March 1835 which was the first declaration of the British Government in the sphere of education in India. The Resolution of March 1835 eventually determined the aim, content and medium of instruction in India.

Promotion of Western science and arts was acknowledged as the avowed object of the British Government in India (Chand, 2007:8 and Sharma and Sharma, 2012:84). On the 7th March 1835 the following Resolution was issued (Sharp, 1920:130-131):

First, His Lordship in Council is of opinion that the great object of the British Government ought to be the promotion of European literature and science among the natives of India; and that all the funds appropriated for the purpose of education would be best employed on English education alone.

Second, But it is not the intention of His Lordship in Council to abolish any College or School of native learning, while the native population shall appear to be inclined to avail themselves of the advantages which it affords, and His Lordship in Council directs that all the existing professors and students at all the institutions under the superintendence of the Committee shall continue to receive their stipends. But his lordship in Council decidedly objects to the practice which has hitherto prevailed of supporting the students during the period of their education. He conceives that the only effect of such a system can be to give artificial encouragement to branches of learning which, in the natural course of things, would be superseded by more useful studies and he directs that no stipend shall be given to any student that may hereafter enter at any of these institutions; and that when any professor of Oriental learning shall vacate his situation, the Committee shall report to the government the number and state of the class in order that the government may be able to decide upon the expediency of appointing a successor.

Third, It has come to the knowledge of the Governor-General in Council that a large sum has been expended by the Committee on the printing of Oriental works; his Lordship in Council directs that no portion of the funds shall hereafter be so employed.

Fourth, His Lordship in Council directs that all the funds which these reforms will leave at the disposal of the Committee be henceforth employed in imparting to the native population a knowledge of English literature and science through the medium of the English language; and His Lordship in Council requests the Committee to submit to government, with all expedition, a plan for the accomplishment of this purpose.

Ultimately, Bentinck was greatly influenced by the views of Macaulay. Bentinck's proclamation gave birth to the following results in Indian education:

- The aims of education in India were determined by the British.
- The promotion of Western arts and sciences was acknowledged as the avowed object.
- The printing of oriental works was to be stopped.
- New grants or stipends to students of oriental institutions were to be stopped in future.
- The medium of education would be English.
- This proclamation promised to supply government with English educated Indian servants cheap but capable at the same time.

In line with the Bentinck's Resolution, 1835, in 1844, Lord Hardinge proclaimed that for services in public offices, preference would be given to those who were educated in English schools. It clearly showed that education was imparted with the limited object of preparing pupils to join services. The emphasis was on producing good clerks (Kochhar, 1982:7). This proclamation had also far-reaching consequences. It gave rise to two new castes in a caste-ridden country – English-knowing caste and non-English knowing mass of people.

But in the words of Professor S. N. Mukherji, "The Proclamation marks a turning point in the history of education in India. It was the first declaration of the educational policy, which the British Government wanted to adopt in this country... The barriers of caste, conservatism and religious orthodoxy which had blocked the cultural progress of the country were done away with and new vistas were opened through the study of English for those persons 'Indian in blood and colour but English in tastes, in opinions, in morals and in intellect'. This brought about the dawn of a cultural renaissance after centuries of confusion and darkness" (Mukherji,1974: 73-74). I am of the opinion that his analysis was not fully acceptable because Bentinck's resolution was not at all cultural renaissance but aggression and earlier centuries of India did not belong to dark ages. It may be, however, said that Bentinck's declaration tried to put an end to the oriental occidental controversy. This minute influenced British's educational policy in this country for more than a century. It must be admitted that the new knowledge through Western learning brought India into contact with scientific researches of the West, and developed Indian languages to standards in which a university education became possible.

Emergence of the Policy of Downward Filtration Theory

In the beginning of nineteenth century the British rulers thoughts that in order to run the British rule in India peacefully, it is essential to make higher classes blind followers of the government. This they wanted to achieve though educating the higher classes. Filtration theory means, "Education is to be filtered to the common people. Drop by drop, the education should go to the common public so that at due time it may take the form of a vast stream which remained watering desert of the society for long times and high class of people should be educated and common people gain influence from it" (Sharma and Sharma, 2012: 85, Aggarwal, 2008: 90). According to this famous doctrine, "Education was to permeate the masses from above. Drop by drop from the Himalayas of Indian life useful information was to trickle downwards, forming in time a broad and stately stream to irrigate the thirsty plains" (Mayhew, 1928:92).

Reasons for Adopting Filtration Theory

- The British rulers needed educated employees to run the commerce and administration.
- The government did not receive sufficient funds for educating the masses.
- The educated people educated on British lines through English medium would get higher post in government services and in return they would use their influence in controlling the masses from going against the government rule.
- After educating some people, the responsibility of educating the masses could be left to them.

Background of the Adoption of Filtration Theory: The Director of the Company in their despatches dated September 29, 1830 had written to Madras Government, "The improvements of education, however, which most effectually contribute to elevate the moral and intellectual condition of a people are those, which concern the education of the higher classes of the persons possessing leisure and natural influence over minds of their countrymen. By raising the standard of education among these classes you would eventually produce a much greater and more beneficial change in the ideas and feelings of the community than you can hope to produce by acting directly on the more numerous class" (Chand, 2007:11 and Aggarwal, 2008: 90). Macaulay is also blamed for supporting the Filtration Theory. Macaulay thought that it was impossible, with the limited means, to educate the masses. So he found it suitable to educate the upper classes only and leave it to them, to spread education among the masses. He mentioned in his Minute, "It would be more suitable to provide higher education to higher classes than to give to elementary education to the mass" (Sharma and Sharma, 2012:85, Aggarwal, 2008: 90). He again on July 31, 1837 said. "At present we don't aim at educating directly the common people. We aim at creating a class of persons who among their countrymen distribute some of the knowledge we gave". Declaring it as government policy, Sir Auckland said, "The government should educate the higher class of the people so that the 'filtered culture' reaches to the public" (Sharma and Sharma, 2012:85). The Committee of Public Instruction in Bengal had also approved the same ideal and expressed its ideas in 1839, "Our efforts should be concentrated first on the education of higher and middle class of people" (Chand, 2017:12). Since then this policy was followed up to 1870 and emphasis was laid on the education of the people of higher classes in the society. Thus, Filtration Theory fulfilled the aim of Lord Macaulay and the Directors of the Company. This theory decided the education policy of India. The immediate aim of getting educated people to run the various jobs in the administration was fully achieved. It also helped in creating a faithful class of people. But the ultimate aim could not be fulfilled as the educated persons were cut off from the common masses and the government was unable to provide jobs to all the educated Indians.

Lord William Bentinck, the Governor-General of India appointed William Adam (1789-1868) in 1835 to survey the state of education in Bengal and Bihar and to suggest reforms. Adam submitted three reports (1835-1838). The second part of the Adam's Third Report provides proposals for the reform of education, especially indigenous. His recommendations were not accepted by the government. Before he submitted his third Report, Macaulay as the chairman of the Committee had pronounced his verdict. Macaulay was Wedded to the Filtration Theory and believed firmly in the superiority of Western civilisation. He observed, "I am little inclined to doubt, however, whether we are at present ripe for any extensive practical measure, which he (Adam) recommends. Our work is to educate the school masters for the generation" (Chand, 2007:19). The Committee regarded Adam's plan as impractical and accepted the views of Macaulay.

Wood's Despatch, 1854

The Charter Act of the East India Company was to be reviewed in 1853 by the British Parliament. Before doing so, the Court of Directors in England decided to lay down a definite policy in regard to educational matters of India. So the British Parliament appointed a Special Parliamentary Committee to suggest a suitable educational policy for India. The Committee made thoroughly an evaluation of educational policy followed by the Company in India. On the basis of this evaluation, a Despatch – a policy document on education was prepared for the functioning of education system in India. The Despatch was prepared by Traivellian Pairy, Marshman, Wilson, Cameron, Duff etc, who had thorough knowledge of Indian education. The Committee reported that the question of Indian education would not be ignored any longer and its development will not be in any case harmful to British Empire. The suggestions of the Committee were favourably considered by the Board of Directors. As Charles Wood was the President of the Board of Control for India, the despatch was christened as "Wood's Educational Despatch". It decided the educational policy of the Company Government.

The objective of the Despatch was "not only to produce a higher degree of intellectual fitness but to raise the moral character and to supply with servants". The function of education was to diffuse

European knowledge – arts, philosophy, science and literature. English and vernacular languages of India would be the media for the diffusion of European knowledge. As 'Filtration Theory' failed, Wood emphasised useful education for the public. The ultimately purpose of the Despatch was just well-guarded attempt to impose Western knowledge and learning and English language on the Indian people (Sharma and Sharma, 2012:107). According to J. Chand (2007), the Despatch visualised India as a market for the supplier of raw materials to Britain and a consumer market for the purchase of finished goods of Britain's industries. Thus, its vocational policy was lopsided (p. 33). However, education under the East India Company ended with the Wood's Despatch of 1854 as the Company ceased to be a political power in 1858 and the Government of India came directly under the Crown.

An immediate outcome of this despatch was the passing of the three University Acts of 1857 establishing universities at Calcutta, Madras and Bombay and creation of an Education Department in each province of British India. But before any further action could be taken the Government of India was transferred from the Company to the Crown. Thus, the centre of interest in education now shifted from London to Calcutta, parliamentary interest in Indian education was reduced to minimum and the Government of India became the most effective authority to deal with important educational issues (Biswas and Agarwal, 1994:29). This period of about five decades between the Despatch of 1854 and the appointment of the Indian Universities Commission in 1902 is described as the Victorian era in Indian Education. The principal educational events comprised the establishment of the Education Departments, development of the system of grant-in-aid, establishment of universities, extension of collegiate and secondary education, westernisation of the content of education etc.

It was the Wood's Despatch that set the framework for expenditure on formal education in India with the observation that - The origin of the present system of education which is prevalent in this country today can be traced to the beginning of the nineteenth century when a controversy had been raging over the issue whether oriental learning and science should be spread through the medium of Sanskrit, Arabic or Persian or Western sciences and literature be spread through English as the medium of instruction. The government conducted surveys of the then prevalent systems of education with a view to re-organising education to suit the needs of the times. Consequent on Macaulay's Minute regarding the educational policy of the future, Lord William Bentinck's Government issues a communiqué wherein it was stated "that the great object of the British Government ought to be the promotion of European literature and science among the natives of India; and that all the funds appropriated for the purpose of education alone". The Government Resolution, however, stated that provision should be made for the continuance of schools and colleges where indigenous learning was being imparted (Raina, 2010).

In 1859, Staley, the Secretary of State for India, passed an order that the Government of India should own responsibility of primary education. Accordingly, the Government of India instructed to levy local taxes for this task. Consequently in 1864, local taxes were levied in various provinces of India for meeting the expenditure on primary education.

The Indian Education Commission, 1882

The educational policies during the period of 1854 and 1902 were formulated by two main documents only – the Despatch of 1854 and the Report of the Indian Education Commission, 1882. There were reasons that prompted the appointment of the Commission. The Resolution of the Government of India dated February 3, 1882 stated that, "while the government acknowledged the mastery and comprehensive outline supplied by the Despatch, they deemed it of importance to review the progress made, and to enquire how far the superstructure corresponded with the original design…Nearly a quarter of a century had since elapsed, and the Governor-General in Council believed that the time had now come for instituting a further and more careful investigation in the existing system, and into the results attained by it, than had hitherto been attempted" (Report of The Indian Education Commission, 1882, p. 2). For this purpose Lord Ripon appointed the Indian Education Commission by the Resolution of Government of India dated February 3, 1882 under the Chairmanship of William Hunter, a member of Viceroy's Legislative Council. Within ten months the Commission submitted a report of about 700 pages after hard labour but it could not give any original suggestion or educational ideas. Its report was a revised and enlarged version of Charles Wood's Despatch of 1854 (Sharma and Sharma, 2012:117). The commission boldly admitted that while every branch of education can justly claim the fostering care of the state, it is desirable, in the present circumstances of the country, to declare the elementary education of the masses, its provisions, extensions, and improvement to be that part of the education system, to which the strenuous efforts of the State should be directed in a still larger measure than heretofore. (Chand, 2007: 37, Mukerji, 1974, p. 145)

The Commission recommended the complete withdrawal of government from direct enterprise and the transfer of all primary schools to the control of local self-government bodies such as municipalities and local boards. Thus, it made the government free from responsibility. With regard to secondary schools and colleges, the Commission was of opinion that the government should withdraw as early as possible from the direct management of secondary and collegiate education.

The Major Recommendations of the Commission

- Encouragement and support to indigenous schools for extending elementary education by declaring elementary education of the masses as the most important priority— area in education to which strenuous government efforts should be directed;
- Freedom to the management committees for choosing vernacular language as a medium of instruction depending on the local needs;
- Establishment of secondary schools by the state, for instruction in English based on the system of grant-in-aid, and setting up of primary schools with the support of local people;
- Gradual transfer of all government secondary schools to local native management committees with due consideration of maintenance of standards and quality of education;

- Bifurcation of secondary education into two streams—one leading to the entrance examination of the universities and the other of a more practical character preparing the students for commercial jobs.

For working out the policy, the Commission suggested two important measures:

(1) It was considered necessary that government should not only curtail the activities of its own educational institutions, but should also withdraw from direct enterprise.

(2) It stressed the need for organising a proper system of grant-in-aid so that private enterprise might get enough room to expand and to feed upon. In the field of primary education, it suggested government should completely withdraw itself from direct enterprise and should hand over all the State schools to local boards. But so far as colleges and secondary schools were concerned, the Commission recommended the gradual transfer of government institutions to efficient private bodies. It further stressed that in future, colleges and secondary schools should be established preferably on the footing of a liberal grant-in-aid system and that reorganised private institutions should enjoy the same status and privileges as government institutions (Mukherji, 1974:144).

If we minutely scrutinise the recommendations, we have found the policy of organising a system based on the happy blending of private and public efforts right from the primary to the university stage. However, the Report encouraged Indian private enterprise and awakened public enthusiasm for the cause of education for the first time in India. The Imperial Government accepted all the recommendations except those in connection with religious education as it was considered difficult to take any step in this direction. The main results were:

(1) The transfer of complete control of primary education to Local Boards and Municipalities;

(2) The state policy of not to open more colleges and secondary schools, though the then existing state institutions of higher education were not actually transferred to private bodies; and

(3) The recognition of the principle that the missionary enterprise can occupy only a subordinate position in a national system of education.

In pursuance of the recommendation of Indian Education Commission (1882-83), the government considered seriously the ways and means to develop primary education, and technical education at high school stage. The progress of education during the period from 1882-83 to 1901-02 was reviewed during the period of Lord Curzon, the then Viceroy of India.

Lord Curzon's Educational Policy

In 1899, Lord Curzon was appointed Governor-General of India. In 1901, Lord Curzon convened at Simla an educational conference attended by a few selected educationists and the Provincial Directors of Public Instruction. The Conference adopted 150 resolutions which touched almost every conceivable branch of education. This was followed by the appointment of a Commission under the presidency of Sir Thomas Raleigh on 27 January 1902 "to enquire into the condition and prospects of the Universities in British India" ; to consider and report upon any proposals which have been, or may be, made for improving their constitution and working, and to recommend to the Governor-General in Council such measures as may tend to elevate the standard of University teaching, and to promote the advancement of learning" (Government of India, 1902, p.1). Evidently, the Commission was precluded from reporting on primary or secondary education. After an exhaustive inquiry, the Commission submitted its report to the Government of India, and its recommendations were incorporated in the Universities Act of 1904. In pursuance of the Educational Conference at Simla in 1901 and with a view to giving a clear cut direction to government's activities as well as to private enterprise, the Government passed a Resolution on Indian Educational Policy in 1904, popularly known as Lord Curzon's Educational Policy.

This resolution expressed a grave concern at the defects of education, as it existed, such as pursuing higher education for entering government jobs exclusively, dominance of examination on teaching, too much emphasis on memory training, neglect of the vernaculars and too much emphasis on literary aspects of the curriculum (Chauhan, 2004:32). Special attention was paid to primary education in the Resolution. In view of the importance of primary education as mass education, it was proposed that it should be expanded and should attract more funds from government revenue. The resolution proposed to strengthen secondary education by laying down certain conditions for recognition, funding, and affiliation to the examining universities. The introduction of diversified courses to meet the demands of industrial development was also proposed.

Regarding learning of languages and medium of instruction at school level, the resolution said: As a general rule, a child should not be allowed to learn English language until he has made some progress in the primary stage of education and has received a thorough grounding in his mother tongue. It is equally important that when the teaching of English has begun, it should not be prematurely employed as the medium of instruction in other subjects.... The line of division between the use of vernaculars and of English as the medium of instruction should, broadly speaking, be drawn at a minimum age of 13.

The Resolution regarding university education proposed to reconstitute Senates and Syndicates of universities by limiting the number of ex-officio fellows and by reducing the maximum number of senators. The colleges seeking affiliation to the universities would be required to fulfil certain minimum requirements as prescribed by the concerned university. Affiliation would be granted only when the colleges had a regular governing body, qualified teachers, adequate building and equipment, staff quarters, sufficient financial resources and a rational fee policy. Affiliation once granted might not be permanent and might be reviewed through a proper inspection. Important proposals were also made to improve technical, vocational, and commercial education in order to make it more practical and relevant to the local needs of the people of India. Agricultural education was also proposed to be expanded. The need for the training of secondary school teachers was emphasised in order to make school teaching more efficient and non-mechanical (Chauhan, 2004, 34).

The Resolution also detailed the chief characteristics of the System of Education in British India: (1) Getting government job was the aim of education; (2). English was encouraged at the cost of vernacular languages; (3) Technical education was neglected; (4) Method of instruction encouraged memorisation and not developing intellect.

However, this Resolution acknowledged the negligence of the government in providing adequate share of funds for elementary education and agreed with the views of the Report of the Education Commission of 1882 that the active expansion of primary education is one of the active duties of the State. In the words of Professor J. M. Sen (1925), "Although a provision in the East India Act of 1813 empowering the Governor-General of India to spend one lakh of rupees each year for the purpose of education was the first legislative admission of the right of education to participate in the public revenues of India, and though the Education Despatch of 1854 issued by the Court of Directors of East India Company (re-affirmed by Lord Stanley, the first Secretary of State for India, in his Despatch of 1859) was the first basis for a state educational programme in India, it is in the Indian Educational Policy of 1904 that we find for the first time the Government of India declaring that the rapid spread of primary education is one of the foremost duties of the State" (p. 4).

Government Resolution on Education Policy, 1913

British Government rejected the Gopal Krishna Gokhale's Bill and refused to recognise the principle of compulsory education for paucity of funds; they promised to extend grants for the widest extension of primary education on a voluntary basis and passed the Resolution on Education Policy on February 21, 1913.

The Resolution advocated three cardinal principles of educational policy: (1) The curricula of primary and secondary schools should be made more practical and useful; (2) Facilities of higher education should be provided in India so that Indian students may not have to go abroad; (3) Instead of increasing the number of existing institutions their standard should be raised (Jain, 2007:7, Biswas and Agarwal, 1994: 41).

The Government Resolution on Educational Policy (1913) also provided for sufficient expansion of lower primary schools with a simultaneous opening of upper primary schools. It proposed to streamline inspection and supervision, appoint trained teachers, subsidise Maktabs and Pathshalas, improve school facilities, and encourage girl's education. The Resolution also provided for expansion of university education considering the existing five universities and 185 colleges as insufficient. The universities were to be relieved of responsibility of granting recognition to high schools, and subjects of industrial importance were to be included in the curriculum. The First World War which broke out the next year delayed the implementation of many recommendations set out in the Resolution.

Calcutta University Commission (1917-19)

Calcutta University Commission was appointed by the Government of India in 1917 to inquire into the condition and prospects of Calcutta University under the chairmanship of Dr Michael Sadler, the Vice-Chancellor of Leeds University. The terms and reference included all aspects of secondary, collegiate and university education.

The major recommendations were –

- Those days, the Matriculation Examination, which marked the end of school stage and constituted an entrance examination to the universities, was conducted by the universities. After two years, another public examination was held (also by the universities) which was called Intermediate Examination. This was followed by the First Degree examination. The problem was studied by the commission in depth and the following conclusions were drawn that the Intermediate stage was really a part of the school course and that the students at this stage could be more effectively taught by school methods than by college methods. So the Intermediate Classes of the university were to be transferred to Secondary Institutions;
- The duration of under-graduate courses for the first degree should be increased to three years with a provision of Honours courses;
- A Board of Secondary and Intermediate Education should be established for the purpose of reorganising High School and Intermediate education on the lines recommended by it and for holding the Matriculation and Intermediate examinations;

- The universities should, thus, be left to their proper sphere, namely, the provision of under-graduate and postgraduate education and holding of examination for the first, second and research degrees;
- The universities should have Departments of Education with provision of teaching "Education" as a subject at B.A. level;
- An Inter-University Board (IUB) should be established to coordinate the work of different Indian universities.

The Commission discussed each and every aspect of Indian education excepting primary education, obviously because of having no connection with the higher education. The recommendations of the Commission introduced a fresh outlook in university education in India and a number of new universities sprang up on the suggested lines. Professor S.N. Mukherji (1974) opined that the suggestion for the creation of a multi-collegiate university on the lines of Oxford or Cambridge in the city of Calcutta was really unique but the Commission did not take into consideration the practical difficulties and complications that the scheme would have evolved. To relieve the degree college and the university from pressure of work and to give a suitable type of education to young students in proper atmosphere was really good. It is universally acknowledged that the Commission has widened the greatest influence on Indian university education for thirty years following its appointment.

If we look at present educational scenario in India, we find some of the important features which Sadler Commission already mentioned in its Report. The beginning of introduction of the New Pattern of Education 10+2+3 in 1975 has been hailed as landmark in the reforms of education in India. It may be recalled that the 12 years of schooling and three years of degree course were recommended by the Sadler Commission (1917-1919). In this sense the Sadler Commission may be said to be fore-runner of the present national educational structure.

Education under Dyarchy (1921 -1937)

In 1918, Mr Edwin Montagu, the Secretary of State for India and Lord Chelmsford, the Viceroy, made thorough inquiries into political problems. In the year 1919, the Government of India passed a resolution known as Government of India Act, 1919, which is otherwise known as Montague-Chelmsford Reform. It was the first time that the British India government had introduced democratic form of government. The provinces of India had been given dyarchy form government or double government rule under transferred subjects and reserved subject. Here subjects mean various administrative functions of the government. Moreover, reserved subjects were given to councillors includes law and order, the police, the land revenue, irrigation where transferred subjects were given to Indian minister includes local self-government, education, public health, public works, agriculture, forest and fisheries. This system of governance was later on ended with the introduction of provincial autonomy in 1935.

The main feature of the Government of India Act of 1919 was the introduction of the principle of dyarchy in the provinces. The Provincial Executive was divided into two parts – the Councillors and the Ministers. The Councillors were British, took charge of what was known as "reserved subjects" while the Ministers who were Indians, took responsibility for "Transferred subjects". Education, a transferred subject, became the direct responsibility of the Indian ministers. These ministers were unable to effect any major changes in education because finance, a reserved subject, was under the control of the English Councillors who were reluctant to give the required amount of money to Indian Ministers. That's why Indian National Congress launched the Civil Disobedience Movement.

As a result of the Montague-Chelmsford Reforms of 1919, the Department of Education was transferred to the control of popular ministries in the various provinces. The Central Government ceased to take direct interest in educational matters and the Department of Education in the Government of India was amalgamated with other departments. Above all, the Central special grants for education liberally sanctioned since 1902 was discontinued. Financial difficulties prevented the provincial governments from taking up ambitious schemes of educational expansion or improvement. During this period expansion of education was mostly made by philanthropic effort. Thus, Mont Ford Reforms introduced the first step towards provincial autonomy in the Indian Constitution and Education was made a Transferred

Subject. But European education was maintained as a Reserved Subject (Mukherji, 1074: 206).

In the words of the educationists A. Biswas and S.P. Agarwal (1994), the Indians first obtained the control of the Education Department in the Dyarchy System dividing Provincial governments into reserved and transferred departments under the Government of India Act, 1919. But the Indian ministers were not able to obtain the funds essential for a large-scale expansion, qualitative improvement and reorganisation of education. The most important thing that happened under Dyarchy System was the rapid development of mass education and the passing of Compulsory Education Acts in most of the provinces.

Transfer of control of education to Provincial Governments not only isolated them from the Central Government but also them from one another. It also deprived the Government of India of the power of guiding and formulating an educational policy for the whole country, and it was no longer possible for it to act as an advisory and co-ordinating agency on problems of all-India importance (Mukherji, 1974: 207). Beginning in 1918, some form of compulsory schooling was gradually introduced just as education was transferred to the control of provincial governments under elected Indian ministers. These changes introduced by the 1919 Montague-Chelmsford reforms mark **the end of direct colonial responsibility for education.**

Central Advisory Board of Education (CABE), 1921

The need for a co-ordinating agency in the matter of education was immediately felt by the Central and Provincial Governments. Consequently, the Central Advisory Board of Education (CABE) was established at the Centre in 1921. The idea that there should be a Central Advisory Board of Education was first put forward by the Calcutta University Commission (1917-19) which felt "that the Government of India can perform an invaluable function by defining the general aims of educational policy, by giving advice and assistance to local governments and to universities" and "by supplying organised information as to the development of educational ideas in the various provinces, and also elsewhere than in India". The chief function of the Board was to offer expert advice on important education matters referred to it. The Educational Commissioner with the Government of India was chairman, and it included a number of eminent educationists, official and non-official, from the provinces. The Board was a body which might have been of real assistance to Ministers in framing a policy suited to advancing India, and to whom complex problems could be submitted for advice (Government of India, 1929:227). But, in 1923, in a time of financial stress, the Board was abolished without even a reference to provincial governments as to the advisability of its continuance, and the Bureau of Education was closed in pursuance of a policy of retrenchment in order to save a total recurring expenditure of only a few thousand rupees on the recommendations of the Inchcape Committee. The policy of retrenchment was further responsible for combining the Department of Education and Health in the Government of India with the Department of Revenue and Agriculture (*Ibid.*, p. 277). The combined Department was termed the Department of Education, Health and Land. The drawback of such an ill-thought out economy became evident very soon and the CABE was revived in 1935 according to the suggestions of the Hartog Committee, 1929. The first meeting of the reconstituted Board was held in New Delhi on the 19th and the 20th of December of 1935. The Bureau of Education was also revived in 1937 on the recommendations of the CABE. It was again reconstituted and strengthened in 1945 (Mukherji, 1974:207).

The Hartog Committee, 1929

The Government of India Act of 1919 devolved considerable responsibility to the provinces. The Act created "Diarchy" or "Rule of Two" leading to greater representation of elected members. In 1921, the Department of Education was transferred to an Indian Minister responsible to Legislature. Being unable to receive sufficient funds from the government, these ministers could not provide the expected results. The continuous pressure for educational improvement resulted in the appointment of Hartog Committee (May, 1928), after his its chairman, Sir Philip Hartog which made wide-ranging proposals for development of both, general and professional education. The Committee submitted its report in September, 1929. The main findings of the Hartog Committee were as follows:

The Committee observed that an increase in number of schools and colleges had led to deterioration of education standards.

The Committee was of the opinion that the rapid expansion of education resulted in the dilution of quality and education became largely ineffective and wasteful. It emphasised the national importance of primary education but condemned the policy of hasty expansion or attempt to introduce compulsion in education. The Committee recommended the policy of consolidation and improvements by reducing the large extent of stagnation and wastage. According the Report, "Primary education is ineffective, unless it at least produces literacy. On the average, no child who has not completed a primary course of at least four years will be permanently literate" (Hartog Report, 1919: 48).

The Committee then examined secondary and university education. They were looked upon as designed to produce competent officials. It pointed out the large failure at the matriculation examination as mere wastage. It recommended the introduction of varied curricula in middle vernacular schools and the retention of a large number of pupils in such schools and diversion of more boys to industrial and commercial careers at the end of the middle school stage.

The Committee also criticised the policy of indiscriminate admission at university level which led to lowering of standards. It recommended that "all efforts should be concentrated on improving university work, on confining the university to its proper function of giving good advanced education to students who are fit to receive it, and, in fact, to making the university a more "fruitful and less disappointing agency in the life of the community" (Hartog Report, 1929:137).

The main conclusion of the report was that the quantitative increase of education inevitably led to deterioration of quality and lowering of standard. Quantity had been gained at the cost of quality and therefore the immediate need was to improve the quality rather than increase the numbers still further. The Committee regarded that the transfer of power from the Central to Provincial Governments had been too sudden. It pointed out the need of establishing a centralising educational agency at Delhi. In its opinion the transfer of control over primary education to local bodies was not desirable (Mukherji, 1974:213).

The Report of the Hartog Committee more or less shaped the educational policy of British Government during the last decades of its existence in India. Words like Wastage and Stagnation have become key words in educational terminology, and a policy of expansion initiated since the beginning of the present period was changed into one for consolidation. The Committee highlighted that a policy of expansion resulted in Wastage and Retention and thus weakened the need for a rapid expansion of primary education irrespective of quality. Briefly speaking, the Report like Macaulay's filtration theory stopped the progress of the growth of primary education.

Education under the Provincial Autonomy

The Act of 1919 made education a subject which was "partly all-India, partly reserved, partly transferred with limitations and partly transferred without limitations" (Ghosh, 2013: 162). But in 1935, the British Parliament passed the Government of India Act. This Act divided all educational activities into two categories only – Federal (Central) and State (Provincial). All matters regarding education of all other categories other than those included in the Federal list fell under State or Provincial Subjects. Besides, the entire administration of the Provinces was transferred to the Executive, which was responsible to the Legislature. Popular Ministers were placed in-charge of provincial subjects. Briefly speaking, the whole field of provincial administration was placed under a ministry. This new system of governance, known as Provincial Autonomy, was introduced in 1937. The Congress party came into power in seven provinces of British India. During their short-term in office, the Provincial ministers dealt seriously with education. They made an attempt to study Indian education from the national point of view (Kochhar, 1982: 13). The Provincial Government undertook certain bold experiment such as Wardha Scheme. The main principle of the scheme was 'Learning through Activity'. The Zakir Hossain Committee worked out the details of the scheme and prepared detailed syllabi for a number of crafts. However, the outbreak of the Second World War in 1939 and the resignation of Congress ministers in 1940 due to differences that arose between the Congress and the British Government of India over the question of war and peace aims of the Allies led to the postponement of the scheme. During this period, several committees were set up by the Central and Provincial Governments for the purpose of discussing various problems of education in India. The Abbot-Wood Report (1936-1937) pointed out that general education and vocational education were not essentially different branches and that vocational students should have an adequate general education.

Post-War Plan of Educational Development (1944)

During the period between 1940-1946, due to absence of popular ministries, domination of the Indian scene by political problems and the preoccupation of the government with war efforts, the pace of educational progress slowed down. After the end of Second World War, the Central Advisory Board of Education (CABE) in India published a comprehensive report on the "Post-War Educational Development in India" in the country. This was the first systematic and national level attempt to review the problems of education as a whole. It is also known as Sargent Plan after John Sargent, the then Educational Advisor to the Government of India. Surprisingly, the report is not known after its **chairman (Sir Jogindra Singh)**, but its one of the members of the Committee – John Sargent (the educational advisor to the Government of India). The object of the Plan was to create in India, in a period of not less than forty years, the same standard of educational attainments as had already been admitted in England. It is worth mentioning here that this plan was proposed by the British Government in order to counter the attempts made by leaders of the freedom movement to evolve a National System of Education (such as Wardha Scheme) (Chauhan, 2004:37). It recommended:

- Pre-primary education for three to six years age group; free, universal and compulsory elementary education for 6-11 years age group; high school education for 11-17 years age group for selected children, and a university course of three years after higher secondary; high schools to be of two types (i) academic and (ii) technical and vocational.
- Adequate technical, commercial and arts education with different curricula.
- Abolition of intermediate course.

- Development of adult education and liquidation of adult illiteracy in 20 years.
- Stress on teachers' training, physical education, education for the physically and mentally handicapped.

Sargent Plan was one of the most comprehensive schemes of education ever proposed by the British Government after the Despatch of 1854. Through this, the government had proposed a detailed outline of the educational programmes to be undertaken by the government during the following 40 years from 1944 to 1984. As the freedom movement was at its full swing those days, this plan could not be implemented because of political turmoil in the country. With India achieving freedom in 1947, this Plan became only a matter of historical significance (Chauhan, 2004:38). The objective was to create within 40 years, the same level of educational attainment as prevailed in England. Although a bold and comprehensive scheme, it proposed no methodology for implementation. Also, the ideal of England's achievements may not have suited Indian conditions. However, hardly had the first steps been taken when the British period in the history of Indian education came to an end on 15th August, 1947. The Sargent Scheme envisaged a 40-year educational reconstruction plan for the country which was reduced to 16 years by the Kher Committee.

References

- Biswas, A, and Agarwal, S. P. (1994). *Development of Education in India – A Historical Survey of Educational Documents before and after Independence.* New Delhi: Concept Publishing Company.
- Chand, J. (2007). *Education in India during British Period.* New Delhi: Anshah Publishing House.
- Chauhan, C.P.S. (2004). *Modern Indian Education - Policies, Progress and Problems.* New Delhi: Kanishka Publishers, Distributors.
- Ghosh, S.C. (1989). *Education Policy in India since Warren Hastings.* Calcutta: Naya Prokash.
- Ghosh, S.C. (2013). *The History of Education in Modern India, 1757-2012.* New Delhi: Orient Black Swan Private Limited.
- Government of India (1883). *Report of the Indian Education Commission, 1882.* Calcutta: Superintendent of Government Printing India.
- Government of India (1902). *Report of the Indian Universities Commission, 1902.* Simla: The Government Central Printing Office.

- Government of India (1929). *Indian Statutory Commission. Interim Report of the Indian Statutory Commission. (Review of Growth of Education in British India by the Auxiliary Committee appointed by the Commission).* Calcutta: Government of India.
- Government of India (1929). *Review of the Growth of Education in British India by the Auxiliary Committee of the Indian Statutory Commission*, Delhi: The Manager Government of India Press.
- Government of India (1947). *Post-War Educational Development in India, Report by the Central Advisory Board of Education, January 1944*. Delhi: The Manager of Publications, Government of India.
- Grover, B.L. and Mehta, Alka (2014). *A New Look at Modern India History*. New Delhi: S. Chand Publishing.
- Hharp, H. (1920). *Selections from Educational Records, Part – I, 1781-1839.* Calcutta: Bureau of Education, Superintendent Government Printing, India.
- Howell, Arthur (1872). *Education in British India Prior to 1854 and in 1870-71*. Calcutta: Superintendent of Government Pritinting.
- Jain, M.K. (2007). *Committees and Commissions Elementary Education – Select Documents*. New Delhi: Shipra Publication.
- Jayapalan, N. (2000). *History of Education in India*. New Delhi: Atlantic Publishers and Distributors.
- Jayapalan, N. (2000). *Social and Cultural History of India since 1556*. New Delhi: Atlantic Publishers and Distributors.
- Kochhar, S. K. (1982). *Pivotal Issues in Indian Education*. New Delhi: Sterling Publishers Private Limited.
- Mayhew, Arthur (1928). *The History of India.* London: Faber and Gwyer Limited.
- Misra, B.D. (1089). *A History of the Secondary Education in Uttar Pradesh 1843-1900*. Delhi: Anamika Prakashan.
- Mukerji, S. N. (1974). *History of Education in India*. Baroda, India: Acharya Book Depot.
- Mukherji, S.N. (1974). *History of Education in India (Modern Period)*. Baroda, India: Acharya Book Depot.
- Nurullah, S. and Naik, J. P. (1964). *A Students' History of Education in India*. London: Macmillan and Company Limited.
- Nururllah, S. and Naik, J. P. (1943). *History of Education in India during the British Period.* New York: The MacMillan Company.
- Purkait, B. R. (1992). *Milestones in Modern Indian Education*. Kolkata: New Central Book Agency.
- Ramana, M.V. (2012). *Right to Education – the Parameters and the Paradoxes*. Unpublished Ph.D. Thesis. Guntur: P.G. Department of Legal Studies and Research, Acharya Nagarjuna University.

- Sen, J. M. (1925). *Primary Education Acts in India – A Study*. Calcutta: Calcutta Young Men's Christian Association (CYMCA).
- Sen, J. M. (2010). *History of Elementary Education in India*. New Delhi: Pacific Publication.
- Sharma, R.N. and Sharma, S.K. (2012). *History of Education in India*, New Delhi: Atlantic Publishers and Distributors (P) Ltd.
- Sharp, H. and Richey, J.A. (eds.) 1920. *Selections from Educational Records*. Vol. I, Calcutta: Superintendent of Government Printing.
- Sharp, H. (1920) (Ed.). *Selections from Educational Records, Part I (1781-1839)*. Calcutta: Bureau of Education, Superintendent Government Printing, 1920. (Reprint) Delhi: National Archives of India, 1965.
- State Platform for Common School System (SPCSS). Chennai Declaration, 2012 *Reconstructing Education,* Vol. 1, No. 4, September-December, 2012 and Vol. 2, No. 1, January-March, 2013, pp. 20-34.
- Thakur, A.S. and Berwal, S. (2008). *Development of Education System in India (A Source Book for Teacher Educators and Teachers-in-Training)*. New Delhi: Shipra Publications.
- Thomas, F. W. (1891). *The History and Prospects of British Education in India*. Cambridge: Deighton Bell and Co.

Chapter - 3

Post-Independence Efforts at UEE

The children of today are the future of tomorrow. This is an age-old adage, yet it has a special significance. In India, children in the age group of 0-14 years comprise one-third of the total population of the country. Every child having a conducive and enabling environment can blossom and shine in all spheres of life. Realising the deprived and vulnerable conditions of children, the law makers of the country have accorded a privileged status to children. The number of rights and privileges given by the Indian Constitution and duly supported by legal protection bears a testimony to this. Despite various initiatives both on legal as well as policy and programme levels the condition of children remains a cause of concern that needs to be addressed urgently.

The education is the process of instruction aimed at the all round development of individuals, providing the necessary tools and knowledge to understand and participate in day-to-day activities of today's world. It dispels ignorance and boosts moral values of the individuals. It is the only wealth which cannot be robbed. It forms the basis for lifelong learning and inspires confidence to face challenges. It provides the skills to individuals to become more self-reliant, enhances the ability to manage health and nutrition and plan for future. Education is also a fundamental requirement in a democracy. Through education people become, more informed and responsible citizens, who are capable of exercising wise choices, and finding their voices in politics. It is essential for eradicating poverty, by allowing people to play more productive roles and to earn better for living. Keeping in view the problems and challenges faced by the Indian children, laws have been introduced and programmes are being implemented for the welfare of children in India. There are a large of child rights in India protected by our Constitution, special laws and commissions. These rights cannot be realised unless the right to education is implemented in full swing as the very right is the main key to unlock the other rights of children. Let us now review them.

Education under Indian Constitution

The role of Universal Elementary Education (UEE) for strengthening the social fabric of democracy through provision of equal opportunities to all has been accepted since the inception of our Republic. The Indian Constitution recognised education as a crucial input for nation building and included a number of Articles specially dealing with education. Several articles in the Constitution of India bring into sharp focus on the development of universal elementary education in the country. Few of them have been cited here for our better understanding. They are -

Article 45 enjoined that "the State shall endeavour to provide, within a period of ten years from the commencement of the Constitution, for free and compulsory education for all children until they complete the age of 14 years" (before the 86th Amendment to Constitution, 2002).

Article 28 (1) mandates that "No religious instruction shall be provided in any educational institution wholly maintained out of State funds".

Article (2) enjoins that "Nothing in clause (1) shall apply to an educational institution which is administered by the State but has been established under any endowment or trust which requires that religious instruction shall be imparted in such institution".

Article (3) states that "No person attending any educational institution recognised by the State or receiving aid out of State funds shall be required to take part in any religious instruction that may be imparted in such institution or to attend any religious worship that may be conducted in such institution or in any premises attached thereto unless such person or, if such person is a minor, his guardian has given his consent thereto".

Article 29 (1) of the Constitution provides that any section of the citizens residing in the territory of India or any part thereof having a distinct language scripts or culture of its own shall have the right to conserve the same.

Article 29 (2) lays down that "no citizen shall be denied admission into any educational institution maintained by the state or receiving aid out of state funds on grounds only of religion, race, caste, language or any of them".

Article 30 (1) enjoins, "All minorities, whether based on religion or language, shall have the right to establish and administer educational institutions of their choice".

Article 30 (1A) states that "In making any law providing for the compulsory acquisition of any property of an educational institution established and administered by a minority, referred to in clause (1), the State shall ensure that the amount fixed by or determined under such law for the acquisition of such property is such as would not restrict or abrogate the right guaranteed under that clause".

Article 30 (2) lays down that "the State shall not in granting aid to educational institutions discriminate against any educational institution on the ground that it is under the management of a minority, whether based on religion or language".

Article 350 (A) enjoins that "it shall be the endeavour of every State and of every local authority within the State to provide adequate facilities in the mother-tongue at the primary stage of education to children belonging to linguistic minority groups".

Article 46 mandates that "State shall promote with special care for the educational and economic interests of the weaker sections of the people. And in particular, of the scheduled tribes (STs) and shall protect them from social injustice and all forms of exploitation".

Article 51 (c) mandates that "The State shall endeavour to foster respect for international law and treaty obligations in the dealings of organised peoples with one another".

The 42nd Amendment to the Constitution in 1976 brought education under the Concurrent List, except for certain specified items in the union list like determination of standards in institutions for higher education or research, establishment and maintenance of central universities as well as specified institutions for scientific or technical education and research. The objective of including education in the concurrent list was to facilitate evolution of – national policies in the field of education by placing a greater responsibility on the Union Government as well as State governments. As per the Constitution (Eighty-Sixth Amendment) Act, 2002, the following three Articles have been inserted into the Indian Constitution.

Article 21A mandates that "To provide free and compulsory education to all children of the age of 6-14 years in such a manner as the State may, by law, determine".

Article 45 enjoins that "The State shall endeavour to provide early childhood care and education for all children until they complete the age of six years".

Article 51 (A) of the Constitution relating to Fundamental duties of the Citizens mandates that "(k) who is parent or guardian to provide opportunities for education to his child, or as case may be, a ward between age of 6-14 years".

Child Rights Provisions under Indian Constitution Upholding UEE

If we now examine the entire gamut of Indian Constitution, there are so many Articles which directly or indirectly safeguard the rights of the Indian children. The Articles dealing with Indian child rights provisions under the Constitution of India have been enforcing and rendering imperatives to the Central Governments and State Governments to ensure the rights of the tender. Especially universal elementary education for all children has put emphasis on the agenda of all governments due to those Articles. They are shown in the following Table - 3.1:

Table 3.1: Child Rights Provisions under Indian Constitution

Sl. No.	*Article*	*Child Rights Provisions*
1.	**Articles 24, 39 and 45**	In the Indian Constitution, prior to the 86th Amendment Act, 2002, three Articles in the Constitution i.e. Articles 24, 39 and 45 dealing with prohibition of children from being employed in factories, mines or in other hazardous employment; development and protection of the tender age of children; and free and compulsory education.
2.	**Article 24**	No child below the age of 14 years shall be employed to work in any factory or mine or engaged in hazardous employment.
3.	**Article 39**	The state shall direct its policy toward securing that the tender age of children is not abused and that citizens are not forced by economic necessity to enter avocation unsuited to their age or strength and that children are given opportunities and facilities to develop in a healthy manner and in conditions of freedom and dignity and that childhood and youth are protected against exploitation and against moral and material abandonment.
4.	**Article 21A**	"The State shall provide free and compulsory education to all children of the age of 6–14 years, in such a manner as the State may, by law determine".
5.	**Article 14**	Right to equality.
6.	**Article 15**	Right against discrimination.
7.	**Article 21**	Right to personal liberty and due process of law.
8.	**Article 23**	Right to being protected from being trafficked and forced into bonded labour.
9.	**Article 46**	Right of weaker sections of the people to be protected from social injustice and all forms of exploitation.
10.	**Article 45**	The State shall endeavour to provide early childhood care and education for all children until they complete the age of six years.
11.	**Article 51 (A)**	"(k) Who is parent or guardian to provide opportunities for education to his child, or as case may be, a ward between age of 6-14 years".

Child Rights under the RTE Act, 2009 for UEE

Constitution (Eighty Sixth) Amendment Act, 2002 has transferred the right to education from the non-justiciable right to enforceable right. This Amendment created a new Article i.e. Article 21A. The Article 21A has opened a new horizon in the domain of universal elementary education. Due to the mandate of the Article 21A, India Government has at last enacted the Right to Education Act, 2009 which seeks to provide free and compulsory education of equitable quality to all children in the age group of six to fourteen years. The salient provisions relating to Indian child rights for universal elementary education embedded in the Act are overviewed as follows:

Section 3 provides for every child of the age of six to fourteen years, the right to free and compulsory education in a neighbourhood school till completion of elementary education.

Section 4 provides for every child above six years of age, the right to admission in a class appropriate to his or her age even if the child has not been admitted before in any school or though admitted, could not complete his elementary education.

Section 5 provides for every child, the right to seek transfer to any other school from a school where there is no provision for completion of elementary education.

Section 12 imposes on schools the responsibility of providing free and compulsory education. Under this section, unaided private schools shall admit 25 per cent children to Class–I from among children belonging to weaker sections and disadvantaged groups for continued education of such children till completion of elementary education.

Section 14 is meant for prohibition of denial of admission of a child for lack of age proof.

Section 15 is meant for prohibition of denial of admission to a child, irrespective of the time in the academic year.

Section 17 provides for prohibition of physical punishment and mental harassment of any child in school.

Section 30 prohibits detention or failing of any pupil in any class till completion of elementary education.

Section 32 provides for remedy for grievances relating to the rights of the child under the legislation.

The landmark passing of the Right of Children to Free and Compulsory Education (RTE) Act 2009 makes a historic movement for the children of India. For the first time in India's history, children are guaranteed their right to quality elementary education by the state. For implementation of the Right to Education and for education to be a meaningful child right, government have to make education available, accessible, acceptable and adaptable. It is very necessary to involve the Panchayati Raj Institutions (RPIs) in rural areas for implementing the RTE Act. To achieve the objectives of the Right to Education, the RTE must be aligned with the Sarva Shiksha Abhiyan (SSA). Given the diversity and complexity of the situations of children, teachers need to have at their disposal a deep fund of empathy, commitment, conviction and ability and motivation to persevere; of knowledge and resources to respond and create meaningful educational experiences for all children. The RTE Act is the only single tool to achieve the long cherished goal of universal elementary education of all the children under the territory of India.

Schemes and Programmes for Achieving the Goal of UEE

Social justice and equity are by themselves a strong argument for providing basic education for all. It is an established fact that basic education improves the level of human well-being especially with regard to life expectancy, infant mortality, and nutritional status of children etc. Apart from these, universal basic education significantly contributes to economic growth (MHRD, 2000). In accordance with the Indian Constitutional commitment to ensure free and compulsory education for all children up to the age of 14 years, provision of universal elementary education has been a significant feature of national policy since independence. This resolve has been spelt out emphatically in the National Policies of Education (NPE, 1968, 1986) and the Programme of Action (POA) 1992. A number of schemes and programmes were launched in pursuance of the emphasis embodied in the NPEs and the POA. These included the scheme of Operation Blackboard (OB); Non Formal Education (NFE); Teacher Education (TE); Mahila Samakhya (MS); State specific Basic Education Projects like the Andhra Pradesh Primary Education Project (APPEP),

Bihar Education Project (BEP), Lok Jumbish Project (LJP) in Rajasthan, Education For All Project in Uttar Pradesh; Shiksha Karmi Project (SKP) in Rajasthan; National Programme of Nutritional Support to Primary Education (MDM); District Primary Education Programme (DPEP). Even before the RTE came into force, the following are the Government of India's efforts towards Universalisation of elementary education in the country. Various schemes undertaken to achieve Universalisation of Elementary Education have been mentioned at first in the following Table 3.2:

Table 3.2: Programmes and Schemes for UUE after Independence

Sl. No.	*Title of the Programmes and Schemes for UUE*
A.	Working Group on UEE, Ministry of Education and Social Welfare, GOI, 1978
B.	Restructuring and Reorganisation of Teacher Education, 1987
C.	Non-Formal Education (NFE), 1988
D.	Mahila Samakhya Programme, 1988
E.	Shiksha Karmi Project (SKP), 1987
F.	Operation Blackboard (OB), 1987-88
G	Programmes of Early Childhood Care and Education (ECCE)
H.	Minimum Levels of Learning (MLL), 1991
I.	Lok Jumbish Project (People Mobilisation), 1992
J.	District Primary Education Programme (DPEP), 1994
K.	Education Guarantee Scheme (EGS) and Alternative and Innovative Education (AIE)
L.	(NP-NSPE)/Mid-Day Meal Scheme (MDMS), 1995
M.	District Information System for Education (DISE), 1994
N.	National Programme for Education of Girls at Elementary Level (NP-EGEL), 2003
O.	Kasturba Gandhi Balika Vidyalaya Scheme (KGBV), 2004-05
P.	National Common Minimum Programme (NCPM), 2004
Q.	Prathmik Shiksha Kosh, 2004
R.	Education Cess for Elementary Education and Mid-Day Meal, 2004-05

(*Contd...*)

S.	Creation of Department of Elementary Education and Literacy under MHRD, 1999
T.	Sarva Shiksha Abhiyan (SSA), 2001
U.	National Elementary Education Mission (NEEM), 1995
V.	Navodaya Vidyalayas, 1986
W.	District Institutes of Education and Training (DIETs)
X.	National Institute of Open Schooling (NIOS), 1989
Y.	Right to Education Act, 2009 (RTE Act, 2009)

Now a brief account of the programmes has been interpreted. Ultimately, objective of each programme is to achieve the long-cherished goal of universal elementary education. They are interrelated. Most of the programmes have been merged under the umbrella of SSA – RTE Programme.

1. Sarva Shiksha Abhiyan (SSA)

The Sarva Shiksha Abhiyan is a historic stride towards achieving the long cherished goal of Universalisation of Elementary Education (UEE) through a time bound integrated approach, in partnership with State. SSA, which promises to change the face of the elementary education sector of the country, aims to provide useful and quality elementary education to all children in the 6 -14 age-group. The SSA is an effort to recognise the need for improving the performance of the school system and to provide community owned quality elementary education in mission mode. It also envisages bridging of gender and social gaps (MHRD, 2000).

Sarva Shiksha Abhiyan is an effort to universalise elementary education by community-ownership of the school system. It is a response to the demand for quality basic education all over the country. The SSA programme is also an attempt to provide an opportunity for improving human capabilities to the poorest children, through provision of community-owned quality education in a mission mode (MHRD, 1999). SSA is a programme to provide useful and relevant elementary education for all children in the age group of 6 to 14 years with the active participation of the community by effectively involving the panchayat institutions, school management committees, village and urban slum level education committees, parent-teacher associations, mother-teacher associations, tribal autonomous councils and other grassroot level structures in the management of schools to bridge social, regional and gender gaps. The programme realised the importance of early childhood care and education and looked at the 0-14 age as a continuum (CAG, 2006).

Genesis of SSA: The Scheme of Sarva Shiksha Abhiyan (SSA) evolved from the recommendations of the State Education Ministers' Conference held in October 1998 to pursue universal elementary education in a mission mode. A National Committee of State Education Ministers under the chairmanship of the then Hon'ble Human Resource Development Minister, Dr Murli Manohar Joshi was set up on the recommendation of the Conference to work out the approach to the mission mode. It submitted its Report in October 1999. The **National Committee's Report on UEE in the Mission Mode 1999 recommended that** UEE should be pursued in a mission mode with a holistic and convergent approach with emphasis preparation of District Elementary Education Plans for UEE. Ultimately a framework for Sarva Shiksha Abhiyan had been finalised in consultation with States. The scheme was approved by the Union Cabinet in its meeting held on 16 November 2000 and became functional from January 2001. It supported the fundamental right to education and desired quick action towards operationalisation of the mission mode towards UEE (CAG, 2006 and MHRD, 2001).

Constitutional Mandates, Legal and National Statements for UEE: The Constitutional and legal mandates and national policies and statements have time and again upheld the cause of universal elementary education. The following are the milestones for SSA shown in the Table 3.3:

Table 3.3: Constitutional Mandates, Legal and National Declarations for UEE

SL. No.	*Constitutional, legal/Directives and national policies*	
1.	**Constitutional Mandate, 1950**	"The State shall endeavour to provide, within a period of ten years from the commencement of this Constitution, for free and compulsory education to all children until they complete the age of 14 years."

2.	**National Policy of Education, 1986**	"It shall be ensured that free and compulsory education of satisfactory quality is provided to all children up to 14 years of age before we enter the twenty first century".
3.	**Unnikrishnan Judgement, 1993**	"Every children/citizen of this country has a right to free education until he completes the age of fourteen years."
4.	**Education Ministers' Resolve, 1998**	"Universal elementary education should be pursued in the mission mode. It emphasised the need to pursue a holistic and convergent approach towards UEE."
5.	**National Committee's Report on UEE in the Mission Mode, 1999**	UEE should be pursued in a mission mode with a holistic and convergent approach with emphasis on preparation of District Elementary Education Plans for UEE. It supported the fundamental right to education and desired quick action towards operationalisation of the mission mode towards UEE.
6.	**Initiation of SSA, 2001**	When launched, the SSA aimed to achieve 100 per cent enrollment in a mission mode by 2010. Newer targets have been set after 2010 to comply with RTE provisions. Now SSA is the main vehicle to implement the Right to Education Act (RTE).

Sarva Shiksha Abhiyan is (MHRD, 1999) -

- A programme with a clear time-frame for universal elementary education.
- A response to the demand for quality basic education all over the country.
- An opportunity for promoting social justice through basic education.
- An effort at effectively involving the Panchayati Raj Institutions, the School Management Committees, the Village Education Committees, the Parents' Teachers' Associations, the Mother Teacher Associations, the Tribal Autonomous Councils in the management of elementary schools.
- A partnership between the Central, State and the local government.
- An opportunity for States to develop their own vision of elementary education.

According to the 86th Amendment to the Constitution Act, 2002, Right to Education is a fundamental right and therefore, elementary education shall be free and compulsory. According to Article 21A, "The State shall endeavour to provide free and compulsory education to all children of the age of six to fourteen years in such manner as the State may, by law, determine". The endeavour therefore of Sarva Shiskha Abhiyan (SSA), has been strengthened to provide universal primary education to all in the country. The Prime Minister heads the National Mission for SSA, which monitors the progress made under the scheme.

Some Main Features of SSA

1. **Promotion of Girls' Education:** SSA promotes girls' education to equalise educational opportunities and eliminate gender disparities. A two-pronged strategy is adopted for the promotion of girls education, namely to make the education system responsive to the needs of girls, and simultaneously to generate a community demand for girls' education. Special effort is also made to bring out-of-school girls, especially girls from the disadvantaged sections, to school. Girls' education has received primacy through two special interventions subsumed under SSA, namely the National Programme for Girls Education at Elementary Level (NPEGEL) and Kasturba Gandhi Balika Vidyalaya (KGBV). Concern for education of socially disadvantaged groups is interwoven in SSA.
2. **Special Focus Groups:** SSA lays a special focus on the children of disadvantaged social groups (SC, ST, OBC and Minority communities). SSA targets geographical areas in districts and blocks with predominance of SC, ST, OBC and Minority population in the matter of allocation of funds and school infrastructure to promote education of those who have been deprived of educational facilities so far, 399 such districts have been identified as special focus districts for targeted interventions under SSA, which include 61 districts with high SC population, 109 districts with high ST population, 88 districts with high Muslim population and over 3000

blocks with low female literacy and highest gender gap called educationally backward blocks (EBB) have also been identified to focus on girls' education.

3. **Inclusive Education:** The key objective of SSA is Universalisation of Elementary Education (UEE). Three important aspect of UEE are access, enrollment and retention of all children in 6 – 14 years of age. A zero rejection policy has been adopted under SSA, which ensures that every child with special needs, irrespective of the kind, category and degree of disability, is provided meaningful and quality education.
4. **Improving Quality:** The programme aims to bring a broad shift towards schools and systems that are child-friendly and inclusive, responsive to each child's needs and able to ensure their learning. Across the country, States are being supported to design and implement comprehensive Quality Improvement Programmes, to bring about overall changes in their teachers, curricula, learning materials, learning processes, learning outcomes, assessment and monitoring systems, in order to ensure that the quality of students' learning is improved.
5. **Basic Components of SSA:** There are three basic components of this scheme. They are -
6. **Universal Provision:** It means that an elementary school should be within an easy walking distance from the home of the child. Further primary schools will be opened throughout the country. Although during the first three Five Year Plans primary schools have been established so as to provide primary school within a distance of one kilometer from the home of the child. The norms for opening primary schools, under SSA, are that it should cover a population of 300, in case of lower primary schools and for upper primary schools it should cover the population of 500.
7. **Universal Enrollment:** It means the enrollment of every child of the prescribed age into class first of a school. It also means facilitating enrollment of all children including girls with special focus on mentally as well as physically challenged

groups and children belonging to schedule castes and schedule tribes.

8. **Universal Retention:** It means the retention of every enrolled child in school till he reaches 14 years of age or completes elementary education. Many children initially enrolled in primary schools but don't complete their primary or elementary schooling because of many reasons. For 100 per cent retention under SSA scheme, community involvement at grossroot level has been encouraged and for this purpose Village Education Committees (VEC's) have been framed.

Scope of the Programme: The initiatives under SSA have broadly been grouped under the following heads (CAG, 2006):

- Preparatory activities for micro-planning, household surveys, studies, community mobilisation, school-based activities, training and orientation at all levels, appointment of teachers,
- Opening new primary and alternative schooling facilities like Education Guarantee Scheme (EGS)/Alternative and Innovative Education centres (AIE),
- Opening of upper primary schools, construction of additional classrooms, schools and other facilities,
- Provision of free textbooks to all girls and SC/ST children, maintenance and repair of school buildings,
- Provision of teaching/learning equipment for primary schools on upgradation of EGS to regular schools or setting up of a new primary school,
- TLE for upper primary school, School grant, Teacher grant, Teacher training,
- Opening of State Institute of Educational Management and Training (SIEMAT), Training of community leaders, Provision for disabled children, Research, Evaluation, Supervision and Monitoring, Management cost,
- Innovative activity for girl's education, early childhood care and education, interventions for children belonging to SC/ST community, computer education especially for upper primary level,

- Setting up Block Resource Centre (BRC)/Cluster Resource Centre (CRC) and Interventions for out of school children.

Organisational Set-up and Funding Pattern: The Prime Minister is the Chairman of the General Council of Sarva Shiksha Abhiyan National Mission. The Minister for Human Resource Development is

Organogram of Sarva Shiksha Abhiyan

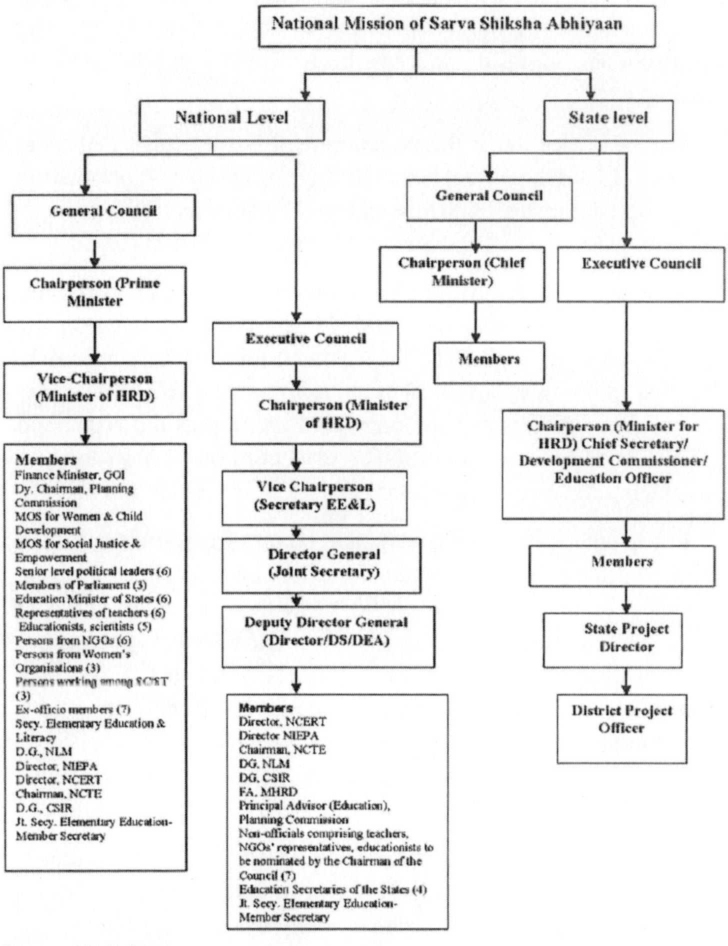

Source: CAG, 2006.

Diagram 3.1: Organisational Set-up of SSA.

the Chairman and the Secretary, Department of Elementary Education, the Vice Chairman of the Executive Committee. A Bureau of Elementary Education has been constituted for overseeing implementation of the scheme. An Implementation Society (SIS) has been established in every State under the chairmanship of the Chief Minister/Education Minister of the State/UT. The district level implementation is overseen by the District Collector/Magistrate/Chief Executive Officer of the Zila Parishad. The District Elementary Education Officer oversees the implementation of the programme at the district level. The Organisational Set-up of SSA has been depicted in the following Diagram 3.1:

The assistance under the programme of Sarva Shiksha Abhiyan was on 85:15 sharing arrangement during the IX Plan, 75:25 sharing arrangement during the Tenth Plan and 50:50 sharing thereafter between the Central Government and State Governments (MHRD, 1999).

Emerging Directions for SSA in Context of the RTE Act, 2009: SSA has been operational since 2000-2001. With the passage of the RTE Act, changes need to be incorporated into the SSA approach, strategies and norms. The changes are not merely confined to norms for providing teachers or classrooms, but encompass the vision and approach to elementary education as evidenced in the shift to child entitlements and quality elementary education in regular schools.

In September 2009, the government set up a Committee under the chairpersonship of Shri Anil Bordia, former Union Education Secretary, to suggest follow up action on SSA vis-à-vis the RTE Act. The Committee had a series of interactions with State Education Secretaries, educationists, representatives of teachers unions, voluntary organisations and civil society organisations. The Committee report, entitled Implementation of RTE Act and Resultant Revamp of SSA, submitted in April 2010, was guided by the following principles (MHRD, 2011: 6):

- Holistic view of education, as interpreted in the National Curriculum Framework 2005, with implications for a systemic revamp of the entire content and process of education with significant implications for curriculum, teacher education, educational planning and management.

- Equity, to mean not only equal opportunity, but also creation of conditions in which the disadvantaged sections of the society - children of SC, ST, Muslim minority, landless agricultural workers and children with special needs, etc. - can avail of the opportunity.
- Access, not to be confined to ensuring that a school becomes accessible to all children within specified distance but implies an understanding of the educational needs and predicament of the traditionally excluded categories - the SC, ST and others sections of the most disadvantaged groups, the Muslim minority, girls in general, and children with special needs.
- Gender concern, implying not only an effort to enable girls to keep pace with boys but to view education in the perspective spelt out in the National Policy on Education 1986/92; i.e. a decisive intervention to bring about a basic change in the status of women.
- Centrality of teacher, to motivate them to innovate and create a culture in the classroom, and beyond the classroom, that might produce an inclusive environment for children, especially for girls from oppressed and marginalised backgrounds.
- Moral compulsion is imposed through the RTE Act on parents, teachers, educational administrators and other stakeholders, rather than shifting emphasis on punitive processes.
- Convergent and integrated system of educational management is pre-requisite for implementation of the RTE law. All states must move in that direction as speedily as feasible.

The revised SSA Framework for Implementation is derived from the recommendations of the **Committee on *Implementation of RTE Act and the Resultant Revamp of SSA***, and is intended to demonstrate the harmonisation of SSA with the RTE Act. It is also based on child centric assumptions emerging from the National Policy on Education, 1986/92 and the National Curriculum Framework (NCF), 2005. The revised SSA Framework for Implementation provides a broad outline of approaches and implementation strategies within which States can frame more detailed guidelines keeping in view their specific social, economic and institutional contexts (MHRD, 2011:7).

The Cabinet Committee on Economic Affairs on 9th September, 2010 approved revision of the existing norms of the SSA programme to conform with the RTE Act (Right of Children to Free and Compulsory Education Act). The Sarva Shiksha Abhiyan (SSA) Programme, a major flagship programme of the Government of India to universalise elementary education in the country, will be the main vehicle for the implementation of the RTE Act. The revisions are as follows (Press Information Bureau, MHRD, 2010):

(i) Revision of SSA norms, including provisions for teachers and classrooms, support for academic supervision, research, evaluation and monitoring, opening of Kasturba Gandhi Balika Vidyalayas (KGBVs) to bring them in conformity with the provisions of the RTE Act and implement the combined RTE-SSA programme. New norms under SSA for uniforms, transportation costs and residential schools to implement the combined RTE-SSA programme have also been included.

(ii) Revision of the funding pattern for the combined RTE-SSA programme between the Centre and the States in the ratio of 65:35 for all States/ UTs; in the case of eight States of NER the existing sharing pattern of 90:10 would however be continue.

The revised SSA Framework for Implementation provides a broad outline of approaches and implementation strategies, within which States can frame more detailed guidelines keeping in view their specific social, economic and institutional contexts. Newer targets having been set after 2010 to comply with RTE provisions, now SSA is the main vehicle to implement the Right to Education Act (RTE).

2. Working Group on UEE, Ministry of Education and Social Welfare, GOI, 1978

Even after three decades, the universalisation of elementary education (UEE) has not been achieved. Therefore, the government have decided to achieve the goal of universal elementary education for all children upto 14 years of age according to a time-bound programme.

The Conference of Ministers of Education of the States and Union Territories held in New Delhi on August 10-11, 1977 recommended that every effort should be made during the Sixth Plan to realise the goal. Accordingly, a Working Group on Universalisation of Elementary Education was set up by the Ministry of Education in collaboration with the Planning Commission to prepare a time bound a feasible plan. The Group considered the matter in depth and submitted its Interim Report.

When the Constitution laid down that free and compulsory education should be provided by 1960, for all children till they reach the age of 14 years, it was expected that an additional 500 lakhs of children would have to be enrolled in elementary schools. Although 27 years have since passed and a very large expansion in enrollment in elementary education has taken place, the task that still remains undone is vast and almost comparable to that in 1950. At the end of 1977-78, total number of children not attending schools would be 4.52 crore : 1.37 crore for Classes I —V and 3.15 crore for Classes VI—VIII.

The Working Group recommends that the target of additional enrollment in the Sixth Plan (1978—83) should be 3.20 crore: 2.20 crore in Classes I—V and 1.00 crore in Classes VI—VIII. It is felt that it will be possible to enrol 220 lakh children in Classes I - V; 100 lakh in full-time schools and 120 lakh children in part-time classes during the Sixth Plan, while at the middle school stage an additional 100 lakh children could be enrolled : 60 lakh in full-time schools and 40 lakh in part-time education.

It has estimated that, to achieve the goal, 452 lakhs of additional non-enrolled children in the age-group 6-14 will require to be covered. The target during the next five years is to cover an additional 320 lakhs of children and to cover the remaining 132 lakhs in another two years, i.e. by 1984-85. The total number of additional children who will have to be enrolled during the five-year period from 1977-78 to 1982-83 will be 320 lakh or 64 lakh per year as against an average additional enrollment of 26 lakh a year during the last four years. This is a task of stupendous magnitude in quantitative terms. This led to the initiation of a Centrally Sponsored Scheme for part-time non-formal education for backward States during the Sixth Five Year Plan.

The Working Group has also suggested that to ensure the achievement of the goal, it will be necessary to provide schools universally after preparing block-level plans within the first three years of the next Plan Period, i.e., by 1980-81. The State Governments have been requested to complete the preparation of the block-level plans immediately so that the national plan for universalisation can be prepared, on a realistic basis, during 1978-79.

The Working Group has identified that eight educationally backward States, namely, Andhra Pradesh, Bihar, Jammu & Kashmir, Madhya Pradesh, Odisha, Rajasthan, Uttar Pradesh and West Bengal have 74 per cent of the total non-enrolled children. The problem in these States is extremely difficult and the success of the entire programme will depend upon what happens or does not happen in these States. Again two-thirds of the non-enrolled children constitute girls. The vast majority of the non-enrolled children are again from weaker sections of the community like Scheduled Castes, Scheduled Tribes and landless agricultural labourers. Such children constitute the hard-core of the problem and do not attend formal schools or even if they do, drop-out soon after joining schools. The Working Group has, therefore, suggested the adoption of large programmes of non-formal part-time education for such children as have dropped out from the formal schools or have not attended any school at all. As concrete evidence of the Centre's concern to bring the eight backward States to the all-India average and to help augment the non-formal part-time education programmes a plan scheme with a provision of Rs four crores has been formulated for implementation during 1978-79. Education in Classes I-V is already free in government schools and in schools run by local bodies in all parts of the country. It is also free in Classes VI-VIII in all States except for boys in Odisha, Uttar Pradesh and West Bengal. All the States except Manipur, Meghalaya, Nagaland, Odisha, Sikkim and Tripura have enacted legislation for compulsory education. As for the Union Territories, such legislation is available in Delhi, Andaman & Nicobar Islands and Chandigarh.

Conference of Education Ministers of States and Union Territories was, in New Delhi on July 13-14, 1978

A Conference of Education Ministers of States and Union

Territories was held in New Delhi on July 13-14, 1978. The resolutions adopted and decisions taken on **Universalisation of Elementary Education** at this Conference are:

The Conference approved a frame-work of action for implementation of universalisation of elementary education on a time-bound basis based on the recommendations of a working group set up in collaboration with the Planning Commission. The framework of action emphasises the following aspects:

- National target of enrollment of 320 lakhs of children in the age group of 6-14 during the next Five Year Plan 1978-83. This will imply enrollment of 90 per cent of the children in the age group of 6-14.
- Location of schools to cover all uncovered habitations within a span of one to three years with priority to rural and backward areas particularly remote tribal areas.
- Enrollment to be planned school-wise and block-wise and district-wise maps to be prepared to identify backward and disadvantaged pockets.
- All out effort to enrol either in formal or non-formal education system, girls and children belonging to under-privileged and backward sections.
- Periodical monitoring of both of enrollment and attendance.
- Optimum utilisation of existing facilities and use of double shifts.
- Academic year and vacations to be planned with reference to local needs.
- Unified elementary educational administration.
- Objectives of universalisation of enrollment and retention emphasised.
- Every child in age group 6-14 shall be enrolled at 6+ and shall continue to learn on full-time basis, if possible, and on part-time basis, if necessary.
- Provide 50 per cent of the State plan budget for elementary education.
- Ensure 30 per cent of this for qualitative improvement.

- Review and revise existing teacher training curricula and in-service programmes and strengthen primary teacher training institutions.
- Central assistance to educationally backward States for innovation and experimentation and non-formal education programmes.

The Conference, while approving these proposals made special mention of the following:

- The provision for voluntary effort in the massive expansion of elementary education particularly in non-formal education.
- That the primary schools have to be provided the necessary facilities, particularly a simple functional building to ensure effective education.
- The quality of the teacher has to be improved and hence teacher education deserves special attention.
- Special efforts needed for enrollment and retention of girls, Scheduled Castes and Scheduled Tribes and wherever necessary special incentives such as mid-day meals, uniforms, attendance scholarships etc., to be provided.
- Since the requirement of funds will be large, efforts should be made to attract private donations for school improvement programmes which should be eligible for income tax rebate.
- Special efforts needed to provide for tackling the problems faced by the Hilly States and desert areas.
- Time-bound programme to be taken up by which NCERT should be able to provide not merely the framework and guidelines but also model instructional material for the non-formal education programmes.

3. Non-Formal Education (NFE), 1988

Non-Formal Education in the Indian context has developed a restricted meaning of an alternative delivery system of education for children who are not able to participate in the formal elementary school. Non-Formal Education has therefore, been limited to providing a second chance to those children who are out-of-school. Broadly speaking, such children are often described as drop-outs. However, a very large number of such children are, in fact, pull-outs from school because of economic and cultural compulsions. Many children may be called stay-outs because the reach of the primary school system in India is not universal. Besides pull-outs and stay-outs, a very large number of children are what may be termed as push-outs. These children do not find the primary school attractive or meaningful.

In order to fulfil the constitutional goal of providing free and compulsory education to all children upto the age of 14, we have to provide education which is both relevant and interesting. For a variety of reasons the formal school system has tended to leave out millions of rural and urban poor children who are not able to attend a full time day-school. Consequently, there is a need for developing a viable alternative system of education which would provide Basic Education for all children in the country. Non-Formal Education has evolved as one such alternative.

Non-Formal Education as an alternative to Formal Elementary Education was experimented with as early as 1976 at which time nine educationally backward states in the country were persuaded to initiate experimental NFE centres. In 1988, following the introduction of the National Policy on Education (1986), a full-fledged scheme of Non-Formal Education supported by the Central Government was introduced primarily in ten educationally backward states, as well as all over the country in urban slums, remote areas, desert and hilly regions. The scheme of Non-Formal Education envisaged widespread participation by State Governments as well as Voluntary Agencies engaged in educational programmes, especially in rural and tribal areas.

Since 1986 there has been a growing National concern for achieving Basic Education for All in the shortest possible time. Several programmes of support to primary and elementary education in the country have been initiated in order to achieve this goal. The experience gathered since 1976 and particularly since 1988 in the area of Non-Formal Education clearly demonstrates that Universal Elementary Education can only be achieved if Non-Formal Education is made available as a viable alternative to formal school education. In 1988, when the Centrally Sponsored Scheme of the Non-Formal Education was formulated by the MHRD, a full-fledged Department of

Non-Formal Education was established in the NCERT prior to 1988, Non-Formal Education functioned as part of other departments. With the establishment of a Department, Non-Formal Education became recognised as an alternative to elementary education. From 1988-1995 the department was also given the responsibility of overseeing Education to Scheduled Castes and Scheduled Tribes since Non-Formal Education emphasised reaching these communities where large number of children was out-of-school. In 1995, the department was re-organised and renamed Department of Education in Non-Formal and Alternative Schooling. This reorganisation has vindicated the significance of Non-Formal Education as an essential alternative to Formal Elementary Education. The department is now poised to play a significant role in the achievement of Universal Elementary Education which has been a goal for the country. Following the 1988 Central Scheme of Non-Formal Education the department was designated as a National Resource Centre for Non-Formal Education. The functions and roles of the department included the following:

- providing academic and technical support to State agencies as well as Voluntary Agencies implementing the scheme of Non-Formal Education;
- evolving training models and providing training for functionaries in Non-Formal Education at all levels;
- developing materials and methodologies for the implementation of Non-Formal Education;
- conducting fundamental and action research in all aspects of Non-Formal Education;
- providing extension services to all agencies (State as well as Voluntary) concerned with Non-Formal Education;
- carrying out programme in pupil evaluation in Non-Formal Education; and
- creating and maintaining capacities at the State level for successful implementation of the scheme of Non-Formal Education.

On 1st April, 2001 the Non-Formal Education (NFE) was converted into Education Guarantee Scheme and Alternative and Innovative Education and it was made a part of SSA.

4. Minimum Levels of Learning (MLL), 1991

A decision was taken in 1991 to identify the minimum level of learning that would be followed by all primary schools in the country. The establishment of MLL was seen as a major step for improving the quality of primary Education. The need to lay down minimum levels of learning (MLL) emerged from the basic concern that irrespective of caste, creed, location or sex, all children must be given access to education of a comparable standard. The MLL strategy is an attempt to combine quality with equity. It lays down learning outcomes in the form of competencies or levels of learning for each stage of elementary education. The strategy also prescribes adoption of measures that will ensure achievement of these levels by children both in formal schools and in non-formal education centres. The focus of the MLL strategy is development of competency-based teaching and learning. Minimum levels of learning in respect of three subjects, namely language, mathematics and environmental studies, have already been laid down for the primary stage. MLLs in terms of learning competencies are expected to be mastered by every child by the end of a particular class or stage of education. Each competency can be further delineated in terms of sub-competencies while specifying the content inputs or while measures of learning. Two basic considerations kept in view while formulating the MLLs are -

- The cognitive capabilities of the children at different classes or grades corresponding to different stage of development.
- The empirical reality in terms of the enabling environmental conditions that characterise the primary education programmes.

Many programmers have been organised to raise the level of learning at national level. Education Commission (1964-66) has emphasised that student of all school should attain the determined level of learning. To take the concerted steps to achieve these levels in institutions got a boost after NPE, 1986. A further momentum was provided by the World conference on EFA, held in Jomtein, in March 1990, which emphasised learning achievement. The report of a committee, set up by the government in 1991, under the chairmanship of Professor R. H. Dave provides a framework and a coherent strategy for achieving MLLs. National Policy on Education 1986 stated as:

- Improving the unattractive school environment, building condition and lack of instructional material.
- Lying down of minimum levels of learning which all students should achieve.

The programme was introduced with the objective of specifying competencies which all primary school students should attain at mastery level in Language, Mathematics and Environmental Studies and to develop curricula and text-books in relation to these. The first phase was implemented through voluntary organisations, research institutions, SCERTs and DIETs. At present, the programme is being implemented in 12 States through 200 DIETs. The MLL approach has been introduced in 50,000 schools in different States. It is now possible to direct effort and resources to schools where the levels of learning have fallen below the prescribed ones.

5. Education Guarantee Scheme (EGS) and Alternative and Innovative Education (AIE)

Education Guarantee Scheme and Alternative and Innovative Education (EGS and AIE) are an important component of Sarva Shiksha Abhiyan (SSA) to bring out of school children in the fold of Elementary Education. EGS addresses the inaccessible habitation where there is no formal school within the radius of one km. and at least 15-25 children of 6-14 years age group. Alternative Education intervention for specific categories of very deprived children e.g., child street children, migrating children, working children, children living in difficult circumstances and older children in the 9+ age group especially adolescent girls are being supported under EGS and AIE all over the country. A sizeable number of out-of-school children are in the habitations where schooling facility is available but these children either did not join the school or dropped out before completing their schooling. These children may not fit into the rigid formal system. To bring such children back to school; back to school camp and Bridge Courses strategies have been implemented. Bridge courses and Back to school camps can be residential or non-residential depending upon the need of children.

The EGS and AIE cover children in the age group of 6-14 years, however, for children with disabilities, it cover children upto the age of 18 years complying with the provisions of Persons with Disabilities (Equal Opportunities, Protection or Rights and Full Participation) Act, 1995 of India. EGS and AIE is based on the assumption that the planning for Universalisation of elementary education (UEE) for all children in the 6-14 years age group should be done in a holistic manner. The EGS and AIE accord a priority to setting up of EGS centres (primary level) in un-served habitations where no school exists within a radius of one km. and at least 15 children in the age group of 6-14 who are not going to schools are available. The funds for EGS and AIE are shared on a 75:25 basis between the Central and State Governments for all state run schools.

6. District Information System for Education (DISE), 1994

The DPEP was initiated in late 1994 as a unique and innovative effort towards achieving the objectives of UPE in educationally backward districts of India. At the project inception stage, it was realised that a sound information base for planning and monitoring of project intervention was an almost non-negotiable requirement. There were many challenges to establish and sustain such a system. This was particularly so as the prevailing system had completely lost its credibility with the data users. The educational statistics collected by the states under the guidance of the MHRD were not only inadequate to meet the growing needs of the decentralised planning but were characterised by inordinate delays, highly aggregative and were not amenable to validation and reliability tests. Since school statistics formed the core of educational statistics, it was rightly recognised that major reforms in school statistics both in terms of their scope and coverage as well as availability and use have to be carried out. Accordingly, NIEPA, now NUEPA took up this as a challenge and accepted the responsibility for designing and implementing such a system for primary education.

The task of developing a school-based statistical system, was initiated by NIEPA during 1995 with the financial assistance from UNICEF, in tune with the spirit of DPEP, the district was selected as a nodal point for collection, computerisation, analysis and use of school level data. The system was later on extended to state and the national level. The state level EMIS cells coordinate the activities of the districts. NIEPA professionals with the involvement of other experts designed and developed the core data capture formats. Accordingly, NIEPA designed software for implementation at the district level and provided the necessary technical and professional support to DPEP districts. A first version of the software named as District Information System for Education (DISE) was released during the middle of 1995. The district level professionals were assisted in the establishment of EMIS units, trained in the data collection, computerisation and analysis using DISE. A major emphasis was on user orientation in the use of educational and allied data for planning, management, monitoring and feedback on the DPEP interventions. DISE is presently operational in more than 200 districts covering 18 DPEP states. Recently, Government of India has decided that the DISE, 2001 will be extended to all the SSA districts with immediate effect and to all the remaining districts of the country by the year 2003–04 data collection. Interaction with the states for implementation of DISE 2001 in non-DPEP states / districts has already started.

DISE is also being developed in regional languages so that the users find it convenient to interpret the data and analyse various types of trends in regional / local language. The distribution of school summary reports in regional languages would be very useful for the school headmasters and the member of the Village Education Committee to understand the progress of their school over the years. Many states are also approaching the MHRD to extend the DISE to cover the whole of school sector. Preliminary work has already been initiated in this regard.

7. (NP-NSPE) / Mid-Day Meal Scheme (MDMS), 1995

The National Programme of Nutritional Support to Primary Education (NP-NSPE), popularly known as the Mid-Day Meal Scheme, was formally launched on 21st August 1995. The programme is designed to give a boost to the universalisation of primary education by impacting upon enrollment, attendance, retention of students of primary schools and also to relate primary education with nutrition, health and integrated child development services (ICDS). From October 2002, the programme has been extended to children studying in Education Guarantee Scheme

(EGS) and other Alternative and Innovative Education (AIE) Learning Centres also. Objectives of Mid-Day Meals Scheme:

(1) Improving the nutritional status of children in Classes I – V in government, Local Body.

(2) Government aided schools, and EGS and AIE centres.

(3) Encouraging poor children, belonging to disadvantaged sections, to attend school more regularly and help them concentrate on classroom activities.

(4) Providing nutritional support to children of primary stage in drought-affected areas during summer vacation.

Rationale

(1) **Preventing classroom hunger:** Many children belonging to disadvantaged sections of society reach school with an empty stomach. Even children, who have a meal before they leave for school, get hungry by the afternoon and are not able to concentrate. Mid-day meal can help children from families, which cannot afford a lunch box or are staying a long distance away from schools to overcome "classroom hunger".

(2) **Promoting school participation:** Mid-day meals have big effect on school participation, not just in terms of getting more children enrolled in the registers but also in terms of regular pupil attendance on a daily basis.

(3) **Facilitating healthy growth of children:** Mid-day meal can also act as a regular source of "supplementary nutrition" for children and facilitate their healthy growth.

(4) **Intrinsic educational value:** A well-organised mid-day meal can be used as an opportunity to impart various good habits to children (such as washing one's hands before and after eating) and to educate them about the importance of clean water, good hygiene and other related matters.

(5) **Fostering social equality:** Mid-day meal can help spread egalitarian values, as children from various social backgrounds learn to sit together and share a common meal. In particular, mid-day meal can help to break the barriers of caste and class among school children. Appointing cooks from SC/ST

communities is another way of teaching children to overcome caste prejudices.

(6) **Enhancing gender equity:** The gender gap in school participation tends to narrow, as the Mid-Day Meal Scheme helps erode the barriers that prevent girls from going to school. Mid-Day Meal Scheme also provides a useful source of employment for women and helps liberate working women from the burden of cooking at home during the day. In these and other ways, women and girl children have a special stake in Mid-Day Meal Scheme.

(7) **Psychological Benefits:** Physiological deprivation leads to low self-esteem, consequent insecurity, anxiety and stress. The Mid-Day Meal Scheme can help address these and facilitate cognitive, emotional and social development.

Presently, MDM scheme in India is the world's largest school lunch programme, reaching to about 113 million children in over 1.26 million schools across the country, with an investment of more than Rs 100 billion "GoI 2012, Mid Day Meal", *Elementary Education*, viewed on 2nd May (http:// mhrd.gov.in/elementaryeducation1). 10.35 crores children studying in 11.55 lakh schools have been covered under the MDMS till 30th September, 2013 (MHRD Annual Report, 2013-2014, GoI).

Development of Mid-Day Scheme (MDMS)

Mid-Day Meal in schools has had a long history in India. In 1925, a Mid-Day Meal Programme was introduced for disadvantaged children in Madras Municipal Corporation. By the mid 1980s three States viz. Gujarat, Kerala and Tamil Nadu and the UT of Pondicherry had universalised a cooked Mid-Day Meal Programme with their own resources for children studying at the primary stage. By 1990-91 the number of States implementing the mid-day meal programme with their own resources on a universal or a large scale had increased to twelve states.

With a view to enhancing enrollment, retention and attendance and simultaneously improving nutritional levels among children, the National Programme of Nutritional Support to Primary Education

(NP-NSPE) was launched as a Centrally Sponsored Scheme on 15th August 1995, initially in 2408 blocks in the country. By the year 1997-98 the NP-NSPE was introduced in all blocks of the country. It was further extended in 2002 to cover not only children in Classes I-V of government, government aided and local body schools, but also children studying in EGS and AIE centres. Central Assistance under the scheme consisted of free supply of food grains @ 100 grams per child per school day, and subsidy for transportation of food-grains up to a maximum of Rs 50 per quintal.

In September 2004 the scheme was revised to provide cooked mid-day meal with 300 calories and 8-12 grams of protein to all children studying in Classes I – V in government and aided schools and EGS/AIE centres. In addition to free supply of food-grains, the revised scheme provided Central Assistance for (a) Cooking cost @ Re 1 per child per school day, (b) Transport subsidy was raised from the earlier maximum of Rs 50 per quintal to Rs 100 per quintal for special category states, and Rs 75 per quintal for other states, (c) Management, monitoring and evaluation costs @ 2 per cent of the cost of foodgrains, transport subsidy and cooking assistance, (d) Provision of mid-day meal during summer vacation in drought affected areas.

In July 2006, the scheme was further revised to provide assistance for cooking cost at the rate of (a) Rs 1.80 per child/school day for States in the North Eastern Region, provided the NER States contribute Re 0.20 per child/school day, and (b) Rs 1.50 per child/ school day for other States and UTs, provided that these States and UTs contribute Re 0.50 per child/school day.

In October 2007, the scheme has been further revised to cover children in upper primary (Classes VI to VIII) initially in 3479 Educationally Backwards Blocks (EBBs). Around 1.7 crore upper primary children were included by this expansion of the scheme. From 2008-09 i.e. w.e.f. 1st April, 2008, the programme covers all children studying in government, Local Body and government-aided primary and upper primary schools and the EGS/AIE centres including Madarsa and Maqtabs supported under SSA of all areas across the country. The calorific value of a mid-day meal at upper primary stage has been fixed at a minimum of 700 calories and 20 grams of protein by providing 150 grams of foodgrains (rice/wheat) per child/school day.

From the Year 2009 onwards: (a) Food norms have been revised to ensure balanced and nutritious diet to children of upper primary group by increasing the quantity of pulses from 25 to 30 grams, vegetables from 65 to 75 grams and by decreasing the quantity of oil and fat from 10 grams to 7.5 grams.

(b) Cooking cost (excluding the labour and administrative charges) has been revised from Rs 1.68 to to Rs 2.50 for primary and from Rs 2.20 to Rs 3.75 for upper primary children from 1.12.2009 to facilitate serving meal to eligible children in prescribed quantity and of good quality. The cooking cost for primary is Rs 2.69 per child per day and Rs 4.03 for upper primary children from 1.4.2010. The cooking cost will be revised prior approval of competent authority by 7.5 per cent every financial year from 1.4.2011.

(c) The honorarium for cooks and helpers was paid from the labour and other administrative charges of Re 0.40 per child per day provided under the cooking cost. In many cases the honorarium was so little that it became very difficult to engage manpower for cooking the meal. A separate component for payment of honorarium @ Rs 1000 per month per cook-cum-helper was introduced from 1.12.2009. Honorarium at the above prescribed rate is being paid to cook-cum-helper. However, in some of the states the honorarium to cook-cum-helpers is being paid more than Rs 1000 through their state fund. Following norms for engagement of cook-cum-helper have been made:

(1) One cook-cum-helper for schools up to 25 students.

(2) Two cooks-cum-helpers for schools with 26 to 100 students.

(3) One additional cook-cum-helper for every addition of upto 100 students.

More than 25.70 lakhs cook-cum-helper are engaged by the State/UTs during 2013-14 for preparation and serving of Mid-Day Meal to Children in Elementary Classes.

(d) A common unit cost of construction of kitchen shed @ Rs 60,000 for the whole country was impractical and also inadequate.

Now the cost of construction of kitchen-cum-store will be determined on the basis of plinth area norm and State Schedule of Rates. The Department of School Education and Literacy vide letter No.1-1/2009-Desk (MDM) dated 31.12.2009 had prescribed 20 sq.mt. plinth area for schools having up to 100 children. For every additional up to 100 children additional four sq.mt plinth area will be added. States/UTs have the flexibility to modify the Slab of 100 children depending upon the local condition.

(e) Due to difficult geographical terrain of the Special Category States the transportation cost @ Rs 1.25 per quintal was not adequate to meet the actual cost of transportation of foodgrains from the FCI godowns to schools in these States. On the request of the North Eastern States the transportation assistance in the 11 Special Category States (Northern Eastern States, Himachal Pradesh, Jammu & Kashmir and Uttarakhand) have been made at par with the Public Distribution System (PDS) rates prevalent in these States with effect from 1.12.2009.

(f) The existing system of payment of cost of foodgrains to FCI from the Government of India is prone to delays and risk. Decentralisation of payment of cost of foodgrains to the FCI at the district level from 1.4.2010 allowed officers at State and National levels to focus on detailed monitoring of the Scheme.

8.41 crore in Primary and 3.36 crore Upper Primary children i.e. a total of 11.77 crore children were estimated to be benefited from MDM Scheme during 2009-10. 11.04 crore children were covered under MDM Scheme during 2009-10. During 2010-11, 11.36 crore children i.e. 7.97 crore children in primary and 3.39 crore children in upper primary had been covered in 12.63 lakhs institutions. During 2011-12 total coverage of children against enrollment was 10.52 crore (i.e. Primary 7.71 crore and Upper Primary 3.36 crore children). During 2012-13, 10.68 crore children (Elementary level) had been covered in 12.12 lakh Schools. 10.45 crore children were covered in 11.58 lakh Schools during 2013-14.

8. District Primary Education Programme (DPEP), 1994

The Centrally sponsored Scheme of District Primary Education Programme (DPEP) was launched in 1994 as a major initiative to revitalise the primary education system and to achieve the objective of Universalisation of primary education. DPEP adopts a holistic approach to universalise access, retention and improve learning achievement and to reduce disparities among social groups. Adopting an area-specific approach with district as the unit of planning, the key sensitivity to local conditions and ensuring full participation of the community. DPEP is based on the principle of 'additionally' and is structured to fill in the existing gaps. The programme components include construction of classrooms and new schools, opening of Non-formal/ Alternative Schooling Centres, appointment of new teachers, setting up early childhood education centres, strengthening of State Councils of Educational Training through District Institute of Education and Training (DIETs), setting up of Block Resource Centres/Cluster Resource Centres, teacher training, development of Teaching Learning Material, Research-based interventions, special interventions for promoting education of disadvantaged groups, girls, SC/ST, etc. initiatives for providing integrated education to disabled children and distance education for teacher training have also been incorporated in the DPEP Scheme. The objectives of the programme are -

- To provide all children with access to Primary Education either in formal system or through Alternative Schooling Centre.
- Provides Reading Writing Materials and free textbooks to all SC and ST children and General girls.
- Providing Access to Primary Education for all children.
- Reducing the Gap among Gender and disadvantaged social groups to less than five.
- Increasing learning achievement of primary school students by 25 per cent.

The District Primary Education seeks to operationalise para 7.4.6 of the POA, 1992 which reads as follows: "Further efforts would be made to develop district specific projects, with specific activities, clearly defined responsibilities, definite time-schedule and specific targets. Each district project will be prepared within the major strategy framework and will be tailored to the specific needs and possibilities in the district. Apart from effective UEE, the goals of each project will include the reduction if existing disparities in educational access, the provision of alternative systems of comparable standards to the disadvantaged groups, a substantial improvement in the quality of schooling facilities, obtaining a genuine community involvement in the running of schools, and building up local level capacity to ensure effective decentralisation of educational planning. That is to say, the overall goal of the project would be reconstruction of primary education as a whole in selected districts instead of a piecemeal implementation of schemes. An integrated approach is more likely to achieve synergies among different programme components."

9. Operation Blackboard (OB), 1987-88

Recognising the unattractive school environment, unsatisfactory condition of school buildings, inadequate physical facilities and insufficiency of instructional materials in primary schools, which function as de-motivating factors for enrollment and retention, a scheme symbolically called "Operation Blackboard" was introduced in 1987-88 with the aim of improving human and physical resources available in the primary schools of the country. The term "Operation" implied that there was urgency in the programme, which had a predetermined time-frame about its implementation and the term "Blackboard" symbolised physical facilities in schools both in terms of man and material. The scheme has been subsumed in Sarva Shiksha Abhiyan (SSA) from 2002-2003. Operation Blackboard has three interdependent components:

- Provision of a building comprising at least two reasonably large all-weather rooms with a deep verandah and separate toilet facilities for boys and girls,
- At least two teachers — one of them preferably a woman — in every school, and
- Provision of essential teaching-learning material including black-boards, maps, charts, toys and equipment for work experience.

Operation Blackboard was to be implemented in phases. However, the pace and extent of implementation have been uneven — constituting a major problem that needs to be addressed. Since the inception of this scheme in 1987, 103,364 teachers (of whom 48 per cent were women) have been recruited and 115,091 classrooms have been constructed. The scope of Operation Blackboard is to be expanded under the Eighth Plan. A third teacher and a third classroom is to be provided to primary and upper primary schools where enrollment levels come up to sufficient levels.

10. Programmes of Early Childhood Care and Education (ECCE)

Early childhood care and education (ECCE) is viewed as a crucial input in the strategy of human resource development, as a feeder and support programme for primary education, and as a support service for working women of the disadvantaged sections of society. Since the age-span covered by ECCE is from conception to six years, emphasis has been given to a child-centred approach and play-way and activity-based learning in place of formal methods of teaching including introduction of the 3 R's. Keeping in mind the role of ECCE as a support service in UEE, it is deliberately directed to the most underprivileged groups, those who are still outside the mainstream of formal education. The aim of ECCE is that every child should be assured access to the fulfilment of all basic needs. It involves the total development of the child in every aspect including the physical, psychomotor, cognitive, language, emotional, social and moral. The present ECCE programmes include:

(1) the integrated child development service (ICDS);

(2) the scheme of assistance to voluntary organisations for running early child education (ECE) centres;

(3) pre-primary schools run by state governments, municipal corporations and other agencies; and

(4) maternal and child health services through primary health centres, sub-centres and other agencies.

The ICDS is today the biggest programme of early childhood development, serving about 15 million children and three million mothers. Appropriate linkages are being established between ECCE programmes, primary schools, NFE centres and other related schemes of UEE. As per the 86th Amendment to Constitution of India, 2002 substituted existing Article 45 of the Constitution and it mandates that 'The State shall endeavour to provide early childhood care and education for all children until they complete the age of six years'. Now early childhood care and education falls under the Directive Principles and it hoped that ECCE will get new momentum.

11. Restructuring and Reorganisation of Teacher Education, 1987

Teacher performance is the most crucial input in the field of education. In the ultimate analysis, the national policies on education have to be interpreted and implemented by teachers as much through their personal example as through teaching-learning processes. With a view to improving the quality and competence of teachers, a centrally sponsored scheme of Restructuring and Reorganisation of Teacher Education (RRTE) was launched in 1987.

During the period 1987-90, nearly 1.8 million teachers were trained under the programme of mass orientation of school teachers (PMOST). Most of them were primary and upper primary teachers. The main objective of the programme was to orient teachers in the main priorities and directions envisaged in the NPE 1986 and to improve their professional competence. Among the other main components of the RRTE, as far as elementary education is concerned, are:

(1) Setting up of District Institutes of Education and Training (DIETs) in all districts to provide good quality pre-service and in-service training to elementary school teachers and adult education/non-formal education personnel and to provide resource support to these systems.

(2) Organising Special Orientation Programmes for Primary Teachers (SOPT) with a view to providing training to teachers in the use of OB materials and orienting them towards MLL strategy with a focus on teaching of language, mathematics and environmental studies.

More than 300 DIETs have already become operational and have started conducting training programmes. The SOPT launched in 1993-94 is now going on in almost all states and more than 115,000 teachers have already been trained. A National Council for Teacher Education

(NCTE) was set up in 1993 with statutory status for the effective implementation of all teacher education and training programmes and to achieve planned and co-ordinated development of the entire teacher education system throughout the country. The regulation and proper maintenance of norms and standards in the teacher education system is the responsibility of the NCTE.

12. Lok Jumbish Project (People Mobilisation), 1992

An innovative project called Lok Jumbish (People's movement for Education for All) with assistance from Swedish International Development Agency (SIDA) has been undertaken in Rajasthan in 1992. The basic objective of the project is to achieve Education for All, through people's mobilisation and their participation. The project is implemented by the Lok Jumbish Parishad (LJP), an autonomous society registered under the Societies Registration Act. Lok Jumbish Project (LPJ) has set-up innovative management structures incorporating the principles of decentralisation and delegation of authority as well as building partnership with local communities and the voluntary sectors, intensive community mobilisation, and schools mapping, processing as well as development of innovative design for community centre school buildings programme. Project interventions were made in several components of primary education like teachers training, minimum levels of learning, opening of new schools, non-formal education centres. It has undertaken environmental technique activities like school mapping, opening new schools and upgradation of primary schools. The Lok Jumbish project has made a positive contribution to quality improvement through the development of improved MLL-based textbooks from Class I-1V, which has been mainstreamed in all government schools of Rajasthan.

13. Shiksha Karmi Project (SKP), 1987

Shiksha Karmi Project was started in Rajasthan in 1987. It was a scheme jointly sponsored by Swedish International Development Agency (SIDA), Government of India and State of Rajasthan. It aimed at universalisation and qualitative improvement of primary education in remote areas and socio-economically backward villages of Rajasthan with primary attention given to girls. It was a unique successful experiment with positive results and minimum costs. SKP of Rajasthan may be an effective alternative strategy. This project sought to solve the problem of teacher absenteeism and identifies it as a major obstacle in achieving the goal of UEE. Under SKP, regular teachers were replaced by local teachers who were less qualified but specially trained. The substitute teachers were known as "*Shiksha karmi*" with a minimum educational qualification of Class VIII for men and Class VI for women. The evaluation of the scheme showed that the level of attainment of the students is comparable to that of those attending formal schools.

14. Mahila Samakhya Programme (MS), 1988

"Education will be used as an agent of basic change in the status of woman. In order to neutralise the accumulated distortions of the past, there will be a well-conceived edge in favour of women. The National Education System will play a positive, interventionist role in the empowerment of women. It will foster the development of new values through redesigned curricula, textbooks, the training and orientation of teachers, decision-makers and administrators, and the active involvement of educational institutions. This will be an act of faith and social engineering..." NPE, 1986.

The Mahila Samakhya programme was launched in 1988 in pursuance of the goals of the New Education Policy (1986) and the Programme of Action as a concrete programme for the education and empowerment of women in rural areas, particularly of women from socially and economically marginalised groups.

Provision of educational opportunities for women and girls has been an important part of the national endeavour in the field of education since Independence. Though these endeavours did yield significant results, gender disparities persist, more so in rural areas and among disadvantaged communities. The National Policy on Education (NPE, 1986) as revised in 1992 was a landmark in the field of policy on women's education in that it recognised the need to redress traditional gender imbalances in educational access and achievement. The NPE also recognised that enhancing infrastructure alone will not redress the problem. It recognised that "*the empowerment of women is possibly the most critical pre-condition for the participation of girls and women in the educational process"*. The Programme of Action (POA, 1992), in the section *"Education for Women's Equality"* (Chapter-XII, pp. 105-107), focuses on empowerment of women as the critical precondition for their participation in the education process. The POA states that education can be an effective tool for women's empowerment, the parameters of which are:

- enhance self-esteem and self-confidence of women;
- building a positive image of women by recognising their contribution to the society, polity and the economy;
- developing ability to think critically;
- fostering decision-making and action through collective processes;
- enable women to make informed choices in areas like education, employment and health (especially reproductive health);
- ensuring equal participation in developmental processes;
- providing information, knowledge and skill for economic independence;
- Enhancing access to legal literacy and information relating to their rights and entitlements in society with a view to enhance their participation on an equal footing in all areas.

These parameters informed the framing of the objectives of the MS programme. In the Mahila Samakhya Programme the empowerment of women is seen as a critical precondition for the participation of women and girls in the education process. The principal strategy identified for ensuring women's participation is through mobilising and organising them into sanghas (collectives). It was decided that the best way to achieve this would be to follow a strategy where the programme would not lay down either targets to be achieved or specific agenda to be followed but would take its programmatic cues from the women in the Sanghas. The predominant composition of the Mahila Sanghas is SC/ST women, women belonging to landless and marginalised families, who are engaged in wage labour. This is the very group that is most alienated from educational and other government programmes and processes. Reaching them has been a difficult but exhilarating process. Launching the programme was a challenge and Mahila Samakhya had to

Table 3.4: The Physical Progress of MS as on March 2014

Sl. No.	*State*	*No. of Districts*	*No. of EBBs*	*No. of Villages*
1.	Andhra Pradesh	14	129	5464
2.	Assam	12	65	3460
3.	Bihar	21	124	8032
4.	Chhattisgarh	6	15	1586
5.	Gujarat	21	76	4335
6.	Jharkhand	11	76	4323
7.	Karnataka	18	66	3725
8.	Kerala	6	12	3020
9.	Uttar Pradesh	19	75	5728
10.	Uttarakhand	7	24	2725
	Total	**126**	**662**	**42398**

adapt and mould itself to the conditions prevailing in each State. In April 1989, Mahila Samakhya Societies were registered and operationalised in different states. Currently, MS coverage exists across 126 districts of 10 States namely AP, Assam, Bihar, Chhattisgarh, Gujarat, Jharkhand, Karnataka, Kerala, Uttar Pradesh and Uttarakhand. An expansion to 60-65 new districts is planned during the XIIth Plan. The physical progress of MS as on March 2014 is as under the Table 4.4.

15. National Programme for Education of Girls at Elementary Level (NP-EGEL), 2003

The National Programme for Education of Girls at Elementary Level (NPEGEL) is a focussed intervention of Government of India, to reach the "Hardest to Reach" girls, especially those not in school. Launched in July 2003, it is an important component of SSA, which provides additional support for enhancing education of under-privileged/disadvantaged girls at the elementary level. The Scheme is implemented in Educationally Backward Blocks (EBBs) where the level of female literacy is below and the gender gap is above the national average in blocks of districts which are not covered under EBBs but have at least five per cent SC/ST population and where SC/ST female literacy is below ten per cent.

16. Kasturba Gandhi Balika Vidyalaya Scheme (KGBV), 2004-05

Apart from NP-EGEL, a new scheme called Kasturba Gandhi Balika Vidyalaya (KGBV) was approved for launching during 2004-05 for setting up 750 residential schools with boarding facilities at elementary level for girls belonging predominantly to the SC, ST and other backward castes (OBC) and minorities in difficult areas. KGBV are residential upper primary schools for girls from SC, ST, OBC and Muslim communities. KGBVs are set up in areas of scattered habitations, where schools are at great distances and are a challenge to the security of girls. This often compels girls to discontinue their education. KGBV addresses this through setting up residential schools, in the block itself. KGBVs provide for a minimum reservation of 75 per cent seats for girls from SC/ST/OBC and minorities communities and 25 per cent to girls from families that live below the poverty line. As of now till 2013-14, 3609 KGBVs have been sanctioned in the country enrolling 347725 girls therein.

17. Prathmik Shiksha Kosh, 2004

An education cess of two per cent on all direct and indirect central taxes has been imposed through the Finance (No. 2) Act, 2004. Soon after the relevant Bill was introduced in Parliament on July 8, 2004, action was initiated for the creation of a separate, dedicated, non-lapsable fund to be named as "Prathmik Shiksha Kosh" and maintained by the Ministry of Human Resource Development, Department of Elementary Education and Literacy. The then Prime Minister, Dr Manmohan Singh, announced the creation of a non-lapsable fund for financing elementary education, including Sarva Shiksha Abhiyan, and the mid-day meal scheme on 18th September, 2004. The fund titled "Prathmik Shiksha Kosh" has been financed from the receipts of the Education Cess levied in the Union Budget 2004-05.

18. National Common Minimum Programme (NCPM), 2004

The United Progressive Alliance government supported by the Left Parties assumed office in May 2004. The constituent parties drew up a National Common Minimum Programme (NCMP) that defined the broad contours of the policies of the UPA government. The UPA made a solemn pledge to provide a government that is corruption-free, transparent and accountable; and to provide an administration that is responsible and responsive at all times, and set out six principles of governance, and seven priorities for policy (Government of India, 2004). It is still an important document as it reveals the intentions of the UPA government, its main priorities, policies and programmes. The intentions of the government with respect to education development have been spelt out under the section of 'Education and health' (Tilak, 2004). The UPA government pledged to raise public spending in education to least six per cent of GDP with at least half this amount being spent of primary and secondary sectors. This will be done in a phased manner. The UPA government also pledged to introduce a cess on all central taxes to finance the commitment to universalise access to quality basic education (Government of India, 2004). This enables better funding of Sarva Shiksha Abhiyan, Prarambhik Shiksha Kosh, Kasturba Gandhi Balika Vidyalaya, Mid-day Meal Scheme, and Nutrition Programme for Adolescent Girls (Government of India, 2005).

19. Education Cess for Elementary Education and Mid-Day Meal, 2004-05

Another major step has been the imposition of the two per cent education cess on all central taxes by the UPA Government in 2004-05 which played a crucial role in augmenting the funds for SSA. The constraints on public resources have had serious implications for the education system in India. A country like India has to make some difficult choices if it is to give expression to its goal of Universalisation of elementary education, which is also a key Millennium Development Goal (MDG) of the UN (Bhaumik and Banik, 2006). An Education Cess @ two per cent on direct and indirect Central taxes has been imposed with effect from April 1, 2004 through Finance (No. 2) Act, 2004, Ministry of Law and Justice (Legislative Department) dated on 10th September "so as to fulfil the commitment of the government to provide and finance universalised quality basic education". The cess is expected to yield about Rs 4,000-5,000 crore per annum. All the proceeds from the cess have been thought to be used for implementation of programmes related to Universal Elementary Education like Sarva Shiksha Abhiyan and Mid-Day Meal Scheme (MHRD, 2005:7).

The then Expenditure Secretary D. Swarup said, "The fund will be non-lapsable and receipts from the education cess will be available on a rollover basis for purposes of financing elementary education and the mid-day meal scheme". Then Prime Minister Manmohan Singh has directed that the entire proceeds from the recently-imposed education cess should go into a non-lapsable fund for primary education and mid-day meals. In line with the PM's directive, the finance ministry has informed the department of elementary education and literacy to set up a fund titled 'Prathmik Shiksha Kosh' to receive the proceeds of the education cess (Malani, 2004). While the allocation for primary education during 03-04 was Rs 2,700 crore, the actual expenditure was Rs 3,200 crore. The allocation for primary education has been hiked to Rs 5,057 crore for 04-05, while that for the mid-day meal scheme has been hiked to Rs 2,907 crore from Rs 1,375 crore in 03-04. On October 6, 2005 the Union Cabinet approved the creation of a non-lapsable Prarambhik Shiksha Kosh (Elementary Education Fund) which would be maintained by the Ministry of Human Resource Development (MHRD), Department of Elementary Education & Literacy (EE&L). Ultimately resources for elementary education, augmented through the Education Cess enables better funding of Sarva Shiksha Abhiyan, Prarambhik Shiksha Kosh, Kasturba Gandhi Balika Vidyalaya, Mid-day Meal Scheme, and Nutrition Programme for Adolescent Girls (Government of India, 2005). Soon after the last Lok Sabha elections, A. P. J. Abdul Kalam had also, inter alia, stated the following in the Parliament on 7th June, 2004:

> "21. India's greatest resource is its people. The full potential of our human resources has yet to be effectively utilised. High priority will, therefore, be accorded to education. The Government will aim at increasing public spending on education so as to ultimately reach at least six per cent of GDP, with half the amount earmarked for primary and secondary education. A cess will be proposed on all central taxes to finance the commitment to universalise access to quality basic education" (MHRD, 2005, p. 7).

20. Creation of Department of Elementary Education and Literacy under MHRD, 1999

A separate Department of Elementary Education and Literacy, headed by an independent Secretary, was created in November 1999 within the Ministry of Human Resource Development. In keeping with the vision of providing education of equitable quality to fully harness the nation's human potential, the Department has laid down the following objectives to:

- Reinforce the national and integrative character of education in partnership with States/UTs.
- Improve quality and standards of school education and literacy towards building a society committed to Constitutional values.
- Universalise elementary education in keeping with the rights conferred under the RTE Act.
- Universalise opportunities for quality secondary education.
- Establish a fully literate society.

The Department presently endeavours to:

- Provide free and compulsory education to all children at elementary level.
- Become a partner with the States and Union Territories to reinforce the national and integrative character of education.
- Build a society committed to Constitutional values with the help of quality school education and literacy.
- Universalise opportunities for quality secondary education (*Source:* http://mhrd.gov.in/overview-se)

21. National Elementary Education Mission (NEEM), 1995

In view of the rapid expansion of the elementary education system and the emerging challenges, the government has been contemplating several structural changes of national and state levels for achieving the good of UEE. Within this background, the commitment made in the revised NPE, 1992, for launching a National Elementary Education Mission (NEEM) has been given final shape. With the objective of mobilising all the resources — human, financial and institutional — necessary for achieving the goal of UEE, a National Elementary Education Mission (NEEM) was set up in August 1995 with the District Primary Education Programme (DPEP) as its core. A major task of such a Mission is to evolve strategies for reaching the unreached and achieving the goals of UEE within a given time frame in a systematic, sustained and integrated manner by involving all segments of civil society in this national endeavour.

The objectives of the Mission are:

- Universal access and enrollment;
- Universal retention of children upto 14 years of age; and
- A substantial improvement in the quality of education to enable all children to achieve essential levels of learning.

The approach and strategy of the Mission would incorporate the following rents:

- Genuine and effective involvement and participation of all people - Political parties, mass organisations, trade unions, peasants, youth groups, women's collectives, individuals, and social activists so as to make UEE a mass movement.
- National arousal and social mobilisation through media - print, theatre, fold culture etc.
- a time bound and decentralised perspective with rigorous planning at district, block and cluster levels for achieving the goal of UEE.
- Accountability and transparency at all levels of the elementary education system.

The political resolve to make the right to elementary education a fundamental right had cast a greater responsibility on the government to achieve UEE. The national Elementary Education Mission was expected to play the role of an overarching body to meet this challenge.

22. District Institutes of Education and Training (DIETs)

As envisaged in National Policy of Education and Programme of Action 1986, the centrally sponsored scheme of restructuring and reorganisation of teacher education was taken up in 1987 to create a viable institutional infrastructure, academic and technical service base for orientation of knowledge, competence and pedagogical skills of elementary school teachers in the country. One of the five components of the Scheme was establishment of DIETs. Draft guidelines for implementing the DIET component were circulated to States in

October 1987 and have, together with certain subsequent circulars, formed the basis for its implementation so far. Till October 1989, Central assistance had been sanctioned under the Scheme for setting up a total of 216 DIETs in the country.

The Scheme envisages setting up of District Institutes of Education and Training (DIETs) in each district to provide academic and resource support to elementary education teachers and non-formal and adult education instructors. It also envisages establishment of CTEs/IASEs to organise pre-service and in-service training for secondary teachers and provide extension and resource support services to secondary schools. IASEs are expected to conduct programmes for preparation of elementary teacher educators, conduct in-service training for elementary and secondary teacher-educators and principals of secondary schools engaged in advance levels and fundamental and applied research especially of inter-disciplinary nature, and provide academic guidance to DIETs and support services to CTEs.

DIETs are established by upgrading existing Elementary Teachers Education Institutions (ETEIs). The land is provided by the states free of cost. The CTEs are set up by upgrading the existing Secondary Teachers Education Institutions (STEs) offering B. Ed. courses and IASEs by upgrading Colleges and University Departments of Education offering M. Ed. courses. DIETs have been identified as the principal technical and professional resource institutions in DPEP districts.

The Rationale for the Introduction of DIETs: The rationale for the introduction of DIETs was that the elementary and adult systems were 'already too vast to be adequately supported by national and State level institutions alone' (MHRD 1989: 3) for the further expansion and qualitative improvement advocated by the policy directive. The DIETs were thus conceived as 'addition of a third – district level – tier to the support system' which would be 'closer to the field, and therefore more alive to its problems and needs' (*ibid*). They were added as a component of an existing top-down, centralised approach to teacher education, adopting similar structures to those already in existence at the State and national levels. It was stressed that the DIETs are part of a larger strategy to achieve national goals in the areas of Elementary and Adult Education. [...] DIETs cannot...afford to view themselves in isolation, and must faithfully discharge their role of supplementing and complementing other parallel initiatives (MHRD 1989: 4).

The official DIET guidelines (MHRD 1989) expected them to pursue three key functions:

- Training and orientation of the following target groups (elementary school teachers; Head Masters, officers of Education Department up to Block level; NFE and adult education instructors and supervisors; members of District Boards of Education and Village Education Committees, other community volunteers; resource persons who will conduct suitable programmes…at the centres other than the DIET).
- Academic and resource support to the elementary and adult education systems in the district in other ways.
- Action research and experimentation to deal with specific problems of the district in achieving the objectives in the areas of elementary and adult education (MHRD 1989: 8).

23. Navodaya Vidyalayas

As part of the programme of action of the new education policy, 1986, Government of India launched the scheme under the pioneer of Shri. Rajiv Gandhi, the then Prime Minister of India to set up Jawahar Navodaya Vidyalayas in all the districts of the country in order to provide opportunities to the children with special talents to proceed at a faster pace by making quality education available to them irrespective of their capacity to pay for it. First established in early 1985, they are the brainchild of the then human resources minister, P. V. Narasimha Rao (who later became Prime Minister of India) and late Prime Minister Rajiv Gandhi to find and foster talented children from the rural parts of India. They were formerly named as Navodaya Vidyalayas and renamed later as "Jawahar Navodaya Vidyalayas in the birth-centenary year of Jawahar Lal Nehru, the first prime minister of independent India.

The Navodaya Vidyalaya Scheme was started during the year 1985-86 and is managed by Navodaya Vidyalaya Samiti, an autonomous organisation under the Department of Education, Ministry of Human Resource Development. Such education would enable students from rural areas to compete with their urban counterparts on an equal footing. The National Policy on Education-1986 envisaged the setting up of residential schools, to be called Jawahar Navodaya Vidyalayas that would bring out the best of rural talent.

In order to provide high quality modern education, including strong component of culture, inculcation of values, awareness of the environment, adventure activities and physical education to the talented children predominantly from the rural areas, without regard to their socio-economic conditions, the Government of India launched the scheme to establish on an average, one Navodaya Vidyalaya (NV) in each district of the country. Navodaya Vidyalayas are fully residential, co-educational institutions, providing education up to Senior Secondary stage. Education in Navodaya Vidyalayas, including boarding and lodging, textbooks, uniforms etc., is free for all students. A couple of states had not then adopted the scheme. Admission to Navodaya Vidyalayas is made at the level of Class VI through a test conducted in the concerned district in which all children who passed Class V from any of the recognised schools in the district are eligible to appear.

24. National Institute of Open Schooling (NIOS), 1989

The National Institute of Open Schooling (NIOS) formerly known as National Open School (NOS) was established in November, 1989 as an autonomous organisation in pursuance of National Policy on Education 1986 by the Ministry of Human Resource Development (MHRD), Government of India. NIOS is providing a number of Vocational, Life Enrichment and community oriented courses besides General and Academic Courses at Secondary and Senior Secondary level. It also offers Elementary level Courses through its Open Basic Education Programmes (OBE). *Vision:* Sustainable inclusive learning with universal and flexible access to quality school education and skill development. *Mission:* (i) Providing relevant, continuing and holistic education up to pre-degree level through Open and Distance Learning System. (ii) Contributing to the Universalisation of School Education. (iii) Catering to the educational needs of the prioritised target groups for equity and social justice.

Open Basic Education (OBE): Programme providing an elementary education at three levels, for school drop-outs and neo-literates, out of school learners through Accredited Agencies. Under its "Sarva Shiksha Abhiyan (SSA)", the Government of India, Ministry of Human Resource Development (MHRD) has been endeavouring to provide Basic Education to all children, youth and adults in the country. The National Institute of Open Schooling (NIOS) has launched the Open Basic Education (OBE) Programme, as an alternative educational programme, equivalent to the Elementary Education Programme of the formal education system. The OBE Programme explores and makes use of the potentialities of Distance Education Mode (DEM) for reaching the unreached. The Foundation Course of NIOS has been subsumed into the Open Basic Education (OBE) Programme. There is a provision of separate OBE programme for children and adults.

Most of the programmes have been merged into the Sarva Shiksha Abhiyan (SSA). Now the existing norms of the SSA have been also aligned with the RTE implementation. In fact, the SSA is now a vehicle for the implementation of the RTE Act, 2009 to universalise the elementary education in India.

References

- Bhaumik, P.K. and Banik, A. (2006, April 8). Making the education cess work, The Economic Times. Retrieved from http://articles.economictimes.indiatimes.com/2006-04-08/news/27454253_1_education-cess-duties-and-service-tax-elementary-education
- Comptroller Auditor General of India (2006). *Performance Audit on Sarva Shiksha Abhiyan. Report No. 15 of 2006.* New Delhi: CAG.
- Government of India (2004). *National Common Minimum Programme of the Government of India May 2004.* New Delhi: GOI. Retrieved from http://architexturez.net/system/files/pdf/cmp_0.pdf
- Government of India (2005). *Government of the United Progressive Alliance Report to People - 1, Implementation of National Common Minimum Programme and Other Initiatives May 2004 – February 2005.* New Delhi: GOI.
- Malani, Gaurav (2004, Sep. 23). Fund for education cess gets finance ministry nod. The Economic Times. Retrieved from http://articles.economictimes. indiatimes.com/2004-09-23/news/27370798_1_education-cess-mid-day-meal-scheme elementary-education

- MHRD (1999). Sarva Shiksha Abhiyan: Framework for Implementation [DRAFT, December 1999]. New Delhi: MHRD, Government of India. Retrieved on 10.09. 2014 from http://www.educationforallinindia.com/SSA1.htm
- MHRD (2000). *Sarva Shiksha Abhiyan: Programme for Universal Elementary Education in India,* New Delhi: Department of Elementary Education and Literacy, MHRD, Government of India.
- MHRD (2001). *Government of India Resolution on Setting Up of National Mission for Sarva Shiksha Abhiyan*, New Delhi: Department of Elementary Education and Litearacy, Ministry of Human Resource Development, Government of India. Retrieved on 12.11.2014 from http://gujarat-education.gov.in/ssa/modules/ssa_guidelines/annexure/annexure-1.htm
- MHRD (2005). *Annual Report 2004-05*. New Delhi: Department of School Education and Literacy, Department of Higher Education, Ministry of Human Resource Development (MHRD), Government of India.
- MHRD (2011). *Sarva Shiksha Abhiyan: Framework for Implementation Based on the Right of Children to Free and Compulsory Education Act, 2009*. New Delhi: Department of School Education and Literacy, Ministry of Human Resource Development, Government of India.
- Ministry of Human Resource Development (2006). *Performance Audit Report on Sarva Shiksha Abhiyan, Report No. 15 of 2006*, New Delhi: Department of Elementary Education and Literacy, MHRD. Retrieved on 10.12.2014 from http://cag.nic.in/html/reports/civil/2006_15_peraud/15%20OF%202006/min_HRD.htm
- Ministry of Statistics and Programme Implementation (2012). *Children in India, 2012 – A Statistical Appraisal,* New Delhi, MOSPI, GOI.
- Mondal, A. and Mete, J. (2012). Right to Education – An Appraisal, *Kurukshetra*, Vol. 60, No. 11, Sept. 2012, pp. 11-14.
- Press Information Bureau, MHRD. (9th September, 2010). Aligning Sarva Shiksha Abhiyan Norms with the Right of Children to Free and Compulsory Education Act, 2009, New Delhi: Press Information Bureau, MHRD, GOI. Retrieved on 20.01.2015 from http://www.educationforallinindia.com/ssa-and-right-to-education.htm
- Tilak, Jandhyala B. G. (2004). Education in the UPA Government Common Minimum Programme, *Economic and Political Weekly*, 39(43), October 23-29, 4717-4721.

Chapter - 4

Development of Free and Compulsory Education under the British Raj

India has a long tradition of education both through formally organised institutions (such as Institutes of Higher Learning at Takshashila and Nalanda) as well as less formal ones like hermitages or 'ashrams' where pupils were under the complete custodial care of their Gurus. A mass education movement, however, began during the age of Jainism and Buddhism when a widespread attempt was made to use the people's spoken language to impart education related to the needs of people.

By the end of the eighteen century, India had a well-developed system of indigenous education. There was, however, no formal school system organised and supported by the State. Professor J. P. Naik (1978) described the traditional educational system in India before the domination of the British colonial rule in the following word – "At the opening of the nineteenth century, we had a limited system of formal education consisting of some institutions of higher learning and much large number of elementary schools. The Hindu institutions of higher learning (the *Tols* and *Pathashalas)* used Sanskrit as the medium of instruction and were open only to the higher castes traditionally authorised to study the Vedas. The institutions of higher learning of the Muslims (the *Madrassahs)* used Arabic and Persian as media of instruction and, though mostly used by Muslims, were open to Hindus as well, and many Hindus did study Persian which was the language of the Moghul court. Both categories of institutions were mediaeval in character and basically oriented to the study of religion. Their enrollments were also small, less than one to a thousand of the total population. The elementary schools were comparatively humbler institutions which taught the three R's to those who wanted to learn them and the Muslim *Maktabs* also taught reading of the Koran in addition... The vast bulk of the people, therefore, were educated in the incidental and non-formal channels of education which initiated them to the essential vocational skills, introduced them to the traditional social culture, and helped them to adjust themselves to their lonely and unenviable station in life (pp. 4-5).

The Charter Act of 1813 – The First Milestone

The development of modern system of education in India may be said to have begun with the Charter Act of 1813 which provided the Clause 43 that *"a sum of not less than one lakh of rupees in each year shall be set apart and applied to the revival and improvement of literature and the encouragement of the learned natives of India, and for the introduction and promotion of a knowledge of the sciences among the inhabitants of the British territories in India;"* (Sharp, 1920, p. 22). The period of modern system of education in India is generally held to have been organised with the Charter Act of 1813 under which Parliament directed East India Company to accept the responsibility for the education of Indian people. In the words of Professor J. M. Sen (1925), "Although a provision in the East India Act of 1813 empowering the Governor-General of India to spend one lakh of rupees each year for the purpose of education was the first legislative admission of the right of education to participate in the public revenues of India, and though the Education Despatch of 1854 issued by the Court of Directors of East India Company (re-affirmed by Lord Staley, the first Secretary of State for India, in his Despatch of 1859) was the first basis for a state educational programme in India, it is in the Indian Educational Policy of 1904 that we find for the first time the Government of India declaring that the rapid spread of primary education is one of the foremost duties of the State" (p. 4). Its Clause 43 contained the first legislative admission of the right of education in India in the public revenues and it laid the foundation of State System of Education in India.

William Adam's Third Report in 1838

The universal compulsory free primary education is essentially a modern concept in Indian education. Its history can be traced back to the year, 1938. No solid efforts were made till the beginning of the twentieth century. The earliest attempt during British Rule for enforcing compulsory primary education was undertaken by William Adam in 1838 (Sharma, 2011, p. 5), a Christian missionary who came to India in 1818. He was the man who understood the function of the Indigenous schools and village Pathsala in 1838. Towards the end of 1838, the General Committee took into consideration the three Reports of William Adam who was appointed by Lord William Bentinck in January 1838 to enquire into the state of vernacular education in Bengal, Bihar and Orissa. In the last 119 pages of third Report, Adam submitted his scheme for the improvement of vernacular education. Adam considered it impossible to introduce compulsory education at that time for more than one reason. He explained it in his Report in the following words:

"The next form in which Government influence may be conceived to be employed **for the promotion of education is by making it compulsory and enacting that every village should have a school**. I hope the time will come when every village shall have a school, but the period has not yet arrived when this obligation can be enforced. Such a law, direct and intelligible, would be preferable to a mere recommendation which might be understood in a double sense, but it would be premature. It would be ordering the people to do what they are too poor and too ignorant to do willingly or well, if at all. It would be neither to follow nor to lead but to run counter to native public opinion. Those who in respect of caste or wealth constitute the higher classes do not need any such coercive means to induce them to instruct their children. Those who in respect of caste may be called the middle classes are convinced of the advantages of education, but they are in general poor and many of them would feel such a measure to be severe and oppressive. The lower classes consisting both of Hindus and Musalmans and of numerous sub-divisions and varieties of caste and occupation greatly exceed the others in number, and they are for the most part by general consent consigned to ignorance. In many villages they are the sole, in others the most numerous inhabitants, and such a compulsory law as I have supposed would be received with universal astonishment and dismay- with dismay by themselves and with astonishment if not derision by the superior classes. A national system of education will necessarily have chiefly ill view the most numerous classes of the population, but ill their present state of moral and social preparation we can approach them only by slow and almost imperceptible steps. We can effectually raise them only by aiding their voluntary efforts to rise; and at present the prejudice against their instruction is nearly as strong and as general in their own minds as in the minds of others. In the preceding pages I have shown that it has begun to give way in Bengal and Behar; and in the records of the General Committee of Public Instruction I find an apt illustration both of the existence of the prejudice ill the North Western Provinces and of the fact that there also it has begun to lose ground.... In any plan, therefore that may he adopted what should he kept in view is to recognise no principle of exclusion, to keep the door open by which all classes may enter, and to abstain from enforcing what their poverty makes them unable and their prejudices unwilling generally to perform (p. 254)".

Adam rejected the idea of instituting model schools on a graded system, beginning from the village schools and ending with the Government Zillah Schools. In order, therefore, to encourage education without compulsion, he recommended a plan of "payment by result". According to this system, rewards were to be given on results of examinations. Adam explained the plan in the following words:

"The question arises in what manner native institutions may be most effectually employed, with a view to the gradual formation of regular system of instruction for the benefit of all classes of the community and the answer which, after mature consideration, I am disposed to give is by proposing the establishment of public and periodical examination to the teachers and scholars of those institutions and distribution of rewards to the teachers proportional to their own qualification and the attainments of their scholars, - the examinations to be conducted, and the rewards bestowed, the officers appointed by government and placed under the authority and control of the General Committee of Public Instruction. This plan appears adapted to the character of the people and to the present condition of native society (p. 260)". The GCPI found Adam's scheme impractical and too expensive and above all, opposed to the idea of filtrating education from the upper and middle classes to the masses. Ultimately, the government rejected the proposal and Adam resigned his appointment.

The Proposal of Captain Wingate, the Revenue Survey Commissioner in Bombay, 1852

A more direct suggestion towards the demand of compulsory education came from Captain Wingate, the Revenue Survey Commissioner in Bombay. In 1852, Captain Wingate when called upon by Government of Bombay to give his views on a proposal to levy a local fund on land revenue, recommended the levy of such cess and suggested that a part of it should be devoted to providing compulsory education to the sons of agriculturists. These proposals did not find favour with other officers most of whom opposed it tooth and nail (Aggarwal, 2002: 123, Pathania and Pathania, 2006: 8). Captain Wingate in a very detailed and finely drafted letter expressed his suggestions on "the purposes for which the proceeds of the tax were to be applied", one of the aspects of the proposal – imposition of additional local tax on land revenue in the following words:

> "I think it should be devoted chiefly to education and to the facilitation of communication between different parts of the country, whether by the construction of roads and bridges...the educational part of the fund should go to provide small salaries of four or five rupees per mensem to school masters...and also to build school-rooms where no accommodation is obtainable".

The schools should be viewed as specially designed for the education of the agricultural class, which is to provide the funds for their support, and none but the children of cultivators should be admitted to them, except on payment of a fee of not less than two annas per mensem, and unless the accommodation is more than sufficient for the former. The trading classes can afford to provide for the education of their children, and should not be allowed to appropriate what is intended for the agricultural class. Every ryot holding land in his own name, and residing in a village having one of these schools, should be required to send all his sons to school on their attaining the age of six or seven years, and be required to keep them for at least three years, under penalty of a fine, nor exceeding 10 rupees per annum to be imposed when a child has not attended school for more than six months out of the 12, unless good and sufficient reasons can be assigned for his absence, unconnected with poverty or the child being required to tend the cattle or work in the field or at home. Any scheme for educating the agricultural class will, I am satisfied, fail, unless it makes the attendance of the children compulsory on the parents (Naik, 1942: 3). Professor J. P. Naik opined that the main flaw in the proposal is its uncritical optimism. It was obviously impossible to finance compulsory primary education out of the proceeds of the Local Fund Cess only (*Ibid*, 5).

Recommendation by Mr T.C. Hope in 1858

Shortly afterwards in 1858, Mr T. C. Hope, the Educational Inspector of Gujarat proposed that a law should be passed empowering the inhabitants of any local area to tax themselves for the establishment of schools (Mukherji, 1964; 68).

In the Report of the Director of Public Instruction, Bombay for the year 1857-58, E.I. Howard, Director of Public Instruction, Bombay drew the attention of John Lord Elphinstone, Governor and President in Council, Bombay to the arguments by which Mr Hope, the educational inspector of Gujarat, who has opposed the voluntary system of school expansion, presses for an enactment to authorise the levy of a compulsory educational rate (Government of Bombay, 1859, p. 56c).

The Report also described the opinion of T.C. Hope about the state of education during 1857-58 in the following words - "that the 'partially self-supporting' or persuading system, as a measure for national education, has proved a total failure... the best substitute appears to be a legislative enactment, to be ready applied, from year to year, to such villages as are judged to be ready for government schools, and throwing the entire cost of the maintenance of the latter on the people themselves" (p. 433). But this proposal was also turned down as premature. **In 1884, Shri Shastri, the Deputy Educational Inspector of Broach**, also suggested the introduction of compulsory primary education in his Annual Administrative Report (Mukherji, 1964: 68). These are the earliest suggestions or attempts for introducing compulsory primary education under the British Raj. But all the suggestions were, however, considered premature.

Indian Education Commission (Hunter Commission), 1882

With the enforcement of compulsory education Act in England in 1870, a demand was raised, in India, to provide similar facilities in its colonies (Juneja, 2003:15). As a result, an emphatic demand for laws to be made to make primary education compulsory was made by **Dadabhai Naoroji and Jyotiba Phule from Bombay Presidency** in their evidence before the Indian Education Commission (Hunter Commission, 1882) which accepted the logic and stated that "while every branch of education can justly claim the fostering care of the state, it is desirable, in the present circumstances to declare the elementary, education of the masses, its provision, extension and improvement, to be that part of the educational system to which the strenuous efforts of the State should now be directed" (Hunter Commission, p. 586 and Government of India, 1993). The Commission also recommended the transfer of the control and administration of elementary education to local bodies, as done, in England.

The first effective step in introducing compulsory primary education was taken only by Dadabhai Naoroji, in his evidence before the Hunter Commission, put forward the demand that four years of compulsory education should be provided to all children (UNESCO, 1984, p. 3). The demand for Universalisation of Elementary Education was first put forward by Indians like Dadabhai Naoroji before the Indian Education Commission (1882) to make the local bodies elected by the Indians responsible for elementary education (Rastogi and Sharma, 1981).

Jotirao Phule also informed the Commission of his views in writing and suggested in his representation to the Education Committee that the responsibility for primary and secondary education should be handed over to the people. He said in his representation that the efforts of Christian missionaries to set up schools are not genuinely patriotic. Their intentions, too, are not strictly restricted to education. Jotirao further said that "There is little doubt that primary education among the masses in this Presidency has been very much neglected. Although the number of primary schools now in existence is greater than those existing a few years ago, yet they are not commensurate to the requirements of the community. Government collect a special cess for educational purpose, and it is to be regretted that this fund is not spent for the purposes for which it is collected...a good deal of their poverty, their want of self-reliance, their entire dependence upon the learned and intelligent classes, is attributable to this deplorable state of education among the peasantry. Even in towns the Brahmins, the Purbhoos, the hereditary classes, who generally live by the occupation of pen, and the trading classes seek primary education. The cultivating and the other classes, as a rule, do not generally avail themselves of the same...**I think primary education of the masses should be made compulsory up to a certain age, say at least 12 years** (Government of India, 1881, p. 142).

The Grand Old Man of India contrasted the "British" policy towards elementary education in England (where the first Parliamentary grant of 20,000 for education was sanctioned in 1833, but further expansion was so rapid that, by 1882, compulsory education laws had already been passed, the total enrollment had increased to 4.657 million or one in seven of the population...) with the "un-British" policy in India (where the first government grant for education was sanctioned twenty years earlier in 1813 but where further expansion was so slow that, by 1882, the total enrollment in elementary schools had increased only to 1.633 million or one in 114 of the population...). He described it as a "sad, sad tale which allowed nearly 25 million children to grow in ignorance". But at this early period, the Commission would not even entertain the concept of universal and compulsory education and all his eloquent pleading was in vain (Naik, 1965: 1).

But the Hunter Commission, 1882 made 36 recommendations regarding the primary education. The notable recommendations have been mentioned for our better understanding -

- That primary education be regarded as the instruction of the masses through the vernacular in such subjects as will best fit them for their position in life, and be not necessarily regarded as a portion of instruction leading up to the University.
- That while every branch of education can justly claim the fostering care of the State, it is desirable, in the present

circumstances of the country, to declare the elementary education of the masses, its provision, extension, and improvement, to be that part of the educational system to which the strenuous efforts of the State should now be directed in a still larger measure than heretofore.

- That an attempt be made to secure the fullest possible provision for, and extension of primary education by legislation suited to the circumstances of each province (Government of India, 1883: 585, Chapter XIII).

In the big volume of its report which runs well over 739 pages, there is no mention of compulsory education at all. The Indian Education Commission at least should have raised the issue especially because several Indian witnesses before it did make a demand for compulsory education (Nurullah and Naik, 1964:201). The principle of compulsion is referred to only in the page number 558, where the Commission observes "One witness advocates compulsory primary education for the city of Bombay". This is all the more surprising because the question was specifically brought before the Commission with a plea either for compulsory maintenance of school or for compulsory attendance. State finances for making primary education universal could be reduced or even ultimately withdrawn, under this doctrine of local self-government introduced in India by Lord Ripon. But local bodies had little resources to take up this burden.

Ultimately the Commission did not recommend making elementary education compulsory, nor did they recommend making free. But they asked the local authorities to admit ascertain portion of pupils as free students on the ground of poverty in all schools managed by the local boards or municipalities (Sen, 2010: 125).

Unfortunately the commission indulged in the speculation of further improvement in a big way and their strenuous efforts in the direction. The report of Indian Education Commission however, is a very disappointing document so far as compulsory education is concerned. Never the less, the report of the Commission paved the way for the organised agitation for the introduction of compulsory education. The educationists and the national leaders realised the gravity of the problem and started systematic movement.

The establishment of Indian National Congress in 1885 further strengthened the movement. The Indian National Congress was rapidly becoming a forum for articulating the seething discontent that has been brewing for sometimes in the heart of the freedom fighters. They, therefore, realised that their demand for Democracy and Home Rule was not likely to be effective unless the masses were educated. Though granted, it would not work successfully unless and until the average men and women were sufficiently educated to discharge their duty and responsibility. Therefore, they agitated for universal education of the masses in order to make it possible for India to become a Free Democratic republic.

On the one hand, Lord Curzon was trying to embitter the condition of primary education in his own way; on the other hand the national leaders under the banner of Indian National Congress were agitating for the introduction of compulsory primary education. In the Calcutta Congress of 1905, it was declared that it is birth right of the people of India to get proper education. This resolution opened a new chapter in the history of the primary education in India.

The struggle to create a national system of education, key-note of this movement is probably best contained in the Resolution on National Education adopted by the 22nd Indian National Congress in 1906, held at Calcutta, 26th, 27th, 28th and 29th December of 1906 which said: "the time has arrived for the people all over the country earnestly to take up the question of national education for both boys and girls, and organise a system of Education- Literary, Scientific and Technical - suited to the requirements of the country, on national lines under national control" (Resolution XI on National Education, pp. iii). The movement thus initiated was kept up till 1947 (Naik, 1978:9).

Again the Resolution X on Education taken in the same Congress was that "This Congress repeats its protest against the policy of the government in respect of high and secondary education as being one of officialising the governing bodies of the universities and restricting the spread of education. The Congress is of opinion that that government should take immediate steps for **(i) making primary education free and gradually compulsory all over the country**, (ii) assigning larger sums of money to secondary education (special encouragement being given, where necessary, to educationally backward classes), (iii) making the existing Universities more free from official control and providing them with sufficient means to take up the work of teaching, and (iv) making adequate provision for technical education in the different Provinces; having regard to local requirements" (pp. iii).

Credit goes to Indian notable Prince **Sir Sahaji Rao Gaikwad of Baroda**. He achieved what the British Government found impossible. He introduced the scheme of free compulsory education as an experimental measure in his Amreli Tuluk of his State in 1893. Being successful in his experimentation he extended the area of compulsion, to his entire state by 1896 (Mukherji, 1964). For his greatest and remarkable contribution for the cause of compulsory education he was often regarded as the 'Prince among the Educators and an Educator among the princes'. The first documented use of the word 'right' in the context of elementary education appeared in a letter written by Rabindranath Tagore to the International League for the Rational Education of Children in 1908, (Niranjanaradhya and Kashyap, 2006:4). In this letter Tagore argued for viewing education as a right which enables individuals and communities to act on reflection (Niranjanaradhya, 2004:70).

Gopal Krishna Gokhale pointed out the following words at the time of introducing the Bill on 16th March, 1911 in the Imperial Legislative Council - "Within the borders of India itself, the Maharaja of Baroda has set an event of enthusiasm in the cause of education... His highness began his first experiment in the matter of introducing compulsory and free education into his State eighteen years ago in ten villages at the Amreli Taluka. After watching the experiment for eight years, it was extended to the whole taluka in 1901, and finally, in 1906, primary education was made compulsory and free throughout the State for boys between the ages of 6 and 12, and for girls between the ages of 6 and 10" (Natesan, 1916, pp. 725-726).

The first organised attempt to introduce compulsory primary education in British India was, however, made in Bombay under **Sir Ibrahim Rahimtoola and Sir Chamanlal Setalwad** (Rai, 1997). As a result of their agitation, the Government of Bombay appointed a Committee in 1906 to examine the feasibility of introducing compulsory education in the city of Bombay. But unfortunately this committee came to the conclusion that the time was not ripe for the introduction of compulsory education (Mukherji, 1964:69). The main argument advance in favour of this policy was that the British Government was a foreign government and hence could not compel the people to send their children to school – an action which an Indian Prince might make (Nurullah and Naik, 1964: 201).

Gopal Krishna Gokhale's Attempts – the Champion of the Right to Education

Gopal Krishna Gokhale was a nationalist leader and the active member of the Indian National Congress. He was also elected as the President of the Indian National Congress in 1905. Gokhale became a non-official member of the British Imperial Legislative Council in 1902. Till that time he was a professor and Principal of Ferguson College, Poona. As a nationalist leader Gokhale visualised the importance of primary education for the socio-political awakening of India. He made heroic efforts to make the government accept the principle of compulsory primary education. The demand for compulsory primary education was strengthened by the fact that the Maharaja Sayaji Rao Gaikwad of Baroda had made primary education free and compulsory within the territories of his state. This attempt inspired Gokhale.

The first definite and vocal demand for the introduction of compulsory education was made by Shri Gopal Krishna Gokhale, the veteran Indian nationalist leader, in the 18 March 1910 when he moved a resolution in the Imperial Legislative Council that "a beginning be made in the direction of making elementary education free and compulsory throughout the country", and that a mixed commission of officials and non-officials be appointed to frame definite proposals. The resolution was overdrawn on an assurance from the government that the whole problem would be fully investigated. Later on, the government accepted only the last three resolutions of Gokhale. A Department of Education was established under the Central Government and the secretary was also appointed. The record of the progress of primary education also started to be published by the government. But the main issue of making primary education free and compulsory remained neglected and unattended by the government.

However, by introduction of this resolution, Gokhale succeeded in putting the case for compulsory education on the National Agenda. It was discussed widely in the newpapers. It was taken note of by both the National Congress and the All India Muslim League. If Gopal Krishna Gokhle, one of the greatest sons of India, would have been alive today, he would have been the happiest person to see his dream of 'Right to Education' for the children of the country come true. It was he who, a hundred years ago, urged the Imperial Legislative Assembly confer such a right on Indian children. That goal has been realised a century later.

On 18th March 1910, Mr Gokhale's Resolution in the Imperial Legislative Council

On 18th March 1910, Mr Gokhale, in moving a Resolution; in the Imperial Legislative Council, recommending that a beginning be made in the direction of free and compulsory education and that a Commission be appointed to frame definite proposals, spoke as follows: I beg to place the following Resolution before the Council for its consideration:

> "My Lord, I trust the Council will note carefully what it is exactly that this resolution proposes. The resolution does not ask that elementary education should be made compulsory at once throughout India. It does not even ask that it should be made free at once throughout the country, though this was the course which the Government of India themselves were decidedly inclined to adopt three years ago. All that the resolution does is to recommend that a beginning should now be made in the direction of making elementary education free and compulsory and that a Commission should be appointed to consider the question and frame definite proposals. In other words, I propose that the State should, now accept in this country the same responsibilities in regard to mass education that the governments of most other civilised countries are already discharging and that a well-considered scheme should be drawn up and adhered to till it is carried out.
>
> My Lord... it is at present universally recognised that a certain minimum of general instruction is an obligation which society owes to all its future members, and in nearly the whole-civilised world every State is trying to meet this obligation only in one way, namely, by making elementary education compulsory and free.

Now the only way that the world has discovered to secure universal education in a country has been by making it compulsory and free. This is the only method that the world has found to be successful and so far there is no other method in the field. Again you make elementary instruction compulsory, it follows that you will have also to make it free, because otherwise compulsion would operate harshly on the poorer classes of the community, The only question therefore that we have to consider is how far we in this country can now adopt that principle which has already been adopted by most countries of the civilised world and which has already produced.

Here let me state at the outset that I do not propose compulsion for the present for *girls;* I propose compulsion only for boys. For girls for the present and for some years to come, education will have to be on a voluntary basis. In some respects girls' education is even more important than that of boys in the India of to-day, and yet in view of the difficulties that surround that question, that education must be maintained for some years to come only on a voluntary basis. At the same time, far more vigorous efforts are necessary, on that voluntary basis, than have so far been made. But I want the Council clearly to understand that the compulsory principle which I advocate to-day is to be confined only to boys. We must therefore first of all ascertain what would be the number of boys that would be at school if education were compulsory in this country. Now I have already pointed out that the standard of 15 per cent of the total population as the school-going population is the standard of England. There the school period is taken to be six to seven years. I propose that we should be satisfied with a compulsory Period of four years only as they have in Japan".

Having pointed, out thus the extent of the problem, I will now come to the actual proposals that I want to make.

(1) My first proposal is that following the example of the Act of 1870, we should pass an Act conferring powers upon local bodies to make elementary education compulsory in their areas. I recognise, my Lord that the unpopularity that will be evoked by the principle of compulsion in certain sections will be considerable; and in view of the special circumstances

attaching to the position of the British Government in this country, I, recognise that this unpopularity should not come to the 'State on account of any direct compulsion introduced by it.' The compulsion introduce therefore should be indirect, through local bodies and not direct by the State.

(2) My second proposal is that compulsion should be only for boys and not for girls.

(3) My third proposal is that the period of compulsion should be between 6 years and 10 years as in Japan.

(4) The fourth proposal is this. In any area where 33 per cent the male population is already at school, there this principle of compulsion should be applied. I should propose 33 per cent as the proportion which should satisfy us that compulsion would not be premature ill any particular area. Where 33 per cent of the boys are actually at school, elementary education should be made (compulsory for all boys in that area. In other areas the attempt should be to work up to this proportion of 33 per cent. As soon as 33 per cent is reached, compulsion should be introduced.

(5) My fifth proposal is that wherever compulsory education is introduced, it should be gratuitous, because otherwise it would be a great hardship on poor people. At any rate the children of those parents whose income is below a certain limit, say, Rs 25 a month, should receive gratuitous instruction.

(6) My sixth proposal is that the extra cost should be divided between the government and the local bodies in the proportion of two to one.

(7) My seventh proposal is that there should now be a separate Secretary for Education in the Home Department. Instead of having a Director-General I would have a Secretary in the Home Department especially for education, and eventually I look forward to the time when a Member will separate charge of education will be included in the Executive Council.

(8) My eighth proposal is that education should now be a divided head instead of its being a purely Provincial head. The root of the mischief, as we see it today, is there. The resources at the disposal of the Provincial Governments are extremely

limited... Education should therefore be a divided charge and there should be a definite programme before the government, just as there is a programme for railways, which should be carried out steadily year by year.

(9) My last proposal in this connection is that a statement describing the progress of education from year to year should be published with the Annual Financial Statement as is done in the case of Army Services and the Railway Board.

These are the nine definite practical proposals that I would like to submit to the consideration of this council (Natesan, 1916: 699-714).

A year later, on 16 March 1911, the Hon'ble Mr Gokhale introduced in the same Council a private Bill "to make better provision for the extension of elementary education in India" (Mukherji, 1964:70 and Sharp, 1914:181). This Bill incorporated most of the suggestions which he had put forward while speaking on his resolution of 1910.

On 16th March 1911, Mr Gokhale, in the Imperial Legislative Council spoke that "My Lord, if the history of elementary education throughout the world establishes one fact more clearly than another, it is this, that without a resort to compulsion no State can ensure a general diffusion of education among its people" (Natesan, 1916: 726). Gokhale presented the Bill in the Legislative Council to make a stronger fight against the government. The Bill, however, was more liberal and humble than the resolutions placed before and the main objective of the bill was to make primary education free and compulsory in a phased manner. The Bill was basically based on the compulsory Education Acts of England, 1870 and 1876 and on the Irish Education Act of 1992. Important clauses of the Bill may be placed below—

- Compulsory primary education should be introduced in those areas where a certain percentage of boys and girls of school-age (6-10) was already receiving instructions. In the words of Gokhale is that "Where one-third of the boys of school-going age were already at school, the question of introducing compulsion might be taken up for consideration by the Local Body".
- The percentage of attendance should be fixed by the Governor General in Council.

- It should be left to the discretion of local bodies whether to apply the Act to certain areas under their jurisdiction or not.
- Local bodies should be given the right to levy educational cess to meet the cost of compulsory primary education.
- Expenditure on education was to be shared by the local bodies and Provincial Government in the ratio of 1:2.
- For the introduction of compulsion, the previous sanction of the Viceroy and the Governor respectively were necessary.
- Compulsory primary education is intended to apply in the first instance only to boys, though later on a local body may extend it to girls also.
- Guardians whose income is less than Rs 10 per month should not be asked to pay any fee for their wards.

However, this bill had three important features which deserve special notice. Firstly, it did not demand the immediate introduction of compulsory education. It only said that Municipalities and Local Boards should be permitted to do so under certain conditions that were to be prescribed under the Act. Gokhale was of the view that the initiative should be left to Local self-government institutions. As he observed:

"My Lord, it is urged by those who are opposed to the introduction of compulsion in this country that though the Gaekwar, as an Indian Prince, could force compulsion on his subjects without serious opposition, the British Government, as a foreign government, cannot afford to risk the unpopularity which the measure will entail. Personally I do not think that the fear which lies behind this view is justified, because the Government in Ceylon is as much a foreign government as that in India, and in Ceylon the authorities have not shrunk from the introduction of compulsion. But to meet this objection, I am quite willing that the first steps in the direction of compulsion should be taken by our Local Bodies, which reproduce in British territory conditions similar to those which obtain in Feudatory States" (Natesan, 1916: 730).

Secondly, Gokhale proposed that cost of compulsion should be shared by government and local bodies in the ratio of two to one. The authors may quote his words:

"It is obvious that the whole working of this Bill must depend in the first instance upon the share, which the, government is prepared to bear, of the cost of compulsory education, wherever it is introduced. I find that in England the Parliamentary grant covers about two-thirds of the total expenditure on elementary schools. In Scotland, it amounts to more than that proportion, whereas in Ireland it meets practically the whole cost. I think we are entitled to ask that in India at least two-thirds of the new expenditure should be borne by the State" (Natesan, 1916, p. 733).

Thirdly, according to Professor J. P. Naik (1943), Gokhale did not contemplate the universal introduction of compulsion at one stroke. He wanted to advance slowly. He suggested that compulsion should be introduced in such areas only where the ground was quite prepared for such an experiment; secondly, he suggested that compulsion may first be introduced in the case of boys only and later on extended to girls when public opinion was sufficiently awakened; and lastly, he suggested proposed to begin with a compulsory education of four years only, with mere attainment of literacy, and to postpone the lengthening of the age-period of compulsion to a time when a more liberal provision of funds would become possible (p. 66).

At last, Gokhale's Bill of 1911 was referred to a Select Committee of 15 members of the Council for detailed examination of the clauses. The Bill was also sent to the Local Governments, the Universities and local education authorities for inviting opinion on it. The Bill was taken up for discussion in legislative council on 17 March, 1912. The Bill was debated for two days (March 17 and 18, 1912). Gokhale had raised powerful arguments in support of the Bill.

From the account of work of the Servants of India Society (1917), founded by the late Mr G. K. Gokhale on the 12th June, 1905 we may get information in this regard that –"In 1911 an elementary education league was formed in Madras to support the Elementary Education Bill introduced by Mr Gokhale into the Imperial Legislative Council in March of that year. The members of the Society issued pamphlets on the subject. in English, Tamil, Telugu and Kanarese and, visited several towns in order to enlighten the public regarding league having been started with the sole object of popularising the Bill ceased to exist when the Bill was thrown out next year by the Legislative Council (p.15)".

However, bureaucrats of the British Government still held the view that education was a charity shown by the English nation to India, and could not yet feel that mass education was a duty which they had ignored too long. The government was not ready to accept the Bill and consequently, it was put to vote and was defeated by 35 votes to 13 in spite of the support of eminent persons like Pandit Madan Mohan Malaviya, Muhammad Ali Jinnah. The grounds for opposition, as expressed in the speeches of the official members, were that (1) no popular demand for compulsory education had been felt; (2) the Local Governments were not in favour of it; (3) a strong minority of educated Indians were against it; (4) the local authorities were unwilling to levy additional rates or increase the existing ones; (5) the attendance committees would not work satisfactorily and the machinery would be disliked by the rate – prayers; and (6) there was still room for the extension primary education on voluntary lines based on the grants-in-aid system (Sen, 1925:17).

Professor J. P. Naik (1942) also pointed out the following amongst others, were the grounds on which the Bill was opposed:

(1) It is a sound maxim of educational policy that persuasion should be exhausted before compulsion is resorted to. It was therefore argued that what the situation needed most was not a hasty enforcement of compulsion, but an expansion of education on a voluntary basis by the provision of additional funds, by opening more schools, by improving schools and teachers and so on.

(2) No popular demand for compulsory education had been felt.

(3) The Provincial Governments were not in favour of the Bill.

(4) A section of educated Indians were entirely opposed to it.

(5) The Local Authorities, it was stated, would be unwilling to increase existing taxes or to impose new ones in order to finance schemes of compulsion (pp. 9-10).

The cautious and conservatives bureaucracy of these days did not accept the principles underlying the Bill as practical propositions. However, this did not come as a surprise to Gokhale. According to

Naik (1943), the majority against the bill is not surprising because at that time, the Imperial Legislative Council had a clear official majority which was strengthened the support of reactionary non-officials (p. 67). Gokhale had anticipated the result correctly and earlier in the debate had already expressed the result of the voting in the following majestic words:

"My Lord, I know that my Bill will be thrown out before the day closes. I make no complaint. I shall not even feel depressed... We, of the present generation of India can only hope to serve our country by our failures. The men and women who will be privileged to serve her by their successes will come later. We must be content to accept cheerfully the place that has been allotted to us in our onward march." (Natesan, 1916:782-783). Thus, the Bill, though defeated, but it was a heroic defeat.

The authors wish to quote the following significant lines of R. P. Paranjpye (1915) regarding Gokhale's Free and Compulsory Education – "A subject on which Gokhale worked very hard was his advocacy of free and compulsory education in India. For the real regeneration of the people this was in his opinion the master talisman and he harped on its necessity on every possible occasion... he brought forward a bill in the Viceregal Council making it possible for any municipality, on the sanction of government, to introduce compulsory education for boys in its area. The Bill was hedged with so many safeguards that it was quite an innocent measure in all conscience... the failure of his actual attempt at legislation need not, however, disappoint us, for everybody now agrees that the objections are mainly of ways and means and even the staunchest "sundried officials" feel that the introduction of free and compulsory primary education in India is only a question of time. Thus, Gokhale's strong advocacy has brought this idea perceptibly hearer. When, a few years hence, it becomes an accomplished fact, to Gokhale will be given the credit of giving the first momentum to the idea and he will go down to posterity as the educator of the people (pp. 57-58)". Gokhale's efforts were not entirely in vain; they had the following direct benefits:

- The creation of Central Department of Education was the direct impact of Mr Gokhale's efforts. It has now developed into the Central Advisory Board of Education.

- Gokhale's efforts had a great propaganda value because they awakened public opinion to the need of mass education.
- His efforts also aroused the government to their duty regarding the education of the masses.

According to Professor J. P. Naik (1943), Gokhale's efforts had lighted a torch that was not born for death and other workers were soon to arise and spread the light all over India. In the meanwhile, government had to define its attitude towards mass education in India. Though Gokhale's attempts on three consecutive years to force the government to pass an Education Act had failed, yet primary education in India received a great impetus when His Majesty the King Empower, George V, while on a visit to India said on 6th January 1912 (Sen, 1925:20). His Most Gracious Imperial Majesty the King Emperor, in replying to the address of the Calcutta University on the 6th January 1912, said:

"It is my wish that there may be spread over the land a network of schools and colleges, from which will go forth loyal and manly and useful citizens, able to hold their own in industries and agriculture and all the vocations in life. And it is my wish, too, that the homes of my Indian subjects may be brightened and their labour sweetened by the spread of knowledge with all that follows in its train, a higher level of thought, of comfort and a health. It is through education that my wish will be fulfilled, and the cause of education in India will ever be very close to my heart" (Indian Educational Policy, 1913, p. 1)." His Majesty's pronouncement, coupled with the attempts of Mr Gokhale's attempts forced the government to pay more attention to primary education.

The Government Resolution on Education Policy dated 21st February, 1913, which was an attempt of the British Government to compensate the demand for compulsory primary education by Gokhale. While rejecting Gokhale's bill of 1911, the government promised to extend recurring and non-recurring grants to primary education as it could not ignore the growing popular demand for the spread of primary education. The education department had declared the new policy in the form of Government of India Resolution on February 21, 1913 covering primary, secondary, and higher and women education.

The Indian Educational Policy, 1913 stated regarding the compulsory education that:

"The propositions that illiteracy must be broken down and that primary education in the present circumstances of India, a predominant claim upon the public funds represent accepted policy no longer open to discussion. **For financial and administrative reasons of decisive weight the Government of India have refused to recognise the principle of compulsory education; but they desire the widest possible extension of primary education on a voluntary basis, regards free elementary education the time has not yet arrived** when it is practicable to dispense wholly with fees without injustice to the many villages, which are waiting for the provision of schools. The fees derived from those pupils who can pay them are now devoted to the maintenance and expansion of primary education, and a total remission of fees would involve to a certain extent a more prolonged postponement of the provision of schools in villages without them. In provinces elementary education is already free and in the majority of provinces liberal provision is already made for giving free elementary instruction to those boys whose parents cannot afford to pay fees. Local Governments have been requested to extend the application of the principle of free elementary education amongst the poorer and more backward sections of the population. Further than this it is not possible at present to go (pp. 9-10)".

Ultimately, the British Administrators had never looked upon education in India as a sacred duty which they had to fulfil. They looked upon the education of Indians as an object of charity and not as a duty. Charity entails no goal, nor a minimum requirement. A duty has both.

In 1915, Gokhle passed away and soon after his demise the campaign for compulsory primary education was again started by the late Sri Vithalbhai Patel. Vithalbhai Patel successfully piloted an Act for the permissive introduction of compulsion in Municipal areas of the Province of Bombay. Mr Patel introduced in 1917 a Bill in the Bombay Legislative Council for permitting Municipalities to introduce compulsion in their areas. This Bill received the ascent of the Governor-General on the 5th February, 1918, and the Bombay Primary Education (District Municipalities) Act of 1918. Mr Vithalbhai Patel was thus responsible for getting the first Law on Compulsory Primary Education in British India passed by the Bombay Legislative Council. This is popularly known as the Patel Act, after its mover. It was broadly based on Gokhle's bill, but made some momentous changes which were mainly responsible for its acceptance by the government. The main difference between the bill of Gokhle and Patel was that the former wanted to extend his experiment to both urban and rural areas, while the later desired to confine it only to municipalities. Secondly, Gokhle's tactical error in insisting that the government should bear two-thirds of the expenditure on compulsory education was rectified by Patel who accepted the suggestion made by the Government of India that it should be left to the discretion of the State government to give grant-in-aid for schemes of compulsory education. These two changes particularly the later, weakened the opposition of the government to the measure and it became law in 1918. However, the Patel Act awakened nation-wide interest in the need of compulsory primary education. It may be asserted that all the compulsory acts in all the provinces of British India are modelled either on Mr Gokhale's Bill or on Patel Act.

Compulsory Education during the Period of 1917-27

After the passing of Government of India Act, 1919, the control of elementary education was transferred to Indian ministers. This ushered in an era of rapid expansion of elementary education (Government of India, 1993). In fact, the decade 1917 to 1927 in the history of compulsory education in British India may rightly be regarded as the boom-period of compulsion. Indian primary education lacked in legislation till 1917. Since 1918, all the State legislatures began passing in acts for introducing Compulsory Primary Education in their respective States. Thanks to Montague-Chelmsford Reforms, the Education portfolio was placed in the hands of an Indian Minister responsible to a legislature with large elected majority. Besides, there was a great awakening among the masses owing to Non-Cooperation Movement and the intelligentsia began to develop sympathy for the masses. These social and political changes gave a great impetus to compulsory education. The concept of compulsory elementary education thus came to be accepted in theory and was incorporated in the laws of the land, especially after the transfer of education to Indian control in 1921. All the compulsory education Acts of British India Provinces except N.W.F. Province were either conceived or passed in this period. The following Table 4.1 gives detailed information regarding.

Thus, the dreams of Mr Gokhale were realised fifteen years after the failure of his own bill for compulsory education. The progress of compulsion prior to the partitioning of the country will be evident from the following Table 4.2:

Table 4.1: Compulsory Education Acts in British India after 1918

Year	*Province*	*Name of Act*	*Whether for*	*Areas boys or girls*
1919	Punjab	P.E. Act	Boys	Rural and Municipal
1919	U.P.	P.E. Act	Both	Municipal
1919	Bengal	P.E. Act	Boys	Municipal
1919	Bihar and Orissa	P.E. Act	Boys	Rural and Municipal
1920	Bombay	City of Bombay P.E. Act	Both	City of Bombay
1920	C.P.	P.E. Act	Both	Rural and Municipal
1920	Madras	Elementary Education Act	Both	Rural and Municipal
1923	Bombay	P.E. Act	Both	Rural and Municipal
1926	Assam	P.E. Act	Both	Rural and Municipal
1926	U.P.	District Boards P.E. Act	Both	Rural
1930	Bengal	Bengal (Rural) P. E. Act	Both	Rural
1932	Bengal	P.E. (Amendment) Act	Girls	Municipal
1939	N.W.F.	P. E. Act	Boys	Rural and Municipal

Source: Naik, 1942, p. 12.

Table 4.2: Compulsory Education in British India, 1921-37

Year	*Municipalities and Urban areas*	*Rural areas*
1921-22	8	-
1926-27	114	1571
1931-32	153	3392
1936-37	167	3034

Source: Mukherji, 1964, p. 73.

The progress had not been very encouraging especially between 1931 and 1937. On the recommendations of the Hartog Report, 1929, the government adopted the policy of consolidation rather than of expansion. The Hartog Committee (an auxiliary Committee of Simon Commission, 1929) observed that "throughout the whole educational system, there is wastage and ineffectiveness." Insufficient schools were rooted out and only the effective schools were allowed to run.

The introduction of Provincial Autonomy in 1937 through the Government of India Act, 1935, gave more powers to Indian Ministers to act independently. With the introduction of Provincial Autonomy, the Indian National Congress assumed the office in seven provinces out of eleven. The education ministers under Provincial Autonomy could command far larger resources than the ministers under Dyarchy ever did. Though detailed plans for large scale expansion of elementary education were developed, the implementation was restricted because of the outbreak of the Second World War. For overcoming the constraints of funds at the disposal of Congress Ministers, Mahatma Gandhi suggested that the plans of mass education need not be held up and that universal, compulsory and free primary education of seven years' duration could be given to every child if the process of schooling could be made self-supporting. With this object in view, Gandhiji formulated the scheme of 'Basic Education' which was discussed and endorsed by the first Conference of National Education held at Wardha in October, 1937 which resolved that free and compulsory education be provided for seven years on a nation-wide scale.

Wardha Scheme of Basic Education, 1937

In the light of the resolutions passed at the National Conference on Education in October 1937 in Wardha, Zakir Hussain committee formulated a detailed national scheme for basic education. The main principle behind this scheme was 'learning through activity'. It was based on Gandhi's ideas published in a series of articles in the weekly Harijan. Gandhi thought that western education had created a gulf between the educated few and the masses and had also made the educated elite ineffective.

The scheme had the following provisions:

- Inclusion of a basic handicraft in the syllabus.
- First seven years of schooling to be an integral part of a free and compulsory nationwide education system (through mother tongue).
- Teaching to be in Hindi from Class II to VII and in English only after Class VIII.

- Ways to be devised to establish contact with the community around schools through service.
- A suitable technique to be devised with a view to implementing the main idea of basic education—educating the child through the medium of productive activity of a suitable handicraft.

The system, rather than being a methodology for education, was an expression of an idea for a new life and a new society. The basic premise was that only through such a scheme could India be an independent and non-violent society. This scheme was child-centred and cooperative. This scheme was adopted in several provinces where the Congress was in power. There was not much development of this idea, because of the start of the Second World War and the resignation of the Congress ministries (October 1939). However, Wardha Scheme of Basic Education of Mahatma Gandhi was also an effort towards the Universalisation of elementary education.

The Post-War Plan of Educational Development in India (1944)

Consequent upon the continued efforts of the leaders, the provision of free and compulsory education to all children till they reached the age of 14 years, was nationally accepted during the early 1940s as the responsibility of the State. The Post-War Plan of Educational Development in India (1944) popularly known as the Sargent Plan, recommended the provision of free and compulsory education to all children in the age group of 6 - 14 years in a phased manner spread over a period of 40 years. However, as per Report of the "Progress of Education in India, 1937-47" Volume 1, p. 73, in 1946-47, compulsion existed in 229 towns and 10,017 villages for boys, and in 10 towns and 1404 villages for both boys and girls.

The Kher Committee, 1948

However, the national leadership was determined to minimise the process. The proposal of the Sargent Plan was examined by a special committee under the Chairmanship of B.G. Kher, the then Chief Minister of Bombay in 1950 accepted the programme of universal, compulsory and free basic education as proposed in the Plan itself but reduced the time span from 40 (1944-84) to 16 years (1944-60). It was this recommendation that formed the basis of Article 45 of the

Table 4.3: Compulsory Primary Education in India, 1946-47

Province	*Age Group under Compulsion*	*Areas with Boys only under Compulsion*		*Areas with Girls only under Compulsion*	
		Number of Towns and Cities	*Number of Villages*	*Number of Towns and Cities*	*Number of Villages*
West Bengal	6-10	1*	-	-	-
Bihar	6-10	17	1	-	-
Bombay	6-11	11	298	9	319
C.P. and Berar	6-11	34#	1031	-	-
	7-12	-	-	-	-
Madras	6-14	10	100	7	1082
	6-12	-	-	-	-
Orissa	6-12	1	24	-	-
	6-10	-	-	-	-
East Punjab	6-11	35	4984	-	-
Sind	6-12	1	2551	1	-
United Provinces	6-11	36	1371	3 @	3
Delhi	5-10	1$	15	-	-

Source: Progress of Education in India 1937-1947 Decennial Review, Vol. 1, Central Bureau of Education, Ministry of Education, Government of India, 1948, p. 73.

[*Introduced only in Ward No. 9 of Calcutta Corporation, # In 11 of these towns certain wards are under compulsion, @ A few wards only under compulsion, $ Nine out of 12 wards of Old Delhi Municipal Committee are under compulsion].

Directive Principles of the Indian Constitution enjoining that the "State shall endeavour to provide within a period of ten years from the commencement of this Constitution for free and compulsory education for all children until they complete the age of 14 years." Ever since, efforts are being made to fulfil the provision of free and compulsory education for all Indian children through successive five-year plans and a host of Central and State Governments' sponsored programmes. Details of Compulsory Primary Education in India for the year 1946-47 are given in the Table 4.3.

Compulsory Primary Education has not been introduced in Assam, North West Frontier and in Centrally Administered Areas except Delhi.

References

- Aggarwal, D. D. (2002). *History and Development of Elementary Education in India*. New Delhi: Sarup & Sons.
- B. C. Rai (1997). *History of Education in India and Problems*. Lucknow: Prakashan Kendra.
- Government of Bombay (1859). *Report of the Director of Public Instruction, Bombay, for the Year 1857-58*. Bombay: The Education Society's Press.
- Government of India (1868). *Adam's Reports on Vernacular Education in Bengal and Behar with a Brief View of its Past and Present Condition by Rev. J. Long*. Calcutta: The Home Secretariat Press.
- Government of India (1881). *Education Commission Bombay Vol. II Evidence taken before The Bombay Provincial Committee, and Memorials addressed to The Education Commission*. Calcutta: The Superintendent of Government Printing, India. Government of India.
- Government of India (1883). *Report of the Indian Education Commission*. Calcutta: The Superintendent of Government Printing.
- Government of India (1915). *Indian Educational Policy, 1913*. Calcutta: Superintendent Government Printing, India.
- Government of India (1950). *Report of the Committee on the Ways and Means of Financing Education Development in India, 1948*. Delhi, Manager of Publications, Bureau of Education, Government of India.
- Government of India (1993). Report of National Development Council Committee on Literacy, Planning Commission 1993. New Delhi: MHRD. Retrieved on 12.09.2012 from http://www.teindia.nic.in/mhrd/50yrsedu/y/3P/45/toc.htm
- Indian National Congress (1906). *Report of the Twenty Second Indian National Congress, held at Calcutta, the 26th to 29th December, 1906*. Calcutta: Indian National Congress.

- Juneja, N. (2003). *Constitutional Amendment to Make Education a Fundamental Right – Issues for a Follow-up Legislation*. New Delhi: NIEPA.
- Mukherji, S. N. (1964). *Education in India – Today and Tomorrow*. Baroda: Acharya Book Depot.
- Naik, J. P. (1942). *History of the Local Fund Cess (Appropriated to Education) in the Province of Bombay*. Bombay: The Local Self-Government Institute.
- Naik, J. P. (1942). *Studies in Primary Education*, First Series. Bombay: The Local Self-Government Institute (Bombay Presidency).
- Naik, J. P. (1965). *Elementary Education in India – The Unfinished Business*. Bombay: Asia Publishing House.
- Naik, J. P. (1975). *Elementary Education in India – A Promise to Keep*. Bombay: Allied Publishers.
- Naik, J. P. (1978). Educational Reform in India: A Historical Review. Bombay: Orient Longman Limited.
- Naik, J.P. (1943). *A Review of Modern Education in India (1813-1942)*. Tilak College of Education, Poona: The Aryabhushan Press.
- Natesan, G. A. (1916). *Speeches of Gopal Krishna Gokhale*. Second Edition. Madras: G. A. Natesan & Co.
- Niranjanaradhya and Kashyap, A. (2006). *The Fundamentals of the Fundamental Right to Education in India*. Bangalore: Books for Change.
- Niranjanaradhya, V. P. (2004). *Legal Aspects of Universalisation of School Education in India – Myth and Reality*. Paper presented in the Second International Conference on Law, Session on Right to Education, Organised by UNESCO, New Delhi and the Indian Society of International Law, New Delhi.
- Nurullah, S. and Naik, J. P. (1964). *A Students' History of Education in India*. Bombay: Macmillan and Co Limited.
- Pathania, A. and Pathania, K. (2006). *Primary Education and Mid-Day Meal Scheme – Results, Challenges and Recommendations*. New Delhi: Deep & Deep Publications Private Limited.
- R. P. Paranjpye (1915). *Gopal Krishna Gokhal*. Reprinted from Fergusson College Magazine, Poona. Published by Natesh Appaji Dravid, the Aryabhushan Press.
- Raina, Vinod (2010). *Education and Knowledge in the Time of Globalisation Inclusion, Quality and Agency*. Shillong: B. M. Pugh Fourth Memorial Lecture, 2010, NERIE, NCERT. Retrieved from http://nerie.nic.in/pdf/txtVinod-Raina-during-IVth-BM-Pugh.pdf. on 10.4.2013.
- Rastogi, K.G. and Sharma, H.L. (1981). *Universalisation of Elementary Education Brochure – V*, New Delhi: NCERT.

- Sen, J. M. (1925). *Primary Education Acts in India – A Study*. Calcutta: Calcutta Young Men's Christian Association (CYMCA).
- Sen, J. M. (2010). *History of Elementary Education in India*. New Delhi: Pacific Publication.
- Sharma, Nirmala (2011). *Universalisation of Elementary Education among Tea-Tribe of Assam with special reference to Jorhat District*. Guwahati, Assam: Assam State Commission for Protection of Child Right.
- Sharp, H. (1914). *Progress of Education in India 1907-1912*. Volume 1. Calcutta: Superintendent of Government Printing, India.
- The Servants of India Society (1917). *A Brief Account of the Work of the Servants of India Society, Poona (from June 1905 to December 1916)*. Poona: The Aryabhushan Press.
- UNESCO (1984). *Towards Universalisation of Primary Education in Asia and the Pacific Country Studies India*. UNESCO Regional Office for Education in Asia and the Pacific: Bangkok.

Chapter - 5

Movement Discourse on Right to Education from Directive Principle to Fundamental Right

The Indian education system is the second largest in the world and is perhaps the most complex in terms of its spatial outreach and profile of students and teachers in terms of their linguistic, social, cultural and economic background. On 26th January 1950 when Indian Constitution came in force, it had in its Article 45 a directive principle promising free and compulsory education for all children until they complete the age of 14 years. This was to be attained within 10 years. But the state could not do so for next five decades. In order to enforce the Unnikrishnan judgement, several public interest litigation petitions were filed in different High Courts. This created tremendous pressure on the parliament for a constitutional amendment to include the right to education as a fundamental right. The Indian State adopted the Eighty Six Amendment Act to the Constitution, thereby conferring on education the status of a fundamental right. Through 86th constitutional amendment, Article 21-a (part III) was inserted in the fundamental right section of constitution under which, "The State shall provide free and compulsory education to all children of the age of 6 to 14 years in such manner as the State may, by law, determine. On the 27th day of August 2009, Right of children to free and compulsory education Act 2009 was notified. The path to the most sought 'Right to Education' was an uphill journey. For understanding it in a better way, this Chapter has tried to explore the movement discourse on the right to free and compulsory education from directive principle to fundamental right.

Why Was the 86th Amendment Act Required? : Before exploring the movement discourse, the authors have intended to explain why the 86th Amendment Act of the Constitution was required. The Right of Children to Free and Compulsory Education Act (RTE Act), 2009 came into force April 1, 2010, pursuant to the 86th Amendment to the Constitution (2002) which guarantees primary education as a fundamental right. The RTE Act and its notification are rightly hailed by many as a landmark in the history of education in post-independence India. But while these are momentous developments, they also highlight — even 60 years after the Constitution came into force — our conspicuous failure to fulfil the Directive Principle 45 of the Constitution (1950) which promised to provide free and compulsory education to all children within a period of ten years. Had the directive principle been implemented in letter and spirit, the need for the 86th Amendment and the RTE Act would not have arisen (Tilak, 2010).

Article 45 which refers to primary education advises the State to endeavour to provide, within a period of ten years from 1950, for free and compulsory education for all children until they complete the age of fourteen years. The irony of the directive principle was that checks and controls on the endeavours were not envisaged. The sincerity of the implementation of the Article 45 was lost because of a provision under Article 41. Article 41 reads as follows: The State shall, within the limits of its economic capacity and development, make effective provision for securing the right to work, to education and to public assistance. It is under the escape route of capacity and development that the State has all along justified its poor performance in regard to elementary education (Seetharamu, 2002).

Movement Discourse after Independence

The period spanning between 1950 - the Unnikrishnan's Case in 1993 saw several legal developments and policy perspectives. A brief flashback to these issues provides us an insight into the historical journey of transformation of right to education from directive principle into a fundamental right. Now we look at the initiatives of the Union Government of India to provide free and compulsory elementary education and include the right to education as fundamental right in Part III of the Constitution after 1950. One of the main problems that faced the Government of India immediately on attaining independence was that of education. The problem was two-fold:

(1) To fight illiteracy, by providing facilities for giving elementary Basic Education to 85 per cent of our population who cannot read and write; and

(2) To nationalise our entire system of education so as to train, equip and direct the youth of the country to take their proper share in building a progressive State.

To solve this two-fold problem government had to contend from the very outset with three main difficulties – restricted finance, paucity of trained teacher and controversial problem of the medium of instruction (Government of India, 1948:1). In order to re-examine the entire problem of education, the Honourable Maulana Abul Kalam Azad, Minister for Education in the National Government, convened an All-India Education Conference in January 16th and 15th, 1948. The then Prime Minister Jawaharlal Nehru in his inaugural address to the All India Educational Conference said that "Great changes have taken place in the country and the educational system must also be in keeping with them. The entire basis of education must be revolutionised" (Biswas and Agrawal, 1986, p. vi). Addressing the conference on All India Education on January 16, 1948, Maulana Azad emphasised: "We must not for a moment forget, it is a birth right of every individual to receive at least the basic education without which he cannot fully discharge his duties as a citizen."

The following decisions related to universal free and compulsory basic education were taken there:

- The period of forty years contemplated by Sargent Plan for the completion of the work of universal compulsory basic education should be substantially curtailed.
- The view of the Central Advisory Board of Education that universal free and compulsory basic education should cover a period of eight years was fully endorsed. In case of financial crisis and other practical reasons, in the first instance, plan for a shorter period not less than five years may be taken.

- The Conference endorsed the recommendations of the CABE to appoint a Committee of Educationists and other experts to consider ways and means of raising the finances, required to expedite and implement Basic Education Plans, including the question of Central grants, the levy of an educational cess and the raising of educational loans.

Committee on the Ways and Means of Financing Education Development in India (B. G. Kher Committee), 1948

The outline of educational development of the country had been laid down in the Report of the CABE known as "Post-War Educational Development in India" published in January 1944. This Report also supplied estimates of the cost of the various programmes and stages of educational development. The practical experiences gained since then signified that the recommendations made in the Report required to be modified in the materialistic perspective. The question of our future programme of education was raised at the 14th Meeting of the CABE, 1948 and at the All India Education Conference held in January 1948. It was generally agreed that the period of 40 years laid down in the Report for including an eight-year course of compulsory education must be curtailed and, if necessary for the purpose, the stage up to which compulsion should be enforced would also be reduced. It was however agreed that the period of compulsion would in no case be less than five years i.e. for the age group 6-11. The estimates of cost as calculated in the Report were also out of date. It was decided to appoint a committee to examine the existing financial resources and the programme for educational development for all Provinces and States and to make suggestions to ensure that educational development may not be held up for want of funds. A Committee entitled "Committee on the Ways and Means of Financing Education Development in India" was appointed by the Government of India in 1948 under the chairmanship of Shri B. G. Kher, Chief Minister of Bombay. For the proper financing of educational development, the Kher Committee recommended that:

- The State must undertake the responsibility of providing at least Junior Basic Education for everybody without, however, detriment to existing facilities for Secondary and Higher

Education. Special attention should be given to the provision of such higher studies as will be necessary for increasing the industrial and agricultural potential of the country.

- The Provinces should aim at introducing universal compulsory education for the children of 6-11 age-groups within a period of ten years but if financial conditions compel, the programme may be extended over a larger period but in no circumstances should it be given up.
- A fixed percentage of Central and Provincial revenues - about 10 per cent of the Central and 20 per cent of the Provincial - should be earmarked for education by the respective governments.
- About 70 per cent of the expenditure on education should be borne by Provincial Governments including Local Bodies, and the remaining 30 per cent by the Centre.
- All contributions for education approved by the Provincial and Central Governments should be exempted from income tax (Government of India, 1950).

When Moulana Azad addressed the meeting of the Central Advisory Board of Education in January, 1949 he spoke of the approach of the National Government towards education. He stated that "the first and foremost task of the National Government is the provision of free and compulsory basic education for all" and he envisaged that universal compulsory basic education could be introduced within a period of 16 years by two five-year and one six-year plans (Chatterjee, 2010:4). Again at the time of address at the Central Advisory Board of Education, Cuttack, January 8, 1950 pointed out the proposal of the Ministry of Education that "our immediate objectives should be four, namely:

(1) The provision of basic education on a universal free and compulsory basis for all our school-going children;

(2) The provision of adult education in order to wipe out the colossal illiteracy of our masses;

(3) The improvement and expansion of technical education in order to solve the problem of manpower for industrial and technical development; and

(4) The reorganisation and improvement of university education from a national point of view."

However, Vinod Raina, one of the chief architects of RTE Act commented that Moulana Azad committed to free and compulsory education but while he recognised that basic education was the birthright of every individual, how much he used his powers of persuasion and clout in transforming this birthright into a legal right in the Constitution was not clear. Because, the Constituent Assembly ultimately decided to drop the draft article that would have made education a fundamental right from the very beginning of the Constitution.

Movement after the Constitutional Era

After Independence, the national and international policies in general and the Directive Principles of Indian Constitution in particular bound the state to provide free and compulsory elementary education to all the children. Despite the constitutional and international commitments, the Indian State has failed to achieve the goal of the Universal Elementary education within the stipulated time mandated by the Constitution. In such a situation, it took more than six decades for the Indian State to frame and implement the Right to Education Act, 2009 and to make the mandate of the Constitution an enforceable right.

Despite the consistent demand for free and compulsory education during the freedom struggle, at the time of drafting the Constitution, there was no unanimous view that the citizens of India should have a right to education as fundamental right. Serious debates and discussions were held to secure the position of right to education in the Constitution of India. Right to education did not secure a position within Part III of the Constitution during its drafting and subsequent enactment in 1950. It was rather secured under Part IV of the Constitution thereby protecting the State from any proceedings in absence of the enforcement of right to education.

A brief flashback to the framing of the Constitution provides us an insight into the historical background with which the framers of our Constitution included Article 45 in it (as it stood before 86th Amendment to the Constitution) which stated that *"The State shall endeavour to provide within a period of ten years from the commencement of this constitution, for free and compulsory education for all children until they complete the age of fourteen years".*

Despite the consistent demand for free and compulsory education during the freedom struggle, at the time drafting the Constitution, there was no unanimous view that the citizens of India should have a right to education, let alone a fundamental right (Constituent Assembly Debates, Volume 1, 11 December, 1946). The framers of the Constitution of India shied away from making education a fundamental right and provided for only a directive to the State under Chapter IV of the Constitution. The Directive Principles of State Policy (DPSP) is not enforceable in the court of law but it shall be the duty of the State to apply these principles in making laws. DPSP forms the pious obligations of the State and is not enforceable in the court as provided under Article 37 of the Indian Constitution.The Article 45 was a Directive Principle of State Policy within India, effectively meaning that it was within a set of rules that were meant to be followed in spirit and the government could be held to court if the actual letter was not followed (Sripati and Thiruvengadam, 2004). As a result of the responsibility of providing education to the children was a directive to the State and not a fundamental right casted upon them. The distinction between Fundamental Rights and Directive Principles of State Policy is well settled under the Indian Constitution. While the former is absolute and legally enforceable, the latter is a directive policy to the State (Government of Bihar, 2007:23). Constitution of India provides for two types of rights: (a) civic and political rights and (b) social and economic rights. Articles 12 to 35 of the Constitution constitute the fundamental rights which are justiciable. Article 32 of the Constitution guarantees 'Remedies for enforcement of civic and political rights'. The 93th Constitutional Amendment has transformed education from its status as a social and economic right to that of a civic and political right (Seetharamu, 2002).

The Constituent Assembly commenced its task from 1946 that continued till the Constitution was adopted in 1950. However, in 1947, the Assembly Sub-Committee on Fundamental Rights placed free and compulsory education on the list of Fundamental Rights. According to its Clause 23:

"Every citizen is entitled as of right to free primary education and it shall be the duty of the State to provide within a period of ten years from the commencement of this constitution for free and compulsory primary education for all children until they complete the age of fourteen years."

But on 23rd April, 1947 the Advisory Committee of the Constituent Assembly rejected free and compulsory education as a fundamental right on the ground that *"what would happen if the State would not have sufficient funds to make arrangements for free and compulsory education of all children?"* and sent this clause to the list of 'non-justiciable fundamental rights' (latter termed as 'Directive Principles of State Policy') [Rao, 1968]. Pandit Govind Ballabh Pant quipped, "It cannot be justiciable. No court can possibly adjudicate". So "this clause be transferred to Part IV (Directive Principles)" [Pal, 2001].

Professor Sadgopal (2010) stated that the recommendation of the Assembly Sub-Committee on Fundamental Rights was considered by the Advisory Committee of the Constituent Assembly (21-22 April 1947) chaired by Sardar Vallabhbhai Patel. The Chairman directed the Advisory Committee to "restrict [ourselves] to the rights which are actually considered necessary…and not go into detailed description of theoretical rights which are not enforceable at all." Taking cue from this caution, a member wondered, "Suppose the government has no money?". Another opined that he would like "deletion of this clause" (p. 18). Ultimately a compromise was worked out.

What appears shocking to many of us today is that there was much apathy to the Directive Principles enunciated in the Constitution (Juneja, 2003:27). In fact, one of the members of the Constituent Assembly in 1947 added a note of dissent to the formation of two types of rights of the people – justiciable and non-justiciable rights. In his view, non-justiciable rights had no meaning. He had wanted the Assembly to unambiguously declare all rights as justiciable for the reason that:

"Once an unambiguous declaration of such a right is made, those responsible for giving effect to it would have to bestir themselves to find ways and means to give effect to it. If they had no such responsibility placed upon them, they might be inclined to avail themselves of every

excuse to justify their own inactivity in the matter, indifference, or worse." — Excerpted from Note of dissent of K.T. Shah to the Report, (April 17-20, 1947) On Right to Work (Rao, 1968).

These words of K.T. Shah proved prophetic. Although Advisory Committee of the Constituent Assembly had distinguished and self-proclaimed liberals and Gandhians like Mr M. R. Masani, only one member, Mr K. T. Shah had the courage of conviction and gave a dissenting note. He said that if a right to education becomes non-justiciable, it "would remain as no more than so many pious wishes". He added that if it does not become "imperative obligations of the state towards the citizen, we would be perpetuating a needless fraud" (Pal, 2001).

On the fate of the Article 45 after independence, the noted Gandhian economist L.C. Jain has observed that "there is not to be found even a passing reference to education let alone to Article 45 in the budget speeches" (Jain, 2001). When Right to Education Act has been passed in 2009 and formally implemented in 2010, it appears as if successive governments during 62 years before the passage of this Act have successfully availed the above said excuses, (Singh, 2012).

The initial framing of Article 36 of the Draft Constitution, which formed Article 45 of the Indian Constitution (before the enactment of the 86th Constitutional Amendment Act, 2002), was found to be problematic. During a debate in the Constituent Assembly in November 1948, the first line of the Article 36 was removed which stated "every citizen is entitled as of right to free primary education and it shall be the duty of the State provide ...." And the new Article replaced it with "The state shall endeavour to provide, within a period of ten years from the commencement of this constitution, for free and compulsory education for all children until they complete the age of fourteen years" (Constituent Assembly Debates, 1948, Vol.7). Here it needs mention that Pandit Lakshmi Kanta Maitra, an eminent member of the Constituent Assembly debate proposed the deletion of the words "every citizen is entitled to". His justification was that all the Articles of the DPSP begin with "the state shall endeavour to" except Article 36 alone and hence does not fit in the framework. Moreover, the wordings of Article 36 resemble fundamental rights mixed with DPSP. Hence, it was proposed to be amended. That effectively put an end to the possible inclusion of Right to Education in the original Constitution itself.

The term "primary education" was removed from the final draft because of the intervention of Babasaheb Ambedkar, the Chairperson of the Assembly as on November 23rd, 1949 when he gave an argument against it ".... a provision has been made in Article 18, to forbid any child being employed below the age of 14. Obviously, if the child is not to be employed below the age of 14, the child must be kept occupied in some educational institution. That is the object of the Article 36" (Constituent Assembly Debates, 1948, Vol.7). Barring this intervention, the Final Article 45 under the Directive Principles would have said *"up to age 11"* rather than *"up to age 14"*.

According to Professor Anil Sadgopal (2010), during the Constituent Assembly debates, a member contended that the commitment made in the draft Article (later to be known as Article 45) to provide "free and compulsory education" to children *upto 14 years of age* should be limited to *only 11 years of age* as India would not have the necessary resources. The dilution would have been made but for Dr Babasaheb Ambedkar's clarity of mind that it is at this age of 11 years that a substantial proportion of children become child labourers. He forcefully argued that the place for children at this age in independent India should be in schools, rather than in farms or factories. The rhetoric of 'resource crunch' for education of the masses guided the Constituent Assembly for even a more crucial decision (pp. 17-18).

Finally, Article 45 of Directive Principles of State Policy accepted – *"The State shall endeavour to provide within a period of ten years from the commencement of this constitution, for free and compulsory education for all children until they complete the age of fourteen years"*.

Never the less, the constitution framers established three things:

(1) A time frame (10 years) for implementation of the Right to free and compulsory education.

(2) An upper age limit (14 years).

(3) No lower age limit because it was never an issue during that period.

The background of this timeframe can be traced back to the Sargent Committee (1944) which had envisaged provision of free and compulsory education in two phases within 40 years (1944), the first phase up to the age of 11 years and second phase up to the age of 14 years which further led to the establishment of Kher Committee (1948) under the chairmanship of B.G. Kher, to explore the means and ways of achieving UEE up to the age of 14 years within ten years at lesser cost.

Now it may be claimed that systematic development of universal elementary education was taken up with the attainment of independence in 1947, particularly with the enactment of the Constitution of India in 1950 and initiation of country-wide economic and social planning in 1951. Article 45 of the Constitution enacted in 1950, enjoins that "the state shall endeavour to provide, within a period of ten years from the commencement of this Constitution, for free and compulsory education for all children until they complete the age of fourteen years". The expression 'State' which occurs in Article 12 is defined to include "The Government and Parliament of India and the Government and the Legislature of each state and all local authorities within the territory of India or under the control of the Government of India". Since then, many documents including every Five Year Plan, the National Policies on Education, and Education Commissions and Committees have attempted to refine India's efforts at Universal Elementary Education (UEE).

Efforts to fulfil this objective were, in the first few years, greatly hampered by the influx and unending stream of refugees from across the border and the difficult position of resources, both financial and human (Government of India, 1965, pp 17-18).

University Education Commission (1948-1949)

The University Education Commission (1948-1949) under the chairmanship of Dr Radhakrishnan recognised that "in a democratic society the opportunity of learning must be open not only to elite but to all those who have to carry the privilege and responsibility of citizenship. Education is a universal right, not a class privilege" (The Report of the University Education Commission (1948-1949, Volume -1, p. 43).

All-India Council of Elementary Education (AICEE), 1957

In order to accelerate the pace of expansion of elementary education and to fulfil the directive of Article 45 of the Constitution, the Government of India had decided that an All-India Council of Elementary Education (AICEE) should be established with effect from July 1, 1957. It served as an advisory body to the Union and State Governments and local bodies on matters relating to elementary education. A Government of India resolution to this effect was published in the Gazette of India on June 29. The Council not only examined and appraised proposals referred to it by the Union and State Governments, but also initiated proposals for the development of elementary education.

Delhi Primary Education Act, 1960

In 1960, fifty years after Gopal Krishna Gokhale had moved his resolution on compulsory education in the Imperial Legislature Assembly, Dr K. L. Shrimali, the Union Minister of Education, moved the Delhi Primary Education Bill in the Parliament. Its primary objective was to provide a compulsory education law for the Delhi Union Territory; but it also included up-to-date provisions regarding enforcement of compulsory attendance, which could be taken as a model by the States for amending their compulsory education laws. The bill became law on the 2nd of October 1960 (Rajkhowa, 1964:39). The State Governments had also initiated action to amend their compulsory education laws on the model of the Delhi Primary Education Act, 1960. Such legislation has been passed in several States. Eighteen States and two Union Territories had their own legislations dealing with compulsory elementary education. Though these Acts were passed, enforcement was not strict. As a result Acts were remained in papers (Sharma, 2011, p. 7).

Report of the Kothari Commission (1964-66)

It took 17 years after independence and four years after the deadline set by Article 45 of the Constitution for providing free and compulsory education to all children up to the age of 14 years to constitute the Kothari Commission (1964-66) - the first Commission to examine the question of elementary education (Class I-VIII) (AIFRTE, 2012; 22).

After the expiry of ten-year period (1950-1960), to achieve the target of providing free and compulsory education to all, the Report of the Education Commission (1944-1966) recommended Common School System of public education based on neighbourhood schools to fulfil the insistent demand for free and universal education of the people. The Commission admitted in its report that the fulfilment of the directive principle contained in Article 45 of the Constitution was to have been achieved by 1960. But in view of the immense difficulties involved, such as lack of adequate resources, tremendous increase in population, resistance to the education of girls, large numbers of children of the backward classes, general poverty of the people and the illiteracy and apathy of parents, it was not possible to make adequate progress in primary education, and the Constitutional Directive has remained unfulfilled. There has, therefore, been an insistent demand that government should fix an early deadline for its fulfilment and prepare a concrete programme of action for the purpose. The commission pointed out that the provision of free and universal education for every child is an educational objective of the highest priority, not only on grounds of social justice and democracy, but also for raising the competence of the average worker and for increasing national productivity. Due to the magnitude of the problem, the uneven development of primary education in the different parts of the country and the need for large financial resources, the commission suggested the following strategy for fulfilling the Constitutional Directive:

(2) Each State, and even each district, should prepare a perspective plan for the development of primary education taking into account the stage of development already reached and the local conditions and problems. The objective of the plan should be to fulfil the Constitutional Directive as early as possible;

(3) Each State and district should be assisted to go ahead at the best pace it can, and the progress in no area should be allowed to be held up merely for want of essential facilities or financial allocations; and

(4) While the Constitutional Directive may be fulfilled in some places such as urban areas or advanced States as early as in 1975-76, all the areas in the country should be able to provide

five years of good and effective education to all the children by 1975-76 and seven years of such education by 1985-86 (Para 7.08).

In short, the Kothari Commission recommended for the implementation of the free and compulsory education of good quality to all children up to the age of 14 years, directed by Article 45 of the Constitution, in a phased manner over a period of time due to the need of immense human and physical resources. This can be done by providing five years of effective education to all children by 1975-76 and seven years of such education by 1985-86.

The 31st CABE Meeting, at Bangalore on October 11 and 12, 1964, under the Chairmanship of Shri M.C. Chagla

Shri M.C. Chagla, the then Union Education Minister and Chairman, Central Advisory Board of Education spoke about the failure of the intention of UEE as envisaged in the Article 45 and suggested few measures at the Presidential Address of the Thirty-first, meeting of the Central Advisory Board of Education was held at Bangalore on October 11 and 12, 1964.

The meeting focused on the vision of education for the future with Child Centric education. Shri M.C. Chagla, the then Union Education Minister said that we cannot be slaves of the past and must move with the processes of change. We need to learn from the past; build on it and create opportunities for the future of our children as also the future of the unborn child. He said that the most precious of all resources are our children and we must ensure that they get all the opportunities for their development. While enunciating his vision of child centric education, Shri M.C. Chagla, recalled the very insightful and perceptive statement. He stated:

> "There has been a tremendous expansion in primary education, which is all to the good. I think the spirit of our men, which has been submerged, put down, which did not find a scope before, we became free, suddenly found a scope for free play and the result has been that boys and girls want to go to schools; parents want to send their children to schools; they want more and more schools, more and more facilities for primary education and we have to encourage that. But with this expansion, and I call it "expansion-

explosion" that we have today, if my figures are correct, there are 60 million students in our primary schools and these are astronomical figures. But along with expansion, along with the emphasis on quantity, we must not wholly forget that some importance has to be attached to quality. In this connection, I would like to mention, that as far as primary schools are concerned, we want better buildings, we want better equipment, we want better teachers, we want laboratories, we want better textbooks, we want playgrounds attached to our primary schools where our boys and girls will be able to play games, for athletics sports, and not to be locked up in a building all the time that they are studying. May I say this? You know of the Article 45 of the Constitution. It is a directive to every State Government and to the Union Government that we must give free elementary education to all boys and girls between the ages 6 and 14. We are very far from complying with that directive. But what I wish to emphasise before you today is that the compliance. Our Constitution fathers did not intend when they enacted Article 45 that we just set-up hovels or any sort of structures, put students there, give them untrained teachers, give them bad textbooks, no playgrounds and say we have complied with Article 45 and primary education is expanding. The compliance that was intended, as I said, by our Constitution fathers, by the founding fathers, by those who drafted the Constitution, was a substantial compliance. They meant that real education should be given to our children between the ages of 6 and 14. Therefore, I appeal to the States not to forget that they are not true to the spirit of the Constitution, merely by submitting to us figures that so many millions are in primary schools. What I want is a statement to satisfy me, not that so many millions are in schools but so many million children are getting real, proper, true education. Then only I would feel that Article 45 has been complied with".

National Policy on Education (NPE), 1968

Immediately thereafter, the National Policy on Education (NPE), 1968 was formed. This policy was the first official document evidencing the Indian Government's commitment towards school education. It dealt with the issues of equalisation of educational opportunity and sought to adopt a common school system in order to promote social cohesion and national integration. However, it was not supported by legal tools that could enforce such policy mandate. The Policy had to state "*strenuous efforts should be made for the early fulfillment of the Directive Principle under Article 45 of the Constitution seeking to provide free and compulsory education for all children up to the age of 14. A suitable programme should be developed to reduce the prevailing wastage and stagnation in schools and to ensure that every child who is enrolled in schools successfully completes the prescribed course*" {para. 4 (1)}.

National Policy for Children, 1974

In 1974, the Government of India adopted a National Policy for Children, declaring the nation's children as 'supremely important assets'. Keeping in view the goals set out the U.N. Declaration of the Rights of the Child, the Government of India adopted the Resolution on the National Policy for Children on 22nd August, 1974. This National Policy affirmed the constitutional provisions and declared that "it shall the policy of the State to provide adequate services to children, both before and after birth and through the period of growth, to ensure their full physical, mental and social development. The State shall progressively increase the scope of such services so that, within a reasonable time, all children in the country enjoy optimum conditions for their balanced growth" (GOI, 1974). The policy in particular, adopted two among other measures towards the attainment of the child's right to education:

(1) "The State shall take steps to provide free and compulsory education for all children up to the age of 14 for which a time-bound programme will be drawn up consistent with the availability of resources. Special efforts will be made to reduce the prevailing wastage and stagnation in schools, particularly in the case of girls and children of the weaker sections of the society. The programme of informal education for pre-school children from such sections will also be taken up.

(2) Children who are not able to take full advantage of formal school education should be provided other forms of education suited to their requirements" (GOI, 1974:1-2).

Shifting Education from State List to Concurrent List, 1976

With the 42nd Amendment in the Constitution which received President's assent on December 18, 1976 education was moved from the 'State' list to the 'Concurrent' list. Government of India Resolution on National Policy on Education, 1968 advocated for making education a concurrent subject – "Considering the key role which education, science and research play in developing the material and human resources of the country, the Government of India will, in addition to undertaking programmes in the Central sector, assist the State Governments for the development of programmes of national importance where coordinated action on the part of the States and the Centre is called for" (NCERT, 1970: xviii).

The amendment was also suggested by a Committee headed by S. Swaran Singh, appointed by the Congress Party. The Committee stated "Agriculture and Education are subjects of prime importance to the country's rapid progress towards achieving desired socio-economic changes. The need to evolve all-India policies in relation to these two subjects cannot be overemphasised. It is, therefore, suggested that Education and Agriculture should be placed in the Concurrent List" (Aggarwal, 2008: 10). As per the Constitution (Forty-Second Amendment) Act, 1976, Entry 25 of the Concurrent List includes, "Education, including technical education, medical education and universities, subject to the provisions of entries 63, 64, 65 and 66 of List I; vocational and technical training of labour."

With its move to the concurrent list education became a responsibility shared between the State Governments and the Centre. Under the Constitution of India, initially, education was a State subject, that is, it was the exclusive responsibility of the States. But, the 42nd Amendment Act of 1976 shifted it from the 'State List' to the 'Concurrent List'. This step gave both Central and State Governments jurisdiction over it concurrently. Till the 42nd Amendment of the Constitution in 1976, education was in the State List, except for certain specified items in the Union List like determination of standards in institutions for higher education or research, establishment and maintenance of Central Universities. The objective of incorporating education in the Concurrent List was to facilitate evolution of all-India policies in the field of education. The concept of concurrency was given an operational meaning by the National Policy on Education, 1986 (NPE). This policy envisages concurrency as "a sharing of responsibility between the Union Government and the States" in the vital area of national life – education. This Policy further stated that "While the role and responsibility of the States in regard to education will remain essentially unchanged, the Union Government would accept a larger responsibility to reinforce the national and integrative character of education, to maintain quality and standards (including those of the teaching profession at all levels), to study and monitor the educational requirements of the country as a whole in regard to manpower for development, to cater to the needs of research and advanced study, to look after the international aspects of education, culture and Human Resource Development and, in general, to promote excellence at all levels of the educational pyramid throughout the country" (Para 3.13). It created an avenue for the Centre's intervention in the field of elementary education. With this change, the elementary education has been able to lay claim to funding not only from the States whose financial resources are limited but also from the Centre.

Education for Our People, 1978

A movement for educational transformation was an essential part of the larger egalitarian movement for social transformation which was implicit in the ideal of total revolution sponsored by Jayaprakash Narayan. An idea of preparing a document entitled 'Education for Our People' relating to a policy frame of educational reform was passed by the Trustees of the J.P. Institute of Human Rights in a meeting held in Bombay on 21st June 1977 under the chairmanship of Jayaprakash Narayan. It was there decided that a framework for educational reform should be prepared under the auspices of the Citizens for Democracy and headed by Dr J.P. Naik, Member-Secretary of the Indian Council of Social Science Research. The proposal was later approved in a meeting of the National Executive Council of the Citizens for Democracy held on 13th August 1977. Dr J.P. Naik undertook the work with characteristic enthusiasm and prepared a tentative policy frame for educational reform by the end of September 1977. This document was published in 1978. This document was the product of a purely non-official effort, and it was submitted to the people at large and only indirectly to the governments at the Centre and in the States. This document suggested that Elementary education (age- group 6-14) should be made universal in an intensive and sustained programme spread over to 5-10 years. Special attention has to be given to the enrollment of girls and children from the poorer sections. The multiple-entry system should be adopted and part-time education should be provided for all children who cannot attend on a full-time basis (Kochhar, 1982: 63).

Draft National Policy on Education, 1979

Twenty one years after becoming independent, the nation had its first National Policy on Education in 1968. After eleven years, in 1979, a Draft National Policy on Education was printed and circulated by the Central Government (DOE, 1979). This draft NPE also laid down that "Highest priority must be given to free education for all up to the age of 14 as laid down in the Directive Principles of the Constitution... While it is necessary to expand the facilities for formal education in elementary schools for all children in the age group 6-14, it is also important to formulate schemes of non-formal education for dropouts and the older children in the age group who have not had any schooling. The aim should be to cover all the children in the age group 6-14 in the next ten years. Steps should be taken to prevent children giving up schooling without completing the course. The problem of wastage should be studied in detail and remedial measures also be taken" (Government of India, 1979).

Inclusion of Education in the Revised 20-Point Programme, 1982

Even in the eighties, there is a loud cry for Universalisation of Elementary Education all over India. In addition to the general programmes of development, a special activity named as the 20-Point Programme was initiated in 1975 by the then Prime Minister Smt. Indira Gandhi with an objective of improving the socio-economic conditions of the weaker sections in the country. Necessitated with the subsequent changes that took place in the economic and social life of the people and the new challenges that arose, a Revised 20-Point Programme was announced by the Prime Minister of India on the 14th January, 1982.

Besides pinpointing areas of special thrust like Irrigation and Farm Technology, Rural Employment, Land Reforms, Minimum Wages, Drinking water, Houses for the poor, Electricity, Family planning, Welfare of women and children, Essential supplies, Industrial Policy and Fight against black money, the programme devoted Point No. 16 to Education.

Point 16 of this Programme states: "Spread Universal elementary education for the age-group 6-14 with special emphasis on girls, and simultaneously involve students and voluntary agencies in programmes for the removal of adult illiteracy". Under Point No. 16 on education the following programme was envisaged:

Elementary Education: Article 45 of the Constitution provides free and compulsory education for all children in the age group 6-14 years by 1960. We have not been able to fulfil the long standing objective despite concerted efforts. By 1990, all the 16.3 crore children estimated in the age group will have to be enrolled in elementary schools, either in the formal or non-formal system of education. At present 9.3 crore children are attending schools. In the next 10 years, seven crore additional children will have to be brought to schools.

This big aspect of education in India has thus found a place in the Prime Minister's New Revised 20-Point Programme. It was restructured three times so far in the years 1982, 1986 and in 2006. The Programmes and Schemes under TPP-2006 are in harmony with the priorities contained in the National Common Minimum Programme, the Millennium Development Goals of the United Nations and SAARC Social Charter.

Objective of Twenty-Point Programme: The basic objective of the 20-Point Programme is to eradicate poverty and to improve the quality of life of the poor and the under-privileged population of the country. The programme covers various socio-economic aspects like poverty, employment, education, housing, health, agriculture and land reforms, irrigation, drinking water, protection and empowerment of weaker sections, consumer protection, environment etc. The 20-points of the Programme and its 66 items have been carefully designed and selected to achieve the above objectives. The TPP further restructured in 2006 had following Points: Poverty eradication, Power to people,

Support to farmers, Labour welfare, Food security, Clean drinking water, Housing for all, Health for all, Education for all, Welfare of SC/ ST/ OBC and minorities, Women welfare, Child welfare, Youth Development, Improvement of slums, Environment protection and afforestation, Social security, Rural Roads, Energising of rural areas, Development of Backward areas, IT enabled and e-governance.

The monitoring of the programme at the Centre has been assigned to the Ministry of Statistics and Programme Implementation, Government of India. The management information system relating to Twenty Point developed by the Ministry consists of a Monthly Progress Report (MPR) and yearly Review of the Programme, Point-wise, Item-wise and State-wise.

Challenge of Education - A Policy Perspective, 1985

Before the formulation of National Policy on Education - 1986, the Prime Minister of India in a national broadcast expressed the desire for a national debate on education and asked the academic community and others interested to give their suggestions in formulating a New National Policy on Education. He also formally expressed his views at various official conferences. Consequent to the Prime Minister's appeal, the Union Education Ministry published a document the "Challenge of Education - A Policy Perspective 1985" intended to serve as the basis for national debate. This document was actually the forerunner to the National Policy on Education 1986. This document stated at the outset:

"The country now stands on the threshold of the twenty-first century. Those who are being born now will finish their elementary, schooling at the turn of the century and enter into a world which will, it is already clear, offer opportunities unprecedented in the history of mankind to those who are equipped to cope with the future challenges and the accelerating pace of change" (Para. 1.1). The document mentioned clearly the present status of UEE in the following words:

> In spite of a specific provision in the Constitution to endeavour to provide free and compulsory education up to the age of 14 by 1960, and several explicit commitments with regard to the achievement of Universal Elementary Education, progress in this

sector is far short of the target. In fact, the target itself has been moving farther and farther to accommodate the failures' arising from inadequacy of resources or sheer lack of a viable strategy (Para. 3.6). If adequate provisions are not made even now for school facilities, requisite number of teachers, restructuring of the curricula and methods of teaching, we will be marching into the twenty first century with an unacceptably large corpus of illiterate people (Para. 3.9). It also pointed out that one of the most important reasons of the present state of affairs in education was the paucity of resources. While budgetary allocations from plan expenditure for education have gone up substantially over the years, these have not kept pace with the growth in enrollments and rise in prices. The provision of minimum outlays required for achieving the constitutional goals in respect of elementary education should be considered a national responsibility. However, it mentioned no word for enforcing free and compulsory education for Indian children.

National Policy on Education, 1986

The National Policy on Education, 1986 while re-affirming the goal of Universalisation of elementary education promised that "effective measures will be taken in the direction of the Common School System recommended in the 1968 Policy" (NPE, 1986, Para 3.2). This policy document once again did not discuss or aim to alter the legal status of Free and Compulsory Education in India, i.e., Free and Compulsory Education continued to remain a non-justifiable Directive Principle of State Policy. The NPE, 1986 attached importance to the fact that enrollment without retention and achievement is of no use. This policy document states that *"The new thrust in the elementary education will emphasise two aspects: (i) universal enrolment and universal retention of children up to 14 years of age, and (ii) a substantial improvement in the quality of education"* (NPE,1986:5.5). *It again resolved that "It shall be ensured that all children who attain the age of about 11 years by 1990 will have had five years of schooling, or its equivalent through the non-formal stream. Likewise, by 1995 all children will be provided free and compulsory up to 14 years of age"* (NPE,1986:5.12). The National Policy on Education 1986 (as modified in 1992) did envisage the alternative modality of non-formal education also for achieving universal elementary education. For instance, its

Para 5.8 stated that "the Non-formal Education Programme, meant for school dropouts, for children from habitations without schools, working children and girls who cannot attend whole-day schools, will be strengthened and enlarged". This Policy has been criticised for having introduced sub-standard Non-Formal Education for the out of school children and therefore having reduced the constitutional obligation of full time schooling (Singh, 2012).

The National Policy of Education, 1986 had aimed to achieve universal elementary education by 1995, the time frame for which was extended by another five years in its 1992 version as mentioned below:

"The New Education Policy will give the highest priority to solving the problem of children dropping out of school and will adopt an array of meticulously formulated strategies based on micro-planning and applied at the grassroots level all over the country, to ensure children's retention at school. This effort will be fully co-ordinated with the network of non-formal education. It shall be ensured that free and compulsory education of satisfactory quality is provided to all children up to 14 years of age before we enter the twenty-first century. A national mission will be launched for the achievement of this goal" [NPE 1986 (as modified in 1992), Para 12.5].

The National Policy on Education 1986 (as modified in 1992) did envisage the alternative modality of non-formal education also for achieving universal elementary education. For instance, its Para 5.8 stated that "the Non-formal Education Programme, meant for school dropouts, for children from habitations without schools, working children and girls who cannot attend whole-day schools, will be strengthened and enlarged".

However, target of universal elementary education as envisaged in the Policy of 1992 could not be achieved even by end of the century (Rajya Sabha Secretariat, Parliament of India, 2008:1).

Jomtien Declaration, 1990

At the international level, the world leaders met at Jomtien in 1990 to charter an agenda for ensuring that all children irrespective of their caste, creed and affiliation acquire at least basic education. Basic education is not only necessary from the viewpoint of human development but is also a fundamental right of all children. **In March 1990, India signed the 'World Declaration on Education For All' and 'Framework For Action To Meet Basic Learning Needs'** adopted at the 'World Conference on Education for All: Meeting Basic Learning Needs', held at Jomtien, Thailand under the joint sponsorship of three UN agencies (UNDP, UNESCO and UNICEF) and the World Bank. The Jomtien declaration renewed the commitment of the world community to achieve the goals of EFA by 2000. India is also active partner in the worldwide movement for education for All that began in 1990 in Jomtien and signatory to the Dakar declaration in 2000.

Report of the Ramamurti Committee, 1990

Among official documents, it was the Ramamurti Committee Report in 1990, on the review of the 1986 National Policy, which first chided the government for not paying attention to the right to education saying, "this problem qualifies for being ranked as the most fundamental problem of our educational system" (Para 6.2.1). The Committee to Review the National Policy on Education, 1986 in its report titled "Towards an Enlightened and Humane Society –NPE 1986-A Review" called for recognition of the right to education as a fundamental right:

"*Now, time has come to recognise 'Right to Education' as one of the fundamental rights of the Indian citizen for which necessary amendments to the Constitution may have to be made and more importantly, conditions be created in society such that right would become available for children of India*" (Para 6.1.3).

The Acharya Ramamurti committee recommended that the right to education should be included as a fundamental right in part III of the constitution. However, this recommendation was not implemented immediately.

Publication of Myron Weiner's Study in a Book, 1991

Myron Weiner's book entitled, **"The Child and the State in India; Child Labour and Education Policy in Comparative Perspective"** created a move among the Indians. In his study, he attempted to provide an explanation for why India's policies toward children in education and employment are different from those of so many other countries. Why the Indian state is unable or unwilling to deal with the high and increasing illiteracy, low school enrollments, high dropout rates, and rampant child labour? Why did government commissions reviewing child labour and education policies as recently as 1985-1986 not call for compulsory education or for legislation to abolish child labour? Why has the state not taken legislative action when the Indian Constitution calls for a ban on child labour and for compulsory primary-school education, positions frequently reiterated in government reports as a long-term objective?

The cardinal proposition of his study is that India's low per capita income and economic situation is less relevant as an explanation for the failure to eradicate child labour and enforce compulsory education than the belief systems of the state bureaucracy, a set of beliefs that are widely shared by educators, social activists, trade unionists, academic researchers, and, more broadly, by members of the Indian middle class. These beliefs are held by those outside as well as those within government, and by those who regard themselves as secular, and by leftists as well as by centrists and rightists.

According to Professor Weiner, at the core of these beliefs, there lies the Indian view of the social order, notions concerning the respective roles of upper and lower social strata, the role of education as a means of maintaining differentiations among social classes, and concerns that "excessive" and "inappropriate" education for the poor would disrupt existing social arrangements.

Ratification of the UN Convention on Rights of the Child, 1992

Since the days of the League of Nations, commitments for the protection of children have been projected in various international treaties and declarations. The Geneva Declaration containing five principles was adopted on 26th September, 1924. It stated that necessary means must be given for the normal development of the child, both materially and spiritually, and specifically provided that a child must be protected against exploitation. Thereafter, the landmark 1948 Universal Declaration of Human Rights proclaimed that children as a category are entitled to special care and assistance. In Article 26, the right to compulsory free education, at least in the elementary and fundamental stages is recognised (Law Commission of India, 1998: 27).

On 20th November, 1959, the Declaration on the Rights of the Child was proclaimed by the General Assembly of the United Nations. It contained 10 principles which enriched and developed the 1924 Geneva Declaration. Specifically Principle 7 mandated "The child is entitled to receive education, which shall be free and compulsory, at least in the elementary stages". Exactly 30 years later, 20th November, 1989 the General Assembly unanimously adopted the Convention on the Rights of the Child. It entered into force 2nd September 1990 having been ratified by the required 20 states. This convention has been recognised as the most complete statement of children's rights with the force of international law. The earlier 1959, UN Declaration on the Rights of the Child, though an international instrument, carried no binding legal obligation, whereas the 1989 Convention demanded "States Parties shall undertake all appropriate legislative, administrative, and other measures for the implementation of the rights recognised in the present Convention" (UNCRC, 1989, Article 4). This convention explicitly mandated – "States Parties recognise the right of the child to education and with a view to achieving this right progressively and on the basis of equal opportunity, they shall, in particular: (a) Make primary education compulsory and available free to all..." (UNCRC, 1989, Article 28). By ratifying the Convention on the Rights of the Child on 2nd December, 1992, the Government of India once again re-affirmed its commitment to children. As a part of this agreement, the UN Convention obligates the Government to -

- Review National and State legislation and bring it in line with provisions of the Convention,
- Develop appropriate monitoring procedures to assess progress in implementing the Convention,
- Involve the concerned Government/Ministries and Departments, international agencies, non-governmental organisations, and the legal profession in the implementation and reporting process,
- Publicise the Convention, and seek public inputs for frank and transparent reporting. (CRC Country Report India, 1997, Para 1.23).

The Convention revalidates the rights guaranteed to children by the Constitution of India, and is, therefore, a powerful weapon to combat forces that deny these rights. Article 51(C) of the Indian Constitution mandates that the State shall endeavour to foster respect for international law and treaty obligations.

The 73th and 74th Constitutional Amendment Acts, 1992

There have been important Constitutional Amendments as well that were intended to give a boost to elementary education. Before 1976, education was the exclusive responsibility of the States. The 42nd Amendment to the Constitution in 1976 brought education, which was largely a state responsibility, into the Concurrent List and made universalising elementary education the responsibility of both the central and state governments.

The 73rd and 74th Constitutional Amendment Acts enacted in 1992, the two pieces of legislation created a key paradigm shift in governance models by invoking decentralisation, paving the way for the participation of local communities and institutions in the planning, implementation, and monitoring of government programmes including those in education. The amendments established the three-tier Panchayati Raj system in the country, with elected bodies at the gram, taluk, and zilla levels to enable the community to actively participate in developmental programmes and ensure more effective implementation. Amongst the 29 subjects identified by the 73rd Amendment Act for transfer to the Panchayats was education - primary and secondary, adult and non-formal, vocational and technical. The institutionalised statutory space provided by the 73rd and the 74th amendment acts makes mechanisms like Community Based Monitoring (CBM) key factors in facilitating movement from "top-down" methods to participatory processes for local engagement in effective governance. The 73rd and 74th Amendments to the Constitution placed a greater role on local bodies for the development of education, among others.

Mohini Jain versus State of Karnataka Case, 1992

A great legal breakthrough was achieved in 1992 when the Supreme Court of India while deciding the *Mohini Jain* versus *State of Karnataka Case* (1992 3 SCC 666) stated that "the 'right to education' is concomitant to fundamental rights enshrined under Part III of the Constitution". And that **"every citizen has a right to education under the Constitution"**.

Unnikrishnan versus State of Andhra Pradesh Case, 1993

The Supreme Court subsequently reconsidered the above-mentioned judgement in the Case of *Unnikrishnan, J. P.* versus *State of Andhra Pradesh* (1993 1 SCC 645). Justice Jeevan Reddy while delivering the judgement of this case entirely changed the status of the Article 45. The Supreme Court judgement said that Article 45 of the Part IV should be read in harmonious construction with Article 21 of Part III (Right to Life) since without education 'Right to Life is Meaningless'. It was also stated in the judgement that "The citizens of this country have a fundamental right to education. The said right flows from Article 21. This right however is not an absolute right. Its contents and parameters have to be determined in the light of Articles 45 and 41. In other words every child /citizen of this country has a right to free education until he completes the age of fourteen years. Thereafter his right to education is subject to limits of economic capacity and development of the state".

Responding to the Court's Verdict

The Unnikrishnan Judgment (1993) – the historic declaration by the Supreme Court in 1993 made India's ruling class evidently uncomfortable. The Central Government undertook a series of steps in the following years designed to extricate itself of the implication of the judgment. The Central Government responded by establishing two committees (Saikia Committee and Tapas Majumder Committee) to investigate both the desirability and financial implications of amending the Constitution to establish elementary education as a fundamental right.

Report of the Saikia Committee, 1997

Community activists and non-government organisations began utilising the verdict as a means of pushing the executive and legislature toward action on primary education. At the same time, the decisions became a catalyst for political advocacy and public sphere debate over the state of primary education in India, galvanizing a number of different children's rights groups into a coalition demanding government implementation of the 'fundamental right to education'.

The 14-party United Front Government (UFG) in 1996 came up with a Common Minimum Programme (CMP) carrying a lengthy title 'Common Approach to Major Policy Matters and a Minimum Programme'. The CPM proposed to make free and compulsory education for children upto 14 years a Fundamental right for achieving Universalisation of elementary education by the turn of the century and enforcing it through its suitable statutory measures.

The pros and cons of the proposal were discussed in the Conference of State Education Ministers and State Education Secretaries held on August 9-10, 1996. The Conference recognised the momentous significance of the proposed Constitutional Amendment and urged the government to consider the financial, administrative, legal and academic implications of the proposal. The Conference recommended the constitution of a Committee of State Education Ministers to consider the implications. Accordingly, the Ministry of Human Resource Department (Department of Education) constituted a Committee of State Education Ministers under the chairmanship of Muhi Ram Saikia, Union Minister of State for HRD (Education).

As per the 'Report of the Committee of State Education Ministers on Implications of the Proposal to make Elementary Education a Fundamental Right' 1997, a Committee of State Education Ministers under the Chairmanship of Shri Muhi Ram Saikia, Union Minister of State for HRD (Education) vide its order No. F.1-53/92-EE dated 29 August, 1996, was constituted "to examine and consider the legal, academic, administrative and financial implications of the Proposal to amend the Constitution to make the right to free and compulsory elementary education a Fundamental Right, to suggest suitable statutory measures to enforce it and to suggest guidelines indicating facilities which if not provided would become, justifiable" (GOI, 1997). The Committee held three meetings on 16 September, 24 October and 30 November, 1996 in New Delhi and concluded its work in its fourth meeting held in Cochin on 10 January, 1997. As regards the proposed constitutional amendment, the Committee recommended that -

"The Constitution of India should be amended to make the right to free elementary education upto 14 years of age a fundamental Right. Simultaneously, an explicit provision should be made in the Constitution to make it a Fundamental Duty of every citizen who is a parent to provide opportunities for elementary education to all children up to 14 years of age. Consequential amendments to the Directive Principles of State Policy as enunciated in Article 45 of the Constitution should also be made".

It also recommended that "In a diverse federal polity such as our's with wide disparities in provision of school education between and within States and the States being the main providers of elementary education, there is no need to enact a Central legislation making elementary education compulsory. States should either amend their existing legislation or enact fresh legislation to give effect to the proposed Constitutional amendments on the lines; of the action taken in regard to implementation of 73rd and 74th Constitutional amendments. The Central Government should issue guidelines providing a broad framework for enactment of fresh legislation on compulsory elementary education. The guidelines should be finalised in consultation with State/UT Governments" (*Ibid*).

Commending the report to the government, the Committee agrees with the view that compulsion is not the only answer to achieve UEE. The government would have to continue with its consensual approach to motivate parents and children involve communities and build up public opinion in favour of UEE. The key elements of this approach have been (i) community involvements; (ii) decentralisation of planning and management of school education to PRIs; (iii) motivation of children to attend schools regularly; (iv) improvement of infrastructure and facilities in schools; (v) development of locally relevant curricula; (vi) improvement in quality of textbooks; (vii) teacher training (viii) child centred learning; and (ix) adoption of minimum level of earning. However, to demonstrate political will and administrative resolve of the country for achieving this task by 2000 AD, it is considered essential that the Constitution be amended and suitable statutory measures taken to operationalise the Constitutional mandate.

The Saikia Committee Report finally resulted in a Bill to amend the Constitution to introduce a new Article 21A, which provided: 'the State shall provide free and compulsory education to all citizens of age six to fourteen years in such manner as the State may, by law, determine.' It also introduced a new Article 51A which imposed a duty on parents and guardians to provide their children with educational opportunities, in the terms recommended by the Saikia Committee. The Bill was tabled in 1997, but would not pass into law until December 2002.

Constitution (83rd) Amendment Bill, 1997

In 1997, the United Front Government introduced Constitution (83rd) Amendment Bill, 1997 which encompassed insertion of Article 21A and omitting Article 45 of the Constitution. This amendment bill had an additional financial memorandum that outlined the costs that would go into making education for children in the six to fourteen age groups a fundamental right for a 10-year period.

In 1997 (July), the Constitution (83rd Amendment) Bill, 1997 was tabled in Lok Sabha the S. R. Bommai, then HRD minister. The Bill proposed to add Article 21A as-

2. "After Article 21 of the Constitution, the following Article shall be inserted, namely:

21A (1) The State shall provide free and compulsory education to all citizens of the age of six to fourteen years.

The right to free and compulsory education referred to in clause (1) shall be enforced in such manner as the State may, by law, determine.

The State shall not make any law for free and compulsory education under clause (2), in relation to the educational institutions not maintained by the State or not receiving aid out of State funds.

3. Article 35 of the Constitution shall be renumbered as clause (1) of that Article and after clause (1) as so renumbered and before explanation following clauses shall be inserted, namely: (2) The competent Legislature shall make the law for the enforcement of right to free and compulsory education referred in clause (1) of Article 21A within one year from the

commencement of the Constitution (Eighty-Third Amendment) Act, 1997:

Provided that a provision of any law relating to free and compulsory education in force in a State immediately before the commencement of the Constitution (Eighty-Third Amendment) Act, 1997 which is inconsistent with the provisions of Article 21A, shall continue to be in force until amended or repealed by a competent legislature or other competent authority or until the expiration of one year from such commencement, whichever is earlier.

4. Article 45 of the Constitution shall be omitted.

(3) 5. Article 51A of the Constitution, after clause (j), the following clause shall be added, namely:

5. (k) to provide opportunities for education to a child between the age of six and fourteen years of whom such citizen is a parent or guardian".

Subsequently, this Bill was referred to the Parliamentary Standing Committee on Human Resource Development. In 1997 (November) the Department-Related Parliamentary Standing Committee on Human Resource Development submitted report to both Houses of Parliament, and recommended that the Bill be passed subject to changes recommended by it. The major recommendations of the committee related to:

- Retention of Article 45 to cater to the 0-6 age group.
- Clause (3) of the proposed Article 21-A relating to private institutions may be deleted.
- The Central Government should prepare one simple legislation with some skeletal framework which may also indicate the Central share in the financial burden. The details can be formulated by the respective States according to their requirements. The Central Government may therefore consider working out the necessary legislation (Para 15.16).

165th Report on Free and Compulsory Education for Children by Law Commission of India, 1998

The Law Commission of India had taken up the subject on "Free and Compulsory Education for Children" having regard to the Directive

Principle of the Constitution of India as well as decision of the Supreme Court of India. In 1998, the Commission prepared a detailed Report on free and compulsory education for all children together with a draft Bill for a central legislation. The Committee has come to the following conclusions:

"If a Central Legislation is enacted as is being proposed by the Commission, it would not require ratification by the State Legislatures, being a subject falling under Entry 25 of Concurrent List of Seventh Schedule to the Constitution of India. Article 254(1) provides that the law made by Parliament with reference to a concurrent subject shall prevail over a law made by the State Legislature on the same subject irrespective of the fact whether the law made by the Parliament is earlier or subsequent to the State enactment" (Para. 6.1.2). This provision is of course subject to Clause (2) of Article 254. Only when an inconsistent law or inconsistent provision (inconsistent with the Central Legislation) is sought to be enacted by the State Legislature that the requirement of President's assent is necessary to make it effective and valid as per Article 254 (2) [Para 6.3.1]. The Commission has identified that 19 States/Union Territories have enacted primary/ elementary education compulsory. These Acts are shown in the following Table 5.1:

Table 5.1: Compulsory Primary /Elementary Education Acts (Law Commission of India, 1998)

Sl. No.	*States/UTs*	*Name of the Act*
1.	Andhra Pradesh	Andhra Pradesh Education Act 1982 (Act No. 1 of 1982
2.	Assam	The Assam Elementary Education (Provinciali-sation) Act, 1974 (Assam Act No. of 1975
3.	Bihar	Bihar Primary Education (Amendment) Act 1959 (Bihar & Orissa Education Act (1 of 1919) as amended by Bihar Act XVI of 1919 and Bihar Act XVII of 1946 and Bihar Act IV of 1959)
4.	Delhi	The Delhi Primary Education Act 1960 Act No. 39 of 1060
5.	Goa	The Goa Compulsory Elementary Education Act, 1995 (Goa Act No. of 4 of 995)
6.	Gujarat	Gujarat Compulsory Primary Education Act, 1961 (Gujarat Act No. XLI of 1961)

(Contd...)

7.	Haryana	Punjab Primary Education Act 1960
8.	Himachal Pradesh	The Himachal Pradesh Compulsory Primary Education Act 1953 (Act No. 7 of 1954)
9.	Jammu & Kashmir	The Jammu and Kashmir Education Act (Act No. XI of 1984)
10.	Karnataka	The Karnataka Education Act 1983 (Karnataka Act No. 1 of 1995)
11.	Kerala	The Kerala Education Act 1958 (Act No. 6 of 1959) (As amended by Acts 35 of 1960, 31 of 1969 and 9 of 1985)
12.	Madhya Pradesh	The Madhya Pradesh Primary Education Act 1961 (Madhya Pradesh Act No. 33 of 1961)
13.	Maharashtra	The Bombay Primary Education Act 1949 (Bombay Act No. LXI of 1949) (As modified up to 30th April, 1986)
14.	Orissa	Orissa Basic Education Act 1951 No. 18, Orissa Primary Education Act 1969 as amended by the provisions of the Orissa Education (Amendment) Act, 1974 & 1975
15.	Punjab	Punjab Primary Education ACT 1960, No. 39
16.	Rajasthan	The Rajasthan Primary Education Act 1964 (Act No. 31 of 1964)
17.	Tamil Nadu	The Tamil Nadu Compulsory Elementary Education Act 1994 (Act No. 33 of 1995)
18.	Uttar Pradesh	United Provinces Primary Education Act 1919 (UP Act No. 7 of 1919)/ United Provinces (Dist. Boards) Primary Education Act 1926 (UP Act No. 1 of 1926) Adapted and modified by the Adaptation of Laws order 1950
19.	West Bengal	Primary Education Act 1973 (West Bengal Act No. 43 of 1973)

Source: 165th Report on Free and Compulsory Education for Children by Law Commission of India, 1998, Annexure - B.

These enactments have three parts:

(1) Power vested in the State Government to notify the area in which the Act can be implemented.

(2) Penalties for not sending children to school.

(3) Power in a vested authority to grant exemption from the legislation.

That's why the Commission finally would like to emphasise the need for immediate central legislation to give effect to right to education without waiting for the Constitutional Amendment to go through in Parliament. The Commission also recommended that -

"...it may not be feasible to bring the private unaided institutions within the perview of the proposed Bill" (Para 6.1.3). In this regard, the Commission recommended that the State or affiliating board may compel the private unaided institutions to admit and impart free education to twenty per cent of the students as a condition for affiliation or for permitting their students to appear for the Government/ Board examination in order to reduce the financial burden upon the State.

"Universal Elementary Education (UEE) cannot be achieved except by the use of a certain amount of compulsion... It needs to be emphasised that constitutional obligation is to provide "free and compulsory education" and all permissible means and measures ought to be employed to achieve the said goal. It may necessitate dispensing with the tuition fee, providing free text books or free uniforms, free lunch, etc. whatever necessary" (Para 6.1.8).

The Report of the Tapas Majumdar Committee, 1999

The Report of the Committee of State Education Ministers on Implications of the Proposal to make Elementary Education a Fundamental Right, 1997 (Saikia Committee) had recommended the setting of a Group Experts to assess the financial resource requirements for operationalising the proposed 83th Amendment Bill, making the Right to Free and Compulsory Education upto 14 years of Fundamental Right. Accordingly, in June 1997, the Department of Education, Ministry of Human Resource Development constituted a group of experts to examine the financial requirements of the states/UTs in this regards. The expert group consisting of 18 Members including Professor Tapas Majumdar submitted its report entitled "Expert Group on Financial Requirements for Making Elementary Education: A Fundamental Right" in 1999.

The Committee chose the right-based approach to providing elementary education. The report said: "From being an incremental development goal in the process of education for all, Universalisation of elementary education has in consequence of the Unnikrishana Judgment, now become the legal right of every Indian child... entitlements sanctioned by the Constitution cannot be deferred by the

State at its convenience. The State has to make the necessary reallocation of resources by superseding other important claims, if necessary, in a manner that the justiciable entitlement can become a reality" (Government of Bihar, 2007, pp. 24). This may call for restructuring of all government spending, forcing the State to cut down even on spending that it would otherwise consider as essential, but which was not covered by any of the Fundamental Rights guaranteed by the Constitution.

The Committee estimated that an additional investment of Rs 1,37,000 crores would have to be made over a 10-year period to bring all out-of-school children into the school system (not parallel streams) and enable them to complete the elementary stage. This works out to an average investment of Rs 14,000 crores a year, which in 1999 amounted to a mere 0.78 per cent of the gross domestic product (GDP); in other words, 78 paise out of every Rs 100 India then earned (GOI, 1999 and Sadgopal, 2003).

Dakar Declaration, 2000

The progress towards these goals was reviewed in Dakar in 2000 (10 years after Jomtien) and mixed type of signals regarding the progress emerged. While it was recognised that considerable progress has been made by different countries but some could not achieve the EFA targets adopted at Jomtien. The Dakar Meet came out with revised targets for the countries where the goals of EFA could not be achieved. The participating countries made the commitment to achieve the following goals by 2015:

(1) **Early childhood care and education:** Expanding and improving comprehensive early childhood care and education, especially for the most vulnerable and disadvantaged children;

(2) **Free and compulsory primary education by 2015**: Ensuring that by 2015 all children, particularly girls, children in difficult circumstances and those belonging to ethnic minorities, have access to and complete, free and compulsory primary education of good quality;

(3) **Life skills for adolescents and youth**: Ensuring that the learning needs of all young people and adults are met through equitable access to appropriate learning and life-skills programmes;

(4) **Improvements in adult literacy by 50 per cent:** Achieving a 50 per cent improvement in levels of adult literacy by 2015, especially for women, and equitable access to basic and continuing education for all adults;

(5) **Eliminate gender disparities:** Eliminating gender disparities in primary and secondary education by 2005, and achieving gender equality in education by 2015, with a focus on ensuring girls' full and equal access to and achievement in basic education of good quality;

(6) **Enhance educational quality:** Improving all aspects of the quality of education and ensuring excellence of all so that recognised and measurable learning outcomes are achieved by all, especially in literacy, numeracy and essential life skills.

Ambani and Birla Committee Report, April 2000

Mukesh Ambani (Convenor) and Kumarmangalam Birla (Member) submitted the report entitled 'Report on a Policy Framework for Reforms in Education' to Prime Minister's Council on Trade and Industry, Government of India in 2000 (April). The report also recommended that "Compulsory and free primary education must be on top of our education agenda. There is no getting away from enforcing the Constitutional commitment to compulsory education till the age of fourteen years, provided by Article 45 and reinforced by a historical Supreme Court judgement declaring education as a fundamental right. Compulsory and free primary education is feasible only through active involvement of local bodies at the panchayat and municipal levels... Compulsory and free primary education will entail increased spending on education. This has to be met by restructuring of inter-sectoral allocations and divestment of loss making public sector companies...There must be a political will and a conviction that compulsory and free primary education is an investment in India's future" (Para 6.1, p. 98).

Millennium Development Goals (MDGs), September 2000

At the September 2000 Millennium Summit, the IMF-World Bank, along with the Organisation for Economic Co-operation and Development (OECD) and the UN agencies, devised a set of eight

Millennium Development Goals (MDGs). In line with the Jomtien-Dakar Framework, one of the eight goals directly relating to education reiterates the agenda of "achiev[ing] universal primary education."

The 93rd Constitution Amendment Bill, 2001

Based on the recommendation of the Parliamentary Standing Committee on Human Resource Development, advice of the Ministry of Law and suggestions of the Law Commission of India, The Ministry of Human Resource Development formulated the revised Constitution Amendment Bill. This Bill known as the 93rd Constitution Amendment Bill had been passed by both Houses of the Parliament and is awaiting Presidential assent. The Constitution (83rd Amendment) Bill, 1997 was amended, and reintroduced as Constitution (93rd) Amendment Bill 2001 in the Parliament with the following provisions:

Insertion of a new Article 21A—'To provide free and compulsory education to all children of the age of 6-14 years in such a manner as the State may, by law, determine'.

Substitution of existing Article 45 of the Constitution—'The State shall endeavour to provide early childhood care and education for all children until they complete the age of six years'.

Insertion of the following new clause in Article 51 (A) of the Constitution relating to Fundamental duties of the Citizens—'(k)—who is parent or guardian to provide opportunities for education to his child, or as case may be, a ward between age of 6-14 years'.

Sarva Siksha Abhiyan (SSA), 2001

The Sarva Shiksha Abhiyan (SSA) launched by the Government of India is the vehicle for implementing the Constitutional obligation under the Constitution (93rd) Amendment Bill 2001. According to the 86th Amendment to the Constitution Act, 2002, Right to Education is a fundamental right. According to Article 21A, "The State shall endeavour to provide free and compulsory education to all children of the age of six to 14 years in such manner as the State may, by law, determine". The endeavour therefore of Sarva Shiskha Abhiyan (SSA), has been strengthened to provide universal primary education to all in the country. The Prime Minister of India heads the National Mission for SSA which monitors the progress made under the Sarva Shiksha Abhiyan. The Executive Committee of the National Mission is chaired by the Minister for Human Resource Development.

The Scheme of Sarva Shiksha Abhiyan (SSA) evolved from the recommendations of the State Education Ministers' Conference held in October 1998 to pursue universal elementary education in a mission mode. A National Committee of State Education Ministers under the chairmanship of the then Hon'ble Human Resource Development Minister, Dr Murli Manohar Joshi was set up on the recommendation of the Conference to work out the approach to the mission mode. It submitted its Report in October 1999. The **National Committee's Report on UEE in the Mission Mode 1999 recommended that** UEE should be pursued in a mission mode with a holistic and convergent approach with emphasis preparation of District Elementary Education Plans for UEE. Ultimately a framework for Sarva Shiksha Abhiyan had been finalised in consultation with States. The scheme was approved by the Union Cabinet in its meeting held on 16 November 2000 and became functional from January 2001.

Report of the National Commission to Review the Working of the Constitution, 2002

The National Commission to Review the Working of the Constitution was set up by the Government of India on 22 February, 2000 to examine, in the light of the experience of the past 50 years, as to how best the Constitution can respond to the changing needs of efficient, smooth and effective system of governance and socio-economic development of modern India within the framework of Parliamentary democracy, and to recommend changes, if any, that are required in the provisions of the Constitution without interfering with its basic structure or features. The Commission submitted its report in two volumes to the government on 31st March, 2002. Commission stated on the subject on Right to Education in the Report, Volume – 1, Chapter 3 that "At the time when the Commission released its Consultation Paper on the subject, Constitution (93rd Amendment) Bill was under consideration. But the proposed Amendment covers the

Right to Free and Compulsory Education only between the years 6 and 14 years. The Commission is of the view that the Right to Free and Compulsory Education should also be extended to the children up to the age of fourteen years and that the right to education beyond the age of 14 years may depend upon the economic capacity and the stage of development of the State (Para. 3.20.1).

The Commission feels that the constitutional commitment for free and compulsory education for all children until the age of fourteen should under no circumstances be diluted and the State should fulfil this solemn obligation to the nation. The responsibility for the Universalisation of elementary education should be entrusted to Panchayats and local self-government institutions. **It is recommended that the relevant provisions in the Constitution (93rd Amendment) Bill, 2001 making the right to education of children from six years till the completion of fourteen years as a Fundamental Right should be amended and enlarged to read as under**:

> 30-C Every child shall have the right to free education until he completes the age of fourteen years; and in the case of girls and members of the Scheduled Castes and the Scheduled Tribes, until they complete the age of eighteen years [Para 3.20.2].
>
> It should also be laid down in Article 45 that the State shall make provision for education beyond the age of fourteen years within the limits of its economic capacity and stage of development [Para 3.30.2].
>
> The Commission also recommended that an independent National Education Commission should be set up every five years to report to Parliament on the progress of the constitutional directive regarding compulsory education and on other aspects relevant to the knowledge society of the new century. The model of the Finance Commission may be usefully looked into [Para 3.31.3].

The Constitution (86th Amendment) Act, 2002

The Constitution (93rd) Amendment Bill, 2001 was discussed and passed in 2002 (12th December) by Indian Parliament as Constitution (86th Amendment) Act, 2002, through which the existing

Article 45 was deleted and added new Articles. The Constitution (86th Amendment) Act, 2002, notified on 13th December, 2002 in the Gazette of India, sought to make the following three changes in the Constitution:

(1) In Part III ("Fundamental Rights"), add the following new article:

(6) "21A. Right to Education - The State shall provide free and compulsory education to all children of the age of six to fourteen years in such manner as the State may, by law, determine."

(2) In Part IV ("Directive Principles of State Policy"), replace the existing Article 45 ("Provision for Free and Compulsory Education for Children"), with the following:

(7) "45. Provision for Early Childhood care and Education to Children below the age of Six Years - The State shall endeavour to provide early childhood care and education for all children until they complete the age of six years."

(3) In Article 51A ("Fundamental Duties"), after clause (j), add a new clause (k) as follows: **"51A Fundamental Duties** - It shall be the duty of every citizen of India:

...(k) Who is a parent or guardian to provide opportunities for education to his child or, as the case may be, ward between the age of six and fourteen years."

With aforesaid amendment, the right to free and compulsory education to the all Indian children between 6-14 years of age group was declared a fundamental right. Below the age of six years, the State shall endeavour to provide early childhood care and education for all children. But the issue relating to children below six years is not justiciable that is a person cannot claim to enforce it. Further, every Indian citizen has duty for providing opportunities for education to his/her ward between 6-14 years. It is also evident from the Article 21 A that the State had to provide free and compulsory education and for this purpose the State was under duty to determine the manner by law. Though the Constitution was amended in 2002 but the Government took more than seven years to think in this respect.

The Free and Compulsory Education for Children Bill, 2003 (Process of Drafting)

After the Bill received the President's assent on 13.12.2002, the Constitution (93rd) Amendment Bill, 2001 became the 86th Constitution Amendment Act (12th December, 2002). It now remains for the **'State' to determine 'by law'**, as required by the new Article 21A, the manner in which free and compulsory education is to be provided to all children in the 6 – 14 age group. Then began the process of drafting the Follow up Legislation to determine the manner in which the state would provide free and compulsory education to all children of the age of 6 -14 years.

In 2003 (October) the first draft of the Free and Compulsory Education for Children Bill, 2003 was posted online by the government inviting comments and suggestions from the public (NDA Government). The Bill began with the words – "A BILL to provide for free and compulsory education for all children from the age of six years to fourteen years and for matter connected therewith and incidental thereto. BE it enacted by Parliament in the Fifty-fourth Year of the Republic of India".

The Free and Compulsory Education Bill, 2004

In 2004, a revised version of this Bill, re-titled the Free and Compulsory Education for Children Bill 2004, was re-posted (NDA Government). The Free and Compulsory Education Bill, 2004 began with the words – "To provide free and compulsory education to all children from the age of six to fourteen years and for matters connected therewith and incidental thereto; BE it enacted by Parliament in the Fifty-fifth Year of the Republic of India".

Right to Education Bill (CABE Bill), 2005

The Government of India had re-constituted the Central Advisory Board of Education (CABE) Vide Resolution dated 6th July, 2004. The first meeting of the re-constituted CABE was held on 10-11 August, 2004 during which some critical issues emerged needing detailed deliberations. It was decided to committees of CABE to examine in detail these critical issues. Accordingly, with the approval of MHRD, a Committee of Central Advisory Board of Education (CABE) on the subject " Free and Compulsory Education Bill and Other Issues Related to Elementary Education" under the chairmanship of Shri Kapil Sibal, the then MHRD minister was constituted vide Order dated 8.9.2004 of the Ministry of Human Resource Development, with the following terms of reference:

"(a) to suggest a draft of legislation envisaged in Article 21-A of the Constitution, and

(b) To examine other issues related to elementary education for achieving the objective of free and compulsory basic education."

Based on the following principles, CABE formulated the draft of the essential provisions of "Right to Education Bill, 2005":

(1) Right to Education should imply that every child has a right to be (a) provided full-time education of satisfactory and equitable quality in a formal school which satisfies at least certain essential norms, and (b) enabled to complete elementary education.

(2) Right to Education also implies that it is the State's obligation to remove whatever obstacles – social, economic, academic, linguistic, cultural, physical, etc. – prevent children from effectively participating in and completing elementary education of satisfactory quality.

(3) Right to Education must be seen not merely as a right for its own or the individual child's sake, but also as an instrument of promoting other constitutional objectives, e.g. equality, justice, democracy, secularism, social cohesion, etc.

(4) Provision of Free and Compulsory Education of satisfactory quality to children from weaker sections is the responsibility not merely of Schools run or supported by the State, but also of Schools which are not dependent on State funds. Schools of the latter kind also need to provide education to such children at least to the extent of 25 per cent of their intake.

(5) One major reason why it has not been possible to universalise elementary education all these years is the dysfunctionality of the delivery system. The Committee has therefore attempted to formulate a number of provisions for the proposed

legislation, essentially aimed at greater decentralisation and accountability, so that the delivery system is able to rise to the challenge.

(6) Although its terms of reference were confined to free and compulsory education for children between the ages of 6-14 years, the Committee has considered the main programme for Early Childhood Care and Education (ECCE), *viz.*, Integrated Child Development Services (ICDS), and proposed convergence to the extent possible (MHRD, 2005, pp. 4-7).

In 2005 (June), the Right to Education Bill, 2005 as drafted by CABE was introduced to give effect to the Constitution (86th) Amendment Act, 2002 (UPA – 1 Government). Even the draft Right to Education Bill, 2005 was circulated to States in August 2005 and comments were received on it from 16 States. But, opposition was raised due to this mandatory provision to provide 25 per cent reservation of disadvantaged group in private schools. Indian Law Commission initially proposed 50 per cent reservation of seats. However, the CABE Sub-Committee held this provision as a significant prerequisite for creating a democratic egalitarian society.

In November 2005, Dr Manmohan Singh, the then Prime Minister appointed the High Level Group (HLG), comprising Minister for Human Resource Development, Finance Minister, Deputy Chairman, Planning Commission, and Chairman, PM's Advisory Council on Economic Affairs, to consider the constitutional, legal and financial implications of the Right to Education. HLG had two meetings (January 2006 and November 2007). In its first meeting the HLG favoured drafting of a Model Bill for State legislation.

In 2006, Central legislation discarded. States were advised to make their own Bills based on the model Right to Education Bill, 2006 (UPA-I Government). Accordingly the model Right to Education Bill, 2006 was circulated to States in June 2006. Total 23 States responded to the Model Bill.

Sachar Committee Report, 2006

On 9 March 2005, the PMO had issued the Notification for constitution of the High Level Committee under the chairmanship of

Justice Rajendra Sachar for preparation of Report on the Social, Economic and Educational Status of the Muslim Community of India. The Committee was unanimous in its view to submit its report by 8 June 2006. The Committee stated that Access to education is critical for benefiting from emerging opportunities that are accompanied by economic growth. The report brings out clearly the educational deprivation experienced by the Muslim community. From lower levels of enrollment to a sharp decline in participation in higher levels of education, the situation of Indian Muslims is indeed very depressing as compared to most other SRCs...the major problems lie in school education; the likelihood of Muslim children completing school education is significantly lower than other SRCs (Socio-religious Category), except SCs/STs, once factors like household expenditure, place of residence, gender etc. are controlled for. Once the "hurdle" of school education is crossed, the differences across most SRCs in the likelihood of completing graduate studies narrow down and are at times not very significant. Therefore, a sharper focus on school education is desirable. Free and compulsory education up to the age of 14 is the responsibility of the State. And the fulfilment of this obligation is critical for the improvements in the educational conditions of Muslims, in fact, of all socio-economically deprived children (Para 3.1, p. 243).

Report of the National Knowledge Commission (NKC), 2007

National Knowledge Commission (NKC), 2007 recognises that the primary responsibility for school education is borne by the State governments, and therefore any policy changes must be with the full participation and involvement of the States. NKC believes that providing universal access to quality school education is a cornerstone of development and a minimum necessary condition for any progress towards making India a knowledge society. However, NKC would responds specifically to the recent initiative of the central government of sending a model Right to Education Bill to the Secretaries of State Education Departments, with incentives for the state governments to enact this bill. NKC has perused the bill and consulted with a wide range of experts and educationists. It considers that the model bill is flawed for a number of reasons, and most importantly that such legislation must be enforced by the central government following upon the commitment made in the Constitutional Amendment Article 21A. However, it feels that this matter can be resolved through an appropriate central legislation which takes into account the following proposals (NKC, 2007: 45-47):

- **Central Legislation:** Legislation at the national level is required to affirm the Right to Education, which is a fundamental right mandated by Article 21A. Since it cannot be dependent upon which state a citizen lives in, a model bill sent to be enacted individually by State Governments is not adequate to meet the constitutional responsibilities of the Government of India. Therefore, a central legislation should be enacted along the lines of the Panchayati Raj (Amendment) Act, requiring the States to enact Right to Education Bills within a specified time period, and with the primary financial responsibility for this resting with the Central Government.
- **Financial commitment:** The Central Government must provide the bulk of the additional funds required to ensure the Right to Education. Therefore, there must be financial provision in the central legislation, requiring the Central Government to share the revenues of the Prarambhik Shiksha Kosh with State Governments and to provide additional resources as required to meet the requirement of ensuring the right to all children.
- **Time frame:** The State-level legislation should specify the period within which universal education of reasonable quality is sought to be achieved, preferably within three years.
- **Schedule of norms and standards:** To ensure a minimum quality of education, it is important to have a schedule of norms for all schools to follow. While ensuring quality is a complex matter, certain norms regarding infrastructure, number of teachers per school and per student, teaching methods and other facilities, must be adhered to as necessary conditions.
- **Specification for teachers:** Since teachers are critical to ensuring the quality of education, it is particularly important to lay down well-defined but flexible norms for the minimum qualifications of teachers.

- **Justiciability and Redressal mechanism:** Any right, including the Right to Education, is only meaningful if it is justiciable. The responsibility of the government, at different levels, must be recognised and made justiciable. To ensure justiciability, a redressal mechanism should be outlined and an appropriate procedure must be set in place for students or parents in case the right is not upheld.
- **Universal schooling:** School education must be provided to all. This necessarily also requires that children of the disadvantaged, landless and minority communities must also be integrated, along with children with disabilities or special needs.

The Right of Children to Free and Compulsory Education Bill, 2008

Central legislation revived. Then Prime Minister, Dr Manmohan Singh took a meeting on 14th February 2008 in which a decision was taken to proceed with the drafting of a Central Legislation on Right to Education, and to introduce it in the budget session of the Parliament.

HRM constituted a Working Group under the chairpersonship of Secretary, DSE&L to review the draft Central legislation (August 2005 version). The Working Group took into account comments received from State Governments on the August 2005 version, and prepared a revised version, which was circulated to concerned Ministries/ Departments for inter-ministerial consultation along with the draft Cabinet Note. The observations received from the concerned Ministries/ Departments and the comments of D/SE&L thereon were made available to the Legislative Department, which prepared the draft Right of Children to Free and Compulsory Education Bill, 2008 for submission to the Cabinet. The Bill was subsequently placed before the Union Cabinet on 30th October 2008 which approved the Bill for introduction in the Parliament (MHRD, 2009, p. 23).

The Right of Children to Free and Compulsory Education Bill, 2008, representing the consequential legislation pursuant to the 86th Constitutional Amendment Act, 2002, was introduced in the Rajya Sabha on 15th December, 2008. The notification for enforcement of the 86th Constitutional Amendment would be issued after the enactment of the Right of Children to Free and Compulsory Education Bill, 2008.

213th Report of the Department-Related Parliamentary Standing Committee on Human Resource Development on the Right of Children to Free and Compulsory Education Bill, 2008

The Right of Children to Free and Compulsory Education Bill, 2008 was introduced in the Rajya Sabha on 15th December, 2008. In pursuance of Rule 270 relating to Department-related Parliamentary Standing Committees, the Chairman, Rajya Sabha, referred the bill on the 18th December, 2008 to the Committee for examination and report within three months. The Department-related Parliamentary Standing Committee made its Draft Report on the Right of Children to Free and Compulsory Education Bill, 2008 on 23rd January, 2009. The Department-related Parliamentary Standing Committee on Human Resource Development under the Chairmanship of Shri Janardhan Dwivedi, M.P., Rajya Sabha presented its Report (213th) on the Right of Children to Free and Compulsory Education Bill, 2008 to both Houses of Parliament on 18th February, 2009.

The Report at the outset stated that "The Right of Children to Free and Compulsory Education Bill, 2008 is a sequel to 86th Constitution Amendment Act passed in 2006 which provided free and compulsory education to all children between the age group of 6-14 years. This Bill is an attempt to provide elementary education to all children including the ones who have dropped out of school before the completion of their elementary education...Presently, 18 States and two Union Territories have their own legislations dealing with compulsory elementary education. The Committee noted that experiences of these States in implementation of their laws have not been very encouraging and to a large extent, they have remained unimplemented. The Committee wonders whether the experiences of these States and UTs have been fully taken into account while drafting the Central legislation. The Committee is of the opinion that problem areas and shortcomings noticed in the implementation of these State laws should be taken into account so that these are ameliorated beforehand in the present legislation. Community involvement and participation is an essential ingredient for the successful implementation of the provisions of the Bill."

Acceptance of the Bill, 2008 both in the Lok Sabha and Rajya Sabha (2009 July and August)

The Right of Children to Free and Compulsory Education Bill, 2008 was passed in the Rajya Sabha on 20th July, 2009 and in the Lok Sabha on 4th August, 2009. It can be said that nearly six years after the Amendment, the Bill was cleared by the Cabinet. On August 4, 2009, the Right to Education Act was officially passed by the Indian Parliament and on 26th August, 2009 received the President's assent. The then Union Human Resources Development Minister Shri Kapil Sibal said, "This is a historic opportunity as there was never such a law in the last 62 years since Independence". The Right of Children to Free and Compulsory Education Act, 2009 on receiving the assent of the President on the 26th August, 2009 was published in the Gazette of India on the 27th August, 2009 for general information.

Section 1(2) of the Constitution (Eighty-sixth Amendment) Act, 2002 provides that "It shall come into force on such date as the Central Government may, by notification in the Official Gazette, appoint". The enforcement of the Constitution of Eighty-Sixth Amendment Act through notification in the Official Gazette was an immediate requirement. The Central Government hereby appointed 1st April, 2010 as the date from which the RTE Act, 2009 came into force by notification in the Official Gazette of India on the 19th February, 2010 envisaged in the above Article 21A. However, the implementation of the RTE Act, 2009 began eight months after the Presidential assent (UPA II Government).

It needs mention here that the word 'Right' was missing in the first two drafts of the Bill and was used from the 2005 CABE bill onwards. The central legislation was dropped in 2006 in preference to state legislations based on a token model bill draft, for the recurring 'lack of central resources' argument, but it was intense public pressure based on independent financial estimates that made it possible to revive and bring back the central legislation in 2008.

Implementation of the RTE Act, 2009 (1st April, 2010)

The Right of Children to Free and Compulsory Education Act as enacted by Parliament comes into force. "We are committed to ensuring that all children, irrespective of gender and social category, have access to education. An education that enables them to acquire the skills, knowledge, values and attitudes necessary to become responsible and active citizens of India," said Prime Minister Manmohan Singh. The 'Right of Children to Free and Compulsory Education Act 2009' (RTE Act) came into 1st of April, 2010, with much fanfare and an address by Prime Minister Manmohan Singh. The RTE Act is a detailed and comprehensive piece of legislation which includes provisions related to schools, teachers, curriculum, evaluation, access and specific division of duties and responsibilities of different stakeholders.

Amendment to the RTE Act, 2009

April 12, 2012: Supreme Court upholds the validity of the RTE Act and makes it clear that the Act would be implemented across the country. The court, however, exempted private unaided minority schools (such as schools run by religious institutions) from the Act stating that it would "infringe upon the fundamental freedom" of such schools.

The Right of Children to Free and Compulsory Education (RTE) Act, 2009 was amended in 2012 and the RTE Amendment Act came into force with effect from 1 August 2012. The Amendment Act *inter alia* provides for: (i) inclusion of children with disability as contained in the Persons with Disabilities Act 2005 and the National Trust Act under the purview of RTE Act and providing them free and compulsory education, and providing option for home-based education for children with severe disability; (ii) protection of the rights of minorities provided under Articles 29 and 30 of the Constitution while implementing the RTE Act; (iii) exemption of Madrasas, Vedic Pathsalas and educational institutions imparting religious instruction from the provisions of the RTE Act.

Does RTE Act, 2009 follow UN's Child Rights Convention?

With heightened political consciousness amongst the deprived and marginalised, never in the history of India has the demand for inclusive education been as enthusiastic as today. Yet even a cursory examination of the RTE Act shows some glaring shortcomings. Like the age of the child. As a signatory to the UN Child Rights Convention (UNCRC), India has accepted the international definition of a child, which is up to age 18. According to the Article 1 of the UNCRC, 1989, a child means every human being below the age of eighteen years unless under the law applicable to the child, majority is attained earlier. The Act provides free and compulsory education to only children from age 6 to 14, clearly excluding and violating the rights of the 0-6 and 14 to 18 year olds. This problem can be traced to the 86th Amendment and its Article 21A, which defines the age from 6 to 14. The 86th Amendment Act, 2002 mandates that "The State shall provide free and compulsory to all children of age of six to fourteen years in such manner as the State may, by law, determine". As the RTE Act flowing out of the Amendment, it is clear that the Act cannot go beyond Article 21A, which makes it imperative that the 86th Amendment must be re-amended to correct this anomaly. The Act needs to bring into its ambit all children in the age group of 0-18 years. It ignores children who are below six years of age.

There are so many Clauses in the RTE Act, 2009 among which some are fully and some are partially familiar with the clauses in the U.N. Convention on the Rights of the Child. As it may be seen from the Table 5.2 below, Section 29 (2) of the Act was unmistakably inspired by Clauses from the Convention, (especially Article 29 of the CRC, which begins with the statement "States Parties agree that the education of the child shall be directed to" :

Table 5.2: Similar Clauses among the RTE Act, 2009 and UNCRC, 1989

	RTE, Section 29(2)	*UNCRC, Article 29*
1.	Conformity with values enshrined in the Constitution [Subsection 29(2)/a].	The development of respect for human rights and fundamental freedoms, and for the principles enshrined in the Charter of the United Nations [Article 29(b)].
2.	All round development [Subsection 29(2)/b].	The development of the child's personality, talents and mental and physical abilities to their fullest Potential [Article 29(a)].

(Contd...)

3.	Building up the child's knowledge, potentiality and talent [Subsection 29(2)/c].	The development of the child's personality, talents and mental and physical abilities to their fullest Potential [Article 29(a)].
4.	Development of physical and mental abilities to the fullest [Subsection 29(2)/c].	The development of the child's personality, talents and mental and physical abilities to their fullest Potential [Article 29(a)].
5.	Learning through activities, discovery and experience in a child-friendly and child-centric [Subsection 29(2)/e].	States Parties recognise the right of the child to rest and leisure, to engage in play and recreational activities appropriate to the age of the child and to participate freely in cultural life and the arts [Article 31(1)].
6.	Medium of instruction shall as far as practicable be in the child's mother tongue [Subsection 29(2)/f].	The development of respect for the child's parents, his or her own cultural identity, language and values, for the national values of the country in which the child is living, the country from which he or she may originate, and for civilisations different from his or her own [Article 29(c)].
7.	Making the child free of fear, trauma and anxiety and helping the child to express views freely [Subsection 29(2)/g].	States Parties shall assure to the child who is capable of forming his or her own views the right to express those views freely in all matters affecting the child, the views of the child being given due weight in accordance with the age and maturity of the child [Article 12(1)].
8.	Comprehensive and continuous evaluation of the child's understanding of knowledge and his or her ability to apply the same [Subsection 29(2)/h].	Not found in the CRC.
9.	The appropriate government shall "ensure that child belonging to weaker section and the child belonging to disadvantaged group are not discriminated against and prevented from pursuing and completing elementary education on any ground" [Section - 8(c)].	States Parties shall take all appropriate measures to ensure that the child is protected against all forms of discrimination or punishment on the basis of the status, activities, expressed opinions, or beliefs of the child's parents, legal guardians, or family members. [Article 2(2)].
10.	Every child... shall have a right to free and compulsory education in a neighbourhood school till completion of elementary education [Section - 3(1)].	States Parties recognise the right of the child to education, and with a view to achieving this right progressively and on the basis of equal opportunity, they shall, in particular: (a) Make primary education compulsory and available free to all [Article 28(1)].

What would be State laws after Central laws? Where do existing State Acts on Education stand in relation to the RTE Act?

Education being in the Concurrent List, Parliament as well as State legislatures is competent to legislate in pursuance of Article 21A. Many States already have laws on free and compulsory education, albeit they pre-date the 86th Amendment. Once a Central legislation is enacted in pursuance of Article 21A, the position of existing State laws on free and compulsory education would be governed by the provisions of Article 254(1), i.e. their provisions would become null and void to the extent they are repugnant to the provisions of the Central legislation. However, it would be possible to enact State amendments to the Central legislation, or enact fresh State laws on the subject, after following the procedure laid down in Article 254(2).

The State Acts would have to be brought in conformity with the Central Act. As per Article 254 of the constitution reproduced below, a state Act can not violate the provisions of the Central Act in a concurrent subject. States could amend such a Central Act, but that would require Presidential assent. However, if the State Act contains anything on which the Central Act is silent, then that may remain as a part of the State Act.

254. (1) If any provision of a law made by the Legislature of a State is repugnant to any provision of a law made by Parliament which Parliament is competent to enact, or to any provision of an existing law with respect to one of the matters enumerated in the Concurrent List, then, subject to the provisions of clause (2), the law made by Parliament, whether passed before or after the law made by the Legislature of such State, or, as the case may be, the existing law, shall prevail and the law made by the Legislature of the State shall, to the extent of the repugnancy, be void.

(3) Where a law made by the Legislature of a State with respect to one of the matters enumerated in the Concurrent List contains any provision repugnant to the provisions of an earlier law made by Parliament or an existing law with respect to that matter, then, the law so made by the Legislature of such State shall, if it has been reserved for the consideration of the President and has received his assent, prevail in that State: Provided that nothing in this clause shall prevent

Parliament from enacting at any time any law with respect to the same matter including a law adding to, amending, varying or repealing the law so made by the Legislature of the State.

The above chapter of the present Study is thus an attempt to equip the stakeholders with an overview of the historical and recent development relating to the task of making free and compulsory education in India a fundamental right. The Right to Education legislation has a long and chequered history, having been subjected to numerous demands, pressures, rounds of heated debates and philosophical and semantic alterations. Following the passage of the 86th Constitutional Amendment in 2002, Education was declared a fundamental right of all children in the age-group of 6-14. The different national approaches to the right to education are reflected in varied constitutional provisions. As Table 5.3 illustrates, there are 43 countries where there is no explicit constitutional guarantee of the right to education, while such a guarantee does exist in 144 countries; that the vast majority of States constitutionally guarantee the right to education reflects the thrust of international human rights law.

Table 5.3: Countries which Guarantee Right to Education under Constitution

Full Constitutional Guarantee	Albania, Algeria, Argentina, Australia, Austria, Azerbaijan, Barbados, Belgium, Belize, Bolivia and Herzegovina, Brazil, Bulgaria, Canada, Cape Verde, Chile, China, Columbia, Congo, Costa Rica, Croatia, Cuba, Denmark, Ecuador, Egypt, Estonia, Finland, France, Gambia, Georgia, Germany, Ghana, Haiti, Honduras, Iceland, **India**, Ireland, Italy, Japan, Latvia, Liechtenstein, Lithuania, Madagascar, Malta, Mauritius, Mexico, Netherlands, Norway, Palau, Panama, Paraguay, Peru, Poland, Portugal, Korea, Moldova, Romania, Russia, Rwanda, Saudi Arabia, South Africa, Spain, Sri Lanka, Suriname, Sweden, Switzerland, Tajikistan, Thailand, Trinidad and Tobago, Tunisia, Ukraine, UAE, UK, Uruguay, Venezuela, Former Yugoslavia.

Partial Constitutional Guarantee	Bangladesh, Belarus, Benin, Bhutan, Cameroon, Comoros, Guinea, Iran, Iraq, Israel, Micronesia, Maldives, Monaco, Mongolia, Myanmar, Namibia, Nepal, Nigeria, Pakistan, Sierra Leone, Sudan, Togo, Uganda, Tanzania, Uzbekistan, Zimbabwe.
Constitutional Guarantee only for citizens / residents	Armenia, Bahrain, Cambodia, Chad, Cyprus, Czech Republic, Korea, Dominican Republic, El Salvador, Equatorial Guinea, Greece, Grenada, Guatemala, Guyana, Hungary, Jordan, Kazakhstan, Kuwait, Kyrgyzstan, Libyan Arab Jamahiriya, Luxembourg, Malawi, Mali, Morocco, New Zealand, Nicaragua, Philippines, Qatar, Sao Tome and Principe, Seychelles, Slovakia, Slovenia, Syrian Arab Republic, Turkey, Turkmenistan, Vietnam, Yemen.
No Constitutional Guarantee	Angola, Antigua and Barbuda, Bahamas, Botswana, Brunei Darussalam, Burkina Faso, Burundi, Central African Republic, Côte d'lvoire, Djibouti, Dominica, Eritrea, Ethiopia, Fiji, Gabon, Indonesia, Jamaica, Kenya, Kirbati, Lao People's Democratic Republic, Lebanon, Lesotho, Liberia, Malaysia, Marshall Islands, Mauritania, Mozambique, Nauru, Niger, Oman, Papua New Guinea, Saint Lucia, Saint Vincent and the Grenadines, Samoa, San Marion, Senegal, Singapore, Solomon Islands, Swaziland, Tonga, Tuvalu, United States of America, Vanuatu, Zambia.

Source: Annual Report of Special Rapporteur on the Right to Education, Commission on Human Rights, 2001, 57th Session, E/CN 4/2001/42, [available at www.un.org].

Table 5.3 has been modified by the author to include India in the list of countries that have full constitutional guarantees of the free and compulsory education after the constitutional Amendment of 2002. Thus, the RTE Act, 2009 is not an imperative for realising rights but it a useful tool, which can assist on the claiming of a right. It is not a determinant of whether or not people have their right to education realised but it can be used as a mobilisation tool to transform rights and policies into reality.

References

- (1997): Report of the Committee of State Education Ministers on Implications of the Proposal to Make Elementary Education a Fundamental Right, (chairman: Muhi Ram Saikia), Ministry of Human Resource Development, Department of Education, New Delhi.
- Aggarwal, J. C. (2008). *Development and Planning of Modern Education*. New Delhi: Vikas Publishing House Pvt. Ltd.
- AIFRTE (2012). Chennai Declaration. *Reconstructing Education*. 22 Vol. 1, No. 4, September-December, 2012 and Vol. 2, No. 1, January-March, 2013.
- B. G. Tilak, Jandhyala (6 July 2010). RTE Act 2009 — illusory promises. Retrieved from http://educationworldonline.net/index.php/page-article-choice-more-id-2288.
- Basu, A.N. (1941). (Ed.). *Adam's Reports of the State of Education in Bengal and Bihar*. Calcutta: University of Calcutta Press.
- Bhaumik, P.K. and Banik, A. (2006, April 8). Making the education cess work, *The Economic Times*. Retrieved from http://articles.economictimes.indiatimes.com/2006-04-08/news/27454253_1_education-cess-duties-and-service-tax-elementary-education
- Biswas, A. and Agrwal, S.P. (1986). *Development of Education in India A historical Survey of Educational Documents Before and After Independence*. New Delhi: Concept Publishing House.
- Chatterjee, S. (2010). Inaugural Address. In Habib, S. Irfan (Ed.). *Maulana Abul Kalam Azad and the National Education System*. New Delhi: NUEPA.
- Committee on the Ways and Means of Financing Education Development in India, 1948, Delhi, Manager of Publications, 1950, Bureau of Education, Pamphlet No. 64.
- Deogirikar, T. R. (1992). *Gopal Krishna Gokhale*, New Delhi: Ministry of Information and Broadcasting, Government of India.
- Department of Education, University of Delhi (1997), Convention on Education as a Fundamental Right, Golden Jubilee Celebrations, Central Institute of Education, University of Delhi, Delhi.
- GOI (1974). *National Policy for Children*. New Delhi: Department of Social Welfare, Government of India.
- GOI (2007). *National Knowledge Commission – Recommendations on School Education*. New Delhi: National Knowledge Commission, Government of India.
- GOI (2008). *Department – Related Parliamentary Standing Committee on HRD: Two Hundred Thirteenth Report on the Right to Free and Compulsory Education Bill, 2008*. New Delhi: Parliament of India, Rajya Sabha Secretariat.

- GOI. (1999). *Expert Group Report on Financial Requirements for Making Elementary Education a Fundamental Right (also known as Tapas Majumdar Committee Report of 1999).*New Delhi: Department of Education, Ministry of Human Resource Development, GOI.
- GOI. (2005). *Report of the Committee of CABE on Universalisation of Secondary Education.* New Delhi: Ministry of Human Resource Development, Government of India.
- Government of Bihar (2007). *Report of the Bihar Common School System Commission.* Patna: Common School System Commission, Govt. of Bihar.
- Government of India (1948). *Education in Free India (August 1947 – August 1948).* New Delhi: The Ministry of Education, Government of India.
- Government of India (1950). *Committee on the Ways and Means of Financing Education Development in India, 1948.* Delhi: Pamphlet No. 64, Manager of Publications, Bureau of Education.
- Government of India (1950).*Committee on the Ways and Means of Financing Education Development in India, 1948.* Bureau of Education, Pamphlet No. 64. Delhi, Manager of Publications, Government of India.
- Government of India (1965). *Education in Eighteen Years of Freedom.* New Delhi: Ministry of Education, Government of India.
- Government of India (1979). *Draft National Policy on Education*, 1979. New Delhi: Ministry of Education and Social Welfare, GOI.
- Government of India (1985). *Challenge of Education – A Policy Perspective.* New Delhi: Ministry of Education, Government of India.
- Government of India (1999). Expert Group on Financial Requirements for Making Elementary Education A Fundamental Right, (Chairman: Prof. Tapas Majumdar) Ministry of Human Resources Development, Government of India, New Delhi.
- Government of India (2000). Report on a Policy Framework for Reforms in Education, New Delhi: Prime Minister's Council on Trade and Industry, Government of India.
- Government of India (2002). *Report of the National Commission to Review the Working of the Constitution.* New Delhi: Ministry of Law, Justice and Company Affairs, Department of Legal Affairs, GOI.
- Government of India (2004). *National Common Minimum Programme of the Government of India May 2004.* New Delhi: GOI. Retrieved from http://architexturez.net/system/files/pdf/cmp_0.pdf
- Government of India (2005). *Government of the United Progressive Alliance Report to People - 1, Implementation of National Common Minimum Programme and Other Initiatives May 2004 – February 2005.* New Delhi: GOI.

- Government of India (2005a). Report of the CABE Committee on Free and Compulsory Education Bill and Other Issues Related to Elementary Education, June 2005. Available at www.education.nic.
- Government of India (2005b). Report of Committee on National Common Minimum Programmes Commitment of Six Per Cent of GDP to Education, (Chairman: Prof. Tapas Majumdar) National Institute of Educational Planning and Administration, New Delhi. Available at www.niepa.org.
- Government of India (2006). *Report on the Social, Economic and Educational Status of the Muslim Community of India*. New Delhi: Ministry of Minority Affairs, Government of India.
- Irfan Habib, S. (2010) (Ed.). *Maulana Abul Kalam Azad and the National Education System*. New Delhi: National University of Educational Planning and Administration (NUEPA).
- Juneja, Nalini. Constitutional Commitments. SEMINAR 464, 1998 (Issue on Right to Education). Juneja, Nalini. Compulsory Education in India: The Policy in Practice. National Institute of Educational Planning and Administration (mimeo).
- Kumar, C. Raj (2004). International Human Rights Perspectives on the Fundamental Right to Education - Integration of Human Rights and Human Development in the Indian Constitution, *Tulane Journal of International and Comparative Law*, Volume 12 (237-286).Available at www.heinonline.org. polar.onu.edu/HOL/Print?collection=journals& handle=hein.journals/tulicl12&id=248
- Law Commission of India (1998). *One Hundred Sixty Fifth Report on Free and Compulsory Education for Children*. New Delhi: Law Commission of India.
- Malani, Gaurav (2004, Sep 23). Fund for education cess gets finance ministry nod. *The Economic Times.* Retrieved from http://articles.economictimes. indiatimes.com/2004-09-23/news/27370798_1_education-cess-mid-day-meal-scheme-elementary-education
- MHRD (1964). *The 31st CABE Meeting, at Bangalore on October 11 and 12, 1964, under the Chairmanship of Shri M. C. Chagla*, Union Education Minister. New Delhi: CABE, MHRD. Retrieved from http://www.teindia.nic.in/mhrd/50yrsedu/g/12/1K/121K0101.htm
- MHRD (1997). *Convention on the Rights of the Child – Country Report, 1997.* New Delhi: Department of Women and Child Department, MHRD. Retrieved from http://wcd.nic.in/crcfebmr.htm
- MHRD (1998). *National Policy on Education 1986 (as modified in 1992)*. New Delhi: Department of Education, Ministry of Human Resource Development, GOI.
- MHRD (2005). *Annual Report 2004-05*. New Delhi: Department of School Education and Literacy, Department of Higher Education, Ministry of Human Resource Development (MHRD), Government of India.

- MHRD (2009). *Fifty Fifth Meeting of the Central Advisory Board of Education Agenda Items and Background Notes*, Dated Tuesday, The 10th February, 2009. New Delhi: Ministry of Human Resource Development, Government of India.
- MHRD. (2005). *Report of the Central Advisory Board of Education (CABE) Committee on Free and Compulsory Education Bill and Other Issues Related to Elementary Education, June 2005*. New Delhi: MHRD, GOI.
- NCERT (1970). *Education and National Development Report of the Education Commission, 1964-66 (Reprinted)*. New Delhi: National Council of Educational Research and Training.
- Pal, R. M. (2001). Denial of the Right to Education: A Human Right's Violation. *Social Action*. Vol. 51, April-June 2001.
- Raina, V. (2010). *Education and Knowledge in the Time of Globalisation Inclusion, Quality and Agency*. B.M. Pugh Fourth Memorial Lecture, 2010, NERIE, NCERT, Shillong.
- Raina, V. (2010). Maulana Azad and Right to Education. In Habib, S. Infan (2010). *Maulana Abul Kalam Azad and the National Education System*. New Delhi: NUEPA.
- Rajkhowa, S. C. (1964). Towads Universal Elementary Education (1921-61). In NCERT (Eds.), *The Indian Year Book of Education 1964 Second Year Book Elementary Education*, (pp. 21-40). New Delhi: NCERT.
- Rajya Sabha Secretariat (2009). *213th Report of the Department-Related Parliamentary Standing Committee on Human Resource Development on the Right of Children to Free and Compulsory Education Bill, 2008*. New Delhi: Rajya Sabha, Parliament of India.
- Sadgopal, A. (2003). Education for too few. *Frontline*, Vol. 20, Issue 24, November 22 - December 05.
- Sadgopal, A. (2010). Right to Education vs. Right to Education Act. *Social Scientist*. 38(9-12) September–December 2010, pp. 17-50.
- Seetharamu, A.S. (2002, February 9). Fundamental Right Status for Education: Opportunity or eyewash? Retrieved from http.// www.deccanherald.com/
- Sharma, Nirmala (2011). *Universalisation of Elementary Education among Tea – Tribe of Assam with special reference to Jorhat District*. Guwahati, Assam: Assam State Commission for Protection of Child Right.
- State Platform for Common School System (SPCSS). Chennai Declaration, 2012 Reconstructing Education, Vol. 1, No. 4, September-December, 2012 and Vol. 2, No. 1, January-March, 2013, pp. 20-34.
- Supreme Court of India. Judgement on J.P. Unnikrishnan v. State of Andhra Pradesh, New Delhi (1993), Reproduced in Journal of Higher Education 16 (2), Spring 1993.

- Supreme Court of India. Judgement on Miss Mohini Jain v. State of Karnataka and Others. New Delhi (30 July 1992). Reproduced in Journal of Higher Education 16 (1), Autumn, 1992.
- Tilak, Jandhyala B. G. (2004). Education in the UPA Government Common Minimum Programme, *Economic and Political Weekly*, 39(43), October 23-29, 4717-4721.
- Universalisation of primary education in South Asia with special reference to Bangladesh http://shodhganga.inflibnet.ac.in/handle/10603/14240
- Weiner, Myron (1991). *The Child and the State in India; Child Labour and Education Policy in Comparative Perspective*. Princeton, NJ: Princeton University Press.

Chapter - 6

RTE in the Light of "Justice Delayed is Justice Denied"

If we analyse the history of free and compulsory education in India, we will find the history of persistent denial. The question on Right to Education was initiated in India by Mahatma Jotirao Phule more than 125 years ago when a substantial part of the memorandum presented by him to the Indian Education Commission (the Hunter Commission) in 1882 dwelt upon how the British government's funding of education tended to benefit "Brahmins and the higher classes" while leaving "the masses wallowing in ignorance and poverty." Mahatma Phule drew attention to the irony that this happened when most of the revenue collected by the British government was generated from the output of the labour of the masses themselves. Things have not fundamentally changed since then.

In 1911, when Gopal Krishna Gokhale moved his Free and Compulsory Education Bill in the Imperial Legislative Assembly, he faced stiff resistance. Instead of supporting the Bill, the members representing the privileged classes from Mumbai, Maharajas and other rulers from princely states and the big landlords from feudal areas talked of the conditions in the country not being ripe for such a Bill and that haste should be avoided. The Maharaja of Darbhanga from Bihar collected 11,000 signatures on a Memorandum from princes and landlords expressing concern about what would happen to their farm operations if all children were required to attend the school!" (Sadgopal, 2010, p. 17).

At the National Education Conference held at Wardha (Maharashtra) in 1937, Mahatma Gandhi had to use all the moral powers at his command to persuade the Ministers of Education of the newly elected Congress governments of seven provinces to give priority to Basic Education (*Nai Talim*) of seven years and allocate adequate funds for this purpose. The ministers kept on pointing out that there was no money. In this context, it would be worthwhile to quote from the widely acclaimed Tapas Majumdar Committee Report (January 1999):

> From being an *incremental* developmental goal in the process of education for all, UEE [Universalisation of Elementary Education] has, in consequence of the [Supreme Court's Unnikrishnan] judgment, now become a *justiciable entitlement* of every Indian child...entitlements sanctioned by the Constitution cannot be deferred by the State at its convenience...The State has to make the necessary reallocation of resources, by *superseding* other important claims, if necessary, in a manner that the justiciable entitlement can become a reality. This may call for restructuring of all government spending, forcing the State to cut down even on spending that it would otherwise consider as essential, but which was not covered by any of the Fundamental Rights guaranteed by the Constitution.

Even the post-independence history stands witness to the persistent denial of Constitutional mandate for achieving the goal of Universal Elementary Education. Clearly, it is not a matter of paucity of funds at all but a matter of socio-political priorities of the Indian State. The State has consistently denied the Fundamental Right to education of the 6-14 year age group children for the past six decades claiming paucity of funds.

- In 1949, as the Constitution was being adopted, the leaders of all parties had thought 1960 was a good deadline for achieving the objective of Article 45.
- The education commission of 1964-66 was barely more pragmatic when it said, "*all* the areas in the country should be able to provide five years of good and effective education to *all* the children by 1975-76 and seven years of such education by 1985-86" (Para 7.08).

- The National Policy on Education, 1986 had envisaged that "by 1995 all children will be provided free and compulsory education up to 14 years of age" (Para 5.12).
- The revised policy formulation of 1992, two years after the Jomtien conference, piously declared "It shall be ensured that free and compulsory education of satisfactory quality is provided to all children up to 14 years of age before we enter the twenty-first century" by launching a national mission (Para 5.12).

In the following Table 6.1 the history of consistent denial of free and compulsory education in India after the Constitution era has been depicted briefly:

Table 6.1: History of Denial of the Original Article 45 (Goal of UEE)

Sl. No.	*Document*	*Area and Level (Only if specified)*	*Target*
1.	Constitution of India, 1950		1960
2.	Report of the Education Commission, 1964-66	Class VII/VIII (In urban areas/ advanced areas)	1975-76
		Class V	1975-76
		Class VII/VIII (Rest if India)	1985-86
3.	National Policy on Education, 1968	"early fulfillment of the Directive Principle under Article 45"	
4.	National Policy on Education, 1986	Class V	1990
		Class VIII	1995
5.	National Policy on Education, 1986 (modified in 1992)	Before 21st Century	
6.	Ramamurti Committee, 1990	*"Now, time has come to recognise 'Right to Education' as one of the fundamental rights of the Indian citizen for which necessary amendments to the Constitution may have to be made"*	
7.	Sarva Shiksha Abhiyan	5 Years of Primary Schooling	2007
8.		8 Years of Elementary Schooling	2010
9.	The Right of Children to free and Compulsory Education Act, 2009	Class V - Class VIII Extended to the whole of India except the State of Jammu and Kashmir	

Source: Sadgopal (2010, pp. 20) and Modified by the Authors.

At last, the free and compulsory education of the children of age of 6 to 14 years became a justifiable fundamental right after 62 years of Independence and 16 years after the historic Unnikrishnan Judgement and it took six years just to frame and pass this Act. The enforcement of this right has a symbolic and historic value, because it was a step ahead in the more than one and half a century long struggle for universalising the elementary education. The Act came into effect in the whole of India except the state of Jammu and Kashmir from the 1st April of 2010.

It is the first time in the history of India a law was brought into force by a speech by the Prime Minister of India. In his speech the history of denial implicitly expressed when Dr Manmohan Singh stated that "About a hundred years ago a great son of India, Gopal Krishna Gokhale, urged the Imperial Legislative Assembly to confer on the Indian people the Right to Education. About ninety years later the Constitution of India was amended to enshrine the Right to Education as a fundamental right. Today, our government comes before you to redeem the pledge of giving all our children the right to elementary education...This demonstrates our national commitment to the education of our children and to the future of India...It is the belief of our government that if we nurture our children and young people with the right education, India's future as a strong and prosperous country is secure. We are committed to ensuring that all children, irrespective of gender and social category, have access to education. An education that enables them to acquire the skills, knowledge, values and attitudes is necessary to become responsible and active citizens of India. I want every Indian child, girl and boy, to be so touched by the light of education. I want every Indian to dream of a better future and live that dream" (GOI, 2010).

The history of consistent denial of the free and compulsory education has also been articulated in the speech of Vinod Raina, one of chief architects of RTE Act at the B.M. Pugh Fourth Memorial Lecture, 2010, organised by NERIE, NCERT, Shillong that

> "Hundred years since Gokhale introduced his private Bill in the Imperial Assembly, seventy-one years since Mahatma Gandhi gave the call for universal education in 1937; sixty-one years since Independence; fifty-eight years since the Constitution instead of making education a fundamental right made it part of the Directive Principles; fifteen years since the Supreme Court ruled in 1993

that the right to education existed; six years after the 86th Constitutional Amendment was passed by the Parliament in 2002 inserting Article 21A that made education a fundamental right for the restricted age group of 6 to 14 years-old children; and four years after the draft Bill was prepared by the CABE committee, the Right to Free and Compulsory Education Bill was introduced in the Rajya Sabha on December 15, 2008. It was passed by the two houses of Parliament and received Presidential assent in August, 2009, and after notification, it is operational since April, 2010. This has undeniably been a momentous event (Raina, 2010)".

With the Right to Education Act coming into force, India became one of the 135 countries to make education a fundamental right of every child. It may be inferred from the above discussion that the Government of India has kept its obligations as advocated by the Apex Court in a number of path-breaking judgements. India has witnessed a long journey in evolving the right to education from the directive principle to fundamental right. The RTE Act is now the first Central legislation on the landscape of elementary education that puts the responsibilities of enrollment, attendance and competition of elementary education of every Indian child on the government. Free and compulsory elementary education for all children in the age group of 6–14 at long last has become a 'so called' legal reality with the implementation of Right of Children to Free and Compulsory Education Act, 2009.

Chapter - 7

Articulation of the RTE in International Treaties as a Human Right

In order to better understand the right to education, it is necessary to situate this discourse within the international treaties as a human right. International legal instruments take the form of a treaty (also called agreement, convention, or protocol) that binds the contracting States to the negotiated terms. When negotiations are completed, the text of a treaty is established as authentic and definitive and is "signed" by the representatives of States. A State can agree to be bound to a treaty in various ways. The most common are ratification or accession. A new treaty is ratified by those States that have negotiated the instrument. A State that has not participated in the negotiations may, at a later stage, accede to the treaty. The treaty enters into force, or becomes valid, when a pre-determined number of States have ratified or acceded to the treaty.

When a State ratifies or accedes to a treaty, that state may make reservations to one or more articles of the treaty, unless reservations are prohibited by the treaty. Reservations may normally be withdrawn at any time. In some countries, international treaties take precedence over national law; in others a specific law may be required to give a ratified international treaty the force of a national law. Practically all States that have ratified or acceded to an international treaty must issue decrees, change existing laws, or introduce new legislation in order for the treaty to be fully effective on the national territory. The binding treaties can be used to force governments to respect the treaty provisions that are relevant for the right to education. The non-binding instruments, such as declarations and resolutions, can be used in relevant situations to embarrass governments by negative public exposure; governments who care about their international image may consequently adopt their policies. India is a signatory to three key international instruments that guarantee the right to elementary education – Universal Declaration of Human Rights, 1948, the International Covenant on Economic, Social and Cultural Rights, 1966 and the Convention on the Rights of the Child, 1989. The right to education has been explicitly enshrined in these conventions. The following are the international conventions which recognise right to education as a human right at global level.

World Commitment on Education as a Right and India is a Signatory

(1) Universal Declaration of Human Rights, 1948: Education is defined as a right in itself, but the text of the UDHR also implies that education is a means to an end, rather than an end in itself. Education is seen as the process through which all citizens can become aware of their rights and responsibilities, so that peace as well as prosperity can be secured for all nations and people. The UDHR's definition of the role of education in and for human rights is reflected in later international standards. UDHR establishes right to education in its Article 26, in the following terms :

(a) Everyone has the right to education. Education shall be free, at least in the elementary and fundamental stages. Elementary education shall be compulsory. Technical and professional education shall be made generally available and higher education shall be equally accessible to all on the basis of merit.

(b) Education shall be directed to the full development of the human personality and to the strengthening of respect for human rights and fundamental freedoms. It shall promote understanding, tolerance and friendship among all nations, racial or religious groups, and shall further the activities of the United Nations for the maintenance of peace.

(c) Parents have a prior right to choose the kind of education that shall be given to their children (UDHR, Article 26).

(2) Declaration of the Rights of the Child, 1959: Principle 7 - The child is entitled to receive education, which shall be free and compulsory, at least in the elementary stages...The best interests of the child shall be the guiding principle of those responsible for his education and guidance that the responsibility lies in the first place with the parents.

(3) UNESCO Convention against Discrimination in Education, 1960: The States Parties to this Convention undertake furthermore to formulate, develop and apply a national policy which, by methods appropriate to the circumstances and to national usage, will tend to promote equality of opportunity and of treatment in the matter of education and in particular:

(a) To make primary education free and compulsory; make secondary education in its different forms generally available and accessible to all; make higher education equally accessible to all on the basis of individual capacity; assure compliance by all with the obligation to attend school prescribed by law;

(b) To ensure that the standards of education are equivalent in all public educational institutions of the same level, and that the conditions relating to the quality of the education provided are also equivalent;

(c) To encourage and intensify by appropriate methods the education of persons who have not received any primary education or who have not completed the entire primary education course and the continuation of their education on the basis of individual capacity;

(d) To provide training for the teaching profession without discrimination [Article 4].

(4) International Covenant on Economic, Social and Cultural Rights (1966): 1. The States Parties to the present Covenant recognise the right of everyone to education. They agree that education shall be directed to the full development of the human personality and the sense of its dignity, and shall strengthen the respect for human rights and fundamental freedoms. They further agree that education shall enable all persons to participate effectively in a free society, promote understanding, tolerance and friendship among all nations and all racial, ethnic or religious groups, and further the activities of the United Nations for the maintenance of peace.

2. The States Parties to the present Covenant recognise that, with a view to achieving the full realisation of this right: (a) Primary education shall be compulsory and available free to all; [Article 13].

(5) Convention on the Right of the Child, 1989: (Article 28(1) - The States Parties recognise the right of the child to education and with a view to achieving this progressively and on the basis of equal opportunity, they shall in particular, (a) Make primary education compulsory and available free to all; (b) Encourage the development of different forms of secondary education, including general and vocational education, make them available and accessible to every child and take appropriate measures such as the introduction of free education and offering financial assistance in case of need; (c) Make higher education accessible to all on the basis of capacity by every appropriate means; (d) Make educational and vocational information and guidance available and accessible to all children; (e) Take measures to encourage regular attendance at schools and the reduction of dropout rates.

(6) World Declaration on 'Education For All' at Jomtien, Thailand, 1990: "...Education is a fundamental right for all people, women and men, of all ages, throughout the world.... Every person — child, youth and adult — shall be able to benefit from educational opportunities designed to meet their basic learning needs.... to be able to survive, to develop their full capacities, to live and work in dignity.... to improve the quality of their lives, to make informed decisions.... Basic education should be provided to all children, youth and adults.... The most urgent priority is to ensure access to, and improve the quality of, education for girls and women, and to remove every obstacle that hampers their active participation. All gender stereotyping in education should be eliminated" (Articles 1 and 3).

(7) The Dakar Framework for Action, Education for All: Meeting our Collective Commitments, Dakar, Senegal, 2000: The six Dakar goals:

- Expanding and improving comprehensive early childhood care and education, especially for the most vulnerable and disadvantaged children;

- Ensuring that by 2015 all children, particularly girls children in difficult circumstances and those belonging to ethnic minorities, have access to and complete, free and compulsory primary education of good quality;
- Ensuring that the learning needs of all young people and adults are met through equitable access to appropriate learning and life-skills programmes;
- Achieving a 50 per cent improvement in levels of adult literacy by 2015, especially for women, and equitable access to basic and continuing education for all adults;
- Eliminating gender disparities in primary and secondary education by 2005, and achieving gender equality in education by 2015, with a focus on ensuring girls' full and equal access to and achievement in basic education of good quality;
- Improving all aspects of the quality of education and ensuring excellence of all so that recognised and measurable learning outcomes are achieved by all, especially in literacy, numeracy and essential life skills.

(8) The Millennium Development Goals, 2002: In September of the year 2000, leaders of 189 countries met at the United Nations in New York and endorsed the Millennium Declaration, a commitment to work together to build a safer, more prosperous and equitable world. The Declaration was translated into a roadmap setting out eight time-bound and measurable goals to be reached by 2015, known as the Millennium Development Goals, namely:

(a) *Eradicate extreme poverty and hunger*

- Reduce by half the proportion of people whose income is less than $1 a day.
- Achieve full and productive employment and decent work for all, including women and young people.
- Reduce by half the proportion of people who suffer from hunger.

(b) *Achieve universal primary education*

- Ensure that all boys and girls complete a full course of primary schooling.

(c) *Promote gender equality and empower women*

- Eliminate gender disparity in primary and secondary education preferably by 2005, and in all levels of education no later than 2015.
- Reduce child mortality
- Reduce by two-thirds the mortality of children under five.

(d) *Improve maternal health*

- Reduce maternal mortality by three quarters.
- Achieve universal access to reproductive health.

(e) *Combat HIV/AIDS, malaria and other diseases.*

- Halt and reverse the spread of HIV/AIDS.
- Achieve, by 2010, universal access to treatment for HIV/AIDS for all those who need it.
- Halt and reverse the incidence of malaria and other major diseases.

(f) *Ensure environmental sustainability*

- Integrate principles of sustainable development into country policies and programmes; reverse the loss of environmental resources.
- Reduce biodiversity loss, achieving, by 2010, a significant reduction in the rate of loss.
- Halve the proportion of people without access to safe drinking water and basic sanitation.
- Improve the lives of at least 100 million slum dwellers by 2020.

(g) *Develop a global partnership for development*

- Develop further an open, rule-based, predictable, non-discriminatory trading and financial system.
- Address special needs of the least developed countries, landlocked countries and small island developing States.
- Deal comprehensively with developing countries' debt.
- In cooperation with pharmaceutical companies, provide access to affordable essential drugs in developing countries.

- In cooperation with the private sector, make available the benefits of new technologies, especially information and communications technologies.

Several Global Agencies Striving for Promotion of Right to Education

Several Agencies around the world which are striving for promotion of Right to Education are :

United Nations Educational, Scientific and Cultural Organisation (UNESCO): The main objective of UNESCO is to contribute to peace and security in the world by promoting collaboration among nations through education, science, culture, and communication. This will further universal respect for justice, for the rule of law, and for the human rights and fundamental freedoms that are affirmed for the people of the world, without distinction of race, sex, language, or religion, by the Charter of the United Nations. The United Nations Literacy Decade (2003–2012) aimed to extend the use of literacy to those who did not currently have access to it. More than 861 million adults were in that position, and over 113 million children were not in school and therefore not in a position to learn to read or write either.

United Nations Children's Fund (UNICEF): Created by the United Nations General Assembly in 1946 to help children after World War II in Europe, UNICEF was first known as the United Nations International Children's Emergency Fund. In 1953, UNICEF became a permanent part of the United Nations system, its task being to help children living in poverty in developing countries. Its name was shortened to the United Nations Children's Fund, but it retained the acronym "UNICEF" by which it is known to this day. Believing in quality education for all, UNICEF helps children get the care and stimulation they need in the early years of life and encourages families to educate girls as well as boys. UNICEF supports young people, wherever they are, in making informed decisions about their own lives, and strives to build a world in which all children live in dignity and security. UNICEF's work is geared toward ensuring that all children realise their right to education, and that every child has the opportunity to develop to his or her full potential. Working with national governments, non-governmental organisations (NGOs), other United Nations agencies and private-sector partners, UNICEF protects children and their rights by providing services and supplies and by helping shape policy agendas and budgets in the best interests of children.

World Bank: Since World Bank lending for education began in 1963, the Bank has played a prominent role in assisting developing countries in their efforts to expand universal elementary education and to improve the quality of institutions and programmes. Since 1963, the World Bank has provided over US $30 billion in loans and credits. It currently finances 153 projects in 79 countries. Working closely with national governments, United Nations agencies, donors, NGOs, and other partners, the Bank helps developing countries in their efforts to reach the Education For All (EFA) goals of achieving universal primary education for all children by 2015 and reducing the education gap between boys and girls by 2005. The World Bank works in partnership a wide range of organisations including the following :

- UNESCO (United Nations Educational Scientific and Cultural Organisation), Secondary Education.
- UNESCO, International Bureau of Education (IBE).
- UNESCO, International Institute of Educational Planning (IIEP).
- OECD, Organisation for Economic Cooperation and Development.
- European Training Foundation.
- Department for International Development (DFID), UK.
- United Nations Children's Fund (UNICEF), Secondary Education and Gender Parity.

International Labour Organisation (ILO): The ILO is the UN specialised agency that seeks the promotion of social justice and internationally recognised human and labour rights. Founded in 1919, it is the only surviving major creation of the Treaty of Versailles, which created the League of Nations. It became the first specialised agency of the UN. The ILO is known for its long-standing work on vocational training policy and structures, but it also has an active programme in education. The ILO's speciality lies in its detailed technical knowledge of what constitutes good employment practices – recruitment, career development, salaries, working conditions, and labour relations – as the basis for education reform and quality. Since the 1950s, ILO's work has focused on researching, promoting, and sharing information on standards and best practices. It is important (though often overlooked in education sector work) because the salaries of educational personal take up 60 to 95 per cent of governments' annual expenditure on education; it is highest in developing countries.

International and Regional Instruments for Protection and Promotion of Right to Education

International legal instruments take the form of a treaty (also called agreement, convention, or protocol) that binds the contracting states to the negotiated terms. When negotiations are completed, the text of a treaty is established as authentic and definitive and is "signed" by the representatives of states. A state can agree to be bound to a treaty in various ways. The most common are ratification or accession. A new treaty is ratified by those states that have negotiated the instrument. A state that has not participated in the negotiations may, at a later stage, accede to the treaty. The treaty enters into force, or becomes valid, when a pre-determined number of states have ratified or acceded to the treaty.

When a state ratifies or accedes to a treaty, that state may make reservations to one or more articles of the treaty, unless reservations are prohibited by the treaty. Reservations may normally be withdrawn at any time. In some countries, international treaties take precedence over national law; in others a specific law may be required to give a ratified international treaty the force of a national law. Practically all states that have ratified or acceded to an international treaty must issue decrees, change existing laws, or introduce new legislation in order for the treaty to be fully effective on the national territory. The binding treaties can be used to force governments to respect the treaty provisions that are relevant for the right to education. The non-binding instruments, such as declarations and resolutions, can be used in relevant situations to embarrass governments by negative public exposure; governments who care about their international image may consequently adapt their policies. The following international instruments protect and promote the right to education :

Apart from **Universal Declaration of Human Rights (1948)**, right to education has been affirmed, protected and promoted in numerous international human rights treaties, such as the following :

Convention concerning Discrimination in Respect of Employment and Occupation (1958): The International Labour Organisation (ILO)'s Convention Concerning Discrimination in Respect of Employment and Occupation declares as its aim the promotion of "equality of opportunity and treatment in respect of employment and occupation, with a view to eliminating any discrimination in respect thereof", and calls upon education to assist in securing this. States are required to "enact such legislation and to promote such educational programmes as may be calculated to secure the acceptance and observance of this policy...." (Article 3).

Convention against Discrimination in Education (1960): UNESCO member states have adopted two treaties aimed at eliminating discrimination in education. These include the 1960 Convention against Discrimination in Education and the Protocol Instituting a Conciliation and Good Offices Commission to be responsible for seeking a settlement of any disputes which may arise between States Parties to the Convention against Discrimination in Education, which was adopted in 1962 and entered into force in 1968.

Convention on the Elimination of all Forms of Discrimination Against Women (1979): The women's rights convention from 1979, known as the Convention on the Elimination of all forms of Discrimination Against Women, and often abbreviated as CEDAW, obliges state parties to: "...take all appropriate measures to eliminate discrimination against women in order to ensure to them equal rights with men in the field of education and in particular to ensure, on the basis of equality of men and women:... The elimination of any stereotyped concept of the roles of men and women at all levels and in all forms of education by encouraging coeducation and other types of education which will help to achieve this aim and, in particular, by the revision of textbooks and school programmes and the adaptation of teaching methods..." (Article 10).

The United Nations Convention on the Right of the Child (1989): UNCRC obliges state parties to: "...recognise the right of the child to education and with a view to achieving this...make primary education compulsory and available free to all..." (Article 28). The convention also mandates that the education of the child shall be directed to: "the development of the child's personality, talents and mental and physical abilities to their fullest potential..." (Article 29).

The right to education has therefore long been recognised by these international treaties as encompassing not only access to educational provision, but also the obligation to eliminate discrimination at all levels of the educational system, to set minimum standards and to improve quality. With respect to applicability of these treaties in India, it is worthwhile to mention that India is a State party to the ICESCR, the CERD Convention, the CEDAW Convention and the Convention on the Rights of the Child.

The right to education has been affirmed in the five key global human rights treaties, presented in Table 7.1, with the number of ratifying states as of December 2003. The Table shows that all states in the world are party to at least one of these. The treaties define different facets of the right to education, as a civil and political, economic, social and cultural right, as well as outlining the right of each child. The large number of states that are party to these treaties demonstrates their global acceptance. The Convention on the Rights of the Child (CRC), for example, has attracted near universal approval with 192 parties, the sole exceptions being the United States of America and Somalia. A smaller number, although still two-thirds of the world, is bound by the International Covenant on Economic, Social and Cultural Rights. Information on the extent to which different states uphold their legal commitments under these treaties is available in the form of government reports, with all five treaties obliging their parties to submit periodic accounts of the practical measures taken to protect human rights, including the right to education.

As the following Table 7.1 shows, not all states have ratified all these treaties, and even when a treaty has been ratified, it is sometimes accompanied by reservations which limit its application in individual countries. Moreover, international treaties are not directly applied in many countries but rather are transformed into domestic legislation, from which national education strategies, routinely developed separately, often differ substantively.

Table 7.1 : Principal Human Rights Treaties and the Number of States Parties

Treaty	*Acronym*	*Adoption*	*Entry into force*	*Number of States Parties*
International Covenant on Civil and Political Rights	ICCPR	1966	1976	151
International Covenant on Economic, Social and Cultural Rights	ICESCR	1966	1976	148
International Convention on the Elimination of Forms of Racial Discrimination	AICERD	1965	1969	169
Convention on the Elimination of All Forms of Discrimination against Women	CEDAW	1979	1981	174
Convention on the Rights of the Child	CRC	1989	1990	192

Source: Tomasevski, K. (2004): *Manual on Rights-Based Education*, p. 6.

To ground an education system on internationally accepted principles of human rights, a unified strategy is needed which spans the entire education sector, as well as exploiting cross-sectoral linkages. The advantages of a rights-based education are far-reaching: through integrated, all-encompassing strategies education becomes associated with all other human rights and fundamental freedoms, such as the right to work, which plays an important role in poverty eradication, the right to marry and raise a family, which has an impact on demographic changes, and the right to political participation, which highlights the importance of education for building all-inclusive societies. Each state party to any of the five key human rights outlined in Table 7.1 is required to submit periodic reports detailing implementation status. These progress reports by individual governments are self-assessments on how well they are meeting their obligations to international human rights in education. The five parallel reporting processes have generated an immense amount of documentation, one of the advantages of which is that there is now a wealth of readily available information on global efforts to turn rights-based education into a reality.

Chapter – 8

Historical Landmarks in the History of RTE in India

Year	***Landmarks in the History of Right to Education in India, 1813-2009***
1813	**The Charter Act of 1813:** The Clause 43 in the East India Act of 1813 empowering the Governor General of India to spend one lakh of rupees each year for the purpose of education was the first legislative admission of the right of education to participate in the public revenues of India.
1838	**William Adam's Third Report in 1838:** "The next form in which Government influence may be conceived to be employed **for the promotion of education is by making it compulsory and enacting that every village should have a school**".
1852	**The Proposal of Captain Wingate, the Revenue Survey Commissioner in Bombay, 1852:** When he was called upon by Government of Bombay to give his views on a proposal to levy a local fund on land revenue, he recommended the levy of such cess and suggested that a part of it should be devoted to providing compulsory education to the sons of agriculturists.
1858	**Recommendation by Mr T.C. Hope in 1858:** In 1858, Mr T. C. Hope, the Educational Inspector of Gujarat proposed that a law should be passed empowering the inhabitants of any local area to tax themselves for the establishment of schools.
1882	**Indian Education Commission (Hunter Commission, 1882):** With the enforcement of compulsory education Act in England in 1870, an emphatic demand for laws to be made to make primary education compulsory was made by **Dadabhai Naoroji and**

	Jyotiba Phule from Bombay Presidency in their evidence before the Indian Education Commission 1882 which accepted the logic and stated that "while every branch of education can justly claim the fostering care of the state, it is desirable, in the present circumstances to declare the elementary, education of the masses, its provision, extension and improvement, to be that part of the educational system to which the strenuous efforts of the State should now be directed."
1884	**In 1884, Shri Shastri, the Deputy Educational Inspector of Broach**, also suggested the introduction of compulsory primary education in his Annual Administrative Report.
	Dadabhai Naoroji in his evidence before the Hunter Commission put forward the demand that four years of compulsory education should be provided to all children.
	Jotirao Phule also pointed out "Government collect a special cess for educational purpose, and it is to be regretted that this fund is not spent for the purposes for which it is collected...I think primary education of the masses should be made compulsory up to a certain age, say at least 12 years".
1885	**Establishment of Indian National Congress in 1885:** The establishment of Indian National Congress in 1885 further strengthened the movement for the introduction of compulsory education. In the Calcutta Congress of 1906, it was declared that it is birth right of the people of India to get proper education. The Resolution on National Education adopted by the 22nd Indian National Congress in 1906, held at Calcutta, 26th, 27th, 28th and 29th December of 1906 pointed out that government should take immediate steps for making primary education free and gradually compulsory all over the country (Resolution XI on National Education, pp. iii).
1893	**Attempt of Sir Sahaji Rao Gaikwad of Baroda:** Indian notable Prince Sir Sahaji Rao Gaikwad of Baroda began his first experiment on the matter of introducing compulsory and free education for boys in ten villages at the Amreli Taluka of his State in 1893. After watching the experiment for eight years, it was extended to the whole Taluka in 1901, and finally, in 1906, primary education was made compulsory and free throughout the State for boys between the ages of 6 and 12, and for girls between the ages of 6 and 10.
1906	**Attempt of Sir Ibrahim Rahimtoola and Sir Chamanlal Setalwad:** The first organised attempt to introduce compulsory

	primary education in British India was made in Bombay under Sir Ibrahim Rahimtoola and Sir Chamanlal Setalwad. As a result of their agitation, the Government of Bombay appointed a Committee in 1906 to examine the feasibility of introducing compulsory education in the city of Bombay. But unfortunately this committee came to the conclusion that the time was not ripe for the introduction of compulsory education.
1910	**Attempts of Gopal Krishna Gokhale (1910-1911):** Gopal Krishna Gokhale became a non-official member of the British Imperial Legislative Council in 1902. Gokhale in the 18 March 1910 he moved a resolution for the introduction of compulsory education in the Imperial Legislative Council in the words "a beginning be made in the direction of making elementary education free and compulsory throughout the country". The resolution was overdrawn on an assurance from the Government that the whole problem would be fully investigated.
	A year later, on 16 March 1911, the Hon'ble Mr Gokhale introduced in the same Council a private Bill "to make better provision for the extension of elementary education in India". The main objective of the Bill was to make primary education free and compulsory in a phased manner.
	At last, Gokhale's Bill of 1911 was referred to a Select Committee. The Bill was taken up for discussion in legislative council on March 17 & 18, 1912. However, the government was not ready to accept the Bill and consequently, it was put to vote and was defeated by 35 votes to 13.
1913	**Resolution on Education Policy, 1913:** The Indian Educational Policy, 1913 stated: "For financial and administrative reasons of decisive weight the Government of India has refused to recognise the principle of compulsory education; but they desire the widest possible extension of primary education on a voluntary basis, regards free elementary education the time has not yet arrived...(pp. 9-10)".
1917	**Attempt of Vithalbhai Patel:** Late Sri Vithalbhai Patel introduced in 1917 a Bill in the Bombay Legislative Council for permitting Municipalities to introduce compulsion in Municipal areas of the Province of Bombay. This Bill received the ascent of the Governor-General on the 5th February, 1918, and the Bombay Primary Education (District Municipalities) Act of 1918 came into effect. This is popularly known as the Patel Act, after its mover. This first Law on Compulsory Primary Education in British India passed by the Bombay Legislative Council.

1918	Since 1918, all the State legislatures began passing in Acts for introducing Compulsory Primary Education in their respective States. Thanks to **Montague-Chelmford Reforms**, the Education portfolio was placed in the hands of an Indian Minister responsible to a legislature with large elected majority.
1919	After the passing of **Government of India Act, 1919**, the control of elementary education was transferred to Indian ministers. The decade 1917 to 1927 in the history of compulsory education in British India may rightly be regarded as the boom-period of compulsion.
1929	**Hartog Committee's Recommendation** for better quality (not quantity) hinders spread and development of primary education.
1937	**Provincial Autonomy in 1937:** The introduction of Provincial Autonomy in 1937 through the Government of India Act, 1935, gave more powers to Indian Ministers to act independently. With the introduction of Provincial Autonomy, the Indian National Congress assumed the office in seven provinces out of eleven. The education ministers under Provincial Autonomy could command far larger resources than the ministers under Dyarchy ever did.
1937	**Wardha Scheme of Basic Education, 1937:** In the light of the resolutions passed at the National Conference on Education in October 1937 in Wardha, Zakir Hussain Committee, 1938 formulated a detailed national scheme for basic education. The scheme had one of the cardinal provisions that first seven years of schooling would be an integral part of a free and compulsory nationwide education system (through mother tongue). This scheme was adopted in several provinces where the Congress was in power. There was not much development of this idea, because of the start of the Second World War and the resignation of the Congress ministries (October 1939).
1944	**The Sargent Plan, 1944:** The Post-War Plan of Educational Development in India (1944) popularly known as the Sargent Plan, recommen-ded the provision of free and compulsory education to all children in the age group of 6 - 14 years in a phased manner spread over a period of 40 years.
1947	**Constituent Assembly Sub-committee on Fundamental Rights places free and compulsory education on list of Fundamental Rights:** "Clause 23 – Every citizen is entitled as of right to free primary education and it shall be the duty of the State to provide within a period of ten years from the commencement of this

	Constitution for free and compulsory education for all children until they complete the age of fourteen years".
1947 April	Advisory Committee of the Constituent Assembly rejects free and compulsory education as a fundamental right. Sends clause to list of "non-justifiable fundamental rights" (later termed as 'Directive Principles of State Policy').
1948	**Report of the B. G. Kher Committee, 1948:** The proposal of the Sargent Plan was examined by the Committee on the Ways and Means of Financing Education Development in India under the Chairmanship of B.G. Kher, the then Chief Minister of Bombay in 1948 and the committee accepted programme of universal, compulsory and free basic education as proposed in the Plan itself but reduced the time span from 40 (1944-84) to 16 years (1944-60). It was this recommendation that formed the basis of Article 45 of the Directive Principles of the Indian Constitution.
1948-49	**The University Education Commission (1948-1949):** "In a democratic society the opportunity of learning must be open not only to elite but to all those who have to carry the privilege and responsibility of citizenship. Education is a universal right, not a class privilege" (The Report of the University Education Commission (1948-1949, Volume -1, p. 43).
1950	On 26th January, when India was declared a Republic, the Article 45 of Directive Principles of State Policy was finally accepted: The state shall endeavour to provide within a period of ten years from the commencement of the constitutions, for Free and Compulsory Education for all children until they complete the age of fourteen years".
1957	**All-India Council of Elementary Education (AICEE), 1957:** In order to accelerate the pace of expansion of elementary education and to fulfill the directive of Article 45 of the Constitution, the Government of India established the All-India Council of Elementary Education (AICEE) with effect from July 1, 1957 to serve as an advisory body to the Union and State Governments and Local Bodies on matters relating to elementary education.
1960	**Delhi Primary Education Act, 1960:** In 1960 Dr K. L. Shrimali, the Union Minister of Education, moved the Delhi Primary Education Bill in the Parliament. Its primary objective was to provide a compulsory education law for the Delhi Union Territory. The bill became law on the 2nd October 1960. The State Governments had also initiated action to amend their compulsory

	education laws on the model of the Delhi Primary Education Act, 1960.
1964	**The Kothari Commission (1964-66) recommended that -** Common School System of public education based on neighbourhood schools to fulfill the insistent demand for free and universal education of the people. While the Constitutional Directive may be fulfilled in some places such as urban areas or advanced States as early as in 1975-76, all the areas in the country should be able to provide five years of education.
1964	**The 31st CABE Meeting, at Bangalore on October 11 & 12, 1964, under the Chairmanship of Shri M. C. Chagla:** Shri M.C. Chagla, then Union Education Minister and Chairman, CABE spoke about the failure of the intention of UEE as envisaged in the Article 45 and suggested few measures at the Presidential Address.
1968	**National Policy on Education (NPE), 1968:** The National Policy on Education (NPE), 1968 was the first official document evidencing the Indian Government's commitment towards school education. The Policy had to state "strenuous efforts should be made for the early fulfillment of the Directive Principle under Article 45 of the Constitution seeking to provide free and compulsory education for all children up to the age of 14. A suitable programme should be developed to reduce the prevailing wastage and stagnation in schools and to ensure that every child who is enrolled in schools successfully completes the prescribed course" {para 4 (1)}.
1974	**National Policy for Children, 1974:** Keeping in view the goals set out the U.N. Declaration of the Rights of the Child, 1959, the Government of India adopted the Resolution on the National Policy for Children on 22nd August, 1974. The policy adopted: "The State shall take steps to provide free and compulsory education for all children up to the age of 14 for which a time-bound programme will be drawn up consistent with the availability of resources".
1976	**Shifting Education from State List to Concurrent List, 1976:** Under the Constitution of India, initially, education was a State subject, that is, it was the exclusive responsibility of the States. With the 42nd Amendment in the Constitution which received President's assent on December 18, 1976 education was moved from the 'state' list to the 'concurrent' list. It created an avenue for the Centre's intervention in the field of elementary education.

1978	**Education for Our People, 1978:** A document entitled 'Education for Our People' relating to a policy frame of educational reform was passed by the Trustees of the J.P. Institute of Human Rights in a meeting held in Bombay on 21st June 1977 under the chairmanship of Jayaprakash Narayan. It was there decided that a framework for educational reform should be prepared under the auspices of the Citizens For Democracy and headed by Dr J.P. Naik, Member-Secretary of the Indian Council of Social Science Research. This document was published in 1978. This document suggested that Elementary education (age-group 6-14) should be made universal in an intensive and sustained programme spread over to 5-10 years.
1979	**Draft National Policy on Education, 1979:** Formulated during the Janata Dal Government at the Centre, the Draft National Policy on Education also laid down that - "Highest priority must be given to free education for all up to the age of 14 as laid down in the Directive Principles of the Constitution...While it is necessary to expand the facilities for formal education in elementary schools for all children in the age group 6-14, it is also important to formulate schemes of non-formal education for dropouts and the older children in the age group who have not had any schooling". With the fall of Janata Dal in 1979, the Draft National Policy on Education lost its significance.
1982	**Inclusion of Education in the Revised 20-Point Programme, 1982:** In the eighties, a special activity named as the 20-Point Programme was initiated in 1975 by the then Prime Minister Smt. Indira Gandhi with an objective of improving the socio-economic conditions of the weaker sections in the Country. The Revised 20-Point Programme was announced on the 14th January, 1982. Among the 20 Points, the Point No. 16 of this programme devoted to Education. Under Point No. 16 on education the following programme was envisaged: [Elementary Education] By 1990 all the 16.3 crore children estimated in the age group will have to be enrolled in elementary schools, either in the formal or non-formal system of education. In the next 10 years, six crore additional children will have to be brought to schools.
1985	**Challenge of Education - A Policy Perspective, 1985:** This document stated that in spite of a specific provision in the Constitution to endeavour to provide free and compulsory education up to the age of 14 by 1960, and several explicit commitments with regard to the achievement of Universal Elementary Education, progress in this sector is far short of the target. In fact, the target itself has been moving farther and farther

	to accommodate the failures' arising from inadequacy of resources or sheer lack of a viable strategy (Para 3.6). However, it mentioned no word for enforcing free and compulsory education for Indian children.
1986	**National Policy on Education, 1986:** This policy document resolved that "It shall be ensured that all children who attain the age of about 11 years by 1990 will have had five years of schooling, or its equivalent through the non-formal stream. Likewise, by 1995 all children will be provided free and compulsory up to 14 years of age" (NPE, 1986:5.12).
1991	**Report of the Ramamurti Committee, 1990:** Among official documents, the Report entitled 'Towards an Enlightened and Humane Society –NPE 1986-A Review" called for recognition of the right to education as a fundamental right: "Now, time has come to recognise 'Right to Education' as one of the fundamental rights of the Indian citizen for which necessary amendments to the Constitution may have to be made and more importantly, conditions be created in society such that right would become available for children of India" (Para 6.1.3). However, this recommendation was not implemented immediately.
1991	**Publication of Myron Weiner's Study in a Book, 1991:** Myron Weiner's book entitled "*The Child and the State in India; Child Labour and Education Policy in Comparative Perspective*" created a move among the Indians. The cardinal proposition of his study is that India's low per capita income and economic situation is less relevant as an explanation for the failure to eradicate child labour and enforce compulsory education than the belief systems of the state bureaucracy, a set of beliefs that are widely shared by all.
1992	**National Policy on Education 1986 (as modified in 1992):** The National Policy on Education 1986 (as modified in 1992) did envisage the alternative modality of non-formal education also for achieving universal elementary education. The National Policy of Education, 1986 had aimed to achieve universal elementary education by 1995, the time frame for which was extended by another five years in its 1992 version as mentioned below: "It shall be ensured that free and compulsory education of satisfactory quality is provided to all children up to 14 years of age before we enter the twenty-first century. A national mission will be launched for the achievement of this goal" [NPE 1986 (as modified in 1992), Para 12.5].

1992	**Ratification of the UN Convention on Rights of the Child, 1992:** The General Assembly of the United Nations, on the 20th November, 1989 unanimously adopted the UNCRC. It entered into force 2nd September 1990 having been ratified by the required 20 States. This convention mandated – "States Parties recognise the right of the child to education and with a view to achieving this right progressively and on the basis of equal opportunity, they shall, in particular: (a) Make primary education compulsory and available free to all…" (UNCRC, 1989, Article 28). By ratifying the UNCRC on 2nd December, 1992, the Government of India once again re-affirmed its commitment to children.
1992	**The 73th and 74th Constitutional Amendment Acts, 1992**: The 73rd and 74th Constitutional Amendment Acts enacted in 1992 established the three-tier Panchayati Raj system in the country. Amongst the 29 subjects identified by the 73rd amendment Act for transfer to the Panchayats was education - primary and secondary, adult and non-formal, vocational and technical. The 73rd and 74th Amendments to the Constitution placed a greater role on local bodies for the development of education, among others.
1992	**Mohini Jain versus State of Karnataka Case, 1992:** While deciding the Mohini Jain versus State of Karnataka Case (1992 3 SCC 666), the Supreme Court of India stated that "the 'right to education' is concomitant to fundamental rights enshrined under Part III of the Constitution". And that "every citizen has a right to education under the Constitution".
1993	**Unnikrishnan versus State of Andhra Pradesh Case, 1993:** Justice Jeevan Reddy while delivering the judgement in the Case of Unnikrishnan, J. P. versus State of Andhra Pradesh (1993 1 SCC 645) entirely changed the status of the Article 45. The Supreme Court judgement said that Article 45 of the Part IV should be read in harmonious construction with Article 21 of Part III (Right to Life) since without education 'Right to Life is Meaningless'. It was also stated in the judgement that "The citizens of this country have a fundamental right to education. The said right flows from Article 21.
1996	**Conference of State Education Ministers and State Education Secretaries, on August 9-10, 1996:** The Conference of State Education Ministers and State Education Secretaries, held on August 9-10, 1996 recognised the momentous significance of the proposed Constitutional Amendment and urged the Government to consider the financial, administrative, legal and academic

	implications of the proposal. Accordingly, the MHRD constituted a Committee of State Education Ministers under the chairmanship of Muhi Ram Saikia, Union Minister of State for HRD (Education).
1997	**Report of the Saikia Committee, (January, 1997):** The Committee of State Education Ministers under the Chairmanship of Shri Muhi Ram Saikia recommended that – "The Constitution of India should be, amended to make the right to free elementary education up to 14 years of age a fundamental right." The Committee also recommended the amendment of existing State legislation on compulsory education.
1997 July	**Constitution (83rd Amendment) Bill, (July, 1997):** In 1997, the United Front Government introduced Constitution (83rd) Amendment Bill, 1997. In 1997 (July), the Constitution (83rd Amendment) Bill, 1997 was tabled in Lok Sabha by the S. R. Bommai, then HRD minister. The Bill proposed to add Article 21 A – "The State shall provide free and compulsory education to all citizens of the age six to fourteen years".
1997 Nov.	**Constitution (83rd Amendment) Bill, (November, 1997):** Subsequently, the 83rd Amendment Bill was referred to the Parliamentary Standing Committee on HRD. In 1997 (24th November) Committee submitted report to both houses of Parliament, and recommended that the Bill be passed subject to changes recommended by it. The major recommendations of the committee: (1) Retention of Article 45 to cater to the 0-6 age group. (2) Clause (3) of the proposed Article 21-A relating to private institutions may be deleted. (3) The Central Government should prepare one simple legislation with some skeletal framework which may also indicate the Central share in the financial burden. The details can be formulated by the respective States according to their requirements. The Central Government may therefore consider working out the necessary legislation (Para 15.16).
1998	**The 165th Report on Free and Compulsory Education for Children by Law Commission of India, (November, 1998):** In 1998 the Law Commission also prepared a detailed Report on free and compulsory education for all children together with a draft Bill for a central legislation. "If a Central Legislation is enacted as is being proposed by the Commission, it would not require ratification by the State Legislatures, being a subject falling

	under Entry 25 of Concurrent List of Seventh Schedule to the Constitution of India."
1999	**The Report of the Tapas Majumdar Committee, 1999:** The expert group consisting of 18 Members including Professor Tapas Majumder submitted its report entitled "Expert Group on Financial Requirements for Making Elementary Education: A Fundamental Right" in 1999. The Committee estimated that an additional investment of Rs 1,37,000 crores would have to be made over a 10-year period to bring all out-of-school children into the school system (not parallel streams) and enable them to complete the elementary stage.
2000	**Dakar Declaration, 2000:** The progress towards these goals was reviewed in Dakar in 2000 (10 years after Jomtien) and the Dakar Meet came out with revised targets for the countries where the goals of EFA could not be achieved. The participating countries made the commitment to achieve the following goal by 2015: 2). Free and compulsory primary education by 2015.
2000	**Ambani and Birla Committee Report, April 2000:** Mukesh Ambani (Convenor) and Kumarmangalam Birla (Member) submitted the report entitled 'Report on a Policy Framework for Reforms in Education' to Prime Minister's Council on Trade and Industry, Government of India in 2000 (April). The report also recommended that "There is no getting away from enforcing the Constitutional commitment to compulsory education till the age of fourteen years, provided by Article 45 and reinforced by a historical Supreme Court judgement declaring education as a fundamental right".
2000	**Millennium Development Goals (MDGs), September 2000:** At the September 2000 Millennium Summit devised a set of eight Millennium Development Goals (MDGs). In line with the Jomtien-Dakar Framework, one of the eight goals directly relating to education reiterates the agenda of "achiev[ing] universal primary education."
2001	**Sarva Siksha Abhiyan (SSA), 2001:** The Scheme of Sarva Shiksha Abhiyan (SSA) evolved from the recommendations of the State Education Ministers' Conference held in October 1998 to pursue universal elementary education in a mission mode. A National Committee of State Education Ministers under the chairmanship of the then Hon'ble Human Resource Development Minister, Dr Murli Manohar Joshi submitted its Report in October 1999 and recommended that UEE should be pursued in a mission

mode with a holistic and convergent approach with emphasis preparation of District Elementary Education Plans for UEE. Ultimately the scheme was approved by the Union Cabinet in its meeting held on 16 November 2000 and became functional from January 2001. This scheme is framed to provide useful and relevant elementary education for all children in the age group of six to fourteen by 2010.

2001 **The 93rd Constitution Amendment Bill, 2001:** Based on the recommendation of the Parliamentary Standing Committee on HRD, advice of the Ministry of Law and suggestions of the Law Commission of India, the MHRD formulated the revised Constitution Amendment Bill. The Constitution (83rd Amendment) Bill, 1997 was amended, and reintroduced as Constitution (93rd) Amendment Bill 2001 in the Parliament with the following provisions:

1. Insertion of a new Article 21A.
2. Substitution of existing Article 45 of the Constitution.
3. Insertion of the following new clause in Article 51 (A) of the Constitution relating to Fundamental duties of the Citizens—(k)

The Constitution (93rd Amendment) Bill, 2001 was discussed and passed by unanimous vote in the Lok Shaba on 27th November, 2001 and by the Rajya Sabha on 14th May, 2002.

2002 **Report of the National Commission to Review the Working of the Constitution, 31st March 2002:** The National Commission to Review the Working of the Constitution was set up by the Government of India on 22 February, 2000 and recommended that the Right to Free and Compulsory Education should also be extended to the children up to the age of fourteen years and that the right to education beyond the age of 14 years may depend upon the economic capacity and the stage of development of the State (Para 3.20.1).

2002 **The Constitution (86th Amendment) Act, 2002:** The Constitution (93rd Amendment) Bill, 2001 was passed as the Constitution (86th Amendment) Act, 2002 on December 12, 2002 after receiving the assent of the President of India. This amendment -

(1) makes education a "Fundamental Right" for those between the ages of six and fourteen and

(2) Deletes the existing Article 45 and added new Articles.

	The Constitution (86th Amendment) Act, 2002 was notified on 13th December, 2002 in the Gazette of India.
2002	**RTE in the Part III ["Fundamental Rights"], 2002:** "21A. Right to Education - The State shall provide free and compulsory education to all children of the age of six to fourteen years in such manner as the State may, by law, determine."
2003	**The Free and Compulsory Education for Children Bill, 2003:** A first draft of the legislation envisaged in the Article 21A under the title of "Free and Compulsory Education for Children Bill, 2003" was posted in October, 2003 online by the government inviting comments and suggestions from the public at large (NDA Government).
2004	**The Free and Compulsory Education Bill, 2004:** In 2004 a revised version of this Bill, re-titled the Free and Compulsory Education for Children Bill 2004, was re-posted on the http://education.nic.in website (NDA Government).
2005	**Right to Education Bill (CABE Bill), 2005:** In 2005 (June), the Right to Education Bill, 2005 as drafted by CABE was introduced to give effect to the Constitution (86th) Amendment Act, 2002 (UPA – 1 Government) and HRD sent it to NAC where Mrs Sonia Gandhi is the Chairperson. NAC sent the Bill to PM for his observation.
2005	In November 2005, Dr Manmohan Singh, the then PM appointed the High Level Group (HLG), comprising Minister of HRD, Finance Minister, Deputy Chairman, Planning Commission, and Chairman, PM's Advisory Council on Economic Affairs, to consider the constitutional, legal and financial implications of the Right to Education. HLG rejected the Bill citing the lack of funds and a Model bill was sent to States for making necessary arrangements.
2006	In 2006, Central legislation discarded. States were advised to make their own Bills based on the model Right to Education Bill, 2006 (UPA-I Government). Accordingly the model Right to Education Bill, 2006 was circulated to States in June 2006. Total 23 States responded to the Model Bill.
2008	**The Right of Children to Free and Compulsory Education Bill, 2008:** Central legislation revived. Then Prime Minister, Dr Manmohan Singh took a meeting on 14th February 2008 in which a decision was taken to proceed with the drafting of a Central Legislation on Right to Education, and to introduce it in the Parliament. The Bill was subsequently placed before the

	Union Cabinet on 30th October 2008 which approved the Bill for introduction in the Parliament.
2008	The Right of Children to Free and Compulsory Education Bill, 2008 was introduced in the Rajya Sabha on 15th December, 2008.
2009	213th Report of the Department – Related Parliamentary Standing Committee on HRD on the Right of Children to Free and Compulsory Education Bill, 2008 was presented to both Houses of Parliament on 18th February, 2009 under the Chairmanship of Shri Janardhan Dwivedi, M.P., Rajya Sabha.
2009	The Right of Children to Free and Compulsory Education Bill, 2008 was passed in the Rajya Sabha on 20th July, 2009 and in the Lok Sabha on 4th August, 2009.
2009	On 26th August the Right of Children to Free and Compulsory Education Bill, 2008 received the President's assent.
2009	On receiving the assent of the President on the 26th August, 2009 the Act was published in the Gazette of India on the 27th August, 2009 for general information.
2010	The Central Government hereby appointed 1st April, 2010 as the date from which the RTE Act, 2009 came into force by notification in the Official Gazette of India on the 19th February, 2010 envisaged in the above Article 21A.

Bibliography

Journals

- Acharya, P. (1994). Problems of Universal Elementary Education. *Economic and Political Weekly.* 29(49): 3098-3105.
- B. G. Tilak, Jandhyala (6 July 2010). RTE Act 2009 — illusory promises. Retrieved from http://educationworldonline.net/index.php/page-article-choice-more-id-2288
- Bharambe, V.S. and Sharma, S.D.(2013). Education for All: Issues, Challenges and Opportunities. *Educationia Confab*, 2(4), 214-116.
- Bordoloi, R. (2011). Challenges in Elementary Education in India: Various Approaches. *Journal of Education and Practice*, 2(7), 39-45.
- Chaudhary, L. (2009). Determinants of Primary Schooling in British India. *Journal of Economic History*, 69(1), 269-302.
- Chowdhury, R. (2010). "The Road Less Travelled": Article 21a and the Fundamental Right to Primary Education in India, *INJlConLaw 2; (2010) 4 Indian Journal of Constitutional Law 24,* pp. 24-46. Retrieved fromhttp://www.commonlii.org/in/journals/INJlConLaw/2010/2.html.
- Desai, F. P. (2010). Tagore's Educational Experiments and Right to Education Bill: A Comparison, *Rupkatha Journal on Interdisciplinary Studies in Humanities*, 2(2): 628-640.
- Devan, K. (2011). Development of the Right to Education in India. *Indian Journal of Adult Education*, 72(2), 93-98.
- Dinda, M. (2010). Literacy: Is It A Human Right? *Anwesa*, Vol. 5, 120-127.
- Gandhi, V. and Yadav, N. (2013). A Study of Awareness among Primary School Teacher's Towards "Right to Education Act, 2009", *Shodh, Samiksha Aur Mulyankan*, IV(48):48-49.
- Garg, P.K. (2013). Fundamental Right of Children to Free and Compulsory Education – Its Implementation and Future Strategies. *International Journal of Basic and Advanced Science,* 2(1), 4-7.

- Ghosh, J. (2011). Public Spending on Education in India, *Frontline* 28(24), 10-12.
- Godbole, M. (2001). Elementary Education as a Fundamental Right – The Issues. *Economic and Political Weekly*, XXXVI(50).
- Gosai, M.R. (2009). The Recent Right to Education and Present State of Primary Education. *University News*, 47(47), 1-6.
- Islam, N. and Chakraborty (2013). A Study on the Awareness of Equitable Quality in the Light of RTE Act' 09 among In-Service School Teachers, *Indian Journal of Applied Research*, 3(6):142-143.
- Jain, P.S. and Dholakia, R.H. (2009). Feasibility of Implementation of Right to Education Act. *Economic and Political Weekly,* XLIV (25), 38-43.
- Jain, P.S. and Dholakia, R.H. (2010). Right to Education Act and Public-Private Partnership. *Economic and Political Weekly,* XLV (8), 78-80.
- Jakhar, J. S. (2010). Right to Education Act, 2009: Salient Features of Major Problems of Implementation. *University News*, 48(47), 06-12.
- Jha, P. and Parvati, P. (2010). Right to Education Act 2009: Critical Gaps and Challenges, *Economic and Political Weekly,* XLV (13), 20-23.
- Juneja, N. (1997). Right of the child to Education and Issues in Implementation of Compulsory Education: Perceptions of Educational Administrators. *New Frontiers in Education*, 27(1), 1-12.
- Kamalakar, G. and Bhojanna, N. (2012). Reservation in Private Schools under the Right to Education Act: Model for Implementation. *International Journal of Management Research and Review,* 2(6), 958-966.
- Kamath, A.K.V.D. (2013). Awareness on Right to Education Act – 2009 among Elementary School Teachers. *Indian Journal of Education Experimentation and Innovation,* 3(5).
- Karande, K. and Gogtay, N. J.(2010). Specific Learning Disability and the Right to Education 2009 Act: Call for Action. *J Postgrad Med*, 56(3), 171-172.
- Kaur, B. (2013). The Right to Children to Free and Compulsory Education Act. *Educationia Confab*, 2(4), 177-181.
- Kaur, R. (2013). Universalisation of Elementary Education in India: The Policy Perspective. *Educationia Confab*, 2(4), 205-213.
- Kothari, V.N. 2004. Challenges of Universalisation of elementary education in India. *Journal of Education Planning and Administration* XVIII (3) 363-378.

- Kumar, J. (2012). Right to Education: Its Problems and Suggestions. *Educationia Confab*, 1(2), 14-19.
- Kumar, N. (2007). British rule and problems of the present education system. *Ghadar Jari Hari.* 1(2): 30-32.
- Kumar, R. Ravi (2012). Primary Educational System in Rural India. A Sociological View. *Indian Journal of Innovations and Developments*, 1(10), 430-432.
- Kurhade, M.S. (2011). Education for All: But When? *University News*, 49(04), 6-8.
- Meenakshi, C. (2012). Universalisation of Education: A Challenging Issue. *Research Journal of Social and Life Science*, 12 – 1 (Year 06), 236-243.
- Mehrotra, S. 2006. Reforming Elementary Education in India. A Menu of options. *International Journal of Educational Development* 26(3).
- Mohanty, T. (2011). Constitutional Provisions and Amendments on Fundamental Duties, Right to Education Act and on Secularism. *Orissa Review*, LXVII (6), 39-41.
- Mondal, A. and Mete, J. (2011). Common School System in the light of Right to Education Act, 2009. *Edusearch*, 2(2), 45-55.
- Mondal, A. and Mete, J. (2011). Education for Minorities and SC / ST in the Context of SSA. *Educational Herald*, 14(14), 14-22.
- Mondal, A. and Mete, J. (2012). Right to Education – An Appraisal. *Kurukshetra*. 60(11). 11-14.
- Nawani, D. (2013). Corporal Punishment in Schools. *Economic and Political Weekly,* XLVII (24), 23-26.
- Nehru, A. and Raghupathi, H. (2008). Massive Funding of Right to Education Bill, *Education World,* October, pp. 76-79.
- Paur, S.S. (2012). Right to Education Act: A Critical Analysis. *International Journal of Educational and Psychological Research*, 1(2), 27-30.
- Ramachandran, V. (2009). Right to Education Act: A Comment. *Economic and Political Weekly,* XLIV (28), 155-157.
- Rana, K.M. (2013). Education for All – Challenges and Opportunities. *Educationia Confab*, 2(4), 241-247.
- Rani, N. (2012). Mid-Day Meals Scheme: Achieving Right to Education and Right to Food Simultaneously. *e – Reflection,* I(III),122-130.
- Rathee, Indu and Rana, S.S. (2012). Education as Human Right: Provisions and Implementation. *Journal of Educational and Psychological Research*, 2(2), 124-129.

- S Ojha, Seema (2013). Implementing Right to Education: Issues and Challenges. *Research Journal Educational Sciences*, 1(2), 1-7.
- Sadgopal, A. (2003). Education for too few. *Frontline*, Vol. 20, Issue 24, November 22 - December 05.
- Sadgopal, A. (2010). Right to Education vs. Right to Education Act. *Social Scientist*, Vol. 38, No. 9-12 September–December 2010, pp. 17-50.
- Sadgopal, A. (2011). Neoliberal Act. *Frontline*, 28(14), 04-09.
- Sarkar, B. (2011). Education – A Basic Human Right: An Analysis in Indian Perspective. *Indian Journal of Human Rights Studies*, 1 (Jan. – Feb. 2011):1-10.
- Savagaon, G. (2012). Elementary Education and Inclusive Development in India. *Abhinav*, 1 (6), 16-23.
- Sharma, H. I. (2013). Universalisation of Elementary Education under Sarva Shiksha Abhiyan in Manipur. *Voice of Research*. L (4): 14-17.
- Sharma, M. K. and Jain, J.L. (2013). Qualitative Education for All: Challenges and Strategies. *Educationia Confab*, 2(4), 187-195.
- Sharma, R. and Saini, R. (2012). Implementation of RTE Act, 2009 in Rural India. *Research Analysis and Evaluation*, III (29), 60-62.
- Sharma, S. and Kumawat, S. R.(2013). Inclusive Education in Right To Education Act 2009. *Research Analysis and Evaluation*, IV (42), 103-104.
- Shukla, P.D. 2000. Non Enforcement of Compulsion in Education in India. *Journal of Indian Education* XXVI (1).
- Siddiqui, S. (2008). Universalisation of Elementary Education in India. *Journal of Educational Research*. 11(1): 4-12.
- Singh, J. (2012). Right to Education: An Assessment. *Indian Streams Research Journal*. 1(XIII), 60-62.
- Singh, R. (2012). Development of Right to Education in India: A Historical Appraisal. *University News*, 50 (30), 16-25.
- Singh, V. P. (2013). The Right of Children to Free and Compulsory Education Act, 2009: An Exploratory Study. *Journal of Indian Research*, 1(1), 118-135.
- Sonia (2012). The Right to Education Act: An Overview. *Indian Stream Research Journal*, 2(11), 1-6.
- Sunita, M. (2010). Teachers Literacy towards the Child Rights. *Edusearch- Journal of Educational Research*: 1(2).

- Tarafdar, M. (2007). Universalisation of Education: A Study in the Indian Context. *Our Education – Journal of Educational Ideas and Research*, Volume-8, pp. 61-62.
- Teltumbde, A. (2012). A Symbolic Gesture, *Economic and Political Weekly*, XLVII (19).
- Thote, P., Mathew, L. and S. Rathoure, D.P. (2013). Right to Education Act: An Analysis of Teachers Awareness in Central India. *International Journal of Advanced Research*, I (3), 184-187.
- Tilak, Jandhyala B. G. (2012). Right to Homeschooling vs Right to Education. *Economic and Political Weekly*, XLVII (41).
- Uma (2013). Right to Education (RTE): A Critical Appraisal. *IOSR Journal of Humanities and Social Science,* 6(4), 55-60.
- Usmani, M. (2012). Right To Education Act 2009: A Dream in the Sunlight or A Divine. *International Journal of Research in Social Sciences and Humanities*, 1(VI), 1-11.
- Vithalrao, M. S. (2011). Child Rights as a Part of Human Rights – A Comparative Study. *International Education E-Journal (Quarterly)*.1(1):13-17.
- Yadav, Raj Kumar (2012). Right To Education in India: A Study. Accessed from http:// ssrn.com/abstract = 2014933 on 12.06.2013.

Books

- Aggarwal, D. D. (2002). *History and Development of Elementary Education in India*. New Delhi: Sarup & Sons.
- Aggarwal, J. C. (2008). *Development and Planning of Modern Education*. New Delhi: Vikas Publishing House Pvt. Ltd.
- Aggarwl, J. C. and Gupta, S. (2010). *Right to Education and Revitalizing Education.* New Delhi: Shipra Publication.
- Aradhya, N. and Kashyap, A. (2006). *The 'Fundamentals' – Right to Education in India*. Bangalore: Books for Change.
- B. C. Rai (1997). *History of Education in India and Problems.* Lucknow: Prakashan Kendra.
- Babu, J. R. (2009). *Universalisation of Elementary Education: A Study of District Primary Education Programme from South India*. UK: Cambridge Scholars Publishing.
- Baneerjee, J.P. (1985). *Education in India – Past Present, Future*, Kolkata: Central Library.
- Bapat, S. and Karandikar, S. (1998). Rural Context of Primary Education Searching for the Roots. In Saraswati, Baidyanath (1998). *The Cultural Dimension of Education.* New Delhi: Indira Gandhi National Centre for the Arts.

- Basu, A. (1982). *Essays in the History of Indian Education*. New Delhi: Concept Publishing Company.
- Basu, A.N. (1941) (Ed.). *Adam's Reports of the State of Education in Bengal and Bihar*. Calcutta: University of Calcutta Press.
- Basu, B. B. (1994). *Human Rights in Constitutional Law*. New Delhi: Prentice Hall of India Pvt. Ltd.
- Basu, B. D. (1935). History of Education in India under the Rule of the East India Company. Calcutta: The Modern Review Office.
- Basu, B.D. (1935). *History of Education in India under Rule of East India Company*. Calcutta: The Modern Review Office.
- Bhattacharya, S. (2000). *National Education Movement – Analysis of the Role of Bengali Intelligentsia and its Impact on Indian Education*. Ph. D. Thesis (Unpublished), Department of Education, University of Kalyani.
- Biswas, A. and Agarwal, S. P. (1994). *Development of Education in India – A Historical Survey of Educational Documents before and after Independence*. New Delhi: Concept Publishing Company.
- Biswas, A. and Agrwal, S.P. (1986). *Development of Education in India -A historical Survey of Educational Documents Before and After Independence*. New Delhi: Concept Publishing House.
- Chand, J. (2007). *Education in India during British Period*. New Delhi: Anshah Publishing House.
- Chatterjee, S. (2010). Inaugural Address. In Habib, S. Irfan (Ed.). *Maulana Abul Kalam Azad and the National Education System*. New Delhi: NUEPA.
- Chauhan, C.P.S. (2004). *Modern Indian Education - Policies, Progress and Problems.* New Delhi: Kanishka Publishers, Distributors.
- Deogirikar, T. R. (1992). *Gopal Krishna Gokhale*, New Delhi: Ministry of Information and Broadcasting, Government of India.
- Desai, D. M. (1993). *Universal Compulsory and Free Primary Education in India.* Bombay: Indian Institution of Education.
- Ghosh, S.C. (1989). *Education Policy in India since Warren Hastings*. Calcutta: Naya Prokash.
- Ghosh, S.C. (2013). *The History of Education in Modern India, 1757-2012*. New Delhi: Orient Black Swan Private Limited.
- Gopalan, K. (1998). Indian Strategies to Achieve Universalisation of Elementary Education. In Saraswati, Baidyanath (1998). *The Cultural Dimension of Education.* New Delhi: Indira Gandhi National Centre for the Arts.

- Grover, B.L. and Mehta, Alka (2014). *A New Look at Modern India History*. New Delhi: S. Chand Publishing.
- Gupta, S. (2009). *What are the different strategies and approaches to realize Right to Education (RTE) in India?* Institute of Development Studies (IDS), University of Sussex.
- Hayre, S.K. (1966). *The Development of Elementary Education in India*. Manhattan, Kansas: School of Education, Kanasas State University.
- Hodgson, D. (1998). *The Human Right to Education*. Aldershot: Dart-mouth Publishing Company Limited.
- Howell, Arthur (1872). *Education in British India Prior to 1854 and in 1870-71*. Calcutta: Superintendent of Government Printing.
- Jayapalan, N. (2000). *History of Education in India*. New Delhi: Atlantic Publishers and Distributors.
- Juneja, N. (2003). *Constitutional Amendment to make Education a Fundamental Right – Issues for a Follow-Up Legislation*. New Delhi: NIEPA.
- Kochhar, S. K. (1982). *Pivotal Issues in Indian Education*. New Delhi: Sterling Publishers Private Limited.
- Lall, M. (2005). *The Challenges for India's Education System*. London: Chatham House, the Royal Institute of International Affairs, Retrieved on 12.09.2013 from http://marielall.com/wp/wp-content/uploads/Chatham-house-indiaeducation.pdf
- Latika C. (2007). *An Economic History of Education in Colonial India*, Hoover Institution. April 28, 2007 Retrieved on 10.03. 2014 fromhttp://economics.ucr.edu/seminars_colloquia/2007/political_economy_development/LatikaChaudhary5-6-07.pdf
- Latika C. (2007). *Determinants of Primary Schooling in British India*, Hoover Institution, August 2, 2007. Retrieved on 23.04.2013 fromhttp://eml.berkeley.edu/~webfac/cromer/e211_f07/chaudhary.pdf
- Mayhew, Arthur (1928). *The History of India*. London. Faber and Gwyer Limited.
- Misra, B.D. (1089). *A History of the Secondary Education in Uttar Pradesh 1843-1900*. Delhi: Anamika Prakashan.
- Mohanty, S. B. (1985). *Universalisation of Elementary Education in India: Lessons of Experience and Pointers for Action*, New Delhi: New Delhi Publication.
- Mukerji, S. N. (1974). *History of education in India*. Baroda, India: Acharya Book Depot.

- Mukherji, S. N. (1964). *Education in India – Today and Tomorrow*. Baroda: Acharya Book Depot.
- Naik, J. P. (1942). *History of the Local Fund Cess (Appropriated to Education) in the Province of Bombay*. Bombay: The Local Self-Government Institute.
- Naik, J. P. (1942). *Studies in Primary Education*, First Series. Bombay: The Local Self-Government Institute (Bombay Presidency).
- Naik, J. P. (1965). Elementary *Education in India – The Unfinished Business*. Bombay: Asia Publishing House.
- Naik, J. P. (1975). *Elementary Education in India – A Promise to Keep*. Bombay: Allied Publishers.
- Naik, J. P. (1978). Educational Reform in India: A Historical Review. Bombay: Orient Longman Limited.
- Naik, J.P. (1943). *A Review of Modern Education in India (1813-1942)*. Tilak College of Education, Poona: The Aryabhushan Press.
- Nanda, N. (1998). The School System in India - A critique, In Saraswati, Baidyanath (1998). *The Cultural Dimension of Education*. New Delhi: Indira Gandhi National Centre for the Arts.
- Narulla, S. and Naik, J.P. (1943). History of Education in India. Bombay: Macmillan.
- Natesan, G. A. (1916). *Speeches of Gopal Krishna Gokhale*. Second Edition. Madras: G. A. Natesan & Co.
- Niranjanaradhya, V. P. and Kashyap, A. (2006). *The Fundamentals of the Fundamental Right to Education in India*. Bangalore: Books for Change.
- Niranjanaradhya, V. P. (2004). *Universalisation of School Education — the Road Ahead*. Bangalore: Books for Change.
- Nurullah, S. and Naik, J. P. (1964). *A Students' History of Education in India*. London: Macmillan and Company Limited.
- Nururllah, S. and Naik, J. P. (1943). *History of Education in India during the British Period*. New York: The MacMillan Company.
- Pathania, A. and Pathania, K. (2006). *Primary Education and Mid-Day Meal Scheme – Results, Challenges and Recommendations*. New Delhi: Deep and Deep Publications Private Limited.
- Planning Commission, GOI. (2008). *Eleventh Five Year Plan (2007-2012), Social Sector, Volume II*. New Delhi: Oxford University Press.
- Purkait, B. R. (1992). *Milestones in Modern Indian Education*. Kolkata: New Central Book Agency.
- R. P. Paranjpye (1915). *Gopal Krishna Gokhal*. Reprinted from Fergusson College Magazine, Poona. Published by Natesh Appaji Dravid, the Aryabhushan Press.

- Rai, Vinay and Kumar, Narendra (2010). *Right to Education: The Way Forward*. New Delhi: Perfect Publications.
- Raina, V. (2010). *Education and Knowledge in the Time of Globalisation Inclusion, Quality and Agency*. B.M. Pugh Fourth Memorial Lecture, 2010, NERIE, NCERT, Shillong.
- Raina, V. (2010). *Education and Knowledge in the Time of Globalisation Inclusion, Quality and Agency*. Shillong: B. M. Pugh Fourth Memorial Lecture, 2010, NERIE, NCERT. Retrieved from http://nerie.nic.in/pdf/txtVinod-Raina-during-IVth-BM-Pugh.pdf. on 10.4.2013.
- Raina, V. (2010). Maulana Azad and Right to Education. In Habib, S. Infan (2010). *Maulana Abul Kalam Azad and the National Education System*. New Delhi: NUEPA.
- Rajkhowa, S. C. (1964). Towards Universal Elementary Education (1921-61). In NCERT (Eds.), *The Indian Year Book of Education 1964 Second Year Book Elementary Education* (pp. 21-40). New Delhi: NCERT.
- Ramachandran, P. and Ramkumar, V. (2005). *Education in India*. New Delhi: National Book Trust.
- Ramana, M.V. (2012). *Right to Education – the Parameters and the Paradoxes*. Unpublished Ph.D. Thesis. Guntur: P.G. Department of Legal Studues and Research, Acharya Nargarjuna University.
- *Rani, S.* (2012). *An Objective Based Evaluation of Rehbar-E-Taleem Scheme in Kashmir Division* (Unpublished Doctoral Thesis). University of Kashmir, Faculty of Education, Srinaga, Kashmir.
- Rao, D.B. (Ed.).(2011). *Right to Education*. Hyderabad: Neelkamal Publications Pvt. Ltd.
- Rastogi, K.G. and Sharma, H.L. (1981). *Universalisation of Elementary Education Brochure – V*, New Delhi: NCERT.
- Saiyidian, K. G., Naik, J. P. and Husain, S. A. (1966). *Compulsory Education in India*. Delhi: Universal.
- Sen, J. M. (1925). *Primary Education Acts in India – A Study*. Calcutta: Calcutta Young Men's Christian Association (CYMCA).
- Sen, J. M. (2010). *History of Elementary Education in India*. New Delhi: Pacific Publication.
- Sharma, M. C. (Ed.).(2013). *Right to Education: Imperative for Progress*. New Delhi: Universal Law Publishing Co.
- Sharma, N. (2011). *Universalisation of Elementary Education among Tea-Tribe of Assam with special reference to Jorhat District. Assam: Assam State Commission for Protection of Child Right Guwahati.*

Retrieved on 12.04.2012 fromhttp://righttoeducation.in/sites/default/files/elementary_education_research.pdf

- Sharma, R.N. and Sharma, S.K. (2012). *History of Education in India*, New Delhi: Atlantic Publishers & Distributors (P) Ltd.
- Shiva Kumar, A. K. and Rustagi, Preet (2010). *Elementary Education in India: Progress, Setbacks and Challenges.* New Delhi: Oxfam India.
- Thakur, A.S. and Berwal, S. (2008). *Development of Education System in India (A Source Book for Teacher Educators and Teachers-in-Training).* New Delhi: Shipra Publications.
- The Servants of India Society (1917). *A Brief Account of the Work of the Servants of India Society, Poona (from June 1905 to December 1916).* Poona: The Aryabhushan Press.
- Thomas, F. W. (1891). *The History and Prospects of British Education in India*. Cambridge: Deighton Bell and Co.
- Tomasevshki, Katerina (2003). *Education Denied: Costs and Remedies.* New York: Zed Books Ltd.
- Tomasevski, K. (2001). *Right to Education Primers No. 3.* Stockholm: Swedish International Development Corporation Agency.
- Trevenlyan, C. E. (1838). *On the Education of the People of India.* London: Longman, Orme, Brown, Green, & Longmans.
- UNESCO (1984). *Towards Universalisation of Primary Education in Asia and the Pacific Country Studies India.* UNESCO Regional Office for Education in Asia and the Pacific: Bangkok.
- Weiner, Myron (1991). *The Child and the State in India; Child Labour and Education Policy in Comparative Perspective.* Princeton, NJ: Princeton University Press.
- Yadav, S.K. (2011). *National Study on Ten Year School Curriculum Implementation.* New Delhi: Department of Teacher Education and Extension, National Council of Educational Research and Training (NCERT).

Reports and Documents

- CABE (2005). *Report of the Central Advisory Board of Education (CABE) Committee on Free and Compulsory Education Bill And Other Issues Related to Elementary Education (Right to Education Bill 2005).* New Delhi: CABE, GOI.
- Government of Bihar (2007). *Report of the Bihar Common School System Commission.* Patna: Common School System Commission, Govt. of Bihar.

- Government of Bombay (1859). *Report of the Director of Public Instruction, Bombay, for the Year 1857-58.* Bombay: The Education Society's Press.
- Government of India (1868). *Adam's Reports on Vernacular Education in Bengal and Behar with a Brief View of its Past and Present Condition by Rev. J. Long.* Calcutta: The Home Secretariat Press.
- Government of India (1881). *Education Commission Bombay Vol. II Evidence taken before The Bombay Provincial Committee, and Memorials addressed to The Education Commission.* Calcutta: The Superintendent of Government Printing, India. Government of India.
- Government of India (1883). *Report of the Indian Education Commission, 1882.* Calcutta: Superintendent of Government Printing India.
- Government of India (1915). *Indian Educational Policy, 1913.* Calcutta: Superintendent Government Printing, India.
- Government of India (1929). *Indian Statutory Commission. Interim Report of the Indian Statutory Commission. (Review of Growth of Education in British India by the Auxiliary Committee appointed by the Commission).* Calcutta: Government of India.
- Government of India (1929). *Review of the Growth of Education in British India by the Auxiliary Committee of the Indian Statutory Commission*, Delhi: the Manager Government of India Press.
- Government of India (1947). *Post-War Educational Development in India, Report by the Central Advisory Board of Education, January 1944.* Delhi: The Manager of Publications, Government of India.
- Government of India (1948). *Committee on the Ways and Means of Financing Education Development in India, 1948*, Delhi: Manager of Publications, 1950, Bureau of Education, Pamphlet No. 64.
- Government of India (1948). *Education in Free India (August 1947 – August 1948).* New Delhi: The Ministry of Education, Government of India.
- Government of India (1948). *Education in Free India (August 1947 – August 1948).* New Delhi: The Ministry of Education, Government of India.
- Government of India (1950). *Committee on the Ways and Means of Financing Education Development in India, 1948.* Delhi: Pamphlet No. 64, Manager of Publications, Bureau of Education.
- Government of India (1965). *Education in Eighteen Years of Freedom.* New Delhi: Ministry of Education, Government of India

- Government of India (1966). *Education and National Development: Report of the Education Commission 1964 - 66*, New Delhi: Ministry Of Education, Govt. of India.
- Government of India (1974). *National Policy for Children.* New Delhi: Department of Social Welfare, Government of India.
- Government of India (1974). *National Policy for Children.* New Delhi: Department of Social Welfare, Government of India.
- Government of India (1979). *Draft National Policy on Education*, 1979. New Delhi: Ministry of Education and Social Welfare, GOI.
- Government of India (1979). *Draft National Policy on Education*, 1979. New Delhi: Ministry of Education and Social Welfare, GOI.
- Government of India (1985). *Challenge of Education – A Policy Perspective*. New Delhi: Ministry of Education, Government of India.
- Government of India (1986). *National Policy on Education*, New Delhi: Department of Education, Govt. of India.
- Government of India (1993). Report of National Development Council Committee on Literacy, Planning Commission 1993. New Delhi: MHRD. Retrieved on 12.09.2012 from http://www.teindia.nic.in/mhrd/50yrsedu/y/3P/45/toc.htm
- Government of India (1998). *Report of the Steering Committee for Formulation of Ninth Plan (1997-2002) on Early Childhood Education Elementary Education (Formal) Non – Formal Education Secondary Education Vocational Education Distance Education Adult Education.* New Delhi: Education Division, Planning Commission, Government of India.
- Government of India (1999). *Expert Group on Financial Requirements for Making Elementary Education A Fundamental Right, (Chairman: Prof. Tapas Majumdar).* New Delhi; Ministry of Human Resources Development, Government of India.
- Government of India (1999), *Expert Group Report on Financial Requirements for Making Elementary Education a Fundamental Right (also known as Tapas Majumdar Committee Report of 1999).* New Delhi: Department of Education Ministry of Human Resource Development, GOI.
- Government of India (2000). Report on a Policy Framework for Reforms in Education. New Delhi: Prime Minister's Council on Trade and Industry, Government of India.
- Government of India (2002). *Report of the National Commission to Review the Working of the Constitution*. New Delhi: Ministry of Law, Justice and Company Affairs, Department of Legal Affairs, GOI.

- Government of India (2004). *National Common Minimum Programme of the Government of India May 2004.* New Delhi: GOI. Retrieved from http://architexturez.net/system/files/pdf/cmp_0.pdf
- Government of India (2005). *Government of the United Progressive Alliance Report to People - 1, Implementation of National Common Minimum Programme and Other Initiative,* May 2004 – February 2005. New Delhi: GOI.
- Government of India (2005). *Report of the Committee of CABE on "Universalisation of Secondary Education.* New Delhi: Ministry of Human Resource Development, Government of India.
- Government of India (2005a). *Report of the CABE Committee on Free and Compulsory Education Bill and Other Issues Related to Elementary Education*, June 2005. Available at www.education.nic.
- Government of India (2005b). *Report of Committee on National Common Minimum Programmes Commitment of Six Per cent of GDP to Education, (Chairman: Prof. Tapas Majumdar).* New Delhi: National Institute of Educational Planning and Administration. Available at www.niepa.org.
- Government of India (2006). *Report on the Social, Economic and Educational Status of the Muslim Community of India.* New Delhi: Ministry of Minority Affairs, Government of India.

- Government of India (2006). *Report on the Social, Economic and Educational Status of the Muslim Community of India.* New Delhi: Ministry of Minority Affairs, Government of India.

- Government of India (2007). *National Knowledge Commission – Recommendations on School Education.* New Delhi: National Knowledge Commission, Government of India.
- Government of India (2008). *Department - Related Parliamentary Standing Committee on HRD: Two Hundred Thirteenth Report on the Right to Free and Compulsory Education Bill, 2008.* New Delhi: Parliament of India, Rajya Sabha Secretariat.
- Government of India (2010). *Prime Minister's Address to the Nation on Fundamental Right of Children to Elementary Education.* New Delhi: Prime Minister's Office, Press Information Bureau, Government of India.
- Law Commission of India (1998). *One Hundred Sixty Fifth Report on Free and Compulsory Education for Children.* New Delhi: Law Commission of India.

- Law Commission of India (1998). *One Hundred Sixty Fifth Report on Free and Compulsory Education for Children.* New Delhi: Law Commission of India.

- MHRD (1997). *Convention on the Rights of the Child – Country Report, 1997.* New Delhi: Department of Women and Child Department, MHRD. Retrieved from http://wcd.nic.in/crcfebmr.htm
- MHRD (1997). Report of the Committee of State Education Ministers on Implications of the Proposal to Make Elementary Education a Fundamental Right, (chairman: Muhi Ram Saikia), Ministry of Human Resource Development, Department of Education, New Delhi.
- MHRD (1998). *National Policy on Education 1986 (as modified in 1992).* New Delhi: Department of Education, Ministry of Human Resource Development, GOI.
- MHRD (2003). *Education for All – National Plan of Action.* New Delhi: Department of Elementary Education and Literacy, MHRD. GOI.
- MHRD (2005). *Annual Report 2004-05.* New Delhi: Department of School Education and Literacy, Department of Higher Education, Ministry of Human Resource Development (MHRD), Government of India.

- MHRD (2005). *Annual Report 2004-05.* New Delhi: Department of School Education and Literacy, Department of Higher Education, Ministry of Human Resource Development (MHRD), Government of India.

- MHRD (2009). *Fifty Fifth Meeting of the Central Advisory Board of Education Agenda Items & Background Notes,* Dated Tuesday, The 10th February, 2009. New Delhi: Ministry of Human Resource Development, Government of India.

- MHRD (2009). *Fifty Fifth Meeting of the Central Advisory Board of Education Agenda Items & Background Notes,* Dated Tuesday, The 10th February, 2009. New Delhi: Ministry of Human Resource Development, Government of India.

- MHRD (2009). *The Right of the Children to Free and Compulsory Education Act, 2009.* New Delhi: Department of Elementary Education and Literacy, MHRD, Government of India.
- MHRD (2011). *Framework of Implementation Based on the Right of Children to Free and Compulsory Act, 2009.* New Delhi: Department of School Education and Literacy, MHRD, Govt. of India.
- MHRD (2012). *Conference of State Education Ministers – Agenda Items and Background Notes.* New Delhi: MHRD, Govt. of India.
- MHRD (2012). *The 2nd Year – The Right of Children to Free and Compulsory Education Act, 2009.* New Delhi: Department of School Education and Literacy, MHRD, Govt. of India.

- MHRD. (2005). *Report of the Central Advisory Board of Education (CABE) Committee on Free and Compulsory Education Bill and Other Issues Related to Elementary Education, June 2005*. New Delhi: MHRD, GOI.
- NCERT (1970). *Education and National Development Report of the Education Commission, 1964-66 (Reprinted)*. New Delhi: National Council of Educational Research and Training.
- Planning Commission, GOI. (2008). *Eleventh Five Year Plan (2007-2012), Social Sector, Volume II.* New Delhi: Oxford University Press.
- Rajya Sabha Secretariat (2009). *213*th *Report of the Department – Related Parliamentary Standing Committee on Human Resource Development on the Right of Children to Free and Compulsory Education Bill, 2008*. New Delhi: Rajya Sabha, Parliament of India.
- Sharp, H. and Richey, J.A. (eds.) 1920. *Selections from Educational Records.* Vol. I, Calcutta: Superintendent of Government Printing.
- Sharp, H. (1914). *Progress of Education in India 1907-1912. Volume 1.* Calcutta: Superintendent of Government Printing, India.
- Sharp, H. (1920) (Ed.). *Selections from Educational Records, Part I (1781-1839).* Calcutta: Bureau of Education, Superintendent Government Printing, 1920. (Reprint) Delhi: National Archives of India, 1965.
- UNESCO (1984). *Towards Universalisation of Primary Education in Asia and the Pacific Country Studies India*. UNESCO Regional Office for Education in Asia and the Pacific: Bangkok.
- University of Delhi (1997). *Convention on Education as a Fundamental Right, Golden Jubilee Celebrations*, Delhi: Central Institute of Education, Department of Education, University of Delhi.

Newspapers

- Bhaumik, P.K. and Banik, A. (2006, April 8). Making the education cess work, The Economic Times. Retrieved from http://articles.economictimes.indiatimes.com/2006-04-08/news/27454253_1_education-cess-duties-and-service-tax-elementary-education
- Malani, Gaurav (2004, Sep 23). Fund for education cess gets finance ministry nod. The Economic Times. Retrieved from http://articles.economictimes.indiatimes.com/2004-09-23/news/27370798_1_education-cess-mid-day-meal-scheme-elementary-education
- Seetharamu, A.S. (2002, February 9). Fundamental Right Status for Education: Opportunity or eyewash? Retrieved from http://www.deccanherald.com.

Websites

(1) http://righttoeducation.in
(2) http://www.isrj.net
(3) http://mhrd.gov.in
(4) http://www.jamiajournal.com
(5) http://www.teacherplus.org
(6) http://www.booksforchange.net
(7) http://www.educationforallindia.com
(8) http://www.right_to_education.org
(9) http://www.unmid.com
(10) http://educationworldonline.net
(11) http://indiacode.nic.in
(12) http://socialissuesindia.worldpress.com
(13) http://indiabudget.nic.in
(14) http://lawmin.nic.in
(15) http://www.education.nic.in
(16) http://nuepa.org.in
(17) http://www.ncte_india.org
(18) http://ncert.nic.in
(19) http://www.azimpremjifoundation.org
(20) http://www.rteindia.com
(21) http://india.gov.in
(22) http://parisar.worldpress.com
(23) http://schoolofeducators.com
(24) http://www.censusindia.gov.in
(25) http://www.indg.org
(26) http://www.un.org
(27) http://undp.org
(28) http://ssa.nic.in
(29) http://asercentre.org
(30) http://rtemonitorcell.info

Primary Sources

(1) National Library of India, Kolkata,
(2) Digital Repository of West Bengal Public Library Network,
(3) Digital Library of Gokhale Institute of Politics and Economics (Pune),

(4) Digital Library of India at Osmania University, Hyderabad,
(5) Shodhganga@INFLIBNET Centre,
(6) Digital Archives of Education Documents (NUEPA),
(7) West Bengal State Archives, Kolkata,
(8) Indira Gandhi National Centre for the Arts (IGNCA),
(9) Archaeological Survey of India, New Delhi,
(10) Digital Library of India hosted by: IISC, Bangalore.

Index

Right to Education in India

Right to Education in India

Vol. II

Act, 2009

Dr Ajit Mondal
Dr Jayanta Mete

GYAN

ISBN : 978-81-212-1337-0

Price : ₹ 2000 (set of 2 Vols)
₹ 1090 (Vol–II)

First Published, 2016

Published by

Gyan Publishing House
5, Ansari Road
Daryaganj, New Delhi-110002
Phones: 9811692060
E-mail: books@gyanbooks.com

Printed at: G. Print Process, Delhi.

Cataloging in Publication Data—DK
Courtesy: D.K. Agencies (P) Ltd. <docinfo@dkagencies.com>

Mondal, Ajit, author.
Right to education in India / Dr Ajit Mondal, Dr Jayanta Mete.
volumes cm
Includes bibliographical references.
Contents: vol. I. History since 1813 — vol. II. Act, 2009.
ISBN 9788121213363 (v. 1)
ISBN 9788121213370 (v. 2)

1. Right to education—India—History. 2. Educational law and legislation—India. 3. India. Right of Children to Free and Compulsory Education Act, 2009. I. Mete, Jayanta, author. II. Title.

KNS1610.M66 2016 DDC 344.54079 23

Contents

Foreword

Education is globally recognised as a fundamental human right, and considered as the bed-rock of all socio-economic development of the nation. Just as food, clothing and shelter are basic necessities for survival, education is equally essential for self-sustenance and growth. It is also an established fact that basic education improves the level of human well-being especially, with regard to life expectancy, infant mortality and nutritional status of children. Education is the fundamental requirement not only for the individual but also for the success of democratic system of government. But sadly, education especially elementary education has remained inaccessible to many and education system at this level is being run in many places all over India like factories where the primary intention of owners is self-interest and profiteering. The failure of the Indian state more than six decades after independence to provide free and compulsory quality education to all children irrespective of all caste, creed, colour and other social discriminations must surely rank among the most dismal and significant failures of the development project in the country. After a continual demand of making the education a fundamental right from all corners, the government made the 86th Amendment of the Constitution of India (2002). This Amendment Act has added a new Article 21-A after Article 21 which makes the right of education of children for the age group of 6-14 years as Fundamental Right. The Right to Education commonly known as RTE (the Right to Free and Compulsory Education Act, 2009) was finally passed by the Parliament on 26th August 2009. This Act came in force with effect from the 1st April, 2010. It is now a matter of satisfaction that RTE is the first legislation in the world that puts the responsibility of enrolment, attendance and competition of education on the government.

The Present book '*Right to Education in India Act, 2009*' has analysed the chequered history of right to education legislation in India as a fundamental right. The book can also be of value for all the stakeholders of education by offering opportunity to delve into the history of the enactment of the RTE Act. I convey my thanks to Dr Ajit Mondal and Dr Jayanta Mete for writing a documentary history on the Right to Education in Indian Act 2009 context.

Professor (Dr) Mita Banerjee
Vice-Chancellor
The West Bengal University of Teachers' Training, Education Planning and Administration
Kolkata, West Bengal

Preface

"Our progress as a nation can be no swifter than our progress in education. The human mind is our fundamental resource."

– John F. Kennedy

Justice B. P. Jeevan Reddy, chairman of the Law Commission of India at the outset of the 265th Report on "Free and Compulsory Education for Children", 1998 stated magnificently the necessity of education in human life. According to him, "Education is essential for all". This is fundamental to our all-round development material as well as spiritual. Education is quintessential for economic, social and human development. It also leads to better healthcare, smaller family norms, greater community and political participation, less income inequality and a greater reduction of absolute poverty. The importance of education in nation building is not a new concern. Post-independence, the Kothari Commission, 1964-66 perceptively highlighted the crucial importance of education in shaping the future of our country. It acknowledged education as a "powerful instrument of social, economic and political change" (Chapter 1, Para 1.04). Thus, there can be no doubt that it is education that will determine our nation's future.

Education is globally recognised as a fundamental human right, and people with access to education can develop the skills, capacity and confidence to secure other rights. The right to education thus acts as an enabling right that functions as the voice through which rights can be claimed and protected. It is therefore considered as the bed-rock of all socio-economic development of the nation. Education is a basic human right and has been recognised since the adaptation of the Universal Declaration of Human Rights (1948, UNO). The Article 26 of the UDHR states that "everyone has the right to education".

Since then numerous international treaties have reaffirmed this right and have supported entitlement to free, compulsory and universal elementary education for all children, irrespective of caste, creed, colour, gender, religion and all other social stratifications across the globe.

Universalisation of elementary education has been one of the most important goals of educational development in India since independence. Universalisation of elementary education in India involves three conditions i.e. Universalisation of Provision, Universalisation of Enrollment and Universalisation of Retention. As per MHRD (2000), Universalisation of elementary education means "100 per cent enrollment and retention of children with schooling facilities in all habitations". India's commitment to universal elementary education dates backs to 1950.

The Right to Education legislation in India has seen a chequered history in evolving from a directive principle to a fundamental right. Attempts to make the right to free and compulsory education available to the Indian child began a little more than a century ago. The Act has its long history and starts from pre-constitutional era. Attempts to make the right to free and compulsory education available to the Indian child began a little more than a century ago. When in the years 1870, 1876 and 1880 Compulsory Education acts were passed in Britain, a demand was raised in India to provide similar facilities in its colonies. From this time onwards began the struggle for making elementary as a right of all children in India and as a duty on the state. After Independence, the national and international policy in general and the Directive Principles of the Indian Constitution in particular bound to provide free and compulsory elementary education to all the children. But despite the constitutional and international commitments, the number of out of school children, particularly from the disadvantaged groups and those engaged in labour, and those receiving poor quality education has continued to remain very large. Even in such a situation it took more six decades for the Indian state to frame and implement the Right to Education Act, 2009 so that the mandate of the Constitution could become an enforceable right. The RTE Act and its notification are rightly hailed by many as a landmark in the history of education in post-independence India. Had the directive principle been implemented in letter and spirit, the need for the 86th Amendment and the RTE Act would not have arisen. The RTE Act is the first Central Act in the domain of elementary education in post-independence India.

The role of Universal Elementary Education (UEE) for strengthening the social fabric of democracy through provision of equal opportunities to all has been accepted since the inception of our Republic. The original Article 45 in the Directive Principles of State Policy in the Constitution mandated the State to endeavour to provide free and compulsory education to all children up to age fourteen in a period of ten years. The National Policy on Education (NPE), 1986 / 92, states "*In our national perception, education is essentially for all. Education has an acculturating role. It refines sensitivities and perceptions that contribute to national cohesion, a scientific temper and independence of mind and spirit – thus furthering the goals of socialism, secularism and democracy enshrined in our Constitution*".

With the formulation of NPE, India initiated a wide range of programmes for achieving the goal of UEE. These efforts were intensified in the 1980s and 1990s through several schematic and programme interventions, such as Operation Black Board (OBB), Shiksha Karmi Project (SKP), Andhra Pradesh Primary Education Project (APPEP), Bihar Education Project (BEP), U.P. Basic Education Project (UPBEP), Mahila Samakhya (MS), Lok Jumbish Project (UP), and Teacher Education which put in place a decentralised system of teacher support through District Institutes of Education and Training (DIET), District Primary Education Programme (DPEP). Currently, the Sarva Shiksha Abhiyan (SSA) is implemented as a Centrally Sponsored Scheme in partnership with State Governments for universalising elementary education across the country.

Over the years there has been significant spatial and numerical expansion of elementary schools in the country. Access and enrollment at the primary stage of education have reached near universal levels. The number of out-of-school children has reduced significantly. The gender gap in elementary education has narrowed and the percentage of children belonging to scheduled castes and tribes enrolled is proportionate to their population. However, quality of learning achievement is not always entirely satisfactory even in the case of children who complete elementary education.

The Constitution (Eighty-sixth Amendment) Act, 2002 inserted Article 21-A in the Constitution of India to provide free and compulsory education of all children in the age group of six to fourteen years as a Fundamental Right in such a manner as the State may, by law, determine. The Right of Children to Free and Compulsory Education (RTE) Act, 2009, which represents the consequential legislation envisaged under Article 21-A, means that every child has a right to full time elementary education of satisfactory and equitable quality in a formal school which satisfies certain essential norms and standards. The need to address inadequacies in retention, residual access, particularly of un-reached children, and the questions of quality are the most compelling reasons for the insertion of Article 21-A in the Constitution of India and the passage of the RTE Act, 2009 in the Parliament. Article 21-A and the RTE Act came into effect on 1 April 2010. The new law provides a justifiable legal framework that entitles all children between the ages of 6–14 years free and compulsory admission, attendance and completion of elementary education. It provides for children's right to an education of equitable quality, based on principles of equity and non-discrimination. Most importantly, it provides for children's right to an education that is free from fear, stress and anxiety. SSA has been operational since 2000–2001. With the passage of the RTE Act, changes need to be incorporated into the SSA approach, strategies and norms. With the recommendation of the Committee on Implementation of RTE Act and the Resultant Revamp of SSA (2010) under the chairperson of Sri Anil Bordia, former Union Education Secretary, the SSA's Framework of implementation has been revised and its norms have been modified to align them with the requirement of RTE Act, 2009. Now let us discuss about the long up-hill journey from 1813 to 2009 of the RTE Act, 2009 and the problems of its effective implementation in detail.

In the wake of the growing awareness about the invaluable right, the authors have made a humble endeavour to explore the journey of right to education from the pre-Constitutional era to the enactment of the RTE Act, 2009. It is necessary to analyse the major events at constitutional level and at policy level after post-independence leading to the 86th Constitution Amendment Act, 2002 to make free and compulsory elementary education a Fundamental Right in India in order to understand some of the problems that one can encounter in attempting to provide education for all children. In this Book the educational policies during the British Period; and the programmes taken after the independence to achieve the goal of UEE have also been critically analysed for building a sound background for the present book.

It is expected that this book will be able to enlighten all types of stakeholders of education about RTE Act, 2009. The present book is designed to serve a reference book under the ambit of RTE Act, 2009. We express our deep gratitude and indebtedness to Professor Vinod Raina, Professor Anil Sadgopal, Professor Nalini Juneja, Professor R. Gobinda and Professor Arun C. Meheta whose valuable articles on RTE Act, 2009 have helped us in incorporating some chapters in this book. Reports and publications from West Bengal Board of Secondary Education, (Sarvasiksha Abhiyan Cell), UNICEF-India, ASER, MHRD, NUEPA, NCERT, NCTE, Bharat Gyan Vigyan Samiti (BGVS), NCPCR have also helped us with invaluable information on the RTE Act. We shall feel rewarded if our dear stakeholders of education find this helpful. We seek any suggestion from all corners for improving the book in future.

Kalyani, West Bengal **Dr Ajit Mondal and Dr Jayanta Mete**
2016

Abbreviations

ABL : Activity Based Learning
AIE : Alternative and Innovative Education
BAS : Baseline Achievement Survey
BE : Budget Estimate
BPL : Below Poverty Line
BRC : Block Resource Centre
BTEC : Basic Teacher Education Centre
CABE Central Advisory Board of Education
CBGA : Centre for Budget and Governance Accountability
CRC : Cluster Resource Centre
CTE : College of Teacher Education
CWSN : Children with Special Needs
DIET : District Institute of Education and Training
DISE : District Information System for Education
DPEP : District Primary Education Programme
EBB : Educationally Backward Block
ECCE : Early Childhood Care and Education
ECE : Early Childhood Education
EDI : Educational Development Index
EFA : Education for All
EGS : Education Guarantee Scheme
GDP : Gross Domestic Product
GOI : Government of India
GP : Gram Panchayat
IASE : Institute of Advanced Studies in Education

ICDS	:	Integrated Child Development Services
KGBV	:	Kasturba Gandhi Balika Vidyalaya
KV	:	Kendriya Vidyalaya
LJP	:	Lok Jumbish Project
MDM	:	Mid-day Meal
MGNREGA	:	Mahatma Gandhi National Rural Employment Guarantee Act
MHRD	:	Ministry of Human Resource Development
MLL	:	Minimum Levels of Learning
MS	:	Mahila Samakhya
MTA	:	Mother Teacher Association
NCE	:	National Commission of Education
NCERT	:	National Council of Educational Research and Training
NCF	:	National Curriculum Framework
NCPCR	:	National Commission for Protection of Child Rights
NCTE	:	National Council of Teacher Education
NDC	:	National Development Council
NFHS	:	National Family Health Survey
NGO	:	Non-Government Organisation
NIEPA	:	National Institute of Educational Planning and Administration
NLM	:	National Literacy Mission
NPE	:	National Policy on Education
NPEGEL	:	National Programme for Education of Girls at Elementary Level
NRHM	:	National Rural Health Mission
NUEPA	:	National University of Educational Planning and Administration
OBB	:	Operation Black Board
OBC	:	Other Backward Community
POA	:	Programme of Action
PRI	:	Panchayati Raj Institution

PROBE	: Public Report on Basic Education
PTA	: Parent Teacher Association
RE	: Revised Estimate
REPA	: Right to Education Protection Authority
RTE	: Right to Education
SC	: Scheduled Caste
SCERT	: State Council of Educational Research and Training
SCPCR	: State Commission for Protect of Children Rights
SES	: Selected Educational Statistics
SIEMAT	: State Institute of Educational Management and Training
SKP	: Shiksha Karmi Project
SMC	: School Management Committee
SRC	: State Resource Centre
SSA	: Sarva Shiksha Abhiyan
ST	: Scheduled Tribe
TET	: Teacher Eligibility Test
TLM	: Teaching Learning Material
UEE	: Universalisation of Elementary Education
UN	: United Nations
UNDP	: United Nations Development Programme
UNESCO	: United Nations Education Scientific and Cultural Organisation
UNICEF	: United Nations International Children's Emergency Fund
URC	: Urban Resource Centre
UT	: Union Territory
VEC	: Village Education Committee

Chapter - 9

The Right of Children to Free and Compulsory Education Act, 2009

सत्यमेव जयते

The Gazette of India

EXTRAORDINARY

PART II – Section I

PUBLISHED BY AUTHORITY

No. 39] NEW DELHI, THURSDAY, AUGUST 27, 2009/BHADRA 5, 1931

Separate paging is given to this Part in order that it may be filed as a separate compilation

MINISTRY OF LAW AND JUSTICE

(Legislative Department)

New Delhi, the 27th August, 2009 / Bhadra 5, 1931 (Saka)

The following Act of Parliament received the assent of the President on the 26th August 2009, and is hereby published for general information: -

THE RIGHT OF CHILDREN TO FREE AND COMPULSORY EDUCATION ACT, 2009

No. 35 of 2009

[26th August, 2009]

An Act to provide for free and compulsory education to all children of the age of six to fourteen years.

Be it enacted by Parliament in the Sixtieth Year of the Republic of India as follows:

CHAPTER I
PRELIMINARY

1. (1) This Act maybe called the Right of Children to Free and Compulsory Education Act, 2009.	Short title, extent and commence-ment
(2) It shall extend to the whole of India except the State of Jammu an Kashmir.	
(3) It shall come into force on such date as the Central Government may, by notification in the Official Gazette, appoint.	
2. In this Act, unless the context otherwise requires, -	Definitions
(a) "appropriate Government" means –	
(i) in relation to a school established, owned or control-led by the Central Government , or the administrator of the Union territory of –	
(A) a State, the State Government;	
(B) a Union territory having legislature, the Government of that Union territory;	
(b) "capitation fee" means any kind of donation or contribution or payment other than the fee notified by the school;	
(c) "child" means or a male of female child of the age of six to fourteen years;	
(d) "child belonging to disadvantaged group" means a child belonging to the Scheduled Caste, the Scheduled Tribe, the socially and educationally backward class or such other group having disadvantage owing to social, cultural, economical, geographical, linguistic, gender or such other factor,	

as may be specified by the appropriate Govern-ment, by notification;

(e) "child belonging to weaker section" means a child belonging to such parent or guardian whose annual income is lower than the minimum limit specified by the appropriate Government, by notification;

(f) "elementary education" means the education from first class to eighth class;

(g) "guardian", in relation to a child, means a person having the care and custody of that child and includes a natural guardian or guardian appointed or declared by a court or a statute;

(h) "local authority" means a Municipal Corporation or Municipal Council or Zila Parishad or Nagar Panchayat or Panchayat, by whatever name called, and includes such other authority or body having administrative control over the school or empowered by or under any law for the time being in force to function as a local authority in any city, town or village.

(i) "National Commission for Protection of Child Rights" means the National Commission for Protection of Child Rights constituted under section 3 of the Commission for Protection of Child Rights Act, 2005.

(j) "notification" means a notification published in the Official Gazette;

(k) "parent" means the natural or step or adoptive father or mother of a child;

(l) "prescribed" means prescribed by rules made under this Act;

(m) "Schedule" means the Schedule annexed to this Act.

(n) "school" means any recognised school imparting elementary education and includes –

   (i) a school established, owned or controlled by the appropriate Government or a local authority;

   (ii) an aided school receiving aid or grants to meet whole or part of its expenses from the appropriate Government or the local authority;

   (iii) a school belonging to specified category; and

(iv) an unaided school not receiving any kind of aid or grants to meet its expenses from the appropriate Government or the local authority;

(o) 'screening procedure' means the method of selection for admission of a child, in preference over another, other than a random method;

(p) 'specified category', in relation to a school, means a school known as Kendriya Vidyalaya, Navodayaya Vidyalaya, Sainik School or any other school having a distinct character which may be specified, by notification, by the appropriate Government.

(q) "State Commission for Protection of Child Rights" means the State Commission for Protection of Child Rights constituted under section 3 of the Commission for Protection of Child Rights Act, 2005.

CHAPTER II

Right to Free and Compulsory Education

3. (1) Every child of the age of six to fourteen years shall have a right to free and compulsory education in a neighbourhood school till completion of elementary education. (2) For the purpose of sub-section (1), no child shall be liable to pay any kind of fee or charges or expenses which may prevent him or her from pursuing and completing the elementary education. Provided that a child suffering from disability, as defined in clause (i) of section 2 of the Person with Disabilities (Equal Opportunities, Protection and Full Participation) Act, 1996, shall have the right to pursue free and compulsory elementary education in a accordance with the provisions of Chapter V of the said Act.	Right to child to free and compulsory education
4. Where a child above six years of age has not been admitted in any school or though admitted, could not complete his or her elementary education, then, he or she shall be admitted in a class appropriate to his or her age; Provided that where a child is directly admitted in a class appropriate to his or her age, then, he or she shall, in order to be at part with others, have a right to receive special training, such manner, and within such time-limits, as may be prescribed:	Special provisions for children not admitted to, or who has not done completed elementary education.

Provided further that a child so admitted to elementary education shall be entitled to free education till completion of elementary education even after fourteen years.	
5. (1) Where in a school, there is no provisions for completion of elementary education, a child shall have a right to seek transfer to any other school, excluding the school specified in sub-clauses (iii) and (iv) of clause (n) of section 2, for completing his or her elementary education.	Right of transfer to other school
(2) Where a child is required to move from one school to another, either within a State of outside for any reason whatsoever, such child shall have a right to seek transfer to any other school, excluding the school specified in sub-clauses (iii) and (iv) of clause (n) of section 2, completing his or her elementary education.	
(3) For seeking admission in such other school the Head-teacher or in-charge of the school where such child was last admitted, shall immediately issue the transfer certificate :	
Provided that delay in producing transfer certificate shall not be a ground for either delaying or denying admission in such other school:	
Provided further that the Head-teacher or in-charge of the school delaying issuance of transfer certificate shall be liable for disciplinary action under the service rules application to him or her.	

CHAPTER III

DUTIES OF APPROPRIATE GOVERNMENT, LOCAL AUTHORITY AND PARENTS

6. For carrying out the provisions of this Act, the appropriate government and the authority shall establish, within such area or limits of neighbourhood, as may be prescribed, a school where it is not so established, within a period of three years form the commencement of this Act.	Duty of appropriate government and local authority to establish school
7. (1) The Central Government and the State Governments shall have concurrent responsibility for providing funds for carrying out the provisions of this Act.	Sharing of financial and other responsibilities

(2) The Central Government and the State Governments shall prepare the estimates of capital and recurring expenditure for the implementation of the provision of the Act.

(3) The Central Government shall provide to the State Government, as grant-in-aid of revenues, such percentage of expenditure referred to in sub-section (2) as it may determine, from time to time, in consultation with the State Governments.

(4) The Central Government may make a request to the President to make a reference to the Finance Commission under sub-clause (d) of clause (3) of article 280 to examine the need for additional resources to be provided to any State government so that the said State Government may provide its share of funds for carrying out the provisions of the Act.

(5) Notwithstanding anything contained in sub-section (4), the State Government shall, taking into consideration the sums provided by the Central Government to a State Government under sub-section (3), and its other resources, be responsible to provide funds for implementation of the provisions of the Act.

(6) The Central Government shall –

(a) develop a framework of national curriculum with the help of academic authority specified under section 29;

(b) develop and enforce standards for training of teachers.

(c) Provide technical support and resources to the State Government for promoting innovations, researchers, planning and capacity building.

8. The appropriate government shall – *Duties of appropriate government*

(a) provide free and compulsory elementary education to every child :

Provided that where a child is admitted by his or her parents or guardians, as the case may be, in a school other than a school established, owned, controlled or substantially financed by funds provided directly or indirectly by the appropriate government or a local authority, such child or his or her parents or guardian, as the case may be, shall not be entitled to make a claim for reimbursement of expenditure incurred on elementary education of the child in such other school.

Explanation – The term "compulsory education" means obligation of the appropriate government to –

(i) provide free elementary education to every child of the age of six to fourteen years; and

(ii) ensure compulsory admission, attendance and completion of elementary education by every child of the age of six to fourteen years.

(b) ensure availability of a neighbourhood school as specified in section 6;

(c) ensure that the child belonging to weaker section and the child belonging to disadvantaged group are not discriminated against and prevented from pursuing and completing elementary education on any grounds;

(d) provide infrastructure including school building, teaching staff and learning equipment;

(e) provide special training facility specified in section 4.

(f) ensure and monitor admission, attendance and completion of elementary education by every child;

(g) ensure good quality elementary education conforming to the standards and norms specified in the schedule;

(h) ensure timely prescribing of curriculum and courses of study for elementary education; and

(i) provide training facility for teachers.

Duties of local authority

9. Every local authority shall –

(a) provide free and compulsory elementary education to every child :

Provided that where a child is admitted by his or her parents or guardian, as the case may be, in a school other than a school established, owned, controlled or substantially financed by funds provided directly or indirectly by the appropriate government or a local authority, such child or his or her parents or guardian, as the case may be, shall not be entitled to make a claim for reimbursement of expenditure incurred on elementary education of the child in such other school;

(b) ensure availability of neighbourhood school as specified in section 6;

(c) ensure that the child belonging to weaker section and the child belonging to disadvantaged group are not discriminated against and prevented from pursuing and completing elementary education on any grounds;

(d) maintain records of children up to the age of fourteen years residing within its jurisdiction, in such manner as may be prescribed;

(e) ensure and monitor admission, attendance and completion of elementary education by every child residing with its jurisdiction;

(f) provide infrastructure including school building, teaching staff and learning material;

(g) provide special training facility specified in section 4;

(h) ensure good quality elementary education conforming to the standards and norms specified in the Schedule;

(i) ensure timely prescribing of curriculum and courses of study for elementary education;

(j) provide training facility for teachers;

(k) ensure admission of children of migrant families;

(l) monitor functioning of schools within its jurisdiction; and

(m) decide the academic calendar.

10. It shall be the duty of every parent or guardian to admit or cause to be admitted his or her child or ward, as the case may be, to an elementary education in the neighbourhood school. — Duties of parents and guardian

11. With a view to prepare children above the age of three years for elementary education and to provide early childhood care and education for all children until they complete the age of six years, the appropriate government may make necessary arrangement for providing free pre-school education for such children. — Appropriate government to provide for pre-school education

CHAPTER IV

RESPONSIBILITIES OF SCHOOLS AND TEACHERS

Extent of school's responsibility for free and compulsory education

12. (1) For the purpose of this Act, a school, -

(a) specified in sub-clause (i) of clause (n) of section 2 shall provide free and compulsory elementary education to all children admitted therein;

(b) specified in sub-clause (ii) of clause (n) of section 2 shall provide free and compulsory elementary education to such proportion of children admitted therein as its annual recurring aid or grants so received bears to its annual recurring expenses, subject to a minimum of twenty-five per cent;

(c) specified in sub-clauses (iii) and (iv) of clause (n) of section 2 shall admit in class I, to the extent of at least twenty-five per cent of the strength of that class, children belonging to weaker section and disadvantaged group in the neighbourhood and provide free and compulsory elementary education till its completion :

Provided further that where a school specified in clause (n) of section 2 imparts pre-school education, the provisions of clauses (a) to (c) shall apply for admission to such pre-school education.

(2) The school specified in sub-clause (iv) of clause (n) of section 2 providing free and compulsory elementary education as specified in clause (c) of sub-section (i) shall be reimbursed expenditure so incurred by it to the extent of per-child expenditure incurred by the State, or the actual amount charged from the child, whichever is less, in such manner as may be prescribed :

Provided that such reimbursement shall not exceed per-child-expenditure incurred by a school specified in sub-clause (i) of clause (n) of section 2.

Provided further that where such school is already under obligation to provide free education to a specified number of children on account of it having received any land, building, equipment or other facilities, either free of cost or at a concessional rate, such school shall not be entitled for reimbursement to the extent of such obligation.

(3) Every school shall provide such information as may be required by the appropriate government or the local authority, as the case may be.

13.	(1) No school or person shall, while admitting a child, collect any captaining fee and subject the child or his or her parents or guardian to any screening procedure. (2) Any school or person, if in contravention of the provisions of sub-section (1),- (a) receives capitation fee, shall be punishable with fine which may extend to ten times the capitation fee charged; (b) subjects a child to screening procedure, shall be punishable with fine which may extend to twenty-five thousand rupees for the first contravention and fifty thousand rupees for each subsequent contraventions.	No capitation fee and screening procedure for admission
14.	(1) For the purposes of admission to elementary education, the age of a child shall be determined on the basis of the birth certificate issued in accordance with provisions of the Births, Deaths and Marriages Registration Act, 1886 or on the basis of such other document, as may be prescribed. (2) No child shall be denied admission in a school for lack of age roof.	Proof of age for admission
15.	A child shall be admitted in a school at the commencement of the academic year or within such extended period as may be prescribed: Provided that no child shall be denied admission if such admission is sought subsequent to the extended period: Provided further that any child admitted after the extended period shall complete his studies in such manner as may be prescribed by the appropriate government.	No denial of admission
16.	No child admitted in a school shall be held back in any class or expelled from school till the completion of elementary education.	Prohibition of holding back and expulsion
17.	(1) No child shall be subjected to physical punishment or mental harassment. (2) Whoever contravenes the provisions of sub-section (1) shall be liable to disciplinary action under the service rules applicable to such person.	Prohibition of physical punishment and mental harassment to child
18.	(1) No school, other than a school established, owned or controlled by the appropriate government or the local authority, shall, after the commencement of this Act, be established or function, without obtaining a certificate of	No School to be established without obtaining certificate of recognition

recognition from such authority, by making as application in such form and manner, as may be prescribed.

(2) The authority prescribed under sub-section (1) shall issue the certificate of recognition in such from, within such period, in such manner, and subject to such condition, as may be prescribed :

Provided that no such recognition shall be granted to a school unless it fulfils norms and standards specified under section 19.

(3) On the contravention of the condition of recognition, the prescribed authority shall, by an order in writing, withdraw recognition :

Provided that such order shall contain a direction as to which of the neighbourhood school, the children studying in the derecognised school, shall be admitted :

(4) With effect from the date of withdrawal of the recognition under sub-section (3), no such school shall continue to function.

(5) Any person who establishes, or runs a school without obtaining certificate of recognition, or continues to run a school after withdrawal of recognition, shall be liable to fine which may extend to one lakh rupees and in case of continuing contraventions, to a fine of ten thousand rupees for each day during which such commencement.

Norms and standards for school

19. (1) No school shall be established, or recognised, under section 18, unless it fulfils the norms and standards specified in the Schedule.

(2) Where a school established before the commencement of this Act does not fulfils the norms and standards at its own expenses, within a period of three years from the date of such commencement.

(3) Where a school fails to fulfil the norms and standards within the period specified under sub-section (2) the authority prescribed under sub-section (1) of section (1) of section 18 shall withdraw recognition granted to such school in the manner specified under sub-section (3) thereof.

(4) With effect from the date of withdrawal of recognition under sub-section (3), no school shall continue to function.

(5) Any person who continues to run a school after the recognition its withdrawn, shall be liable to fine which

	may extend to one lakh rupees and in case of continuing contraventions, to a fine of ten thousand rupees for each day during which such contravention continues.	
20.	The Central Government may, by notification, amend the Schedule by adding to, or omitting there from, any norms and standards.	Power to amend schedule
21.	(1) A school, other than a school specified in sub-clause (iv) of clause (n) of section 2, shall continue a School Management Committee consisting of the elected representative of the local authority, parents or guardians of children admitted in such school and teachers : Provided that at least three-fourth of members of such Committee shall be parents or guardians : Provided further that proportionate representation shall be given to the parents or guardians of children belonging to disadvantaged group and weaker section : Provided also that fifty per cent of Members of such Committee shall be women. (2) The School Management Committee shall perform the following function, namely (a) monitor the working of the school; (b) prepare and recommended school development plan; (c) monitor the utilisation of the grants received from the appropriate Government or local authority or any other source; and (d) perform such other functions as may be prescribed.	School Management Committee
22.	(1) Every School Management Committee, constituted under sub-section (1) of section 21, shall School Development Plan, in such manner as may be prescribed. (2) The School Development Plan so prepared under sub-section (1) shall be the basis for the plans and grants to be made by the appropriate government or local authority, as the case may be.	School Develop-ment Plan
23.	(1) Any person possessing such minimum qualifications, as laid down by an academic authority, authorised by the Central Government, by notification, shall be eligible for appointment as a teacher. (2) Where a State does not have adequate institutions offering courses or training in teacher education, or teachers possessing minimum qualification as laid down	Qualification for appoint-ment and terms and conditions of service of teachers

under sub-section (1) are not available in sufficient members, the Central Government may, if it deems necessary, by notification, relax the minimum qualifications required for appointment as a teacher, for such period, not exceeding five years, as may be specified in that notification :

Provided that a teacher who, at the commencement of this Act, does not possess minimum qualification as laid down under sub-section (1), shall acquire such minimum qualifications within a period of five years.

(3) The salary and allowances payable to, and the terms and condition of service of, teachers, shall be prescribed.

Duties of teachers and redressal of grievances

24. (1) A teacher appointed under sub-section (1) of section 23 shall perform the following duties, namely :

(a) maintain regularity and punctuality in attending school;

(b) conduct and complete the curriculum in accordance with the provisions of sub-section (2) of section 29;

(c) complete entire curriculum within the specified time;

(d) assess the learning ability of each child and accordingly supplement additional instructions, if any, as required;

(e) hold regular meetings with parents and guardians and arise them about the regularity in attendance, ability to learn, progress made in learning and any other relevant information about the child; and

(f) perform such other duties as may be prescribed.

(2) A teacher committing default in performance of duties specified in sub-section (1), shall be liable to disciplinary action under the service rules applicable to him or her :

Provided that before taking such disciplinary action, reasonable opportunity of being heard shall be afforded to such teacher.

(3) The grievances, if any, of the teacher shall be redressed in such manner as may be prescribed.

Pupil-Teacher Ratio

25. (1) Within six months from the date of commencement of this Act, the appropriate government and the local authority shall ensure that the Pupil-Teacher Ratio, as specified in the Schedule, is maintained in each school.

	(2) For the purpose of maintaining the Pupil-Teacher Ratio under sub-section (1), no teacher posted in a school shall be made to serve in any other school or office or deployed for any non-educational purpose, other than those specified in section 27.	
26.	The appointing authority, in relation to a school established, owned, controlled or substantially financed by funds provided directly or indirectly by the appropriate government or by a local authority, shall ensure that vacancy of teacher in a school under its control shall not exceed ten per cent of the total sanctioned strength.	Filling up vacancies of teachers
27.	No teacher shall be deployed for any non-educational purposes other than the decennial population census, disaster relief duties or duties relating to elections to the local authority or the State Legislatures or Parliament, as the case may be.	Prohibition of deployment of teachers for non-educational purposes
28.	No teacher shall engage himself or herself in private tuition or private teaching activity.	Prohibition of private tuition by teachers

CHAPTER V

CURRICULUM AND COMPLETION OF ELEMENTARY EDUCATION

29.	(1) The curriculum and the evaluation procedure for elementary education shall be laid down by an academic authority to be specified by the appropriate government, by notification. (2) The academic authority, while laying down the curriculum and the evaluation procedure under sub-section (1), shall take into consideration the following, namely : (a) conformity with the values enshrined in the Constitution; (b) all round development of the child; (c) building up child's knowledge, potentiality and talent; (d) development of physical and mental abilities to fullest extent;	Curriculum and evaluation procedure

(e) learning through activities, discovery and exploration in a child friendly and child-centred manner;

(f) medium of instructions shall as far as practicable, be in child's mother tongue;

(g) making the child free of fear, trauma and anxiety and helping the child to express views freely;

(h) comprehensive and continuous evaluation of child's understanding of knowledge and his or her ability to apply the same.

Examination and completion certificate

30. (1) no child shall be required to pass any board examination till completion of elementary education.

(2) Every child completing his elementary education shall be awarded a certificate, in such form and in such manner, as may be prescribed.

CHAPTER VI

PROTECTION OF RIGHT OF CHILDREN

Monitoring of child's education

31. (1) The National Commission for Protection of Child Rights constituted under section 3, or as the case may be, the State Commission for Protection of Child Rights constituted under section 17, of the Commission for Protection of Child Rights Act, 2005, shall, in addition to the functions assigned to them under that Act, also perform the following function, namely :

(a) examine and review the safeguards for rights provided by or under this Act and recommend measures for their effective implementation;

(b) inquire into complaints relating to child's right to free and compulsory education; and

(c) take necessary steps as provided under section 15 and 24 of the said Commission for Protection of Child Rights Act.

(2) The said Commission shall, while inquiring into any matters relating to child's right to free and compulsory education under clause (c) of sub-section (1), have the same powers as assigned to them respectively under sections 14 and 24 of the said Commission for Protection of Child Rights Act.

(3) Where the State Commission for Protection of Child Rights has not been constituted in a State, the appropriate government may, for the purpose of performing the

functions specified in clauses (a) to (c) of sub-section (1) constitute such authority, in such manner and subject to such terms and conditions, as may be prescribed.

Redressal of grievances

32. (1) Notwithstanding anything contained in section 31, any person having any grievance relating to the right of a child under this Act may make a written complaint to the local authority having jurisdiction.

(2) After receiving the complaint under sub-section (1), the local authority shall decide the matter within a period of three months after affording a reasonable opportunity of being heard to the parties concerned.

(3) Any person aggrieved by the decision of the local authority may prefer and appeal to the State commission for Protection of Child Rights or the authority prescribed under sub-section (3) of section 31, as the case may be.

(4) The appeal preferred under sub-section (3) shall be decided by State Commission for Protection of Child Rights or the authority prescribed under sub-section (3) of section 31, as the case may be, as provided under clause (c) of sub-section (1) of section 31.

Constitution of National Advisory Council

33. (1) The Central Government shall constitute, by notification a National Advisory Council, consisting of such number of Members, not exceeding fifteen, as the Central Government may deem necessary, to be appointed from amongst person having knowledge and practical experience in the field of elementary education and child development.

(2) The functions of the National Advisory Council shall be to advise the Central Government on implementation of the Provisions of the Act in an effective manner.

(3) The allowances and other terms and condition of the appointment of members of the National Advisory Council shall be such as may be prescribed.

Constitution of State Advisory Council

34. (1) The State Government shall constitute, by notification, a State Advisory Council consisting of such number of Members, not exceeding fifteen, as the State Government may deem necessary, to be appointed from amongst person having knowledge and practical experience in the field of elementary education and child development.

(2) The functions of the State Advisory Council shall be to advise the State Government on implementation of the provisions of the Act in an effective manner.

(3) The allowances and other terms and conditions of appointment of Members of the State Advisory Council shall be such as may be prescribed.

CHAPTER VII

MISCELLANEOUS

35. (1) The Central Government may issue such guidelines to the appropriate government or, as the case may be, the local authority, as it deems fit for the purposes of implementation of the provisions of this Act. — *Power to issue directions*

(2) The appropriate government may issue guidelines and give such directions, as it deems fit, to the local authority or the School Management Committee regarding implementation of the provisions of this Act.

(3) The local authority may issue guidelines and give such directions, as it deems fit, to the School Management Committee regarding implementation of the provisions of this Act.

36. No Prosecution for offences punishable under sub-section (2) of section 13, sub-section (5) of section 18 and sub-section (5) of section 19 shall be instituted except with the previous sanction of an officer authorised in this behalf, by the appropriate government, by notification. — *Previous sanction for prosecution*

37. No suit or other legal proceeding shall lie against the Central Government, the State government, the National Commission for Protection of Child Rights, the State Commission for Protection of Child Rights, the local authority, the School Management Committee or any person, in respect of anything which is in good faith done or intended to be done, in pursuance of this Act, or any rules or order made thereunder. — *Prosecution of action taken in good faith*

38. (1) The appropriate government may, be notification, make rules, for carrying out the provisions of this Act. — *Power of appropriate government to make rules*

(2) In particular, and without prejudice to the generality of the foregoing powers, such rules may provide for all or any of the following matters, namely :

(a) the manner of giving special training and the time-limit thereof, under first proviso to section 4;

(b) the area or limits for establishment of a neighbourhood school, under section 6;

(c) the manner of maintenance of records of children up to the age of fourteen years, under clause (d) of section 9;

(d) the manner and extent of reimbursement of expenditure, under sub-section (2) of section 12;

(e) any other document for determining the age of child under sub-section (1) of section 14;

(f) the extended period for admission and the manner of completing study of admitted after the extended period, under section 15;

(g) the authority, the form and manner of making application for certificate of recognition, under sub-section (1) of section 18;

(h) the form, the period, the manner and the conditions for issuing certificate recognition, under sub-section (2) of section 18;

(i) the manner of giving opportunity of hearing under second proviso to sub-section (3) of section 18;

(j) the other functions to be performed by School Management Committee under clause (d) of sub-section (2) of section 21;

(k) the manner of preparing School Development Plan under sub-section (1) of section 22;

(l) the salary and allowances payable to, and the terms and conditions of service of, teacher, under sub-section (3) of section 23;

(m) the duties to be performed by the teacher under clause (f) of sub-section (l) of section 24;

(n) the manner of redressing grievances of teachers under sub-section (3) of section 24;

(o) the form and manner of awarding certificate for completion of elementary thereof, under sub-section (2) of section 30;

(p) the authority, the manner of its constitution and the terms and conditions thereof, under sub-section (3) of section 31;

(q) the allowances and other terms and condition of appointment of Members of the National Advisory Council under sub-section (3) of section 33;

(r) the allowances and other terms and condition of appointment of Members of the State Advisory Council under sub-section (3) of section 34.

(3) Every rule made under this Act and every notification issued under section 20 and 23 by the Central Government shall be laid, as soon as may be after it is made, before

each House of Parliament, while it is in session or in two or more successive sections, and if, before the expiry of the session immediately following the session or the successive sessions aforesaid, both Houses agree in making any modification in the rule or notification shall thereafter have effect only in such modification or annulment shall be without prejudice to the validity of anything previously done under that rule or notification.

(4) Every rule or notification made by the State Government under this Act shall be laid, as soon as may be after it is made, before the State Legislatures.

THE SCHEDULE

(Sec sections 19 and 25)

Norms and Standards for a School

Sl. No.	*Item*		*Norms and Standards*
1.	Number of teachers	**Admitted children**	**Number of teachers**
(a)	For first class to fifth class	Up to sixty	Two
		Between sixty-one to ninety	Three
		Between ninety-one to one hundred and twenty	Four
		Between one hundred and twenty-one to two hundred	Five
		Above one hundred and fifty children	Five plus one Head teacher
		Above two hundred children	Pupil –Teacher Ratio (excluding Head teacher) shall not exceed forty
(b)	For sixth class to eight class	(1) At least one teacher per class so that there shall be at least one teacher each for – (i) Science and Mathematics; (ii) Social Studies (iii) Languages (2) At lest one teacher for every thirty-five children (3) Where admission of children is above one hundred – (i) a full time head-teacher; (ii) part time instructors for – (A) Art Education; (B) Health and Physical Education; (C) Work Education	
2.	Building	All-weather building consisting of – (i) at least one class-room for every teacher and an office-cum-store-cum-Head teacher's room; (ii) barrier-free access; (iii) separate toilets for boys and girls; (iv) safe and adequate drinking water facility to all children; (v) a kitchen where mid-day meal is cooked in the school;	

		(vi) playground; (vii) arrangements for securing the school building by boundary wall or fencing.
3.	Minimum number of working days / instructional hours in an academic year	(i) two hundred working days for first class to fifth class; (ii) two hundred and twenty working days for sixth class to eighth class; (iii) eight hundred instructional hours per academic year for first class to fifth class; (iv) one thousand instructional hours per academic year for sixth class to eight class.
4.	Minimum number of working hours per week for the teacher	forty-five teaching including preparation hours
5.	Teaching learning equipment	shall be provided to each class as required
6.	Library	there shall be a library in each school providing newspaper, magazines and books on all subjects including story-books.
7.	Play material, games and sports equipment	shall be provided to each class as required

Source: MHRD, GOI.

T. K. VISWANATHAN
Secretary to the Govt. of India

Structural Framework of RTE Act, 2009: This Act has got seven chapters. They are divided in Thirty Eight Sections. Each section has got more than one sub-section. Each sub-section expands and explains the particular section of the Act. The sub-sections are again divided into clauses. Such as, the section 38 is divided into two sub-sections and the second sub-section is re-divided into eighteen clauses (a – r). The features of six chapters are as follows :

CHAPTER – I	:	Clarification / Definition
CHAPTER – II	:	Right to Free and Compulsory Education
CHAPTER – III	:	Duties of Appropriate Government, Local Authority and Parents
CHAPTER – IV	:	Responsibilities of School and Teachers
CHAPTER – V	:	Curriculum and Completion of Elementary Education
CHAPTER – VI	:	Protection of Right of Children
CHAPTER – VII	:	Miscellaneous (Notification of Responsibilities of State as well as Central Government).

This framework was laid on the Principles of Equity, Access and Quality.

Chapter - 10

Model Rules of the Right of Children to Free and Compulsory Education Act, 2009

On the basis of the RTE Act, 2009 the Government of India has framed subordinate legislation called Model Rules as guidelines for implementation of the Act.

Model Rules of the Right of Children to Free and Compulsory Education Act, 2009

Part I - Preliminary

Short title, extent and commencement

1. (1) These Rules may be called the Right of Children to Free and Compulsory Education Rules, 2009.
   (2) They shall come into force from (Date)
   (3) They shall extend to the whole of (Name of State)

Definitions

2. (1) In these rules, unless the context otherwise requires, -
   (a) "Act" means the Right of Children to Free and Compulsory Education Act, 2009.
   (b) "Anganwadi" means an Anganwadi Centre established under the Integrated Child Development Scheme of the Ministry of Women and Child Development of the Government of India.

(c) "appointed date" means the date on which the Act comes into force, as notified in the Official Gazette

(d) "Chapter", "section" and Schedule" means respectively Chapter, section of, and Schedule to, the Act.

(e) "Child" means any child of the age of 6 to 14 years

(f) "Pupil Cumulative Record" means record of the progress of the child based on comprehensive and continuous evaluation

(g) "school mapping" means planning school location to overcome social barriers and geographical distance

(2) All references to "forms" in these Rules shall be construed as references to forms set out in Appendix I hereto.

(3) All other words and expressions used herein and not defined but defined in the Act shall have the same meanings respectively assigned to them in the Act.

Part II – Right of Children to Free and Compulsory Education

Special Training for the purposes of first proviso to section 4

3. (1) The School Management Committee/ local authority shall identify children requiring special training and organise such training in the following manner, namely:

(a) The special training shall be based on specially designed, age appropriate learning material, approved by the academic authority specified in section 29(1).

(b) It shall be provided in classes held on the premises of the school, or through classes organised in safe residential facilities.

(c) It shall be provided by teachers working in the school, or by teachers specially appointed for the purpose.

(d) The duration shall be for a minimum period of three months which may be extended, based on periodical assessment of learning progress, for a maximum period not exceeding two years.

(2) The child shall, upon induction into the age appropriate class, after special training, continue to receive special attention by

the teacher to enable him/her to successfully integrate with the rest of the class, academically and emotionally.

Part III – Duties of State Government, Local Authority

Areas or limits for the purposes of section 6

4. (1) The areas or limits of neighbourhood within which a school has to be established by the State Government shall be as under -

(a) In respect of children in classes I - V, a school shall be established within a walking distance of one km of the neighbourhood.

(b) In respect of children in classes VI - VIII, a school shall be established within a walking distance of three km of the neighbourhood.

(2) Wherever required, the State Government shall upgrade existing schools with classes I – V to include classes VI – VIII. In respect of schools which start from class VI onwards, the State Government shall endeavour to add classes I – V, wherever required.

(3) In areas with difficult terrain, risk of landslides, floods, lack of roads and in general, danger for young children in the approach from their homes to the school, the State Government/Local Authority shall locate the school in such a manner as to avoid such dangers, by reducing the limits specified under sub-rule (1).

(4) For children from small hamlets, as identified by the State Government/Local Authority, where no school exists within the area or limits of neighbourhood specified under sub-Rule (1) above, the State Government/Local Authority shall make adequate arrangements, such as free transportation, residential facilities and other facilities, for providing elementary education in a school, in relaxation of the limits specified under sub-Rule (1).

(5) In areas with high population density, the State Government/ local authority may consider establishment of more than one neighbourhood school, having regard to the number of children in the age group of 6-14 years in such areas.

(6) The Local Authority shall identify the neighbourhood school(s) where children can be admitted and make such information public for each habitation within its jurisdiction.

(7) In respect of children with disabilities which prevent them from accessing the school the State Government/Local Authority will endeavour to make appropriate and safe transportation arrangements for them to attend school and complete elementary education.

(8) The State Government/Local Authority shall ensure that access of children to the school is not hindered on account of social and cultural factors.

Duties of State Government and Local Authority for the purposes of Sections 8 and 9

5. (1) A child attending a school of the State Government or local authority referred to in sub-clause (i) of clause (n) of section 2, a child attending a school referred to in sub-clause (ii) of clause (n) of section 2 in pursuance of clause (b) of sub-section (1) of section 12, and a child attending a school referred to in sub-clause (iii) and (iv) of clause (n) of section 2 in pursuance of clause (c) of sub-section (1) of section 12 shall be entitled to free text books, writing materials and uniforms.

Provided that a child with disabilities shall also be provided free special learning and support material.

Explanation: In respect of the child admitted in pursuance of clause (b) of sub-section

(1) of section 12 and a child admitted in pursuance clause (c) of sub-section (1) of section 12, the responsibility of providing the free entitlement shall be of the school referred to in sub-clause (ii) of clause (n) of section 2 and of sub-clauses (iii) and (iv) of clause (n) of section 2, respectively.

(2) For the purpose of determining and for establishing neighbourhood schools, the State government/local authority shall undertake school mapping, and identify all children, including children in remote areas, children with disabilities, children belonging to disadvantaged groups, children

belonging to weaker sections and children referred to in section 4, within a period of one year from the appointed date, and every year thereafter.

(3) The State government/local authority shall ensure that no child is subjected to caste, class, religious or gender abuse in the school.

(4) For the purposes of clause (c) of section 8 and clause (c) of section 9, the State Government and the Local Authority shall ensure that a child belonging to a weaker section and a child belonging to disadvantaged group is not segregated or discriminated against in the classroom, during mid-day meals, in the play grounds, in the use of common drinking water and toilet facilities, and in the cleaning of toilets or classrooms.

Maintenance of records of children by local authority for the purposes of clause (d) of section 9

6. (1) The Local Authority shall maintain a record of all children, in its jurisdiction, through a household survey, from their birth till they attain 14 years.

(2) The record, referred to in sub-Rule (1), shall be updated each year.

(3) The record, referred to in sub-Rule (1), shall be maintained transparently, in the public domain, and used for the purposes of clause (e) of section 9.

(4) The record, referred to in sub-Rule (1) shall, in respect of every child, include

(a) name, sex, date of birth, (Birth Certificate Number), place of birth;

(b) parents' / guardians' names, address, occupation;

(c) pre-primary school/Anganwadi centre that the child attends (upto age 6);

(d) elementary school where the child is admitted;

(e) present address of the child;

(f) class in which the child is studying (for children between age 6-14), and if education is discontinued in the territorial jurisdiction of the Local Authority, the cause of such discontinuance;

(g) whether the child belongs to the weaker section within the meaning of clause (e) of section 2 of the Act;

(h) whether the child belongs to a disadvantaged group within the meaning of clause (d) of section 2 of the Act;

(i) details of children requiring special facilities / residential facilities on account of migration and sparse population; age appropriate admission; disability.

(5) The Local authority shall ensure that the names of all children enrolled in the schools under its jurisdiction are publicly displayed in each school.

Part IV – Responsibilities of Schools and Teachers

Admission of children belonging to weaker section and disadvantaged group for the purposes of clause (c) to section 12 (1)

7. (1) The school referred to in clauses (iii) and (iv) of clause (n) of section 2 shall ensure that children admitted in pursuance of clause (c) to section 12 (1) shall not be segregated from the other children in the classrooms nor shall their classes be held at places and timings different from the classes held for the other children.

(2) The school referred to in clauses (iii) and (iv) of clause (n) of section 2 shall ensure that children admitted in pursuance of clause (c) to section 12 (1) shall not be discriminated from the rest of the children in any manner pertaining to entitlements and facilities such as text books, uniforms, library and ICT facilities, extra-curricular and sports.

(3) The areas or limits of neighbourhood specified in Rule 4 (1) shall apply to admissions made in pursuance of clause (c) to section 12 (1).

Provided that the school may, for the purposes of filling up the requisite percentage of seats for children referred to in clause (c) to section 12 (1), extend these limits with the prior approval of the State Government.

Reimbursement of per-child expenditure by the State Government for the purposes of section 12(2)

8. (1) The total annual recurring expenditure incurred by the State Government, whether from its own funds, or funds provided by the Central Government or by any other authority, on elementary education in respect of all schools established, owned or controlled by it or by the local authority, divided by the total number of children enrolled in all such schools, shall be the per-child expenditure incurred by the State Government.

Explanation - For the purpose of determining the per-child expenditure, the expenditure incurred by the State Government or local authority on schools referred to in sub-clause (ii) of clause (n) of section 2 and the children enrolled in such schools shall not be included.

(2) Every school referred to in clauses (iii) and (iv) of clause (n) of section 2 shall maintain a separate bank account in respect of the amount received by it as reimbursement under subsection (2) of section 12.

Documents as age proof for the purpose of section 14

9. Wherever a birth certificate under the Births, Deaths and Marriages Certification Act, 1886 is not available, any one of the following documents shall be deemed to be proof of age of the child for the purposes of admission in schools –

(a) Hospital / Auxiliary Nurse and Midwife (ANM) register record

(b) *Anganwadi* record

(c) Declaration through an affidavit of the age of the child by the parent or guardian.

Extended period for admission for the purposes of section 15

10. (1) Extended period of admission shall be six months from the date of commencement of the academic year of a school.

(2) Where a child is admitted in a school after the extended period, he or she shall be eligible to complete studies with the help of special training, as determined by the head of the school.

Recognition of schools for the purposes of section 18

11. (1) Every school, other than a school established, owned or controlled by the State Government or Local Authority,

established before the commencement of this Act shall make a self declaration within a period of three months of the commencement of the Act, in Form No. 1 to the concerned District Education Officer regarding its compliance or otherwise with the norms and standards prescribed in the Schedule and the following conditions:

(a) the school is run by a society registered under the Societies Registration Act, 1860 (21 of 1860), or a public trust constituted under any law for the time being in force;

(b) the school is not run for profit to any individual, group or association of individuals or any other persons;

(c) the school conforms to the values enshrined in the Constitution;

(d) the school buildings or other structures or the grounds are used only for the purposes of education and skill development;

(e) the school is open to inspection by any officer authorised by the State Government/ Local Authority;

(f) the school furnishes such reports and information as may be required by the Director of Education/District Education Officer from time to time and complies with such instructions of the State Government/ Local Authority as may be issued to secure the continued fulfillment of the condition of recognition or the removal of deficiencies in working of the school;

(2) Every self declaration received in Form 1 shall be placed by the District Education Officer in public domain within fifteen days of its receipt.

(3) The District Education Officer shall conduct on-site inspection of such schools which claim in Form No. 1 to fulfill the norms and standards and the conditions mentioned in sub-Rule (1) within three months of the receipt of the self declaration.

(4) After the inspection referred to in sub-Rule (3) is carried out, the inspection report shall be placed by the District Education Officer in public domain and schools found to be conforming to the norms, standards and the conditions shall be granted

recognition by the District Education Officer in Form No. 2 within a period of 15 days from the date of inspection.

(5) Schools that do not conform to the norms, standards and conditions mentioned in sub-rule (1) shall be listed by the District Education Officer through a public order to this effect, and any time within the next two and a half years, such schools may request the District Education Officer for an on-site inspection for grant of recognition.

(6) Schools which do not conform to the norms, standards and conditions mentioned in sub-rule (1) after three years from the commencement of the Act, shall cease to function.

(7) Every school, other than a school established, owned or controlled by the State Government or local authority established after the commencement of this Act shall conform to the norms and standards and conditions mentioned in sub-Rule (1) in order to qualify for recognition.

Withdrawal of recognition to schools for the purposes of sections 18(3) and 12(3)

12. (1) Where the District Education Officer on his own motion, or on any representation received from any person, has reason to believe, to be recorded in writing, that a school recognised under Rule 12, has violated one or more of the conditions for grant of recognition or has failed to fulfill the norms and standards prescribed in the Schedule, he shall act in the following manner:

(a) Issue a notice to the school specifying the violations of the condition of grant of recognition and seek its explanation within one month.

(b) In case the explanation is not found to be satisfactory or no explanation is received within the stipulated time period, the District Education Officer may cause an inspection of the school, to be conducted by a Committee of three to five members comprising of educationists, civil society representatives, media, and government representatives, which shall make due inquiry and submit its Report, along with its recommendations for continuation of recognition or its withdrawal, to the District Education Officer.

(c) The District Education Officer shall forward the Report of the Committee, along with his comments, to the State Commission for Protection of Child or the Right to Education Protection Authority, as the case may be, with a copy to the State Education Department.

(2) The State Commission for Protection of Child Rights or the Right to Education Protection Authority, as the case may be, shall, after seeking explanation from the concerned school and after due examination, prepare and send its recommendations to the State Education Department.

(3) The State Education Department, shall, on the basis of the recommendations referred to in sub-Rule (2) convey its decision to the District Education Officer.

(4) The District Education Officer shall, on the basis of the decision of the State Education Department, pass an order cancelling the recognition granted to the school. The order of derecognition shall be operative from the immediately succeeding academic year and shall specify the neighbourhood schools to which the children of the de-recognised schools shall be admitted.

Part V – School Management Committee

Composition and Functions of the School Management Committee for the Purposes of Section 21

13. (1) A School Management Committee shall be constituted in every school, other than an unaided school, within its jurisdiction, within six months of the appointed date, and reconstituted every two years.

(2) Seventy five per cent of the strength of the School Management Committee shall be from amongst parents or guardians of children.

(3) The remaining twenty five per cent of the strength of the SMC shall be from amongst the following persons:

(a) one-third members from amongst the elected members of the local authority, to be decided by the local authority;

(b) one-third members from amongst teachers from the school, to be decided by the teachers of the school;

(c) remaining one-third from amongst local educationists / children in the school, to be decided by the parents in the Committee

(4) To manage its affairs, the School Management Committee shall elect a Chairperson and Vice-Chairperson from among the parent members. The Head teacher of the school or where the school does not have a head teacher, the seniormost teacher of the school, shall be the ex-officio Member-Convener of the School Management Committee.

(5) The School Management Committee shall meet at least once a month and the minutes and decisions of the meetings shall be properly recorded and made available to the public.

(6) The School Management Committee shall, in addition to the functions specified in clauses (a) to (d) of section 21 (2), perform the following functions, for which it may constitute smaller working groups from amongst its Members :

(a) communicate in simple and creative ways to the population in the neighbourhood of the school, the rights of the child as enunciated in the Act; as also the duties of the State Government, local authority, school, parent and guardian;

(b) Ensure the implementation of clauses (a) and (e) of section 24 and section 28;

(c) Monitor that teachers are not burdened with non-academic duties other than those specified in section 27;

(d) Ensure the enrollment and continued attendance of all the children from the neighbourhood in the school;

(e) Monitor the maintenance of the norms and standards prescribed in the Schedule;

(f) Bring to the notice of the local authority any deviation from the rights of the child, in particular mental and physical harassment of children, denial of admission, and timely provision of free entitlements as per section 3(2);

(g) Identify the needs, prepare a Plan, and monitor the implementation of the provisions of Section 4;

(h) Monitor the identification and enrollment of, and facilities for learning by disabled children, and ensure their participation in, and completion of elementary education;

(i) Monitor the implementation of the Mid-Day Meal in the school;

(j) Prepare an annual account of receipts and expenditure of the school.

(7) Any money received by the School Management Committee for the discharge of its functions under this Act, shall be kept in a separate account, to be made available for audit every year.

(8) The accounts referred to in clause (j) to sub-Rule (6) and sub-Rule (7) should be signed by the Chairperson/ Vice-Chairperson and Convenor of the School Management Committee and made available to the local authority within one month of their preparation.

Preparation of School Development Plan for the Purpose of Section 22

14. (1) The School Management Committee shall prepare a School Development Plan at least three months before the end of the financial year in which it is first constituted under the Act.

(2) The School Development Plan shall be a three year plan comprising three annual sub-plans.

(3) The School Development Plan, shall contain the following details –

(a) Estimates of class-wise enrollment for each year;

(b) Requirement, over the three year period, of the number of additional teachers, including Head Teachers, subject teachers and part time teachers, separately for Classes I to V and Classes VI to VIII, calculated, with reference to the norms specified in the Schedule.

(c) Physical requirement of additional infrastructure and equipments over the three year period, calculated, with reference to the norms and standards specified in the Schedule.

(d) Additional financial requirement over the three year period, year-wise, in respect of (b) and (c) above, including additional requirement for providing special training facility specified in section 4, entitlements of children such as free textbooks and uniforms, and any other additional financial requirement for fulfilling the responsibilities of the school under the Act.

(4) The School Development Plan should be signed by the Chairperson/Vice-Chairperson and Convenor of the School Management Committee and submitted to the local authority before the end of the financial year in which it is to be prepared.

Part VI – Teachers

Minimum Qualification for the Purposes of Section 23(1)

15. (1) The academic authority notified in pursuance of sub-section (1) of section 23, shall, within three months of such notification, lay down the minimum qualifications for persons to be eligible for appointment as a teacher in an elementary school.

(2) The minimum qualifications laid down by the academic authority referred to in sub-Rule (1) shall be applicable for every school referred to in clause (n) of section 2.

Relaxation of minimum qualification for the purposes of section 23(2)

16. (1) The State Government shall estimate the teacher requirement as per the norms in the Schedule for all schools referred to in clause (n) of section 2 within the State, within six months from the commencement of the Act.

(2) Where a State does not have adequate institutions offering courses or training in teacher education, or persons possessing minimum qualifications as laid down under sub-Rule (2) of Rule 15 are not available in sufficient numbers in relation to the requirement of teachers estimated under sub-Rule (1), the State Government shall request, within one year of the

commencement of the Act, the Central Government for relaxation of the prescribed minimum qualification.

(3) On receipt of the request referred to in sub-Rule (2), the Central Government shall examine the request of the State Government and may relax the minimum qualifications by way of a Notification.

(4) The Notification referred to in sub-Rule (3) shall specify the nature of relaxation and the time period, not exceeding three years, but not beyond five years from the commencement of the Act, within which the teachers appointed under the relaxed conditions acquire the minimum qualifications prescribed by the academic authority notified under sub-section (1) of Section 23.

(5) After six months after the commencement of the Act, no appointment of teacher for any school can be made in respect of any person not possessing the minimum qualifications prescribed by the academic authority notified under sub-section (1) of Section 23 without the notification referred to in Sub-Rule (3).

(6) A person appointed as a teacher within six months of the commencement of the Act, must possess at least the academic qualifications not lower than higher secondary school certificate or equivalent.

Acquiring minimum qualifications under proviso to section 23(2)

17. (1) The State Government shall provide adequate teacher education facilities to ensure that all teachers in schools referred to in sub-clauses (i) and (iii) of clause (n) of section 2, who do not possess the minimum qualifications laid down under sub-Rule (2) of Rule 15 at the time of commencement of the Act, to acquire such minimum qualifications within a period of five years from the commencement of the Act.

(2) For a teacher, of any school referred to in sub-clause (ii) and (iv) of clause (n) of section 2, who does not possess the minimum qualifications laid down under sub-Rule (2) of Rule 15 at the time of commencement of the Act, the management of such school shall enable such teacher to acquire such

minimum qualifications within a period of five years from the commencement of the Act.

Salary and allowances and conditions of service of teachers for the purpose of section 23(3)

18. (1) The State Government or the local authority, as the case may be, shall notify terms and conditions of service and salary and allowances of teachers in order to create a professional and permanent cadre of teachers.

(2) In particular and without prejudice to sub-rule (1), the terms and conditions of service shall take into account the following, namely -

(a) Accountability of teachers to the School Management Committee constituted under section 21.

(b) provisions enabling long-term stake of teachers in the teaching profession 11

(3) The scales of pay and allowances, medical facilities, pension, gratuity, provident fund, and other prescribed benefits of teachers, including those employed for the purpose of imparting special training as specified in Section 4, shall be that of regular teachers, and at par for similar work and experience.

Duties to be performed by teachers for the purpose of clause (f) to section 24(1)

19. (1) In performance of the functions specified in sub-section (1) of section 24(1) and in order to fulfill the requirements of clause (h) of sub-section (2) of section 29, the teacher shall maintain a file containing the pupil cumulative record for every child which will the basis for the awarding the completion certificate specified in sub-section (2) of section 30.

(2) In addition to the functions specified in clauses (a) to (e) of sub-section (1) of section 24, a teacher may perform the following duties assigned to him or her, without interfering with regular teaching:

(a) Participation in training programmes;

(b) Participation in curriculum formulation, and development of syllabi, training modules and textbook development.

Grievance Redressal mechanism for teachers for the purposes of section 24(3)

20. (1) The School Management Committee constituted under section 21 shall be the first level of grievance redressal of teachers of schools specified therein.

(2) The State Government shall constitute School Tribunals at the State, District and Block levels which would act as the grievance redressal mechanism for the teachers.

Maintaining Pupil-Teacher Ratio in each school for the purposes of section 25

21. (1) Sanctioned strength of teachers in a school shall be notified by the State Government or the local authority, as the case may be, within a period of three months of the appointed date.

Provided that the State Government or the local authority, as the case may be, shall, within three months of such Notification, redeploy teachers of schools having a strength in excess of the sanctioned strength prior to the Notification referred to in sub-Rule (1).

(2) If any person of the State Government or the local authority violates the provisions of sub-section (2) of section 25, he or she shall be personally liable for disciplinary action.

Part VII – Curriculum and Completion of Elementary Education

Academic Authority for the purposes of section 29

22. (1) The State Government shall notify the State Council of Educational Research and Training (or its equivalent), as the academic authority for the purposes of section 29.

(2) While laying down the curriculum and evaluation procedure, the academic authority notified under sub-Rule (1) shall

(a) formulate the relevant and age appropriate syllabus and text books and other learning material,

(b) develop in-service teacher training design, and

(c) prepare guidelines for putting into practice continuous and comprehensive evaluation.

(3) The academic authority referred to in sub-rule (1) shall design and implement a process of holistic school quality assessment on a regular basis.

Award of certificate for the purposes of section 30

23. (1) The Certificate of completion of elementary education shall be issued at the school/block/district level within one month of the completion of elementary education.

(2) The Certificate referred to in sub-rule (1) shall–

(a) certify that the child has completed all courses of study prescribed under section 29.

(b) contain the Pupil Cumulative Record of the child and also specify achievements of the child in areas of activities beyond the prescribed course of study and may include music, dance, literature, sports, etc.

Part VIII – Protection of Right of Children

Performance of functions by the State Commission for Protection of Child Rights, for the purposes of section 31

24. (1) In respect of a State which does not have a State Commission for Protection of Child Rights, the State Government may take immediate steps to set up the Commission.

(2) Till such time as the State Government sets up the Commission, it shall constitute an interim authority known as the Right to Education Protection Authority (REPA) for the purposes of performing the functions specified in sub-section (1) of section 31, within six months of the commencement of Act or the constitution of the State Commission for Protection of Child Rights, whichever is earlier.

(3) The Right to Education Protection Authority (REPA) shall consist of the following, namely –

(a) A chairperson who is a person of high academic repute or has been a High Court Judge or has done outstanding work for promoting the rights of children; and

(b) Two Members, of whom at least one shall be a woman, from the following areas, from amongst persons of eminence, ability, integrity, standing and experience in –

(i) education;

(ii) child healthcare and child development;

(iii) juvenile justice or care of neglected or marginalised children or children with disabilities;

(iv) elimination of child labour or working with children in distress;

(v) child psychology or sociology; or

(vi) legal profession.

(4) The National Commission for Protection of Child Rights Rules, 2006 shall, so far as pertains to the terms and conditions, mutatis mutandis apply to Chairperson and other Members of the REPA.

(5) All records and assets of the REPA shall be transferred to the State Commission for Protection of Child Rights immediately after its constitution.

(6) In performance of its functions, the State Commission for Protection of Child Rights or the REPA, as the case may be, may also act upon matters referred to it by the State Advisory Council.

(7) The State Government shall enable constituting a Cell in the State Commission for Protection of Child Rights or the REPA, as the case may be, which may assist the Commission or the REPA in performance of its functions under the Act.

Manner of furnishing complaints before the State Commission for Protection of Child Rights

25. (1) The State Commission for Protection of Child Rights, or the REPA, as the case may be, shall set up a child help line, accessible by SMS, telephone and letter, which would act as the forum for aggrieved child/guardian to register complaint regarding violation of rights under the Act, in a manner that records her identity but does not disclose it;

(2) All complaints to the helpline should be monitored through a transparent 'alert and action' online mechanism by the State Commission for Protection of Child Rights, or the REPA, as the case may be.

Constitution and Functions of the State Advisory Council for the purpose of section 34

26. (1) The State Advisory Council shall consist of a Chairperson and fourteen Members.

(2) The Minister in-charge of the Ministry/Department of School Education in the State Government shall be the ex-officio Chairperson of the Council.

(3) Members of the Council, shall be appointed by the State Government from amongst persons having knowledge and practical experience in the field of elementary education and child development, as under

(a) At least four members should be from amongst persons belonging to SCs, STs and Minorities;

(b) At least one member should be from amongst persons having specialised knowledge and practical experience of education of children with special needs;

(c) One member should be from amongst persons having specialised knowledge in the field of pre-primary education;

(d) At least two members should be from amongst persons having specialised knowledge and practical experience in the field of teacher education;

(e) Fifty per cent of such members shall be from amongst women.

(4) The Department of School Education shall provide logistic support for meetings of the Council and its other functions.

(5) The procedure for transaction of Business of the Council shall be as under.

(i) The Council shall meet regularly at such times as the Chairperson thinks fit but three months shall not intervene between its last and the next meeting.

(ii) The meeting of the Council shall be presided by the Chairperson. If for any reason the Chairperson is unable to attend the meeting of the Council, he may nominate a member of the Council to preside over such meeting. Quorum of the meeting of the Council shall be considered complete if at least 50 per cent of its members are present.

(6) The terms and conditions for appointment of Members of the Council shall be as under

  (a) Every member shall hold office as such for a term of two years from the date on which he assumes office. Provided that no member shall hold office more than two terms.

  (b) The member may be removed from his office by an order of the State Government on the ground of proved misbehaviour or incapacity, or on the happening of any one or more of the following events:

    (i) Is adjudged an insolvent; or

    (ii) Refuses to act or become incapable of acting; or

    (iii) Is of unsound mind and stands so declared by a competent Court; or

    (iv) Has so abused his office as to render his continuance in office detrimental to the public interest; or

    (v) Is convicted for an offence by a competent Court; or

    (vi) Is without obtaining leave of absence from the Council, absent from two consecutive meetings of the Council.

  (c) No Member shall be removed from his office without being given an adequate opportunity of being heard.

  (d) If vacancy occurs in the office of Members, whether by reason of his death, resignation or otherwise, such vacancy shall be filled within a period of 120 days by making a fresh appointment in accordance with the provisions of sub-Rule (2).

  (e) Members of the Council shall be entitled to reimbursement of travelling and daily allowances for official tours and journeys in accordance with the orders issued by the State Government in relation to non-official members of the Committees and Commissions and such like categories of persons. [*Source:* MHRD, GOI.]

Chapter - 11

Objectives and Provisions of the RTE Act, 2009

Though the main objective of the RTE Act, 2009 is completion of eight years of schooling in the elementary level, the following objectives may be jotted down :

- The objective of the act is to enable every child to get free and compulsory admission, attendance and completion of elementary education in a neighbourhood school.
- The act is to provide for a stress-free environment and anxiety-free education with prohibition of corporal punishment and any sort of mental harassment.
- The scope of the Act is limited to elementary education, i.e. from class 1 to class 8.
- The act is to acknowledge the duties and responsibilities that teachers are to follow, establishing a system of accountability and ensuring that students get maximum benefits from the teaching-learning process.
- The act makes provisions for a non-admitted child within age group 6 to 14 years to be admitted to an age appropriate class along with getting special training.
- The act prohibits for children in 6–14 age groups – screening procedures for admission, capitation fees, private tuition by teachers, running of schools without recognition.
- It specifies the duties and responsibilities of appropriate governments, local authority and parents in providing free

and compulsory education, and sharing of financial and other responsibilities between the Central and State Governments.

- The act lays down the norms and standards relating to Pupil Teacher Ratios (PTRs), building infrastructure, school working days, and teacher working hours.
- The act provides for rational deployment of teachers ensuring that there is practically no urban-rural imbalance in teacher postings. It also prohibits deployment of teachers for non-educational work, other than decennial census, elections to local authority, state legislature and parliament, and disaster relief.
- The act provides for appointment of appropriately trained teachers.
- The act provides for development of curriculum in consonance with the values enshrined in the constitution and age and learning levels of the children.
- The act contains provisions for establishing School Management Committees and ensuring management and supervision of schools with community support.
- It aims at eradicating the issue of child labour in the country. It provides for protection and monitoring of the child's right to free and compulsory education and redressal of grievances by the National and State Commissions for protection of Child Rights, which shall have quasi-judicial powers and can function as a civil court.
- It mandates a system of evaluation to be done throughout the year and not be based on an annual examination. There will be no failure till completion of elementary cycle and evaluation should reflect all facts, talents including music, theatre, leadership skills etc.
- All private schools are required to admit in their incoming class 25 per cent children from weaker sections and socially disadvantaged groups from their neighbourhood.
- The RTE in different sections makes reference to gender equity both explicitly and implicitly. Some of the relevant provisions are – no discrimination against children from 'disadvantaged groups' and 'weaker sections' on any ground

whatsoever, inclusion of women in school monitoring committees, provision of equity issues etc.

- It is the obligation of the government to ensure not just enrollment but attendance and completion of elementary education. It implies that the government must identify all children those are out of school or dropped out and ensure that they complete the elementary cycle of education eight years free and compulsory schooling at elementary level. If a child is admitted to elementary education shall be entitled to free education till completion of elementary education even after fourteen years.
- The Central as well as State governments will have the concurrent responsibility for providing funds necessary to meet the expenses under the Act.
- No admitted child can be held back in a class or expelled until completion of elementary education.
- Several penal provisions are also prescribed in the Act towards non-compliance.
- The Act also makes it compulsory for the parents of the children in the given age range to admit their children in the schools.
- The Act makes it mandatory for all schools to follow the guidelines of the Act to be eligible for continuity of operation or for start of a new school. Three years moratorium period has been provided to school to implement all that is required of them.
- The Act specifically bans any type of capitation fees or any screening procedure for admission to a school.

Salient Provisions of the RTE Act

The Right to Education Act, 2009 seeks to provide free and compulsory education of equitable quality to all children in the age group of six to fourteen years. The salient provisions of the Act are overviewed as follows:

(1) Section 3 provides for every child of the age of six to fourteen years, the right to free and compulsory education in a neighbourhood school till completion of elementary education.

(2) **Section 4** provides for every child above six years of age, the right to admission in a class appropriate to his or her age even if the child has not been admitted before in any school or though admitted, could not complete his elementary education.

(3) **Section 5** provides for every child, the right to seek transfer to any other school from a school where there is no provision for completion of elementary education.

(4) **Section 6** provides for duty of the appropriate government and the local authority to establish school, where it is not so established, within a period of three years from the commencement of the Act.

(5) **Section 7** seeks to provide for financial and other responsibilities of the Central Government and the State Governments and for developing by the Central Government of a national curriculum and the standards for training of teachers.

(6) **Section 8** stipulates the duty of every parent or guardian to admit his or her war or child to an elementary education in the neighbourhood school.

(7) **Section 12** imposes on schools the responsibility of providing free and compulsory education. Under this section, unaided private schools shall admit 25 per cent children to Class–I from among children belonging to weaker sections and disadvantaged groups for continued education of such children till completion of elementary education.

(8) **Section 13** provides for prohibition of capitation fee and screening in admission procedure and for punishment for contravention of these provisions.

(9) **Section 14** is meant for prohibition of denial of admission of a child for lack of age proof.

(10) **Section 15** is meant for prohibition of denial of admission to a child, irrespective of the time in the academic year.

(11) **Section 16** prohibits the holding back in any class or expelling a child from school till the completion of elementary education.

(12) **Section 17** provides for prohibition of physical punishment and mental harassment of any child in school.

(13) **Section 19** mandates fulfilment of norms and standards by schools for recognition, withdrawal of recognition and imposition of fine in case of contravention.

(14) **Section 21** seeks to spell out the constitution and functions of a school management committee.

(15) **Section 22** formulates a provision for a school development plan by the school management committee.

(16) **Section 23** seeks to ensure qualifications and terms and conditions of service of teachers.

(17) **Section 24** seeks to provide for duties of teachers, disciplinary action against them and redressal of their grievances.

(18) **Section 25** provides for maintenance of pupil-teacher ratio by appropriate governments and local authorities.

(19) **Section 26** seeks to compel filling up of vacancies of teachers in schools.

(20) **Section 27** prohibits deployment of teachers for non-educational purposes, except for decennial population census, disaster relief, elections to local authority, state legislature and Parliament.

(21) **Section 28** seeks to provide for prohibition of private tuition by teachers.

(22) **Section 29** provides for curriculum and evaluation procedure for elementary education to be laid down by an academic authority.

(23) **Section 30** prohibits detention or failing of any pupil in any class till completion of elementary education.

(24) **Section 31** provides for certain additional functions to be performed and powers to be exercised by the National and State Commissions for Protection of Child Rights in pursuance of the provisions of this Act.

(25) **Section 32** provides for redressal of grievances relating to the rights of the child under the legislation.

(26) **Section 33** seeks to provide for the constitution of a National Advisory Council to give expert advice to the Central Government on the implementation of the provisions of the RTE Act, 2009.

(27) **Section 34** provides for the constitution of a State Advisory Council to advise the State Governments on implementation of the provisions of the Act in an effective manner.

(28) **Section 35** gives the power to the appropriate government to issue guidelines as well as directions for purpose of implementation of the provisions of the Act.

(29) **Section 37** prohibits the suit or legal proceedings against the Central Government, State Government, NCPCR, and SCPCR, the local authority, SMC or any rules or order made there under.

(30) **Section 38** empowers the appropriate government may, by notification, make rules, for carrying out the provisions of this Act.

Overview of the RTE Act

The RTE Act is a detailed and comprehensive piece of legislation which includes provisions related to schools, teachers, curriculum, evaluation, access and specific division of duties and responsibilities of different stakeholders. Education is a fundamental human right, essential for the empowerment and development of an individual and the society as a whole. According to the UNESCO's 'Education for All Global Monitoring Report 2010', about 135 countries have constitutional provision for free and non-discriminatory education for all. The enforcement of the Right to Education Act brings the country closer to achieving the objectives and mission of the Millennium Development Goals (MDGs) and Education for All (EFA) and hence is a historic step taken by the Government of India. An examination of the RTE Act, 2009 reveals salient features as discussed below:

1. **Right to Free and Compulsory Education:** The sections 3 to 5 under Chapter II explain the Right of Child to free and compulsory education. Every child of the age of six to fourteen shall have a right to free and compulsory education in a neighbourhood school till completion of elementary

education. The Act is flexible on the age of entry in the school by stating that :

Where a child above six years of age has not been admitted in any school or though admitted, could not complete his / here elementary education, then, he / she shall be admitted in a class appropriate to his / her age. It further provides that where a child above six years of age is directly admitted in a class appropriate to his / her age, he / she shall, in order to be at par with others, have a right to receive special training. Such a child shall be entitled to free education till completion of elementary education even after fourteen years. As per Section 5(1) where in a school, there is no provision for completion elementary education, a child shall have a right to seek transfer to any other school, excluding Kendriya Vidyalaya, Navodaya Vidyalaya, Sainik School etc. (specified category) and unaided private schools, for completing his/her elementary education.

RTE Implementation Authorities

↓

Union Government (Sections 6 to 8 and 35 to 28)

State / UT Government (Sections 6 to 8 and 35 to 38)

National / State Commission for Protection of Child Rights (Sections 31 – 32)

National / State Advisory Council (Sections 33 – 34)

Local Authorities (Section 9)

School Management Committee (Sections 21 to 23)

Schools (Sections 12 to 20)

Teachers (Sections 25 to 28)

2. **Governance for Free and Compulsory Education: Duties, Responsibilities and Functions:** The RTE Act makes an

elaborate arrangement to spell out the jurisdiction and obligations of various administrative authorities responsible for implementation of the Act, These are (Jakhar, 2010).

2.1 Duties of Appropriate Government: As per the definition of the Act, Central Government, Administrators of UTs, State Government, Municipal Corporation, Municipals Council, Zila Parishad, Nagar Panchayat or Panchayat or other name for PRIs, have been called as appropriate governments. The central government and the state governments shall have concurrent responsibility for providing funds for carrying out the provisions of this Act. The Central Government shall workout the estimates of capital and recurring expenditure. Besides, the central government shall provide to the state governments, as grants-in-aid of revenues, such percentage of expenditure referred from time to time, in consultation with the State Governments. The Central Government may make a request to the President to make a reference to the Finance Commission of India to examine the need for the additional resources to be provided to any State Government so that the said State Government may provide its share of funds for carrying out the provisions of the Act.

The Central Government shall:

(a) Develop a framework of national curriculum with the help of academic authority.

(b) Develop and enforce standards for training of teachers.

(c) Provide technical support and resources to the State Government for promoting innovations, researchers, planning and capacity building.

In addition to specific functions to the Central Government, the appropriate governments shall be responsible for :

(i) Providing free elementary education to every child of the age of six to fourteen years;

(ii) Ensuring compulsory admission, attendance and completion of elementary education by every child of the age of six to fourteen years;

(iii) Ensuring availability of a neighbourhood school;

(iv) Ensuring that the child belonging to weaker section and the child belonging to disadvantaged group are not discriminated against and prevented from pursuing and completing elementary education on any grounds;

(v) Providing infrastructure including school building, teaching staff and learning equipment;

(vi) Providing special training facility specified in section 4;

(vii) Ensuring and monitoring the admission, attendance and completion of elementary education by every child;

(viii) Ensuring good quality elementary education conforming to the standards and norms specified in the Schedule;

(ix) Ensuring timely prescribing of curriculum and courses of study for elementary education; and

(x) Providing training facility for teachers.

Local Authority shall:

- Provide free and compulsory elementary education to every child;
- Ensure availability of a neighbourhood school;
- Ensure that the child belonging to weaker section and the child belonging to disadvantaged group are not discriminated against and prevented from pursuing and completing elementary education on any grounds;
- Maintain records of children up to the age of fourteen years residing within its jurisdiction;
- Ensure and monitor admission, attendance and completion of elementary education by every child residing within its jurisdiction;
- Provide infrastructure including school building, teaching staff and learning material; and special training facility;
- Ensure good quality elementary education conforming to the standards and norms specified in the schedule;
- Ensure timely prescribing of curriculum and courses of study for elementary education;
- Provide training facility for teachers;

- Ensure admission of children of migrant families;
- Monitor functioning of schools within its jurisdiction; and
- Decide the academic calendar.

2. Protection of Right of Children by National / State Government: The National Commission for Protection of Child Rights constituted under section 3, or as the case may be, the State Commission for Protection of Child Rights constituted under section 17, shall, in addition to the functions assigned to them under that Act, also perform the following functions, namely:

(a) Examining and reviewing the safeguards for rights provided by or under this act and recommend measures for their implementation;

(b) Inquiring into complaints relating to child's right to free and compulsory education; and

(c) Taking necessary steps for protection of children rights.

Any person having any grievance relating to the right of a child under this Act may make a written complaint to the local authority having jurisdiction. After receiving the complaint under Sub-section (I), the local authority shall decide the matter within a period of three months after affording a reasonable opportunity of being heard to the parties concerned. Any person aggrieved by the decision of the local authority, may prefer an appeal to the Commission for protection of child rights or the authority prescribed under Sub-section (3) of Section 31, as the case may be.

4. Constitution of National/State Advisory Councils: The Central/ State Governments shall constitute, by notification, a National/ State Advisory Council, consisting of such number of members, not exceeding fifteen, as the Central / State Governments has deem necessary, to be appointed from amongst persons having knowledge and practical experience in the field of elementary education and child development. The functions of the National / State Advisory Council shall be to advise the Central / State Governments on implementation of the provisions of the Act in an effective manner.

5. School Management Committee: A school, other than a school specified in sub-section (iv) of section (n) of Section 2, shall constitute a School Management Committee (SMC) consisting of the elected representatives of the local authority, parents or guardians of children admitted in such school and teachers. In the committee, at least three-fourth of members shall be parents or guardians and 50 pe cent women and proportionate representation to the parents or guardians of children belonging to disadvantaged group and weaker section.

6. Responsibilities of Schools: A school under the Act is assigned onerous task to provide free and compulsory elementary education to all children admitted therein. An aided school shall provide free and compulsory elementary education to such proportion of children admitted therein as its annual recurring aid or grants so received bears to its annual recurring expenses, subject to a minimum of twenty five per cent. A school belonging to specified category and an unaided school shall admit in class I, to the extent of at least twenty five per cent of the strength of that class, children belonging to weaker section and disadvantaged group in the neighbourhood and provide free and compulsory elementary education till its completion. The Act lays down specific obligations for school, namely :

- No school or person shall, while admitting a child, collect any capitation fee and subject the child or his or her parents or guardian to any screening procedure.
- Any school or person, if in contravention of the provisions, receives capitation fee, shall be punishable with fine which may extend to twenty-five thousand rupees for the first contravention and fifty thousand rupees for each subsequent contravention.
- No child shall be denied admission in a school for lack of age proof.
- No child admitted in a school shall be held back in any class or expelled from school till the completion of elementary education.
- No child shall be subjected to physical punishment or mental harassment.
- No school, other than a school established, owned or controlled by the appropriate government or the local authority, shall, after the commencement of this Act, be established or function,

without obtaining a certificate of recognition from such authority by making an application in such form and manner, as may be prescribed.

- No school shall be established or recognised under Section 18, unless it fulfils the norms and standards specified in the schedule.

7. Teachers: Qualifications for Appointment, Terms and Conditions, Duties and Redressal of Grievances: The teachers, subject to rules made by appropriate governments, act as hub of the RTE. As per the Provision 23 of the Act : Any person possessing such minimum qualification, as laid down by an academic authority, authorised by the central government, by notification, shall be eligible for appointment as a teacher. It further says that where a state does not have adequate institutions offering courses or training in teacher education, or teachers possessing minimum qualifications as laid down under Sub-section (I) are not available in sufficient numbers, the Central Government may, if it deems necessary, by notification, relax the minimum qualifications required for appointment as a teacher, for such period, not exceeding five years, as may be specified in that notification.

Any teacher who, at the commencement of this Act, does not possess minimum qualifications as laid down under Sub-section (I), shall acquire such minimum qualifications within a period of five years. The salary and allowances payable to, and the terms and conditions of service of teachers shall be such as may be prescribed.

7.1 A teacher shall perform the following duties

- Maintaining regularity and punctuality in attending school;
- Completing the curriculum in accordance with the provisions of Sub-sections (2) of Section 29;
- Completing entire curriculum within the specified time;
- Assessing the learning ability of each child and accordingly supplement additional instructions, if any, as required;
- Holding regular meetings with parents and guardians and apprise them about the regularity in attendance, ability to learn, progress made in learning and any other relevant information about the child; and

- A teacher committing default in performance of above duties shall be liable to disciplinary action under the service rules applicable to him or her provided that before taking such disciplinary action, reasonable opportunity of being heard shall be afforded to such teacher.
- The grievances, if any, of the teacher shall be redressed in such manner as may be prescribed. For the purpose of maintaining the pupil-teacher ratio under sub-section (I) of section 25 no teacher posted in a school shall be made to serve in any other school or office or deployed for any non-educational purpose, except population census, disaster relief and election duties.
- The appointing authority shall ensure that vacancy of teacher in a school under its control shall not exceed ten per cent of the total sanctioned strength.
- No teacher shall engage himself or herself in private tuition teaching activity.

References

- Aradhya, N. and Kashyap, A. (2006). *The 'Fundamentals' – Right to Education in India,* Books for Change, Bangalore.
- Ghosh, Jayati (2011). Public Spending on Education in India, *Frontline* 28(24), 2–5 July 2011, pp. 10-12.
- Gosai, M. R. (2009). The Recent Right to Education and the Present State of Primary Education, *University News*, 47 (47), Nov. 23 – 29, 2009, pp. 1-6, New Delhi.
- Jakhar, J. S. (2010). 'Right to Education Act, 2009: Salient Features of Major Problems of Implementation', *University News,* 48(47) : 06 – 12, New Delhi.
- Jha, P. and Parvati, P. (2010). Right to Education Act 2009 : Critical Gaps and Challenges, *Economic and Political Weekly,* Vol. XLV, No. 13, pp. 20-22.
- Juneja, Nalini (1997). Right of the child to Education and Issues in Implementation of Compulsory Education: Perceptions of Educational Administrators, *New Frontiers in Education* 27(1), pp. 1-12.
- MHRD (2009). The Right of the Children to Free and Compulsory Education, 2009, Department of Elementary Education and Literacy, MHRD, Government of India, New Delhi.

- Mondal, A. and Mete, J. (2011). Common School System in the light of Right to Education Act, 2009, *Edusearch*, Vol. 2, No. 2, pp. 45-55.
- Mondal, A. and Mete, J. (2011). Education for Minorities and SC / ST in the Context of SSA, *Educational Herald*, Vol. 14, No. 14, pp. 14-22.
- Mondal, A. and Mete, J. (2012). Continuous Comprehensive Evaluation and West Bengal Board of Secondary Education: An Overview, *Journal of Education and Culture*, Vol. 4, pp. 45-55.
- Mondal, A.and Mete, J. (2012). Right to Education – An Appraisal, *Kurukshetra*, Vol. 60, No. 11, Sept. 2012, pp. 11-14.
- NCERT (2005). National Curriculum Framework 2005, NCERT, New Delhi.
- Sadgopal, A. (2010). Right to Education vs. Right to Education Act, *Social Scientist*, Volume 38, No. 9/12 (Sept. – Dec., 2010), pp. 17-50.
- Sadgopal, A. (2011). 'Neoliberal Act', *Frontline*, India's National Magazine, 28(14) : 04-09, Chennai.
- Sharma, R. and Saini, R. (2012). Implementation of RTE Act, 2009 in Rural India, *International Referred Research Journal*, Vol. III, Issue 29, pp. 60-62.
- Singh, J. (2012). Right to Education: An Assessment, *Indian Streams Research Journal*, Vol. 1, Issue XIII. Feb, 2012.
- Singh, R. (2012). Development of Right to Education in India : A Historical Appraisal, *University News,* 50 (30), July 23 – 29, 2012, pp. 16-25, New Delhi.
- Tomasevski, K. (1999). Children's rights, adult's duties. International Consultative Forum on Education for All. *Education – a right or a priviledge? Student journalists report on the right to education worldwide*. 1999, p. 3.
- Tomasevski, K. (2001). Right to Education Primers No. 3, Swedish International Development Corporation Agency, Stockholm, Sweden.
- Tomasevski, K. (2003). *Education denied: costs and remedies.* London: Zed Books, 2003.
- Tomasevski, K. (2004). Manual on right-based education: global human rights requirements made simple, UNESCO, Bangkok.

Chapter - 12

Frequently Asked Questions (FAQs) on the RTE Act, 2009

[FAQs, PART – I]

The Right to Free and Compulsory Education Act, 2009 was passed by the Parliament in August 2009, and after receiving Presidential assent immediately thereafter, it was notified for implementation from April 1, 2010. The 86th amendment that provides the children of India, in the age group 6 to 14 years, a fundamental right to free and compulsory education was simultaneously notified the same day. It has now been two years since the implementation of the Act but questions are still looming in the minds of people. The Act is still a puzzle to many. To ease the understanding of the Act, Vinod Raina, a member of the CABE Committee that drafted the Act, has put together a few FAQs.

I. Hundred years of Right to Education: From 1911 to 2010

Q1. When was the first demand for RTE made in the country?

"I beg to place the following resolution before the council for its consideration.... the state should accept in this country the same responsibility in regard to mass education that the government of most civilised countries are already discharging and that a well considered scheme should be drawn up and adhered to till it is carried out.. The well being of millions upon millions of children who are waiting to be brought under the influence education depends upon it..." The above words are the part of the resolution which Gopal Krishna Gokhale moved in the Imperial Legislative Council on 18th March, 1910 for

seeking provision of 'Free and Compulsory Primary Education" in India. This initiative must however be seen as part of the following sequence of events:

1870: Compulsory Education Act passed in Britain.

1882: Indian Education Commission: Indian leaders demand provision for mass education and Compulsory Education Acts.

1893: Maharaja of Baroda introduces Compulsory Education for boys in Amreli Taluk.

1906: Maharaja of Baroda extends Compulsory Education to rest of the state.

1906: Gopal Krishna Gokhale makes a plea to Imperial Legislative Council for introduction of Free and Compulsory Education.

1910: Gokhale proposes Private members Bill (Rejected).

1917: Vithalbhai Patel is successful in getting the Bill passed - First Law on Compulsory Education passed (Popularly Known as Patel Act).

1918: Every Province in British India gets Compulsory Education Act on its.

1930: Statute Book.

1930: Hartog Committee Recommendation for better quality (less focus on quantity) hinders spread and development of primary education.

Many of these initiatives, however, were not seriously implemented; lack of resources and enforcement being the chief reasons.

Q2. What was Mahatma Gandhi's contribution to the demand?

The situation worsened over the years forcing Mahatma Gandhi to give a stirring call for universal education in 1937. His plea for adequate finances for universal education was met with a response that if at all, the way out was to utilise revenues from liquor sales. That meant he had to either give up his stand on prohibition, or his plea for universal education with state support, which he expressed quite plainly:

"the cruelest irony of the new reforms lies in the fact that we are left with nothing but liquor revenue to fall back upon in order to give our children education (*Harijan* 5, 222)'. He solved what he called the 'Educational Puzzle' by proposing self-funded education, in what came to be known *nai talim* later.

Q3. How was the original Article 45 of the Constitution arrived at?

1946: Constituent assembly began its task.

1947: Ways and Means (Kher) Committee set up to explore *ways and means* of achieving Universal Elementary Education within ten years at lesser cost.

1947: Constituent Assembly Sub-Committee on Fundamental rights places free and compulsory education on list of Fundamental Rights: *"Clause 23- Every citizen is entitled as of... right to free primary education and it shall be the duty of the State to provide within a period of ten years from the commencement of this Constitution for free and compulsory primary education for all children until they complete the age of fourteen years."*

1947 (April): Advisory Committee of the Constituent Assembly **rejects** free and compulsory education as a fundamental right (costs being the reason). Sends clause to list of "non-justifiable fundamental rights" later termed as 'Directive Principles of State Policy'.

1949: Debate in Constituent Assembly Removes the First Line of 'Article 36'..."*Every citizen is entitled as of right to free primary education and it shall be the duty of the State to...*" and replaces it with *"The State shall endeavour to..."*

Why was the word 'primary' education removed?..."A provision has been made in article 18, to forbid any child being employed below the age of 14. Obviously if the child is not to be employed below the age of 14, the child must be kept occupied in some educational institution. That is the object of article 36.." -Sh B. R. Ambedkar, 23rd Nov. 1949

1950: Finally, Article 45 of Directive Principles of State Policy accepted: *"The State shall endeavour to provide, within a period of ten years from the commencement of this Constitution, for free and compulsory education for all children until they complete the age of fourteen years."*

This denied a justifiable right. The inadequacy of the final Article 45 was foreseen by K.T. Shah in his note of dissent in April 1947 thus: "Once an unambiguous declaration of such a (justiciable) right is made, those responsible for it would have to find ways and means to give effect to it. If they had no such obligation placed upon them, they might be inclined to avail themselves of every excuse to justify their own inactivity in the matter, indifference or worse.

These words of K. T. Shah proved prophetic. On the fate of Article 45 after independence, the noted Gandhian economist L.C. Jain has observed that there was no reference to education in any of the budget speeches during the ten year period after the adoption of the Constitution, which was the time target envisaged by Article 45. It should therefore be clear that the plea of lack of resources made even Gandhi think of alternative methods, and Babasaheb Ambedkar to accept dropping the draft Article 36 from the final Constitution. Many shortcomings of the 2009 Act, like excluding the 0-6 and 14-18 age groups stem from the same lack of resources argument, and even the fate of the implementation of the 2009 Act will crucially depend on the availability and proper utilisation of adequate finances. In this context, where as it is heartening that the Prime Minister in his unprecedented address to the nation on the Act on April 1, 2010 said that financial availability will not be allowed to hamper the implementation of the Act, one hopes that this promise to the nation will inform state policy in the coming years.

Q4. What did the Supreme Court have to say?

The Supreme Court in 1993 held free education until a child completes the age of 14 to be a right (Unnikrishnan and others Vs State of Andhra Pradesh and others) by stating that: *"The citizens of this country have a fundamental right to education. The said right flows from Article 21. This right is, however, not an absolute right. Its content and parameters have to be determined in the light of Articles 45 and 41. In other words, every child/citizen of this country has a right to free education until he completes the age of fourteen years. Thereafter his right to education is subject to the limits of economic capacity and development of the State."*

Q5. What is the 86th Amendment?

Spurred by the Unnikrishnan judgment and a public demand to enforce the right to education, successive governments from 1993 worked towards bringing a constitutional amendment to make education a fundamental right. That led to the 86th amendment in December 2002 which inserted the following articles in the Constitution:

1. Insertion of new article 21A- After article 21 of the Constitution, the following article shall be inserted, namely:-

   Right to education.- "21A. The State shall provide free and compulsory education to all children of the age of **six** to **fourteen** years in such manner as the State may, by law, determine."

2. Substitution of new article for article 45- For article 45 of the Constitution, the following article shall be substituted, namely: Provision for early childhood care and education to children below the age of six years.

   "45. The State shall endeavour to provide early childhood care and education for all children until they complete the age of six years."

3. Amendment of article 51A- In article 51A of the Constitution, after clause (J), the following clause shall be added, namely:-

   "(k) who is a parent or guardian to provide opportunities for education to his child or, as the case may be, ward between the age of six and fourteen years."

Q6. It is said that the 86th amendment diverted from the Unnikrishnan judgment; how?

The original Article 45 of the Directive Principles had used the term 'up to 14 years' and the Unnikrishnan judgment said 'till he completes the age of 14 years'. Both these definitions contain the age group 0-6 years. Article 21A restricted the age group from 6 to 14, thereby removing the 0-6 age group from the right; relegating it to the new article 45 of Directive Principles. The Unnikrishnan judgment had further observed that the right to education *existed* and would not be contingent upon the economic capacity of the state up to 14 years of age. Article 21A said that it would come into force 'in such manner as the State may, by law, determine'. So it was made contingent on a law that the state *may* bring in. This Act is that law, and it took another eight years to come since the 86th amendment was passed. So it took seventeen years for the right to be enforced since the Unnikrishnan judgment, that too for the restricted age group of 6 to 14 years. It may be noted here that it was the Parliamentary Standing Committee on Education that recommended the age group 6 to 14 years for the eventual 86th constitutional amendment, paving the way for the restricted age group.

Q7. What was the sequence of events leading to the 2009 Act?

After the 86th amendment in December 2002 the following actions took place:

- 2003: The Free and Compulsory Education For Children Bill, 2003 (NDA government)
- 2004: The Free and Compulsory Education For Children Bill, 2004 (NDA government)
- 2005: The Right to Education Bill, 2005 (June) (CABE Bill) (UPA I government)
- 2005: The Right to Education Bill, 2005 (August) (UPA I government)
- 2006: Central legislation discarded. States advised to make their own Bills based on The Model Right to Education Bill, 2006 (UPA I government)
- 2008/9: Central legislation revived. The Right of Children to Free and

Compulsory Bill, 2008, **introduced/ passed in Rajya Sabha and Lok Sabha. President's assent in August 2009.** However, the notification of the Act and the 86th amendment, issued on Feb 19, 2010 in the Gazette of India, stating that implementation will begin from April 1, 2010, eight months after the Presidential assent. (UPA-II Government). Notice that the word 'Right' was missing in the first two drafts of the Bill and was used from the 2005 CABE bill onwards. The central legislation was dropped in 2006 in preference to state legislations based on a token model bill draft, for the recurring 'lack of central resources' argument, but it was intense public pressure based on independent financial estimates that made it possible to revive and bring back the central legislation in 2008.

Q8. Will the Act apply everywhere in India? Why is J&K left out?

Under article 370 of the Constitution, many central Acts do not automatically apply to J&K. The J&K state legislature can however pass a Bill to come at par with the rest of the country. Otherwise the Act will apply to all other states and UTs of India.

Q9. Does the Act cover minority institutions as defined under articles 29 and 30 of the constitution?

As it stands, the Act does cover such institutions too; with an amendment that has recently been introduced in the Parliament (see Q. for proposed amendments to the Act).

Q10. Where do existing State Acts on Education stand in relation to the RTE Act?

They would have to be brought in conformity with the central Act. As per article 254 of the constitution reproduced below, a state Act can not violate the provisions of the Central Act in a concurrent subject. States could amend such a Central Act, but that would require Presidential assent. However, if the state Act contains anything on which the central Act is silent, then that may remain as a part of the state Act.

254. (1) If any provision of a law made by the Legislature of a State is repugnant to any provision of a law made by Parliament which Parliament is competent to enact, or to any provision of an existing law with respect to one of the matters enumerated in the Concurrent

List, then, subject to the provisions of clause (2), the law made by Parliament, whether passed before or after the law made by the Legislature of such State, or, as the case may be, the existing law, shall prevail and the law made by the Legislature of the State shall, to the extent of the repugnancy, be void.

(2) Where a law made by the Legislature of a State with respect to one of the matters enumerated in the Concurrent List contains any provision repugnant to the provisions of an earlier law made by Parliament or an existing law with respect to that matter, then, the law so made by the Legislature of such State shall, if it has been reserved for the consideration of the President and has received his assent, prevail in that State: Provided that nothing in this clause shall prevent Parliament from enacting at any time any law with respect to the same matter including a law adding to, amending, varying or repealing the law so made by the Legislature of the State.

Q11. Does Right to Education under the Act include home-based education, alternative education or education at other alternative sites? Could a child studying at home seek expenditure from the state?

No, the Act does not recognise a child's right to free education at a site other than a school defined in the Act. In that sense, the Act is more like a "Right to Free and Compulsory *Schooling*'. Schooling would in fact be compulsory for all children.

Q12. Would special schools run by NGOs qualify as legal schools under the Act?

Not unless they attain the norms and standards as defined in the Act; within three years of notification of the Act.

Q13. Would education through the open schooling system be deemed to be equivalent to formal education as envisaged under the RTE?

Open schooling provides external certification at various levels in the 6 to 14 age group, even when a child is either not in a school, or is in an informal or non-formal school. Since the Act replaces board examinations by Comprehensive and Continuous Evaluation (CCE) in this age group, and makes education in a neighbourhood school of minimum norms and standards provided by the schedule of the Act compulsory, open school certification would no longer be admissible under the Act. The National Institute of Open Schooling has already withdrawn its certification process for the 6 to 14 age group. All children not in school, or previously under an open school situation have a right to be admitted to age-appropriate class to a neighbourhood school, without having to produce any certification of their earlier education.

II. Definitions in the Act

Q14. What is 'appropriate Government'?

Education being a concurrent subject under the constitution, meaning both the Central and State Governments have responsibility for it, appropriate government in the Act refers to either of these governments, or the government of a Union Territory with a legislature (like Delhi). The full definition is at 2(a) in the Act.

Q15. How was the definition (age) of the child decided?

As mentioned earlier, by confining the Act to Article 21A. The government's decision to do so has obviously got Parliamentary approval with this Act. The original Article 45, and the Unnikrishnan verdict both include the age group 0-6. The Juvenile Justice Act defines a child up to age 18. The United Nation's Child Rights Convention (UNCRC), to which India is a signatory, also defines a child from 0 to 18. In principle, by referring to the JJ Act, the UNCRC and Article 21 (right to life) in the Aims and Objects of the RTE Act, the age could have been defined from 0-18. However, citing economic compulsions, the present Act has been confined to the age group 6-14 as contained in Article 21A. A great deal of public pressure would need to be kept up in order to have the Act amended to incorporate the 0-18 as the age of the child.

Q16. What is 'local authority'?

The Act makes school education a tripartite partnership between the community (school management committees), the PRIs, and the government. As is evident from definition 2(h), the purpose of defining a local authority is to decentralise administrative control by bringing in panchayati raj institutions. However, since differing situations exist in states, the term is flexible and it is left to the state governments to notify an appropriate local authority. For example, Jharkhand continues to be a state where panchayat elections have still not been held, and West Bengal already has a Primary Education Council that it may decide to designate as the local authority. Similarly NE states like Meghalaya have District Councils, which they may want to retain as 'local authority'.

Q17. What about a child without parents or guardian?

Section 2(k) only defines the parents of a child, and section 10 also refers to parent's duty in ensuring education of their children. However, since under Section 8 (explanation (i)), the 'compulsion' is on the state and not on parents, the appropriate government shall have to take the responsibility to ensure education of children without parents.

Q18. What does 'prescribed' mean?

Where ever the word 'prescribe' occurs, it implies that the appropriate government shall make relevant rules.

Q19. How is the 'school' defined?

At section 2(n), four categories are defined: (i) funded and managed by the government or local authority, (ii) private but aided by the government or local authority, (iii) schools defined under special category, like Kendriya Vidyalaya, Navodaya Vidyalaya, Sainik School, school under the Central Tibetan Schools Association and similar others, and (iv) private schools receiving no aid from the government or local authority.

Q20. What does 'screening procedure' mean?

Any test or interview/interaction of the child or interview/ interaction of parents would constitute a screening procedure to admit one child over another. Section 2(o) along with Section 13(2)(b) prohibits any of these screening procedures and calls for only random procedures to be used for admitting a child to school. Random procedure implies that if the number of children applying to a school exceeds the available seats, an open lottery system shall be used to fill the seats. This applies to all categories of schools. Various methods could be employed for the open lottery system, the easiest being having name/number for each child that applied on a folded paper slip in a container, out of which children themselves fish out one each randomly, in the presence of parents in an open transparent manner.

Q21. Who are 'disadvantaged children' and children belonging to 'weaker sections'?

Children belonging to disadvantaged groups are defined at 2(d). These include children from SC/ST, and other socially and educationally backward categories based on cultural, economical, social, geographical, linguistic, gender or other categories that the appropriate governments can separately notify. Appropriate governments can for example notify different categories in different districts and sub-districts of the state, educationally backward religious communities, for example as identified by the Sachar Committee and so on. Weaker sections as defined at 2(e) are children belonging to weaker economic categories that the appropriate governments have to notify, based on a minimum annual income of the parents/guardians.

III. Right to Free and Compulsory Education

Q22. What is the implication of 'free education' in the Act?

Free education is often meant to imply waiver of tuition fees. But tuition fee is only a part of educational expense, and poor families are often not able to raise other expenses needed for education. These could include textbooks, copies and writing material, uniforms, transportation, educational and support materials for disabled children (hearing aids, spectacles, Braille books, crutches and so on), or even library fee, laboratory fee, etc. which are not covered under tuition fee. The phenomenon of drop-outs in particular is related to inability of parents to meet the educational expense of their children, often daughters, somewhere during the course of elementary education. Keeping this in mind, the Act at Section 3(2) enlarges the term 'free' by mandating that "no child shall be liable to pay any kind of **fee** or **charges** or **expenses** which may prevent him or her from pursuing and completing elementary education". A list of free entitlements is made explicit in 5(1) of the Model Rules, but it is not restrictive; as per Section 3(2) of the Act, if any other charge or expense, other than that listed in Model Rules 5(1), for example, free residential facilities for children whose parents migrate, prevents a child from pursuing or completing elementary education, the state shall have to provide it.

Q23. On whom does 'compulsion' lie?

As per Section 8 (explanation) (1) and (2), the state is compelled to provide free education and ensure compulsory admission, attendance and completion of elementary education. The implication is that if a child in the age group 6-14 is working at a tea shop, agricultural field and so on, cooking at home or simply wandering around when the school is functioning the government is violating his/her fundamental right. It is the government that must ensure that all children are attending, and complete elementary education. This has immediate impact on child labour. If the child is engaged in child labour and is not in school, it is the government now that is in violation of law. Consequently, the Child Labour Act 1986 is no more in coherence with this Act and there is already pressure building on the Labour Ministry to review and amend the 1986 Act to bring it in harmony with the Right to Education Act.

Q24. Why not on parents?

In a country like India where such a large majority of parents are poor, migrate for work, do not have support systems, putting compulsion on them, with punishment, would imply punishing them for being poor – which is not their choice. As the well-known educationist J.P. Naik once jocularly remarked, if parents are sent to jail for not sending their children to schools, there may be more parents in jails than children in schools!

Q25. If parents don't send children to schools...?

Section (10) of the Act makes it the duty of the parents to ensure that their children go to schools, without prescribing any punishment.

This implies that SMC members, local authorities and community at large must persuade reluctant parents to fulfill their duty. For child labour and street children, the government would have to ensure that they are not compelled to work and provide schools for them, perhaps residential in many instances. Parents and communities who traditionally forbid their adolescent girls from going to school, or indulge in child marriage would have to be persuaded, or the child marriages act would need to be invoked against them. Civil society interventions would be crucial here.

Q26. Is the Act targeted only for weaker sections?

No, it is universal. Any child who is a citizen of India, rich or poor; boy or girl; born to parents of any caste, religion or ethnicity shall have this right. If a rich parent decides to send his/her child to a school owned by the government/local authority, that child would also have a right to all the free entitlements. Only those children who are sent by their parents to a school that charges fees (private aided/unaided) will surrender their right, as per Section 8(a) of the Act, to free entitlements; they can not claim reimbursement from the government for their educational expenditure (except for the obligatory 25 per cent quota for children of disadvantaged groups and weaker sections to unaided schools, described later).

Q27. Have the disabled children been adequately addressed in the Act?

There are deficiencies in the Act as it was passed in August 2009 in relation to children with disabilities. They should have been included in the definition of disadvantaged groups, but were inadvertently left out. The Act says that their education shall follow the provisions of the Disabilities Act 1996, but that Act has deficiencies in as much that it does not include mental disabilities. The central government has acknowledged these lacunae and promised to bring appropriate amendments in the Budget 2010 session of Parliament, as also to amend the Disabilities Act 1996 appropriately. The proposed amendments are at Q82.

Q28. Would home-based education to the severely disabled come within the purview of the Act?

As the Act stands, education would be inclusive for all categories of disability, including severe and profound.

Q29. What about children not in schools right now?

The Act, at Section 4 lays down that all children who are out of school, as never enrolled or drop outs (in the 6-14 age group), would have to be admitted in age appropriate class in regular schools, and they would have a right to complete elementary education even after crossing age 14.

Q30. What does 'age appropriate class' mean?

It means giving admission in a class where the child would normally be if she had joined school from class 1 at six years of age. So if a child is 11 years old and has never been to school, she will be admitted to class 5, but shall be given special education to make her come to the level in a time frame ranging from three months to two years (model rules 3(1)).

Q31. The model rules provide for such special training through residential facilities and by teachers specially engaged for the purpose 3 (1) (b) and (c). What about involving NGOs that have in the technical background to do so?

If NGO's qualify as per the teacher qualifications and other norms, they could be associated, but as part of the regular school where the children are first admitted, and not as running separate residential or non-residential non-formal centres.

Q32. Can children actually be made equal to age appropriate class in two years?

Pioneering work by groups like the MV Foundation has shown that it is indeed possible to do so. However certain flexibility could be used after the duration of special training. If a child after completing special training is 13 years old and should be in class 7 by the age appropriateness criterion, but the teacher/school feels that it would be better for the child, in terms of coping, to be in class 6, they could advise the child/parents accordingly.

Q33. What if children admitted after age 6 complete age 14 before completing class 8?

They would have the right to get free education till they complete class 8, even if they exceed age 14. This would apply, for example, to a 13 year never enrolled child who may take five years to complete class VIII, up to the age of 18 years, or more.

Q34. What about age proof and transfer certificates?

In the absence of a regular birth certificate issued under the Births, Deaths and Marriages Registration Act 1886, a certificate based on hospital/ANM record, *anganwadi* record or an affidavit by the parents/ guardian would suffice (Model Rule 9). However, under section 14(2) of the Act, if none of these are available, including a notarised affidavit, a child would not be denied admission, meaning if the parents say the child is six years or more, admission would have to be given, while any of the above mentioned documents is simultaneously arranged. The head teacher would have to immediately issue a transfer certificate to a child moving away from the school, or face disciplinary action in case of delay. However, no child shall be denied admission in the absence of a transfer certificate, (Sections 5 (2) and (3) of the Act).

IV. Duties of Governments and Local Authority

Q35. What kind of a school shall be provided to children and when?

The Act lays down minimum norms and standards for all schools, government and private, through a mandatory schedule. This includes number of teaching days per year, number of teaching hours per day, number of rooms, availability of teaching learning materials, library, toilets, safe drinking water, playground, kitchen for mid-day meals, Pupil Teacher Ratio, subject teachers in classes 6 to 8, part time art, work and physical instructors and so on. Governments and private managements have three years to upgrade their existing schools to these minimum norms, barring which they will not be allowed to operate. Governments have to provide such a neighbourhood school to all children within three years, i.e. by March 31, 2013. The prescribed norms are minimum, which implies that nothing stops state governments/managements to have higher norms than those listed in the schedule. In particular, if some schools already have higher norms, it does not imply that they reduce those norms to match the schedule.

Q36. Why is not 'neighbourhood school' defined in the Act? Why leave it to Rules?

To ensure that instead of a rigid national norm, the states define it in terms of their geographical, social and cultural realities. The Model Rule (4) indicates these realities, like difficult terrain, risk of landslides, floods, lack of roads, and in general, danger to young children where the one km and three km norm could be reduced. For children of small hamlets, it could mean free transportation by extending the distance limits, or residential schools. The Rules also prescribe that governments will have to take responsibility to ensure children with disabilities are helped to reach school, as also to ensure that social and cultural barriers, like low caste children and young girls not being able to access their schools due to social interference, are taken care of. The model rules for neighbourhood and access could be further improved by the state governments in terms of their realities.

Q37. The Act still allows different schools; why? Isn't that in variance with the common school prescriptions of the Kothari Commission Report?

It is a common misconception that the Kothari Commission Report recommended that the common school concept that it envisioned would be implemented by having just one kind of 'common' school. The Report accepted that there would be ordinary government and government aided schools, but their quality would be raised to a minimum standard; about 10 per cent government schools would be of better quality (like the Navodaya and Kendriya Vidyalayas); and private schools would exist; which would have to be kept out of the common school system. Here is what the Kothari Commission said:

A nation-wide programme of school improvement should be organised with three objectives: (a) to raise all schools to at least to a minimum prescribed level; (b) to assist every school to rise to the highest level of which it is capable; and (c) during the next ten years, to raise at least **ten per cent of the institutions to an optimum standard**.

Raising all schools to a minimum prescribed level is what the mandatory schedule of norms and standards in the Act is intended for. As for private schools, the Kothari Commission acknowledged that: *"The right to establish private schools for any purpose whatsoever has also been given to all citizens under clauses (c) and (g) of Article 19 which provide that all citizens shall have the right 'to form associations' and to 'practice any profession, or to carry on any occupation, trade or business' and which obviously covers the right of individuals and groups to establish and conduct educational institutions of their choice. Private schools may, therefore, be established under the provisions of the Constitution and, if they do not seek aid or recognition from the State, they will have to be treated as being outside the national system of public education."*

Common school is defined as part of the National System of Education in the Report. The Act is very much in line with these prescriptions; perhaps better because it mandates private schools would be obliged to take 25 per cent children from disadvantaged groups from their neighbourhoods, without screening; whereas the Kothari Commission Report suggested that talented children should be sent on scholarships to these schools, that would entail admission tests.

Q38. The duties of the appropriate government and local authority seem to be mixed up in the Act; why? What are their respective responsibilities?

There is a certain overlap and complementarities in their functions. Essentially however, the appropriate government shall lay down policy, prescribe curriculum, make arrangements for teacher recruitment and their proper deployment, and make financial arrangements, and provide technical support. The local authority on the other hand will ensure the enumeration, admission and attendance of children, school mapping and availability of neighbourhood schools, and monitoring. For example, to ensure proper school mapping and availability of neighbourhood schools, a GIS mapping of schooling facilities could assist the appropriate governments to understand the geographic dispersal of schools, the distance to schools from the habitations and the physical barriers, if any, as some state governments are already doing. This would require the appropriate government and the local authority to work in unison.

Q39. Is there a financial estimate for the Act? Why it was not attached when the Bill was introduced in the Parliament?

Financial estimates made by the National University for Educational Planning and Administration suggest that an additional 1.71 lakh crore rupees (about thirty four crore rupees per year) shall be required to implement the Act in the next five years. Since the Bill was introduced in the Rajya Sabha first, a financial estimate was not attached (only a financial memorandum was, which committed funds from the consolidated funds of the government). With an attachment of financial estimates, the Bill would have had to be introduced in the Lok Sabha first (as a Money Bill), where it would have lapsed since it was not passed before the end of the term of the last Lok Sabha.

Q40. Who will bear most of the expenses? How will the centre and state sharing be determined?

A sharing pattern will be arrived at through mutual negotiations between the central and state governments. The SSA norms and sharing patterns will need to be reviewed. For example, the RTE-SSA harmonisation committee's report has already recommended a 75:25 sharing pattern between the centre and the states instead of the present 55:45 sharing ratio under the SSA.

Q41. What does the reference to Finance Commission in section 7(4) imply?

It implies that on the basis of a reference by the central government through the President, the Finance Commission could sanction monies directly to states for the Act, which would be in addition to the sharing ratio of the centrally sponsored scheme operating the Act. It provides an additional window for central funds to be allocated to states that need them most. The 13th Finance Commission has since made allocations of Rs 24068 crore over a five year period specifically for elementary education. This will help States meet their 15 per cent state share towards SSA – from the sliding scale of 65:35 in 2008-09 to 50:50 in 2011-12, but may be inadequate to meet the RTE requirements.

Q42. Who will decide the academic calendar of the school?

As per the Act, the local authority also has the right to do so. This opens up the possibility of decentralised school calendars suiting local conditions.

Q43. Will all double shift schools become single shift?

The implications of the number of hours for which a school shall function per day indicate that. This would go a long way in forcing children out of labour since double shifts allow them to go to schools as also to engage in labour.

Q44. What will happen in places where government land is not available for building a neighbourhood school?

Many states face this problem in urban areas in particular, but in rural areas too, as in Bihar where most of the land is in private hands. Since a school is a fundamental right of children now, the government will have to hire accommodation for schools, or consider acquiring or buying land, as it does for other projects of national importance.

Q45. Will the Act put an end to recent trends in big cities to close government schools and transfer prime land for promoting commercial real estate?

Since the governments have to provide a neighbourhood school to every child in three years, which includes a vast number of children who are out of school today, the need for land and school buildings should force the governments to refrain from removing schools on prime lands in big cities for making land available for commercial purposes. In any case it will require vibrant civil society interventions, as were seen in Indore, Karnataka and other places. Since such transfer of land has also been reported in PPP kind of school arrangements (in Mumbai), it should be clear that all memorandums for PPPs if at all signed, would be under the purview of the provisions of this Act for the age group 6 to 14. They can not be exempted from this Act. The government can not seek PPPs for schools catering to the age group 6 to 14 since providing a neighbourhood school to all children in three years is a compulsion on the State. But, as it appears, if the government signs MoUs for 3500 secondary schools which have classes 1 to 8 attached to them, then the provisions of the Act, like admission tests, capitation fees, CCE etc. would apply to these classes of such schools.

Q46. How will children of migrant families receive education?

There are two options; if children migrate with parents, particularly small children, the schools in the migrated areas have to admit all children even if they can not produce transfer certificates. Or if the parents demand that their children be given education in their native place while they are away for work, appropriate governments/local authorities shall have to ensure the availability of free residential schools.

Q47. Whose responsibility is it to ensure children, particularly of the disadvantaged groups, are not discriminated against?

Legally, of the appropriate governments, local authorities and the schools; monitored by the SMCs, civil society groups and the NCPCR/SCPCRs. Model Rule 5, (3) and (4) explains this in clear terms: *(3) The State government/local authority shall ensure that no child is subjected to caste, class, religious or gender abuse in the school. (4) For the purposes of clause (c) of section 8 and clause (c) of section 9, the State Government and the Local Authority shall ensure that a child belonging to a weaker section and a child belonging to disadvantaged group is not segregated or discriminated against in the classroom, during mid-day meals, in the play grounds, in the use of common drinking water and toilet facilities, and in the cleaning of toilets or classrooms.*

Q48. Who will ensure good quality education?

The governments and the academic institutions under them, like the NCTE, NCERT, SCERTs and so on, by ensuring that the norms and standards of the schools are adhered to within three years, all teachers are professionally trained in a maximum of five years, curriculum, content and process follows principles laid out in Section 29, a comprehensive and continuous evaluation system is in place, and children learn in an atmosphere free of fear, anxiety and trauma. The governments would be well advised to seek collaboration from university education departments and civil society groups that have experience in quality elementary education in this effort. These would be monitored by the NCPCR/SCPCRs and civil society institutions.

In addition, as per the model rules 21(3), the appropriate governments must undertake systemic quality reviews periodically through institutions of renown, which are not confined only to testing children's achievement scores, but include assessment of teacher quality, curricular issues, social discrimination, infrastructure and other parameters that impact on quality. The involvement of institutions of higher learning on a continuous basis would be critical in this respect.

V. Schools and Teachers

Q49. What does the 25 per cent quota obligation of private schools imply? Can a private school admit more than 25 per cent? What is the obligation of aided schools?

All private schools have to admit 25 per cent children from disadvantaged groups from their neighbourhoods for free education, which can be extended if the number is not filled up within the customary one km radius; every year in the class in which they induct new children. If the induction class is class 1, then 25 per cent children will be admitted therein each year, but if the induction is done in pre-school, then the quota will be filled there. The Act says 'at least 25 per cent' instead of 'at least and no more', which implies that a school could offer to take more than 25 per cent children.

Private aided schools shall have to admit children from similar backgrounds in the proportion of aid they receive from the government, in the induction class each year, and will not receive any extra reimbursement for these children. For example, if the total annual contribution from the government to an aided school is 70 per cent of its total recurring expenditure for a particular year, it will have to admit 70 per cent children in the induction class that year. Either of these admissions each year shall be in the induction class only, and not for each class of the elementary stage.

Q50. How will it be administered? How will they be paid by the Governments?

As for payments, the appropriate government shall work out its per-learner cost by adding up all the recurring costs it incurs in one year, from its own and central funds including mid-day meals, and divide it by all the children enrolled in its schools. It will reimburse the unaided school admitting 25 per cent children at this rate, or the fee of the school, which ever is less. If the school is already obliged to admit a certain number of children by a separate MoU, for subsidised land or other benefits it obtained from the state, then it will not receive reimbursement for the percentage of children covered by the MoU. The detailed procedure is outlined in Model Rules (7) and (8).

Q51. What are the other regulations for private schools?

They will have to adhere to the norms and standards prescribed by the schedule and have three years to do so. Their teachers shall also be required to have the nationally prescribed teacher qualifications, within five years. They will have to get recognition within the three years period; if they don't have recognition after three years, they can not function, and heavy fines will be imposed on them if they do. They can not take tests or interview children or parents for giving admission; all admissions have to be based on random selection and violations will lead to financial punishments. They must announce at the beginning of the term the fees they will charge, after that they can not ask for other charges during the year (capitation fees).

Q52. When can a child be admitted to a school during the year?

At any time of the year when he/she attains six years of age, or is an older out of school child.

Q53. Is it true that no child can be expelled or failed?

No school, governmental or private, can detain (fail) or expel any child at the elementary stage. The Delhi High Court has already given a verdict on this on the basis of the Act (April 7, 2010), against St. Xavier's School, Delhi, which had to take back all the children they had declared failed and expelled from the school.

Q54. Will that not affect the quality of education since children will advance even if they are not learning?

This is a common perception since it is difficult to see beyond the centuries old custom and culture of failing and expelling children. That the learning level of a child who is punished by failure at any time in the elementary stage shall improve the next year has no educational or research backing. If at all, the social stigma of failure, particularly for a child coming from a poor home is more likely to ensure that the failed child shall drop off from the next year. It is a method to weed out children who are harshly judged for being 'weak' or 'dull', which may have a lot to do with the learning environment of the school, the psychological and coping stress on the child, rather than any innate deficiency in the child. More often, failure and expulsion of the child hides the deficiencies of the learning environment of the class room. That is why the CCE, which continuously monitors the learning levels of the child and helps in timely intervention is far superior educationally to annual or board examination based punishments of failure and expulsions. CCE also takes into account the interests, abilities and talents of the child beyond the school subjects that must be recorded while issuing the completion certificate at the end of the elementary stage (see also Q70). Properly implemented, CCE will ensure that children do not advance without learning better than mindless testing of children. Private schools in particular use the failure and expulsion route to weed out what they call 'dull' and 'weak' in order to keep their school brand at a premium to charge more fees. The Act attempts to prohibit this malpractice, which has been upheld by the Delhi High Court decision in relation to a prominent private school of Delhi, mentioned previously.

Q55. Do the norms and standards of a school apply only to private schools?

No, all schools must adhere to the norms. As per section 19 (1), no school shall be established (by the government), or recognised (private), if it does not fulfill the norms and standards prescribed by the Act.

Q56. What if a government school lacks the prescribed norms and standards?

If the problem is not rectified locally, the matter can go to NCPCR/ SCPCR or the courts, as a serious violation of the law.

Q57. Can the norms and standards (schedule) be improved or changed?

Yes, and that shall not require a parliamentary amendment. As per Section 20 it can be done by the central government through a notification. Most likely, the National Advisory Council shall be assigned the task of reviewing the schedule periodically.

Q58. Are all schools required to have a School Management Committee?

All government, government-aided and special category schools shall have to constitute SMCs as per Section 21 of the Act; since private schools are already mandated to have management committees on the basis of their trust/society registrations, they are not covered by Section 21. A proposed amendment (see Q82) makes the SMC an advisory rather than a statutory body for schools covered under Article 29 and 30 of the constitution (minority schools).

Q59. How will the SMCs be formed?

The detailed procedure for the formation of SMCs is outlined in Model Rule 13. State governments may modify the procedure if they deem necessary. Apart from the statutory requirement that 75 per cent members shall be parents of children studying in the school, 50 per cent of the total members women, the model rule prescribes that the Chair and Vice-Chairpersons should be from amongst the parents; it should meet at least once a month, the minutes of its meetings should be made public and so on.

Q60. What is the School Development Plan that the SMCs will prepare?

It is elaborated in Model Rule 14. It will be a three-year plan estimating student strength, teacher requirement under the prescribed PTR, additional infrastructural, financial requirements and so on. The requirement is that the combined school development plans of a local authority will identify requirements in a bottom up decentralised manner, for each panchayat, rather than in a top down centralised manner, as is the common practice.

Q61. Does the Act define a 'Teacher'? Who will prescribe teacher qualifications?

Yes, it does at Section 23(1). An academic institution of the central government shall prescribe teacher qualifications that all teachers of the country must have within five years. This will include both the academic and professional qualifications. The central government has already notified that the National Council for Teacher Education shall prescribe teacher qualifications. A broader committee under MHRD has already sent its suggestions to the NCTE regarding the new teacher qualifications

Q62. Can a 'para' teacher exist after the Act comes into force?

The term 'para' has many connotations. In terms of qualifications, all teachers will have to have the same qualification in five years, so there can be no less qualified 'para' teachers after five years. It can also mean contractual. That is covered by service rules and conditions, and since teachers are mostly state government employees (except for Kendriya, Navodaya or similar schools of the central government) that is a preserve of state governments and as per the Act will be prescribed by them. The Model Rules however mandate that the service conditions prepared by the states provide for and enable long-term stake of teachers in the teaching profession. Short term teaching contracts would therefore not be compatible with such a principle.

Q63. What about salaries of teachers?

These too are within the purview of the state governments and are to be prescribed by them. The Model Rule 18 (3) however lays down the principle that salaries and other benefits of teachers, including those handling out-of-school children, shall be that of regular teachers, and at par for similar work and experience.

Q64. What if the teacher remains absent or does not teach properly?

Disciplinary action can be taken against the teacher (Section 24(2)). Under Model Rules 18(2) (a), it is prescribed that the service rules of teachers should mandate the accountability of teachers to the School Management Committees.

Q65. How long do governments have to ensure the PTR as given in the schedule?

There is a certain ambiguity about this in the Act. Section 25(1) says that the PTR ratio shall be maintained in each school within six months of notification of the Act. However, for implementing the schedule of norms and standards of the school, that prescribes the PTR ratio, a three years time period has been given. States like Bihar, UP, Assam and Orissa that need to recruit a huge number of new teachers could use this ambiguity by sanctioning all the required posts and redeploying teachers in the first six months, and complete all the recruitments as early as possible, within the three years time frame.

Q66. Why not disallow election duties of teachers since they take away a lot of teacher time?

The Act bans all non-academic work by teachers, except elections, decennial census and disaster related tasks. Where as census involves work once in ten years, and disasters are rare, increasingly frequent elections do keep teachers away from schools for long periods of time, particularly the preparation of electoral rolls, and can violate the child's right to quality education. Whereas disallowing election duties for teachers would therefore be very desirable, the constitution however mandates that all central and state employees could be drafted for election work, which the Supreme Court has upheld:

> Article 324(6) of the Constitution of India read with Section 159 of the Representation of the People Act, 1951 makes it obligatory that the President (the Government of India), or the Governor (the Government of any state) as well as every local authority shall, when so requested by the Election Commission, make available to the Election Commission or to a regional Commissioner or to the Chief Electoral Officer or the Returning Officer, as the case may be, such staff as may be necessary for the performance of any duties in connection with an election.
>
> In Election Commission of India, vs. State Bank of India, the Supreme Court has made it abundantly clear that the services of those government servants who are appointed to public services and posts under the Central or State Governments as well as those who are employees of the local authorities will have to be made available for the purpose of election and any such government servant or employee of the local authority who shall defy the requisition, may receive suitable punishment.
>
> Now that education is a fundamental right of children, the state governments could ensure, when requested by the Election Commission, to make available to the Commission staff other than school teachers, or for a minimal amount of time that does not interfere with their primary task of teaching.

Q67. Is private tuition banned for all teachers?

It is banned for all teachers as defined under this Act, working in government or private elementary schools. Since this Act does not apply to secondary school teachers, the ban on tuitions under this Act shall not extend to them, though there might be other laws and service conditions at the state level that disallow tuitions for secondary school teachers, which will continue to remain in force.

VI. Curriculum, Content and Process

Q68. Does the Act mandate a national curriculum framework?

Yes, under Section 7(6a), the central government has to develop a framework of national curriculum with the help of academic authorities of state governments. This is significant since the present practice of the NCERT preparing the NCF was of an advisory nature; under the Act, it has become mandatory, and shall involve the state governments too.

Q69. Who will prescribe the curriculum and evaluation systems at the state level?

The state governments shall have to specify academic authorities that will lay down curriculum and evaluation procedures at the state level. These could be SCERTs or other academic institutions of the state. The state curriculums must however be prepared according to certain common principles of content and process described in Section 29(2).

Q70. What are the main thrusts of academic quality and processes under the Act?

The Act upholds internationally accepted research and academic practice that says:

- All children have similar potential for learning. If one child is doing better than the other, the problem is not with the child, but the different nurturing processes and systemic inputs. It therefore puts the onus of learning on the school and the system, and does not prescribe punishing the child through failure, detention and expulsion.
- Failing in examinations psychologically demotivates and socially humiliates children. Instead of improving their scholastic quality, failure and detention is more likely to result in pushing small children out of the school system, as dropouts.

- The Act prescribes a learning environment that does not cause fear, anxiety and trauma to children, promotes their all round development rather than only excellence in school subjects, building up child's knowledge, potentiality and talent, imbibing values enshrined in the Constitution, learning through activities, discovery and exploration in child friendly and child-centred manner, using the mother tongue as medium of instruction as far as possible, and Comprehensive and Continuous Evaluation, rather than Board examinations.

The Act more or less legalises the principles enunciated in the National Curriculum Framework 2005. As for implementation of these principles, the approaches described in the NCF 2005 and its accompanying 22 focus group reports, as also the text books, curricular material, in-service teacher training modules, CCE manuals etc. produced by the NCERT and a few other states would be a vital input for future implementation for quality improvement.

Q71. If there are no Board examinations, how will children be certified when they complete elementary education?

The procedure for certification is described at Model Rule 23. The certificate will include the Pupil Cumulative Record of a child which will contain the talents and abilities of the child beyond school subjects. The implication is that such a cumulative record, spanning eight years of elementary stage shall be kept for each child, and teachers shall be facilitated through trainings and other means to fulfill this task.

Q72. Who will enforce standards of teacher trainings?

Under Section 7(6b), the central government shall 'develop and enforce standards for training of teachers'.

Q73. What about innovation and research?

Providing technical support and resources to the state governments for promoting innovations, research, planning and capacity building is a task assigned to the central government (Section 7(6c)). Model Rule 19(2)(b) prescribes that a teacher may perform the tasks of curriculum formulation, development of syllabi, preparation of training modules and textbook development, in a manner that these tasks do not interfere with his/her regular teaching.

VII. Protection and Monitoring of Children's Right

Q74. If a child is denied admission, beaten up or discriminated against, or his/her right is violated in any other manner, what will be the redressal mechanism?

One may assume that a number of complaints would be settled at the school and SMC level itself, through the intervention of civil society groups. If that does not happen, the next step would be for the complaint to be filed with the local authority. The complainant could appeal to the SCPCR if the action of the local authority does not redress the complaint satisfactorily.

Q75. Can NCPCR/SCPCR act on their own, even if a complaint has not been filed?

Yes, both the NCPCR and the SCPCRs can move on their own, *suo moto*, without any one specifically filing a complaint. As per Model Rule 25, SCPCRs shall set up child helplines, accessible by SMS, telephone and letter for receiving and registering complaints.

The problem at present (April 2010) is that the NCPCR is in the process of being reconstituted, and only five states have constituted their SCPCRs, that too with varying capacities. The exact rules and procedures for redressal shall have to be worked out by the NCPCR when it again becomes properly functional, and it will have to assist the SCPCRs to do the same. The reconstituted NCPCR is expected to carry forward its earlier initiatives of linking and networking with civil society organisations for monitoring, appointing state commissioners for the enforcement of the Act (on the lines of Supreme Court Commissioners for Right to Food), networking with other Commissions like the one's for Human Rights, Women and Minorities, set up helplines and set up a separate division for enforcing the Right to Education.

The Model Rules provide that in states that do not have SCPCR at present (which is set up by the Women and Child department), the education department shall constitute a Right to Education Protection Authority (REPA) till the SCPCR comes into force.

Q76. What kind of powers does the NCPCR/SCPCR have? Can they punish?

Under the NCPCR Act 2005, the NCPCR and SCPCRs have quasi-judicial powers whereby they can investigate, summon and recommend cases to the courts. They can not, however, pass judgments and hand out punishments.

Q77. What about the courts? Which court can one go to and who can go?

As a law flowing out of a fundamental right, it is justiciable from the lowest to the highest court of the country. One can file a case in the lowest civil court, or the Supreme/High Court, depending on the nature of complaint.

Q78. Is there any role for NGO's/civil society groups in monitoring?

NCPCR has already initiated moves to work through civil society groups in a variety of ways. Independent of that, NGOs and other civil society groups can on their own bring violations to the notice of authorities and courts. An example of that is the civil society group Social Jurist working in Delhi. They can ensure opening of neighbourhood schools, monitoring teacher availability, and help in local redressal mechanisms.

Q79. What if the problems are not local but of higher levels, like unavailability of funds, insufficient teacher recruitment and so on?

Since the 'compulsion' in the Act is on the governments, the NCPCR/SCPCR and the courts shall have to investigate where the onus of a particular violation rests, and judge accordingly.

VIII. Other Issues

Q80. Who makes the Rules; centre or state governments?

Since both the central and state governments are involved, both shall have to make rules. The central rules have already been finalised, and a set of model rules for the states have been circulated by the centre to the states. The states can either accept the model rules as circulated or make appropriate changes in them. Finally, the central government has to place the rules in the Parliament, and the states in their respective legislatures. The rules can be modified by the centre or the states as and when necessary.

Q81. What will happen to the Sarva Shiksha Abhiyan from April 1, 2010?

The SSA would have to be harmonised with the RTE. That shall require changing various norms, working out a new fund sharing pattern and necessary changes in the governance structure. RTE, unlike the present SSA is not a scheme. If SSA remains the vehicle of implementation of RTE, it shall have to shed its project character. A RTE-SSA harmonisation committee has considered these issues and its 217 page report is now public. It is like a blueprint for the implementation of the Act. It is hoped that the MHRD shall make available bulk copies of the report at the earliest.

Q82. What will be the role of the NAC and SACs?

They shall act as advisory bodies. They could also facilitate research and studies and systemic evaluation to help improve the implementation of the Act. The NAC is also likely to be the body that will monitor the norms and standards of a school contained in the schedule attached to the Act, and suggest changes to it whenever necessary.

Q83. What are the proposed amendments to the Act at this stage?

A set of amendments have already been introduced in the Parliament during the 2010 budget session, which are likely to be incorporated during the following monsoon session. They are:

(i) To insert in Section 2(d) after the word "means", the words "a child with a disability or"

(ii) After clause 2(e) insert the following clause: '(ee) "child with disability includes" namely – (A) a child with "disability" as defined in clause (i) of the Persons with Disabilities Act 1995, (B) a child, being a person with disability as defined in clause (j) of section 2 of the National Trust for Welfare of Persons with Autism, Cerebral Palsy, Mental Retardation and Multiple Disabilities Act, 1999; (C) a child with "severe disability" as defined in clause (o) of section 2 of the National Trust Act, 1999.

(iii) In Section 21 of the Act, in sub-section (2), the following proviso shall be inserted, namely: "Provided that the School management Committee constituted under sub-section (1) in respect to a school established and administered by minority, whether based on religion or language, shall perform advisory functions only."

Section 3 of the Act has also been amended to reflect the amendments (i) and (ii) and Section 22 has also been appropriately amended to reflect amendment (iii).

IX. Immediate Tasks of the Central Government

1. Promulgate central rules.
2. Notify teacher qualifications.
3. Come out with a modified SSA in harmony with the Act, with revised norms (the Report of the concerned committee is already out, it needs to made available widely).
4. Set up the National Advisory Council.
5. Work out an appropriate fund sharing pattern with the states.
6. Facilitate academic support to states in CCE, curriculum and classroom transaction.
7. Facilitate defining content of professional teacher qualifications after point 2 is finalised
8. Work out appropriate teacher education facilities and strategies in order to achieve the five-year teacher qualification target.
9. Incorporate the promised amendments relating to disabled children (already introduced in the Parliament).

10. Undertake a vigorous public campaign in collaboration with civil society groups to prepare the SMCs, local authorities and other concerned agencies to effectively implement the Act. Work out appropriate mechanisms to involve universities and non-government agencies with appropriate expertise in areas like quality improvement, curricular design, teacher trainings and so on. Facilitate that the state governments also undertake similar work with these agencies.

X. Immediate Tasks of the State Governments

1. Finalise and promulgate state rules.
2. Work out teacher requirements and complete teacher deployment in order to ensure prescribed PTR ratio in each school within six months.
3. Commence detailed school mapping under the neighbourhood definition in the model rules to plan for neighbourhood school for each child in ten years. The states may take recourse to GIS mapping and child tracking methods for the purpose.
4. Notify local authorities.
5. Commence the process of setting up of School Management Committees.
6. Scrap board examinations and switch over to CCE.
7. States that have a seven year elementary cycle need to switch over to a eight year cycle and states that enroll children at age five have to rethink about making age six as the admission age.
8. States that don't have SCPCRs need to set up interim Right to Education Protection Agencies (REPA) at the earliest. Design a multi-level redressal mechanism involving concerned agencies/institutions.
9. Plan for teacher educators/mentors and institutions.
10. Notify 'disadvantaged groups' and 'weaker sections'.

[PART – II, FAQs on the RTE Act, 2009]

National Commission for Protection of Child Rights (NCPCR, New Delhi, 2010) has also formulated a good number of FAQs on the RTE Act, 2009 for better understanding of the Act. The FAQs made by the Commission have been assembled below:

I. PRELIMINARY

Q1. What is the coverage of the Act?

The entire country is covered by the Act, with the exception of Jammu and Kashmir.

Q2. Which schools are covered by the Act?

The Act applies to all schools, government and private. However, there are some specific provisions that apply to only government schools and some that apply only to private schools. "Specified category" schools that are exempt from some of the provisions include:

(i) Kendriya Vidyalayas, Navodaya Vidyalaya, Sainik schools.

(ii) Any other school having a distinct character which may be specified by notification by the appropriate government. [Section 2(p)]

Q3. What happens to the existing State Acts, in light of the RTE Act, 2009?

Once the new Central RTE Act comes into force, all other Acts are superseded. The states would be able to issue guidelines and state Rules, but not separate Acts.

II. RIGHT TO FREE AND COMPULSORY EDUCATION

Q4. What does the Act guarantee?

Free and Compulsory Education to all children between the age of 6-14 years covering the elementary cycle of education in a neighbourhood school. Further it guarantees education of a specified standard, subscribing to norms of school infrastructure, hours of instructional time and days of school functioning, pupil-teacher ratios and teacher quality.

Q5. What happens to children under the age of 6?

The Act does not specifically cover this age group of children. However, it says that the "local authorities" may provide free and compulsory education at the pre-primary stage.

Q6. What is meant by "free" education in the Act?

According to the Act (section 3.2) free refers to any fees or charges that may prevent a child from pursuing and completing the elementary cycle of education. It implies that any kind of tuition or other fees (sports, development, examination, etc.,) cannot be charged from any child. Further, any expenses that may prevent a child from participating in the education process from transport facilities to physical aides such as spectacles, crutches or hearing aides are included in the entitlement of free education for a child.

Q7. What does "compulsory" education mean in the Act?

By compulsory is meant that it is entirely the obligatory on the State to provide free elementary education to every child in the 6-14 years age group and ensure not just admission, but attendance and completion of the elementary cycle of schooling as well.

Q8. What is meant by a neighbourhood school?

By neighbourhood is meant a specified walking distance from the habitation of a child. The Model Rules will define more specifically different categories of situations where the definition of neighbourhood may need to be varied to accommodate children in remote areas, conflict ridden areas or children from migrant families etc.

Q9. Is there any compulsion on the parents as well to send their children to school?

The law makes it clear that the compulsion is on the state and not on the parents to ensure completion of the elementary cycle of schooling. It says that it is the duty of every parent to admit their children in a neighbourhood school, but the responsibility of the government to ensure quality education and the retention and completion of elementary education by child in school. There are no penalties on parents for not sending their children to school.

Q10. Many children work, so can they be accommodated in a second shift?

No. According to the norms laid out in the Act, all schools must provide a minimum of four hours of instruction every day if primary and 4.5 hours if upper primary. It is also suggested that schools function for a minimum of six hours daily to enable children to participate in extra-curricular activities as well. This schedule makes it difficult to run two shifts a day in a school. Besides, an underlying objective of the right to education is to wean children away from working and into schools. Hence, second shifts which encourage child labour are made infeasible under the Act.

Q11. What about children from migrant families?

Children from migrant families have the same right to free and compulsory education in a neighbourhood schools as other children. In order to fulfill this right for children who are part of migratory families the government may provide residential schooling facilities.

Q12. What if a child is older than six years and has never been to school? Can she be enrolled now? If yes, in what class?

Yes. No child in the age group 6-14 years can be refused admission in school.

She would be enrolled in a class "appropriate to her age". By this is meant that if she is 10 years old she will be admitted to class 4.

Q13. How will she cope with the studies of class 4 if she has never been to school?

The Act makes it the responsibility of the school to provide her with "special training" in the school premises to enable her to come up to her age appropriate class. In other words, a 10 years old has the right to be enrolled in class 4 while she attends remedial classes provided by the school in the same premises till she is able to be mainstreamed. This could take three months to two years.

Q14. If a 13 years old child wants to join school, will she be asked to leave in one year when she attains 14 years of age?

No. The Act guarantees the completion of elementary education. It means therefore that the child can continue to study till she has completed class 8, irrespective of her age at that time.

Q15. Who will provide the special training or remedial classes for children to be able to be in age-appropriate classes?

It is the responsibility of the government (or school) to provide the special classes, as far as possible within the school premises itself, so that the child can feel a part of the school in which she/he is enrolled.

Q16. Does this mean that non-governmental organisations that have been running bridge courses will have to stop running them?

No. It does not mean that. Nothing in the Act prevents the government from taking the assistance of a non-governmental organisation to run the special classes. The bridge courses could become part of the school programme if the government decides to do that. The overall responsibility for providing these classes however, will remain that of the government.

Q17. If the parents of a child bring the child to school for admission in the month of November, when admissions are normally over, the school can refuse admission, can't it?

No. Admission cannot be refused to any child at any time. However, since the child would have missed many classes she/he may need special coaching to cope with the syllabus of the class she is enrolled in. These special classes are also to be provided by the school on its premises.

Q18. If the village school goes only up to the primary section, what happens to education beyond that?

According to the Act a child has the right to seek transfer to any school (apart from private unaided schools and the special category schools mentioned in the Act) for completing elementary education. It is the responsibility of the local authority to ensure that the child (and in fact all children of that primary school) are seamlessly transferred to the nearest upper primary school in time. Alternatively the primary school can upgrade its facilities to the upper primary level.

Q19. What if the school delays issuing the transfer certificate?

No child can be denied admission, transfer certificate or not. In fact, disciplinary action can be taken against a Head teacher who delays issuing the Transfer Certificate.

Q20. What about schools that have facilities below the standard specified in the Act?

The schools have been given three years to upgrade their standards and bring them at par with the norms specified in the Act. After that action can be taken against them for not meeting the standards.

Q21. What happens to the existing norms, such as those of SSA?

The RTE norms would override all other norms. SSA norms would have to be revised to accommodate RTE norms, even in the transition period of three years.

III. DUTIES OF APPROPRIATE GOVERNMENT, LOCAL AUTHORITY AND PARENTS

Q22. What is the role of the Central Government in implementing the Act?

The Central Government role is three fold:

(i) Developing a National Curriculum Framework with the help of an appointed Academic Authority [section 6(a)].

(ii) Developing and enforcing standards of teacher qualification and training [section 6(b)].

(iii) Providing technical and financial support and resources to the State governments for innovation, research, planning and capacity building [section 6(c)].

Q23. What is the role of the state education department?

(i) Provide free and compulsory elementary education to all children.

(ii) Ensure availability of a neighbourhood school with requisite infrastructure, teachers, and learning equipment as specified in the Act.

(iii) Ensure admission, attendance and completion of elementary education for every child.

(iv) Prevent discrimination against any child on any grounds.

(v) Ensure quality education conforming to standards specified in the Schedule of the Act.

Q24. What is the role of the local authority?

(i) Maintain records of all children up to the age of 14 years residing in its jurisdiction.

(ii) Ensure admission of all children, including migrant children.

(iii) Ensure that no child is discriminated against.

(iv) Decide the academic calendar.

(v) Monitor functioning of schools in its jurisdiction.

Q25. What are the quality norms guaranteed by the Act?

(i) Pupil-Teacher Ratio of 30:1; with minimum instructional hours of 4/day and minimum working days of 200/annum (4.5 and 220 for Upper primary sections).

(ii) Buildings [all-weather, barrier-free access, boundary wall; one classroom for every teacher; separate room for Head teacher; separate toilets; safe drinking water, kitchen for mid-day meal; and playground].

(iii) Teaching learning materials.

(iv) Library.

(v) Play and sports equipment.

Q26. What if the teachers are not available to meet the norms of the pupil-teacher ratio?

The number of vacancies in a school cannot exceed 10 per cent of the sanctioned strength following the pupil-teacher norms. If the requisite number of qualified teachers cannot be found in a particular area the qualification norms may be modified to suit the purpose, but only for a period not exceeding five years.

Q27. By when do they have to be in place?

The PTR has to be in place within six months of the Act coming into force. The other norms have to be in place within three years.

Q28. Who will provide the money for this upgradation?

The Central and State governments will together provide the funds for implementing the Act. For this the Central Government will do the following:

(i) Prepare estimates of capital and recurring expenditure for the implementation of the Act and providing grants-in-aid to the State governments for RTE [Section 7 (2) and 7 (3)].

(ii) Request the Finance Commission to examine the need for extra grants to state governments for provisions related to RTE.

IV. RESPONSIBILITIES OF THE SCHOOLS

Q29. Does the Act imply that the private schools can no longer charge fees?

No. Private schools and schools in the specified category can continue to charge fees as before. However, they are required to admit in their incoming class, at least 25 per cent children from disadvantaged and weaker sections of society, without charging any fees.

Q30. Private schools would have to ensure admission to some students from poor families? How many such students will they required to admit?

Twenty five per cent of the incoming class must include children from disadvantaged and weaker sections.

Q31. These children will not pay fees, but what about other costs of schooling?

These children shall have the full extent of a free and compulsory education as guaranteed in the Act for all other children. The schools will be reimbursed by the government to the extent of the expenditure incurred by a child in the government school.

Q32. What about capitation fees?

No capitation can be charged by any school, government or private or specified category.

Q33. Does this apply to the special category schools as well, such as the Kendriya Vidyalayas, Navodyayas, Sainik Schools and other such?

These schools are also required to take in at least 25 per cent children in their incoming class from weaker sections but will NOT be reimbursed by the government, as in the case of private unaided schools.

Q34. What about private aided schools?

These schools are required to provide free education to children in proportionate relationship to the grants-in-aid they receive, subject to a minimum of 25 per cent. They too will not be reimbursed by the state.

Q35. What about minority institutions?

If the minority institutions are not receiving any aid from the state they will follow the rule of private unaided schools, and if receiving aid they will follow the rule of aided schools.

Q36. Will this clause also hold for those schools that have already provided subsidised education to children of poor families, in lieu of land and other resources received at subsidised rates?

In these cases the schools shall have to fulfil the 25 per cent reservation criteria but will not be reimbursed to the extent of expenditures in a government school.

Q37. What does the Act say about admission procedures, such as tests, interviews and other such?

The Act prohibits the use of any screening procedures for admission for all schools.

Q38. What documentation would then be required at the time of admission ?

Proof of age document would be required at the time of admission to determine which class she is to be admitted, since age-appropriate education is the provision of the RTE. Birth certificate or such other document issued by a statutory body may be sued for proof of age.

Q39. Since the Act talks about age-appropriate enrollment, but no documents are required at the time of admission, how would the age of the child be determined?

The Act does not specify a procedure. The Rules are likely to make that clear. However, written submissions by parents on the age of the child may be accepted as age-proof at the time of admission.

Q40. How would admission be done, if there are no tests and no documentation required?

No admission can be denied for lack of any documentation, including proof of age.

Q41. What if a school uses capitation fees as a method of screening?

The school can be penalised to the extent of 10 times the capitation fee charged or Rs 25,000 for using a screening procedure. If a screening procedure is used a second time by the school, the penalty doubles to Rs 50,000 and so on.

Q42. What is the deadline for admission? What if the deadline is missed?

A child should be admitted at the start of the academic year, but no child can be denied admission at any later date either.

Q43. Can a child be failed in any class?

No. A child cannot be failed or expelled from any class till he/she completes eight years of schooling.

Q44. How can it be assured that a child is learning, if promotion is automatic and there are no tests?

According to the Act, the Academic Authority specified by the appropriate government shall lay down an evaluation procedure that is based on the principle of "continuous and comprehensive evaluation" for every child. Thus, the child will be evaluated but not through a single end-of-year exam but through a process that is continuous and looks at all aspects of the child's learning and abilities.

Q45. Can a child be expelled from school for, say, misbehaviour?

No.

Q46. A large number of schools exist without recognition. What does the Act say about them?

No school other than a wholly government school can function without recognition after the commencement of the Act.

Q47. On what basis would recognition be granted ?

Must fulfil norms and standards mentioned in the Schedule, or within thre years of notification of Act if school already in existence.

Q48. What if the school decides to run anyway, without recognition?

Such a school will be liable to pay a fine of Rs 1 lakh and if it continues to contravene, the fine will go up to Rs 10,000/day.

Q49. What happens to children in currently un-recognised schools?

These children will have to be admitted to the nearest neighbourhood schools at the earliest.

Q50. What about schools run by NGOs?

They too will have to subscribe to the stated norms.

Q51. Is there any role of parents in the school ?

The Act requires that a School Management Committee be set up consisting of at least three-fourth parent-members, with adequate representation of parents of children from disadvantaged communities and at least 50 per cent members to be women.

Q52. What is the role of the SMCs?

The SMC's have been given the following functions:

(i) monitor the working of the school

(ii) prepare and recommend the school development plan

(iii) monitor the utilisation of grants

(iv) perform other functions as may be prescribed.

Further, in the model rules teachers have been made accountable to the SMCs. This will have a far reaching impact on the performance of teachers.

V. TEACHERS

Q53. What is the minimum qualification specified for a teacher in the Act?

These are to be specified by the Academic Authority. If there are no teacher education institutions in an area or sufficient numbers of teachers cannot be made available at the required level of qualifications, these norms may be relaxed, but only for a period not exceeding five years.

Q54. What about existing teachers in existing schools that do not meet these qualifications?

Those teachers that can be trained and brought up to the standards required by the Academic Authority that sets the standards, they can be retained and provided the adequate training to enable them to be at par within the 3[5] years that is required to comply with the norms of the Act.

Q55. What are the specific duties of the teachers under this Act?

(i) Maintain regularity and punctuality in school.

(ii) Complete entire curriculum in specified time.

(iii) Assess the learning ability of each child and provide supplementary additional instruction if required.

(iv) Hold regular meetings with parents and apprise them of regularity in attendance, learning abilities, progress and other issues concerning the child.

Further, the model rules suggest that teachers report absence of children that goes beyond seven days to the SMCs so that they can be tracked and brought back into school.

Q56. What happens if a teacher is absent?

A teacher contravening any of the duties as laid down in the Act, which includes absenteeism, shall be liable to disciplinary action according to service rules. In fact, a teacher not performing any of the duties that are prescribed for teachers in the Act [section 24(1)] is liable for disciplinary action.

Q57. Many teachers engage in private tuition and there is pressure for students to join their tuition classes. How can we deal with that situation?

Teachers are prohibited by the Act to give private tuitions or private teaching activity.

Q58. Can the curriculum that is taught vary from place to place?

The curriculum must follow some basic principles which have been laid down in the Act, including be in line with Constitutional values and designed to develop a child's full potential.

VI. GRIEVANCE REDRESSAL

Q59. If any of the rights are not being met, where can a complaint be lodged ?

Complaints can be lodged at the Gram Panchayat or Block Education Office. Or even at the SCPCR or NCPCR. Finally, complaints can also be taken to the courts, as education is now a justiciable fundamental right of all children in the age group 6-14 years. NCPCR is setting up a centralised helpline, on which complaints can be received. This helpline will simultaneously register the complaint at the appropriate education office as well, so that follow up can be efficiently monitored.

Chapter - 13

Explanation of the Terms in the RTE Act

Some terms used in the RTE Act, 2009 have been explained for better understanding about the RTE Act, 2009.

(A) Appropriate Government: Appropriate government in the Act refers to either central or state government, or the government of a Union Territory with a legislature (like Delhi). The full definition is at Section 2(a) in the Act.

(B) Definition (Age) of the Child: The Juvenile Justice Act defines a child up to age 18. The United Nation's Child Rights Convention (UNCRC), to which India is a signatory, also defines a child from 0 to 18. In principle, by referring to the Juvenile Justice Act, the UNCRC and Article 21 (**right to life**) in the Aims and Objectives of the RTE Act, the age could have been defined from 0 – 18. However, citing economic compulsions, the present Act has been confined to the age group as contained in Article 21A [2(c)]. Revised Article 45 takes notice of the children in the age group 0 – 6 years stating that "The state shall endeavour to provide early childhood care and education for all children until they complete the age of six years.

(C) Local Authority: The Act school education a tripartite partnership between the communities (School Management Committees), the PRIs, and the government. As is evident from definition 2(h), the purpose of defining a local authority is to decentralise administrative control by bringing in Panchayati Raj Institutions. However, the term is flexible and it is left to the state government, to notify an appropriate local authority like "Primary Education Council" in West Bengal or "District Council" in North Eastern states like Meghalaya.

(D) Parents or Guardian: Section 2(k) only defines the parents of a child in the way that parent means either the natural or step or adoptive father or mother of a child. The guardian of a child section 2(g) is a person having the care and custody of that child and includes a natural guardian or guardian appointed or declared by a court or a statute. Section 10 refers to parents' or guardian's duty in ensuring education of their children. However, Section 8 states that the appropriate government shall have to take the responsibility to ensure elementary education to every child of the age of six to fourteen years.

(E) Prescribed: Wherever the word 'Prescribe' occurs, it implies that the appropriate government shall make relevant rules.

(F) School: At section 2(n), four categories are defined: (i) funded and managed by the government or local authority (ii) private but aided by the government or local authority (iii) schools defined under special category, like Kendriya Vidyalaya, Navodaya Vidyalaya, Sainik School, School under the Central Tibetan School Association and similar others, and (iv) private schools receiving no aid from the government or local authority.

(G) Implications of "Free Education" in RTE: Free Education is often meant to imply waiver of tuition fees. But tuition fee is only a part of educational expenses. Besides tuition fees, there are other expenses which include textbooks, copies and writing material, uniforms, transportation, educational and support materials for disabled children (hearing aids, spectacles, Braille books, crutches and so on), or even library fee, laboratory fee, etc. which are not covered under 'tuition fee'. Children from poor families are often not able to afford them. The phenomenon of drop-outs in particular is related with the inability of parents to meet the educational expenses of their children. Often in our country girl children face the problem of drop-out somewhere during the course of elementary education. Keeping this in mind, the Act at section 3(2) enlarges the term "free" by mandating that "no child shall be liable to pay any kind of fee or charges or expenses may prevent him or her from pursuing and completing elementary education". A list of free entitlements is made explicit in 5(1) of the model rules, but it is not restrictive; as per section 3(2) of the Act, if any other charge or expense other than that listed in Model Rules 5(1), for example, free residential facilities for children whose parents migrate, prevents a child from pursuing or completing elementary education, the state shall have to provide it.

(H) Compulsory Elementary Education: The word 'compulsory' has implications for the government alone. In other words while it is the duty of the parents to send their children to school (Article 15k), it is the obligation of the government to ensure not just enrollment but attendance and completion of elementary education. This implies that the government:

(a) Must identify all children that are out of school or dropped out.
(b) Make sure that they are enrolled in school.
(c) Make sure they attend school on a regular basis.
(d) Make sure they complete the elementary cycle of education.
(e) If parents are reluctant to send their children it is the responsibility of the government to find a way of convincing the parents, without use of force / violence / pressure to send their children to school.

(I) Screening Procedure: Any test or interview / interaction of the child or interview / interaction of parents would constitute a screening procedure to admit one child over another. Section 2(O) along with section 13(2) prohibits any of those screening procedure and calls for only random procedures to be used for admitting a child to school. This prohibition would apply to all schools, private or special category schools like Navodaya schools too. Random procedure implies that if the number of children applying to a school exceeds the available seats, an open lottery system be used to fill the seats. This applies to all categories of schools.

(J) Disadvantaged Children and Children belonging to 'weaker sections': Children belonging to disadvantaged groups are defined at 2(d). These include children from SC / ST, and other socially and educationally backward categories based on cultural, economical, social, geographical, linguistic, gender or other categories that the appropriate governments can separately notify. Weaker sections as defined at 2(e) are children belonging to weaker economic categories that the appropriate governments have to notify, based on a minimum annual income of the parents / guardians. Through amendments in the RTE Act children with disabilities have been included in the definition of 'children belonging to disadvantaged group' in Section 2(d) of the Act.

(K) Age Appropriate Class: It means arranging admission in a class where the child would normally be if he / she had joined school from Class I at six years of age. So, if a child is 11 years old and has never been to school, she / he will be admitted to class V, but shall be given special training in order to be at par with others.

(L) Children not in Schools Right Now: The Act, at section 4 lays down that all children who are out of school, as never enrolled or dropouts (in the 6 – 14 age group), would have to be admitted in age appropriate class in regular schools, and they would have a right to complete elementary education even after crossing age 14.

(M) Elementary Education: Elementary education is eight years of education corresponding to classes 1–8. This in most cases includes children between 6–14 years, but in states that start at five years and go up to class 7, RTE would still extend to class 8.

(N) Neighbourhood School: The neighbourhood has been given a wide definition in the Model Rules of the Act. Ordinarily it is one km. walking distance from the habitation of a child at the primary level and three km for upper primary level. However, in areas with sparse populations, or those prone to natural disasters or with difficult terrain or civil unrest, this limitation may be changed and transportation or residential facilities provided to children so that their education is not interrupted or disrupted.

(O) Quality Norms for All Schools: The Act lays out some basic norms for all schools (government and private) :

(a) Pupil-Teacher Ratio (cannot exceed 1: 30).

(b) Minimum days of school functioning in a year (200 and 250 for primary and upper primary respectively).

(c) Minimum hours of instruction in school (four and five hours a day for primary and UP).

(d) Minimum working hours for the teacher (45 hours a week)

(e) Separate subject teachers and head-teacher.

(f) One room for every teacher.

(g) Separate and functional toilets; clean and adequate drinking water.

(h) Playground, boundary wall, library and kitchen.

(P) Qualifications for Teachers:

(a) Para Teachers banned.

(b) All teachers must subscribe to minimum qualifications and training norms laid out by Academic Authority within five years.

(c) Teacher education and Teacher training institutes to be upgraded to enable fulfilment of quality and qualification norms for teachers.

(Q) Curriculum in line with Constitution:

(a) This means that curriculum, syllabus and books must conform to Constitutional values. It implies that communal and harmful agendas cannot be part of the materials used and taught in ANY school of the country.

(b) Syllabus and books must also take into account age and learning levels of children.

(R) Evaluation system to be based on principle of Continuous and Comprehensive Evaluation (CCE):

(a) No failure till completion of elementary cycle.

(b) Evaluation to be done throughout the year and not be based on an annual exam.

(c) Teachers to maintain **Pupil Cumulative Record (PCR)** for every child.

(d) Evaluation to be "comprehensive" performance of child, reflecting all facets, talents of the child and not be based on just a few subject areas. The PCR to include music, theatre, leadership skills, social skills etc., as well.

(S) Role of Panchayati Raj Institutions (PRIs):

(a) The PRIs have been given a wide range of functions related to the implementation of the provisions of the RTE, such as identification of out of school children; neighbourhood-wise school mapping; maintenance of child records (child-tracking) public display of information; education of children from migrant families; participation in School Management Committees (SMCs).

(b) PRIs have also been made responsible for grievance redressal in matters related to violations of the rights of the child under RTE.

(T) Participation of Civil Society:

(a) School Management Committees consisting largely of parents (75 per cent) and of PRIs officials and civil society partners have been given a wide range of functions under the Act, including the preparation of the School Development Plan.

(b) Teachers have been made accountable to the SMCs.

(U) Reservation in Private Schools:

(a) All private schools are required to admit in their incoming class 25 per cent children from weaker sections and socially disadvantaged groups from their neighbourhood.

(b) Private schools to be reimbursed for these children by the government at the rate of per learner costs of government schools in the state.

(V) Separation of Implementation and Monitoring Agency:

(a) Implementation responsibilities lie with the education departments in conjunction with the PRIs.

(b) Monitoring role has been given to the National Commission for Protection of Child Rights (NCPCR) and the corresponding State Commissions.

(c) This separation is very important and a first in the history of such legislations and allows for independent monitoring of the implementation of the Act.

(d) NCPCR / SCPCR have quasi-judicial powers and can function as a civil court. Complaints and grievances can be addressed to them as well.

Chapter - 14

Section-wise Clarification of the RTE Act, 2009

Ministry of Human Resource Development, Govt. of India has made section-wise clarification on provisions of the RTE Act, 2009. This clarification has been reproduced here for our better understanding about the RTE. The following are the Section-wise Clarifications.

Chapter I: Preliminary

Section 2 defines words and expressions used in the Act.

Chapter II: Right to Free and Compulsory Education

Section 3 provides to every child of the age of six to fourteen years the right to free and compulsory education in a neighbourhood school till the completion of elementary education. The idea of neighbourhood schools can be traced to the National System of Education as elaborated in the Kothari Commission report, whereby the neighbourhood school is meant to be a common space, where all children cutting across caste, class, gender lines learn together in the best inclusive manner. It is, therefore, meant to be a site for inclusion, so that the school becomes a common space for education. This concept has been incorporated in the RTE Act. In providing for the right of every child to free and compulsory education in a *neighbourhood* school, the RTE Act does not restrict the choice of the child to seek admission in a school which may not be in the *neighbourhood* of the child's residence. In other words, there is no compulsion on the child to seek admission only in the school in his or her *neighbourhood*. The term 'free education' is explained to mean that no child shall be liable to pay any kind of fee or charges or expenses which may prevent him or her from pursuing and completing elementary education. The term 'free education' must be read in consonance with the provisions of section 12(1) (a)-(c) which specify the extent of the school's responsibility for free and compulsory education. It further provides that the provisions of the Persons with Disabilities (Equal Opportunities, Protection and Full Participation) Act, 1996 will apply in the case of children suffering from disability as defined under that Act.

Section 4 provides children above six years, who have either not been admitted to any school or, having been admitted have not completed elementary education and have dropped out, the right to be admitted to a school in a class appropriate to his or her age for completing elementary education. A majority of out-of-school children belong to disadvantaged communities: scheduled castes, scheduled tribes, Muslim minorities, migrants, children with special needs, urban deprived children, working children, children in difficult circumstances, for example, those living in difficult terrain, children from displaced families, and areas affected by civil strife, etc. This provision in the RTE Act enables these out-of-school children to be admitted to an age-appropriate class and complete elementary education. The overall objective of age appropriate admission for these children is to save them from the humiliation and embarrassment of sitting with younger children. When older children are forced to sit in a class younger than their age, they tend to be teased, taunted, suffer lower self-esteem, and consequently drop out. The Act facilitates a child admitted to an age appropriate class to be given Special Training to enable him or her to be at par with other children. Given the varied life experiences of these children, it is recognised in the field of education that their mental capabilities are higher than that of entry level six-year old children, and that they are indeed capable of accelerated learning. At the end of the Special Training, the child will be assessed and his/her suitability for being placed in a particular class will be reviewed. For example, if a 10-year old child was admitted to class IV, and received two years of Special Training till age 12, an assessment may be made as to whether the child could cope better in class V or VI in the formal school, and the child appropriately placed. If such child is found suitable for class V, she/he will be placed in class V, rather than mechanically being placed in class VI – because if she/he is mechanically placed in class VI, she/he might again drop-out, and that would defeat the whole purpose of this provision. That is the rationale for the provision that allows the child to be provided free and compulsory education even beyond age 14. Even after a child is appropriately placed in the formal school she may continue to receive special attention by the teacher to enable her to successfully integrate with the rest of the class, academically and emotionally. The SSA Framework of Implementation has been revised to provide support for Special Training as envisaged under the RTE Act to ensure that out-of-school children are integrated into the school system. Such support will be in the form of residential or nonresidential courses, as needed and such children will continue even beyond 14 years of age to complete elementary education. The country is committed to creating an educated citizenry and environment, and therefore it would not be appropriate to impose an age ceiling for these children to complete elementary education. The obligation under section 4 is on the schools established by the State Government and local authority. Private aided and unaided institutions have no obligations under section 4.

Section 5 provides children the right to seek transfer from a government or government-aided school to another such school in order to complete elementary education and for immediate issue of Transfer Certificate to a child seeking admission to another school. It provides that delay in producing Transfer Certificate shall not be a reason for denying or delaying admission in another school. This provision should lead to States instituting reform to remove procedural barriers to obtaining Transfer Certificates.

Chapter III: Duties of Appropriate Government, Local Authority and Parents

Section 6: The rationale of this provision is to provide all children access to elementary education. Universal access requires schooling facilities within reasonable reach of all children. If schools are not located in or near the habitations where children reside, children may not complete schooling, even if they are formally enrolled in schools, on account of distance factors. The RTE Act therefore mandates the appropriate governments and local authorities to provide for children's access to elementary schools within the defined area or limits of *neighbourhood.* The RTE Act deliberately does not define the limits or area of *neighbourhood* as a centralised norm, but requires the appropriate government to notify such limits or area in the RTE Rules. This is on account of the very diverse geographical, climatic terrain and the varied development requirements of the different States, and the conscious decision that States would be better placed to define the '*neighbourhood*', keeping the best interests of different children in mind. However, the Central Government has attempted to exemplify this in the Model RTE Rules circulated to States, which provide for distance norms of one kilometer for children in classes I-V, and three kilometers for children in classes VI-VIII, as also provision for relaxation of norms in places with difficult terrain where there may be risk of landslides, floods, lack of roads and in general, danger for young children in the approach from their homes to the school. The Model Rules also provide that access of children to school should not be hindered on account of social and cultural factors. Such norms should be laid down keeping in view local contexts and requirements, rather than centrally prescribed through a law. These have also been incorporated in the Central RTE Rules applicable to all UTs without Legislature. States /UTs need to arrive at a clear picture of current availability of schools within defined area or limits of neighbourhoods. In order to do this, State/UTs need to (i) define the neighbourhood norms keeping in view that all primary and upper primary schools and composite schools (with primary and upper primary sections), established by the State Government and local bodies would be *neighbourhood* schools for the purpose of section 3(1), and (ii) map the neighbourhoods or habitations and link them to specific schools. It is possible that a neighbourhood may be linked to more than one school. Similarly, a school may be linked to more than one neighbourhood. The mapping exercise will help identify gaps and areas where new schools need to be opened to ensure universal access.

Section 7(1)–(5) provides for financial and other responsibilities of the Central Government and the State Governments for carrying out the provisions of the proposed Act. The Central Government has estimated a total requirement of Rs 2.31 lakh crore over a five-year period from 2010-11 to 2014-15 to implement the RTE Act. Separately, the 13th Finance Commission has also provided a grant of Rs 24,068 crore specifically for elementary education. The grant of the 13th Finance Commission is released directly on an annual basis to the State Governments from the Finance Ministry. This amount is deducted from the overall estimate of Rs 2.31 lakh crore, and the balance amount of Rs 2.07 lakh crore will be shared between the Central and State Governments in the 65:35 ratio for the implementation of RTE through the SSA programme. In the case of States in the North East Region, the fund sharing pattern will be in the 90:10 ratio.

Section 7(6) provides for the formulation of a National Curriculum Framework. The Central Government has notified the NCERT as the designated authority for this purpose. The National Curriculum Framework, 2005, formulated by the NCERT has been hailed nationally and internationally as trend-setting in defining learning processes, assessment, quality and integration of various aspects of education geared towards producing a creative citizen of the country, and has been accepted as the Curriculum Framework under the RTE Act.

Section 8 assigns duties to the appropriate government to ensure that it provides free and compulsory elementary education to every child, in a neighbourhood school. The term 'compulsory education' is explained to mean obligation of the appropriate government to provide free elementary education and ensure compulsory admission, attendance and completion of elementary education. It further provides that where a child is not admitted to a school which is established, owned, controlled or substantially funded by the appropriate government or local authority, such child or his or her parents will not be entitled to claim reimbursement of the cost of elementary education. It lays down the duties of the appropriate government to ensure *inter alia* that children belonging to weaker sections and disadvantaged groups are not discriminated against and prevented from pursuing and completing elementary education, that admission, attendance and completion of elementary education by every child is monitored, that school building, teaching staff and learning equipment are provided, good quality elementary education conforming to norms and standards is provided, curriculum and courses of study are prescribed in a timely manner, and teachers are trained.

Section 9 assigns duties to the local authority to ensure that it provides free and compulsory elementary education to every child, in a neighbourhood school. It lays down the duties of the local authority to ensure *inter alia* that children belonging to weaker sections and disadvantaged groups are not discriminated against and prevented from pursuing and completing elementary education, maintain records of children residing within its jurisdiction, ensure and monitor admission, attendance and completion of elementary education by every child, including migrant children, ensure that school building, teaching staff and learning equipment and good quality elementary education conforming to norms and standards is provided, decide on the academic calendar.

Section 10: This provision casts a moral responsibility on every parent/guardian to admit their children/wards to school, and ensure that children are not deprived of their right to elementary education. This includes, for example, child labour, children in ecologically deprived areas where they are required to fetch fuel, water, fodder and do other household chores, children in very poor slum communities and uprooted urban habitations, children of families of scavengers and other such stigmatised professions, children of itinerant or seasonal labour who have mobile and transient lifestyle like construction workers, road workers and workers on large construction sites, children of landless agriculture labour who are required to augment family incomes. This provision should be read together with the responsibility of the appropriate Government and local authority to provide free and compulsory elementary education in a *neighbourhood* school. It is not the intention of this provision to compel parents/guardians and children/wards, who do not wish to avail of free and compulsory education, to necessarily admit their children/wards in *neighbourhood* school. Suggestions were made to incorporate penal provisions against parents/guardians who do not send their children to school, but the fact remains that the maximum number of children who do not attend school are children from weaker sections and disadvantaged groups. Penalising their parents would be tantamount to penalising poverty and deprivation.

Further, there are many first generation learners, who are deprived of a learning environment at home, and dropout on account of difficulties in coping with the curriculum. Inflicting penalties on parents because their children have dropped out or have been pushed out of the education system would be discriminatory. Therefore, it is a conscious decision to abstain from imposing penal provisions against parents and guardian. Instead the RTE Act casts a duty or compulsion on the appropriate government to ensure admission, attendance and completion of elementary education. This would lead to significant systemic reform in universalising elementary education. In many instances however, the government would have to collaborate with the civil society in persuading parents who experience genuine problems in sending their wards to school for them to fulfil their duty to ensure that their children do attend schools regularly, particularly in the case of older girls.

Section 11 provides that the appropriate government *may* make necessary arrangements for pre-school education.

Chapter IV: Responsibilities of Schools and Teachers

Section 12 explains the responsibility of schools for providing free and compulsory education to children, namely:

(a) All government schools shall provide free and compulsory education to all children.

(b) Government-aided institutions shall provide free and compulsory education to such percentage of students in elementary classes which equals the percentage of recurring aid received by it from the government to the annual recurring expenditure incurred by the school, subject to a minimum of 25 per cent.

(c) Private unaided institutions and special category schools shall provide free and compulsory education to at least 25 per cent children belonging to disadvantaged groups and weaker sections admitted to class I or pre-primary classes. Such schools would be entitled to reimbursement at the per-child cost incurred by the government. It has also since been clarified that residential private unaided schools, which do not start at class I, would not be required to admit 25 per cent children from disadvantaged groups and weaker sections in their schools.

There have been misgivings among certain groups about the admission of children from disadvantaged groups and weaker sections in class I in private unaided schools. In this context it is important to refer to the Statement of Objects and Reasons (SOR) attached to the Right of Children to Free and Compulsory Education Bill, 2008, which states: *The Right of Children to Free and Compulsory Education Bill, 2008, is anchored in the belief that the values of equality, social justice and democracy and the creation of a just and humane society can be achieved only through provision of inclusive elementary education to all. Provision of free and compulsory education of satisfactory quality to children from disadvantaged and weaker sections is, therefore, not merely the responsibility of schools run or supported by the appropriate governments, but also of schools which are not dependent on government funds.* The idea that schooling should act as a means of social cohesion and inclusion is not new; it has been oft repeated. Inequitable and disparate schooling reinforces existing social and economic hierarchies, and promotes in the educated sections of society an indifference towards the plight of the poor. The currently used term 'inclusive' education implies, as did earlier terms like 'common' and 'neighbourhood' schools, that children from different backgrounds and with varying interests and ability will achieve their highest potential if they study in a shared classroom environment. The idea of inclusive schooling is also consistent with Constitutional values and ideals, especially with the ideals of fraternity, social justice and equality of opportunity. For children of socio-economically weaker backgrounds to feel at home in private schools, it is necessary that they form a substantial proportion or critical mass in the class they join. The relevant universe in which the proportion needs to be considered is the class/section. It is for this reason that the RTE Act provides for admission of 25 per cent children from disadvantaged groups and weaker sections in class I only. This implies that these children cannot be pooled together in a separate section or afternoon shift. Any arrangement which segregates, or treats these children in a differentiated manner vis-à-vis the fee-paying children will be counter- productive. The rationale for

25 per cent lies in the fact that the composition of caste/class indicated in the Census is fairly representative of the composition of children who are seeking admission under this provision. As per Census 2001, SCs constitute 16.2 per cent, and STs constitute 8.2 per cent (total 24.4 per cent) of the population. Further, the Tendulkar Committee, set up by the Planning Commission to measure poverty, has estimated the below poverty line (BPL) population to be 37.2 per cent. It is a fact that much of the population that suffers economic deprivation also suffers from social disadvantage. Thus, taken together, the figure of 25 per cent for admission of children from disadvantaged groups and weaker sections is considered reasonable. Any lower proportion would jeopardise the long-term goal of the policy which is to strengthen social cohesion and bring out the best human resource potential inherent in our society as a whole. A smaller proportion would serve only a token purpose, and it will run the serious risk of creating the feeling of alienation among the children belonging to disadvantaged groups and weaker sections. Their participation in classroom interaction will be neither strong nor sufficiently manifest to enrich the overall experiential learning taking place in any given subject area. Only a critical mass can play such a role. The RTE Act provides for admission of 25 per cent children from disadvantaged groups and weaker sections in Class I, not across the whole school. As children admitted to class I move to class II, new children will be admitted to class I, and so on till completion of eight years of elementary education. The rationale for admission in class I only must be appreciated in human terms. Teachers who are used to a selective, homogeneous classroom environment cannot be expected to develop the required positive attitude and professional skills to deal with a diversified class overnight. The same applies to children. Children who have grown up to an age of nine or ten in a homogeneous or segregated environment have been socialised into a structure of norms and behaviour. They cannot be transformed on demand. Also, the overall school ethos cannot be expected to respond to a new policy in a positive manner all of a sudden. Education is indeed an act of faith and social engineering – but not quick-fix social engineering. In view of the fact that children take time to socialise and teachers take time to develop new attitudes and pedagogic skills, the RTE Act provides for admission of disadvantaged and poor children at

the entry level, covering pre-school and Class I. With these children moving up, and a new cohort of children entering pre-school and Class I in each successive year, the school will gradually have a more diverse population spread across all classes. Progression at this pace will allow children the opportunity to grow up together and create bonds: bonds that can survive social walls. Progression at this pace can allow the school to develop the professional capacity to respond to the intellectual and emotional needs of children from diverse backgrounds. Children who are younger than eight years of age are yet to develop a stable social identity. Their values are still forming, and their motivation to derive meaning from experience, both concrete and social is very strong. Therefore, it is a valid argument that the policy of mixing children from different socio-economic strata has the best chance of succeeding if it starts from the formative years of nursery/kindergarten and Class I. Diversity enhances learning and development, while segregation impoverishes the classroom environment of all schools, private or government. Admission of 25 per cent children from disadvantaged groups and weaker sections in the neighbourhood is not merely to provide avenues of quality education to poor and disadvantaged children. The larger objective is to provide a common place where children sit, eat and live together for at least eight years of their lives across caste, class and gender divides in order that it narrows down such divisions in our society. The other objective is that the 75 per cent children, who have been lucky to come from better endowed families, learn through their interaction with the children from families, who haven't had similar opportunities, but are rich in knowledge systems allied to trade, craft, farming and other services, and that the pedagogic enrichment of the 75 per cent children is provided by such intermingling. This will of course require classroom practices, teacher training, etc. to constantly bring out these pedagogic practices, rather than merely make children from these two sections sit together. The often voiced concern about how the 25 per cent children from disadvantaged groups and weaker sections can cope in an environment where rich children exist can be resolved when the teaching learning process and teachers use these children as sources of knowledge so that their esteem and recognition goes up and they begin to be treated as equals.

Section 13 provides that no school or person shall collect capitation fee or subject a child to any screening procedure, and prescribes a penalty for contravention of these provisions. On the issue of screening procedure for admission, government had consultation with several private school Principals, and has since issued guidelines under section 35(1). The Guidelines explain that the objective of the provisions of section 13(1) read with section 2(o) is to ensure that schools adopt an admission procedure that is non-discriminatory, rational and transparent, and that schools do not subject children and their parents to admission tests and interviews in order to decide whether they will admit a child or not. Extensive educational research the world over recognises that children are born with equal potential to learn and become creative adults. The colonial beliefs that men have better brains than women, or whites have better brains than blacks, implying thereby that there were intrinsic differences in the potential to learn and in intelligence, have long been discarded and debunked. The most obvious proof of that is the acquisition of language, without which no learning can take place. All children acquire language without the agency of a school at around the same age of two years. This is held as an intrinsic stage of child brain development, which has nothing to do with caste, class, gender, high/low IQ and such other differentiation. What is well recognised, however, is that from infancy, it is the processes of nurturing at home and later during pre-school and school, that determines the depth and extent of learning. Therefore, tests and other screening procedures can only reveal differences in nurturing, rather than any intrinsic differences of the potential to learn. In such a situation it would be particularly necessary, and indeed the obligation of the State and society to provide for better nurturing through good schools to children from poor and disadvantaged sections of society.

The guidelines issued under section 35(1), therefore, explicitly state that tests and interviews are generally a tool for profiling and eliminating children, and therefore screening to assess a child's 'intelligence should be prohibited'. Availability of equal opportunities for children belonging to different social and economic backgrounds will reinforce the idea of equality enshrined in our Constitution, and ensure that children are not discriminated on the basis of their social and economic background. The guidelines also refer to the importance of moving towards composite classrooms with children from diverse backgrounds, rather than homogenous and exclusivist schools: heterogeneity and diversity in classrooms lead to greater inter-learning, respect for differences, tolerance and creativity. Thus, in respect of 25 per cent children representing disadvantaged groups and weaker sections for admission in class I, the guidelines provide for random selection out of applications received. For admission to the remaining 75 per cent, the guidelines give schools the freedom to formulate their own admissions policy. Such policy should include the criteria for categorisation of applicants in terms of the objectives of the school on a rationale, reasonable and just basis. There should be no profiling of the child based on parental educational qualifications. This policy should be in the public domain, explicitly stated in the school prospectus and given wide publicity. There shall be no testing or interviews for any child/parent, and selection should be on random basis.

Section 14 seeks to provide for proof of age certificate of a child and that admission cannot be denied in its absence. The rationale for this provision is that birth certificates under the Births, Deaths and Marriages Certification Act, 1886 are often not available, and in their absence, children and their parent often have to run from pillar to post to obtain age proof. Thus, other documents can be deemed to be proof of age of the child for the purposes of admission in schools. Examples of other documents are (i) ANM register record, (ii) Anganwadi record, (iii) declaration of age of the child by the parent or the guardian. State Governments will identify documents, which may be in the form of affidavits or certificates that can be used for determining the age of the child for admission and suitably provide for them in the delegated legislation. Clause 14 (2) however, makes it explicit that since the child has a *right* to education, that *right* cannot be denied for lack of age proof. Therefore, admission would be given even in the absence of age proof, while an appropriate document of age proof would simultaneously be acquired.

Section 15 prohibits schools from denial of admission to a child, irrespective of the time in the academic year in which admission is sought. Admission of a child in school is a fundamental right and it cannot be denied at any point of time. Ideally, all children should be enrolled in school at the beginning of the academic session.

However, in the case of children in difficult circumstances, including children affected by migration, displacement or ill-health, etc schools may need to be flexible to allow admission at any time during the session. The Central RTE Rules provide that children admitted after six months of the beginning of the academic session may be provided Special Training as determined by the Head Teacher of the school to enable him/her to complete studies. Private unaided schools need not be concerned about this provision, especially with respect to the 75 per cent admission, because if they have filled all seats at the beginning of the academic year the question of any-time admission would not arise.

Section 16 prohibits holding back and expulsion of a child from school till the attainment of elementary education. There have been some misgivings on the provisions relating to 'no detention' and 'no expulsion'. The 'no detention' provision is made because examinations are often used for eliminating children who obtain poor marks. Once declared 'fail', children either repeat grade or leave the school altogether. Compelling a child to repeat a class is demotivating and discouraging. Repeating a class does not give the child any special resources to deal with the same syllabus requirements for yet another year. Parents and friends of such children also tend to view them as being 'fit for failure', thereby reinforcing the perception which the school has already used for declaring a child 'fail'. The 'no detention' provision in the RTE Act does not imply abandoning procedures that assess children's learning. The RTE Act provides for putting in place a continuous and comprehensive evaluation procedure – a procedure that will be non-threatening, releases the child from fear and trauma of failure and enables the teacher to pay individual attention to the child's learning and performance. Such a system has the best potential to improve quality, rather than punishment, fear of failure and detention. Consistent with the arguments provided under section 13 that each child has the same potential for learning, a 'slow', 'weak' learner or a 'failed' child is not because of any inherent drawback in the child, but most often the inadequacy of the learning environment and the delivery system to help the child, realise his/her potential, meaning thereby that the failure is of the system, rather than of the child. This requires addressing the improvement of the quality of the system rather than punishing the child through detention. There is no study of research that suggests that the quality of the learning of the child improves if the child is failed. In fact, more often than not the child abandons school/ learning altogether. As regards expulsion, there are many who give examples of deviant and aberrant behaviour of some children, adversely influencing other children, and that such deviant children should be 'expelled' in order that the others may be protected. But the implications of expulsion are that the education system has *refused* to serve the child. The notion of 'expulsion' is not compatible with the concept of 'right'. No civilised country in the world expels children from elementary school for any reasons: there are no valid grounds for doing so. If the child – and remember we are talking about 6-14 years old, not older children – does not respond to the existing system and resorts to 'deviant' activities, then the education system must address the child differently – through counselling or by providing different curricular and co-curricular activities, which enable the child to develop self-awareness, address deep rooted fears and problems and consequently change patterns of behaviour.

Section 17 prohibits any child being subjected to physical punishment or mental harassment. There is a mistaken notion that 'discipline' of children comes from punishment and fear. Educationists the world-over are clear that what matters for creating a mature citizen is the provision of a 'learning environment' in the formative years, which is what the school must become, and not a 'correctional' centre, which has the connotations of a jail. Physical punishment and mental trauma are counter-productive, and may cause a child to become even more defiant and rebellious than before. The concept of childhood implies a period of impressionability and vulnerability. Both these attributes of childhood enjoin upon the adult society to treat childhood as a part of life, which requires protection and nurturance. Children's bodies are tender and vulnerable. A minor punishment can result in injury: even a slap may result in a child going deaf. There are many examples of grievous injury to children on account of physical punishment. Physical punishment is invariably accompanied by mental trauma. All physical punishment and mental trauma is potentially unsafe and injurious to health. Article 39 (f) of the Constitution of India states: Art 39 (f): '*The state shall ensure that children are given opportunities* *to develop in a healthy manner and in conditions of freedom and dignity and that childhood and youth are protected against exploitation and against moral and material abandonment'*. There is explicit use of the word 'dignity' in Article 39(f). It is not conceivable for dignity and punishment to co-exist.

Further, the National Policy on Education (NPE) 1986/1992 also prohibits corporal punishment. It states: *Corporal punishment will be firmly excluded from the education system.* India is a signatory to the United Nations Convention on Child Rights (UNCRC). Article 19 of the UNCRC states: State parties shall take all appropriate legislative, administrative, social and educational measures to protect the child from all forms of physical or mental violence, injury or abuse, neglect or negligent treatment, maltreatment or exploitation, including sexual abuse, while in the care of parents, legal guardians or any other person who has the care of the child. Thus, the provisions in the RTE Act banning corporal punishment and mental harassment are in consonance with the spirit of Article 39 (f) of the Constitution, the National Policy on Education, and the UNCRC.

Section 18 stipulates that no private school should be established or can function without obtaining a Certificate of Recognition, and that such Certificate of Recognition would be issued to schools that fulfil the prescribed norms and standards. The Act does not have a provision for recognition of government schools, since that would amount to government giving recognition to its own schools, however section 19 clearly states that government schools must meet the requirements of the schedule.

Section 19 lays down the norms and standards for schools. Any school, whether government or private that does not fulfil the prescribed norms and standards shall do so within a period of three years from the date of commencement of the proposed Act. There appears to be a misconception that government schools do not require to meet the norms and standards prescribed under the Act on account of a wrong insertion of a comma in the RTE Bill when it was introduced in Parliament. This has since been corrected and the provision for meeting norms and standards is applicable to all schools, ensuring that these schools also meet the norms prescribed will be monitored by the NCPCR.

Section 20 provides power to Central Government to amend the schedule on norms and standards.

Section 21 provides for constitution and functions of a School Management Committee in certain categories of schools. The setting up of such Committees has been a recommendation of nearly all previous education commissions and policies. The reason is that if the community has to be involved in the vast school system of the country, and if the parents are to be recognised as primary stakeholders in the education of their children, they must be involved in a meaningful manner in the monitoring and management of schools. The RTE Act therefore envisages that parents would form a majority in the School Management Committees, which would also include elected members of the Panchayat and school teachers. There is reason to believe that like the mother's committees that have functioned exceptionally well in some parts of the country, the parent-dominated SMC's will lead to overall improvement of the schooling system. Private unaided institutions are exempted from the constitution of School Management Committees. Government has also introduced an Amendment Bill in the Parliament, which provides that the School Management Committee in respect of private unaided and minority institutions will only have an advisory role.

Section 22 provides for preparation of a School Development Plan (SDP) by the School Management Committee. The SDP is visualised as a comprehensive plan focusing on all aspects of school e.g. protection of children's rights, infrastructure, teacher availability, classroom transaction and child assessments, inclusiveness, etc. Private unaided institutions are not expected to prepare SDPs envisaged under the RTE Act. Further, the Amendment Bill referred to in previous paragraph provides that private unaided and minority institutions will also not be required to prepare SDPs.

Section 23 provides for qualifications and terms and conditions of service of school teachers. The Central Government has notified NCTE as the academic authority for prescribing teacher qualifications. NCTE has laid down the requisite teacher qualifications as per its notification dated 23rd August 2010.

Section 24 provides for duties of teachers. This includes *inter alia* that teachers attend school regularly and transact the syllabus in a timely manner, that they provide supplementary support to children who need such support, that they make an assessment of children's learning, and interact with parents.

Section 25 seeks to provide for maintenance of pupil-teacher ratio, by the appropriate government and local authority. An apparent contradiction between this provision, which requires that the pupil-teacher ratio shall be maintained within a period of six months, vis-à-vis the provision under section 19 mandating that the norms and standards prescribed in the Schedule should be met within three years, is proposed to be corrected through the Amendment Bill introduced in the Parliament. The proviso to this section also provides that teachers shall not be deployed for nonacademic work, barring those specified in section 27, viz., (i) decennial population census, (ii) disaster relief and (iii) elections to Parliament, State Legislatures and Local Bodies.

Section 26 provides that vacancies in schools should not exceed 10 per cent of the teacher strength for that school. This provision will ensure that States take steps to fill up existing teacher vacancies as also rationalise deployment of teachers in schools to remove urban-rural imbalances in teacher deployment.

Section 27 prohibits deployment of teachers for non-educational purposes, other than decennial population census, disaster relief duties or duties relating to elections to local authority, state legislatures and parliament. This provision will ensure that more time is available to teachers for school/ classroom transaction, and that teachers are not deployed for work that takes them away from their classroom responsibilities.

Section 28 prohibits private tuition by teachers. Private tuition is one of the ills affecting Indian education, which needs to be addressed. This provision will ensure that teachers do not use their position for commercial gain through private tuition, which is a source of harassment to children and parents.

Chapter V: Curriculum and Completion of Elementary Education

Section 29 provides for curriculum and evaluation procedure in elementary schools. State Governments are required to prescribe the academic authority to lay down the curriculum and evaluation procedure. In doing so the academic authority must ensure adherence to eight factors stated in the RTE Act. These eight factors are:

1. Conformity with Constitutional values;
2. All round development of the child;
3. Building the child's knowledge, potentiality and talent;
4. Development of physical and mental abilities to the fullest extent;
5. Learning through activities, discovery and exploration in a child-friendly and child-centred manner;
6. The child's mother tongue serving 'as far as practicable' as the medium of instruction;
7. Making the child free of fear, trauma and anxiety and helping the child to express views freely; and
8. Comprehensive and continuous evaluation of the child's understanding and knowledge and the ability to apply it. These factors, which have become part of educational legislation, provide comprehensive coverage of the indicators of child-centred curricular policy for the elementary stage of education spelt out in the National Policy on Education (NPE), 1986/92 and elaborated in the NCF – 2005.

Section 30 provides that no child shall be required to pass Board examinations till completion of elementary education. Board examinations induce tremendous stress and anxiety among children – especially young children. The National Curriculum Framework, 2005, while emphasising the need for flexibility in assessment, states: "*Under no circumstances should board- or state level examinations be conducted at other stages of schools, such as class V, VIII or XI. Indeed, Boards should consider, as a long-term measure, making the Class X examination optional, thus permitting students continuing in the same* *school (and who do not need a board certificate) to take an internal school exam instead".*

Chapter VI: Protection of Right of Children

Section 31 provides an institutional mechanism for protection of rights of the child through the National/ State Commissions for Protection of Child Rights. For children in school, monitoring will involve the following issues:

(i) Provision of neighbourhood school

1. Requisite number of classrooms and infrastructure facilities,
2. Appropriate PTR,
3. School hours.

(ii) Access to school: physical and social.

(iii) Admission process

1. Denial of admission, 2. Capitation Fee, 3. Screening procedure, 4. Demand for Affidavits, 5. Any time Admission.

(iv) Entitlements

1. Textbooks, 2. Uniforms, 3. Library with books, newspapers, magazines, 4. Sports equipment, 5. Play material, 6. Mid-day Meal, 7. Special Training for age-appropriate education, 8. Transfer Certificates, 9. Completion Certificates, 10. Other expenses.

(v) Classroom Transaction

1. No discrimination, 2. No corporal punishment, 3. Appropriate Teaching methods, 4. Appropriate Evaluation Systems.

(vi) School Management Committee

1. Appointments as per rules, 2. Regular meetings, 3. Teacher Accountability Preparation of School Development Plan, 4. Other Responsibilities.

For Children in Private Aided and Unaided Schools

Admission of children from Weaker Sections and Disadvantaged Groups. In addition NCPCR/SCPCR would monitor out-of-school children to facilitate their access and participation in the schooling system. This would include children who have never enrolled or have dropped out, children who are temporarily absent, and children who are permanent migrants, who migrate seasonally with their parents.

Section 32 provides a mechanism for redressal of grievance relating to rights of the child under the proposed Act.

Section 33 provides for constitution of a National Advisory Council to give expert advice to the Central Government on implementation of provisions of the proposed Act. This Council has since been constituted and has commenced its work.

Section 34 provides for the constitution of State Advisory Councils to advise the State Governments on the implementation of the Act.

Chapter VII: Miscellaneous

Section 35 provides for the Central Government to issue guidelines and directions to the appropriate government or local authority for effective implementation of the proposed Act. It also provides for the appropriate Government to issue guidelines and directions to Local Authorities, and for Local Authorities to give guidelines to School Management Committees.

Section 36 provides for previous sanction of an authorised officer for prosecution of offences.

Section 37 provides protection, against any legal suit or proceedings, to appropriate government, local authority, etc for any action taken in good faith.

Section 38 provides powers to the appropriate government to make rules, and for laying of Rules and notifications made, before each House of Parliament.

Chapter - 15

Child Rights in the Context of the RTE Act, 2009

The children of today are the future of tomorrow. This age-old adage, yet it has a special significance. In India, children in the age group of 0 – 14 years comprise one-third of the total population of the country. Every child having a conducive and enabling environment can blossom and shine in all spheres of life. Realising the deprived and vulnerable conditions of children, the law-makers of the country have accorded a privileged status to children. The number of rights and privileges given by the Indian Constitution and duly supported by legal protection bears a testimony to this. Despite various initiatives both on legal as well as policy and programme levels the condition of children remains a cause of concern that needs to be addressed urgently. There is no denying the fact that children hold the key to the nation's future and as such due priority must be given to look into their needs and requirements, by giving them access to a range of opportunities for their holistic and all-round development. In this backdrop, the Right of Children to Free and Compulsory Education Act, 2009 commonly known as RTE Act is the first central legislation in the landscape of elementary education that puts the responsibility on thé state to provide free and compulsory elementary education to every child in the age group 6–14. Education as a right for the Indian children is now constitutionally guaranteed. The present chapter is a modest attempt to analyse the child rights in India from educational point of view, especially in the context of the RTE Act, 2009.

Education is the fourth necessity for man after food, clothing and shelter, in today's competitive world. The education is the process of instruction aimed at the all-round development of individuals, providing the necessary tools and knowledge to understand and participate in day-to-day activities of today's world. It dispels ignorance and boosts moral values of the individuals. It is the only wealth which cannot be robbed. It forms the basis for lifelong learning and inspires confidence to face challenges. It provides the skills to individuals to become more self-reliant, enhances the ability to manage health and nutrition and plan for future. Education is also a fundamental requirement in a democracy. Through education people become, more informed and responsible citizens, who are capable of exercising wise choices, and finding their voices in politics. It is essential for eradicating poverty, by allowing people to play more productive roles and to earn better for living. Keeping in view the problems and challenges faced by the Indian children, laws have been introduced and programmes are being implemented for the welfare of children in India. The RTE Act provides for children's right to an education of equitable quality, based on principles of non-discrimination and equity. There are a large of child rights in India protected by our Constitution, special laws and commissions. These rights cannot be realised unless the right to education is implemented in full swing as the very right is the main key to unlock the other rights of children. Let us now review the child rights in India as a whole and in the context of the RTE Act in particular.

Who is a Child?

The International Covenant on Economic, Social and Cultural Rights (1966, ICESCR) while failing to prescribe an age limit, states that primary education should be compulsory for all. It also states that secondary education should be made available and accessible to all in a progressive manner. However, the ILO permits flexibility in upper age limit with respect to right to education, allowing countries which are not educationally and economically developed to set the minimum age at fourteen International Labour Organisation (ILO), Minimum Age Convention, C138, 26 June 1973. C138, Art. 4. "Notwithstanding the provisions of paragraph 3 of this Article, a Member whose economy and educational facilities are insufficiently developed may, after consultation with the organisations of employers and workers concerned, where such exist, initially specify a minimum age of 14 years."

In India, childhood has been defined in the context of legal and constitutional provisioning, mainly for aberrations of childhood. It is thus a variable concept to suit the purpose and rationale of childhood in differing circumstances. Essentially they differ in defining the upper age-limit of childhood. Biologically, childhood is the span of life from birth to adolescence. According to Article 1 of UNCRC (United Nation's Convention on the Rights of the Child), "A child means every human being below the age of 18 years unless, under the law applicable to the child, majority is attained earlier". According to the Section 2(c) the RTE Act, 2009, "Child means a male or female child of the age of six to fourteen years". A child domiciled in India attains majority at the age of 18 years. However, various legal provisions address children with differing definitions. The different definitions of child in some laws and acts have been shown in the Box 15.1. The age-groups of 0-14 years, 15-59 years and 60 and above years form a commonly accepted standard in reporting demographic indicators.

Box – 15.1: Indian Children with Differing Definitions at a Glance

- Different Acts under Labour Laws declare different age criteria :

– The Apprentices Act (1961)	'A person is qualified to be engaged as an apprentice only if he is not less than fourteen years of age....'.
– The Factories Act (1948)	'A child below 14 years of age is not allowed to work in any factory. An adolescent between 15 and 18 years can be employed in a factory only if he obtains a certificate of fitness from an authorised medical doctor....'.
– The Child Labour Prohibition and Regulation Act (1986)	'Child means a person who has not completed his fourteenth year of age'.

- Prohibition of Child Marriage Act (2006) declares 'Child means a person who, if a male, has not completed twenty-one years of age and, if a female, has not completed eighteen years of age'.
- The Juvenile Justice (Care and Protection of Children) Act 2000, amended in 2006, 2010 declares "juvenile or "Child" means a person who has not completed eighteenth year of age".
- Indian Penal Code in its Criminal law states Nothing is an offence which is done by a child under age of 7 years. The age of criminal responsibility is raised to 12 years if the child is found to have not attained the ability to understand the nature and consequences of his / her act".
- Article 21A: Right to Education mandates "The State shall provide free and compulsory education to all children of the age of 6 – 14 years, in such a manner as the State may, by law determine".

Source: Children in India, 2012 – A Statistical Appraisal, MSPI, GOI.

Constitutional Provisions for Education in India

The role of Universal Elementary Education (UEE) for strengthening the social fabric of democracy through provision of equal opportunities to all has been accepted since the inception of our Republic. The Indian Constitution recognised education as a crucial input for nation building and included a number of Articles specially dealing with education. Article 29 states that the minorities shall have the right to preserve their distinct language, script of culture. Article 29(2) declares that "no citizen shall be denied admission into any educational institution maintained by the state or re-achieving aid out of state fund on grounds any or religion, race, caste, language, or any of them". Article 30 gives protection to religious and linguistic minorities. They have the right to establish and administer institutions of their choice. Article 30(1-A) says that in case of any property of an educational institution established and administered by a minority being acquainted by the state, the state shall ensured that the amount fixed for such acquired property should be such as would not restrict or abrogate the rights of the minority. Article 30(2) prohibits state from discriminating in granting aid to educational institutions managed by the religions and linguistic minorities. Article 28(1) prohibits religious instruction in any educational wholly maintained out of the state funds. Article 28(2) says that nothing in clause (1) shall apply to an educational institution which is administered by the state but has been established under any endowment or trust which requires the religions instruction shall be imparted in such institution. Article 28(3) says that no person attending any educational institution recognised by the state be required to take part in any religious institution that may be imparted in such institution or any premises attached thereto unless such a person is a minor, his guardian has given consent thereto. Article 46 deals education of the socially and educationally backward classes of citizen. Article 350A deals facilities for instruction in mother tongue or in primary stage.

Constitutional Provisions for Protecting Child Rights

In the Indian Constitution, prior to the 86th Amendment Act, 2002, three Articles in the Constitution had the child as their specific focus. These were Articles 24, 39 and 45 dealing with prohibition of children from being employed in factories, mines or in other hazardous employment; development and protection of the tender age of children; and free and compulsory education.

Article 24: No child below the age of 14 years shall be employed to work in any factory or mine or engaged in hazardous employment.

Article 39: The state shall direct its policy toward securing that the tender age of children is not abused and that citizens are not forced by economic necessity to enter avocation unsuited to their age or strength and that children are given opportunities and facilities to develop in a healthy manner and in conditions of freedom and dignity and that childhood and youth are protected against exploitation and against moral and material abandonment.

Article 45: The state shall endeavour to provide within a period of ten years from the commencement of the Constitution for free and compulsory education for all children until they complete the age of 14 years.

Article 21A: "The State shall provide free and compulsory education to all children of the age of 6–14 years, in such a manner as the State may, by law determine".

Besides these, they also have rights as equal citizens of India, just as any other adult male or female:

- Right to equality (Article 14).
- Right against discrimination (Article 15).
- Right to personal liberty and due process of law (Article 21).
- Right to being protected from being trafficked and forced into bonded labour (Article 23).
- Right of weaker sections of the people to be protected from social injustice and all forms of exploitation (Article 46).

Research, documentation and interventions by government and the civil society groups in the past have clearly brought forth some of the following child protection issues and categories of children that deserve special protection : gender discrimination, caste discrimination, disability, female foeticide, infanticide, domestic violence, child sexual abuse, child marriage, child labour, child prostitution, child trafficking, child sacrifice, corporal punishment in schools, examination pressure and student suicides, natural disasters, war and conflict, HIV / AIDS.

National Policies and Programmes for Indian Children

Further, the Nation is implementing a number of Child centric policies addressing the issues of Child Survival, Child Development and Child Protection. The important among them are –

1. **National Policy for Children 1974** is the first policy document concerning the needs and rights of children. It recognised children to be a supremely important asset to the country. The goal of the policy is to take the next step in ensuring the constitutional provisions for children and the UN Declaration of Rights are implemented. It outlines services the state should provide for the complete development of a child, before and after birth and throughout a child's period of growth for their full physical, mental and social development.
2. **National Policy on Education, 1986** was called for "special em-phasis on the removal of disparities and to equalise educational opportunity," especially for Indian women, Scheduled Tribes (ST) and the Scheduled Castes (SC) communities. To achieve these, the policy called for expanding scholarships, adult education, recruiting more teachers from the SCs, incentives for poor families to send their children to school regularly, development of new institutions and providing housing and services. The NPE called for a "child-centred approach" in primary education, and launched "Operation Blackboard" to improve primary schools nationwide.
3. **National Policy on Child Labour, 1987,** contains the action plan for tackling the problem of child labour. It envisaged a legislative action plan focusing and convergence of general development programmes for benefiting children wherever possible, and Project-based plan of action for launching of projects for the welfare of working children in areas of high concentration of child labour.

4. **National Nutrition Policy, 1993**, was introduced to combat the problem of under-nutrition. It aims to address this problem by utilising direct (short-term) and indirect (long-term) interventions in the area of food production and distribution, health and family welfare, education, rural and urban development, woman and child development etc.
5. **National Population Policy 2000:** The national population policy 2000 aims at improvement in the status of Indian children. It emphasised free and compulsory school education up to age 14, universal immunisation of children against all vaccine preventable diseases, 100 per cent registration of birth, death, marriage and pregnancy, substantial reduction in the infant mortality rate and maternal mortality ratio etc.
6. **National Health Policy 2002:** The main objective of this policy is to achieve an acceptable standard of good health amongst the general population of the country. The approach is to increase access to the decentralised public health system by establishing new infrastructure in deficient areas, and by upgrading the infrastructure in the existing institutions. Overriding importance is given to ensuring a more equitable access to health services across the social and geographical expanse of the country.
7. **National Charter for Children (NCC), 2003,** highlights the Constitutional provisions towards the cause of the children and the role of civil society, communities and families and their obligations in fulfilling children's basic needs. Well-being of special groups such as children of BPL families, street children, girl child, child-care programmes, and educational programmes for prevention from exploitation find special mention in the NCC. It secures for every child its inherent right to be a child and enjoy a healthy and happy childhood, to address the root causes that negate the healthy growth and development of children, and to awaken the conscience of the community in the wider societal context to protect children from all forms of abuse, while strengthening the family, society and the Nation. The Charter provides that the State and community shall undertake all possible measures

to ensure and protect the survival, life and liberty of all children. For empowering adolescent, the Charter states that the State and community shall take all steps to provide the necessary education and skills to adolescent children so as to equip them to become economically productive citizens.

8. **National Plan of Action for Children (NPA), 2005** was adopted by Government of India in the pursuit of well-being of children. NPA has a significant number of key areas of thrust out of which the one's relating to child protection are:
   - Complete abolition of female foeticide, female infanticide and child marriage and ensuring the survival, development and protection of the girl child,
   - Addressing and upholding the rights of children in difficult circumstances,
   - Securing for all children legal and social protection from all kinds of abuse, exploitation and neglect.
9. **The Commissions for the Protection of Child Rights Act, 2005** provides for the Constitution of a National and State Commissions for Protection of Child Rights in every State and Union Territory. The functions and powers of the National and State Commissions will be to:
   - Examine and review the legal safeguards provided by or under any law for the protection of child rights and recommend measures for their effective implementation;
   - Inquire into violations of child rights and recommend initiation of proceedings where necessary;
   - Spread awareness about child rights among various sections of society;
   - Help in establishment of Children's Courts for speedy trial of offences against children or of violation of Child Rights.

The various Schemes / Programmes are implemented by different Central Ministries, following the guidance of the national policies. They are aiming to tackle the issues relating to the overall welfare of children work independently as well as hand in hand. The State/ UT Governments also execute numerous programmes from time to time for improving the lot of children.

Important Schemes for Well-being of Children

(1) Integrated Child Development Service Scheme.

(2) Integrated Child Protection Scheme.

(3) National Awards for Child Welfare.

(4) Rajiv Gandhi Manav Seva Awards for Service to Children.

(5) Balika Samriddhi Yojana.

(6) Nutrition Programme for Adolescent Girls.

(7) Early Childhood Education for 3-6 age group children.

(8) Welfare of working children in need of Care and Protection.

(9) Rajiv Gandhi National Crèche Scheme for Children of Working Mothers.

(10) UJJAWALA : A Comprehensive Scheme for Prevention of Trafficking and Rescue, Rehabilitation and Re-integration of Victims of Trafficking and Commercial Sexual Exploitation.

(11) Sarva Shiksha Abhiyan (SSA).

(12) Rashtriya Madhyamik Shiksha Abhiyan (RMSA).

(13) National Rural Health Mission.

(14) Rajiv Gandhi Scheme for Empowerment of Adolescent Girls – SABLA.

In spite of several focused initiatives addressing the various needs of children in India, there is a lot need to be done to improve their condition in all realms of child survival, child development and child protection. The gender inequality is also wide in these areas, calling for special attention on girl child.

The importance of education in India is indeed rising with passing time. Though India has always been a great source of learning for many years, it still needs to improve not just on the quality of education but also on the number of people being educated. In India, still many are deprived of education mainly due to poverty and less accessibility educational services. The lack of education, adds to the vulnerability of children for forcing them into social evils of child labour and crime.

The Indian education landscape saw significant developments during the Eleventh Plan. There was a surge in school enrollments, and gender and social category gaps in enrollments narrowed considerably. Expansion of school infrastructure and facilities significantly widened access to schooling, and incentives and child entitlements, such as textbooks, mid-day meals and uniforms began reaching a considerably large number of children. The most significant development, however, was that Article 21-A, inserted in the Constitution of India through the Constitution (86th Amendment) Act, 2002 to make elementary education a fundamental right, and its consequential legislation, the Right of Children to Free and Compulsory Education (RTE) Act, 2009, became operative on 1st April 2010. This development has far reaching implications for elementary education in the years to come: it implies that every child has a right to elementary education of satisfactory and equitable quality in a formal school which satisfies certain essential norms and standards.

There has been substantial spatial and numerical expansion of primary and upper primary schools; access and enrollment at the primary stage of education have reached near universal levels; the gender gap in enrollment has narrowed. However, there remains much to achieve in universalising education at the upper primary stage. Despite various initiatives both on legal as well as policy and programme levels the condition of children remains a cause of concern that needs to be addressed urgently. The programme and policy initiatives like Sarva Shikha Abhiyan (SSA) and Right to Education (RTE) have contributed to a new vibrancy, meaning and urgency in the country's efforts to universalise elementary education, and are expected to infuse new life in the schooling system in the years to come. However, the issue of drop-outs continues as a major issue in all levels of education. Urgent and more focused measures are required to address and tackle these enduring issues in the education sector of the country. There is a large number of child rights which cannot be met unless the right to education is addressed as the key to unlock other child rights.

The Right to Education Act, 2009: The Genesis

The right to education is not only a human right in itself but also quintessential for the exercise of all other human rights. It is an important tool in improving the quality of life. Education operates as multiplier, enhancing the enjoyment of all individual rights, freedom where the right to education is effectively guaranteed. The right to education is a fundamental human right. Every individual, irrespective of race, gender, nationality, ethnic or social origin, and religion or political, age or disability, is entitled to a free elementary education. This right is explicitly stated in the United Nations' Universal Declaration of Human Rights (UDHR), adopted in 1948: "Everyone has the right to education. Education shall be free, at least in the elementary and fundamental stages. Elementary education shall be compulsory. Technical and professional education shall be made generally available and higher education shall be equally accessible to all on the basis of merit...." (Article 26).

With the Right to Education Act, 2009 coming into force, India has joined the league of over 130 countries which have legal guarantees to provide free and compulsory education to children. According to the UNESCO's Education for All Global Monitoring Report 2010, about 135 countries have constitutional provisions for free and non-discriminatory education for all. The framers of the Constitution of India in their wisdom chose to include education in the Directive Principles of State Policy and not in the section on fundamental rights and correspondingly Article 45 stated that "The State shall endeavour to provide, within a period of ten years from the commencement of the Constitution, for free and compulsory education for all children until they complete the age of fourteen years". However, education remained a neglected area of state policy with universalisation of elementary education continuing to be a distant goal. Efforts from educationists, academics and civil society groups that focused on a right-based approach finally yielded results in 2002, when the 86th Constitutional Amendment was passed by Parliament and Article 21A, which makes right to education a fundamental right, was included in the Constitution. In so doing it put the Right to Education on par with the Right to Life stated in Article 21. Article 21A states: "the state shall provide free and compulsory education to all children of the age of 6 to 14 years as the state may, by law determine". Following from this a Right to Free and Compulsory Education Act (RTE) was drafted and passed in Parliament on August 27, 2009 (notified on February 16, 2010) to come into effect from April 1, 2010.

Provisions of Child Rights under the RTE Act

The Right to Education Act, 2009 seeks to provide free and compulsory education of equitable quality to all children in the age group of six to fourteen years. The salient provisions relating to Indian children embedded in the Act are overviewed as follows:

- **Section 3** provides for every child of the age of six to fourteen years, the right to free and compulsory education in a neighbourhood school till completion of elementary education.
- **Section 4** provides for every child above six years of age, the right to admission in a class appropriate to his or her age even if the child has not been admitted before in any school or though admitted, could not complete his elementary education.
- **Section 5** provides for every child, the right to seek transfer to any other school from a school where there is no provision for completion of elementary education.
- **Section 12** imposes on schools the responsibility of providing free and compulsory education. Under this section, unaided private schools shall admit 25 per cent children to Class–I from among children belonging to weaker sections and disadvantaged groups for continued education of such children till completion of elementary education.
- **Section 14** is meant for prohibition of denial of admission of a child for lack of age proof.
- **Section 15** is meant for prohibition of denial of admission to a child, irrespective of the time in the academic year.
- **Section 17** provides for prohibition of physical punishment and mental harassment of any child in school.
- **Section 30** prohibits detention or failing of any pupil in any class till completion of elementary education.
- **Section 32** provides for remedy for grievances relating to the rights of the child under the legislation.

Child Rights Provisions under the Context of RTE Act, 2009 – A Critical Appraisal

- Every child of the age of 6-14 years shall have Right to Free and Compulsory Education in a neighbourhood school till completion of elementary education. **[Section 3 (1)]**
- No child shall be liable to pay any kind of **fee** or **charges** or **expenses** which may prevent him or her from pursuing and completing the elementary education. **[Section 3 (2)]**
- An out of school child above six years of age, not enrolled or dropout, shall be admitted in a class appropriate to his or her age. **(Section 4)**
- A child admitted in a class appropriate to his or her age shall have arrived to receive Special Training and shall be entitled to free education till completion of elementary education even after 14 years. **(Provisos of Section 4)**
- A child shall have a right to sick transfer to any other school except private un-aided and special category school if there is no provision for completion of elementary education in his/ her school. **[Section 5(1)].**
- Where a child is required to move from one school to another, either within a state or outside**, for any reason whatsoever,** the child shall have right to seek transfer to any other school, except private aided and special category school, for completing elementary education. **[Section 5 (2)].**
- The head teacher or in-charge of the school shall immediately issue the transfer certificate to a child seeking transfer to any other school and the delay in producing transfer certificate shall not be a ground for either delaying or denying admission in such other school. **[Section 5 (3)].**
- No child shall be denied admission in a school for lack of age proof. **[Section 14 (2)]**
- No child or his/her parents shall be subjected to any screening procedure and shall be made to pay any capitation fee. **(Section 13)**
- A child shall be admitted in a school at the commencement of the academic year or within such extended period as may be

prescribed: provided further no child shall be denied admission if such admission is sought subsequent to the extended period. **(Section 15)**

- No child admitted in a school shall be held back in any class or expelled from school till the completion of elementary education. **(Section 16)**
- No child shall be subjected to physical punishment or mental harassment. **(Section 17)**
- No child shall be required to pass any board examination till completion of elementary education. **(Section 30)**
- The Academic Authority while laying down the curriculum and evolution procedure shall take into consideration *inter-alia* that the child is free from fear, trauma and anxiety and is helped to express views freely. **[Section 29 (2) (g)]**

Basic Premises of the Rights Based Approach

- The 'compulsion' is on the State to ensure completion of elementary education by each and every child of 6-14 years.
- A child cannot be held responsible for failing to access school or complete elementary education.
- There should be a school in the neighbourhood for each and every child.
- The appropriate government/local authority will have to create an enabling environment and adequate facilities to facilitate completion of elementary education by each and every child.
- There should be institutional mechanisms in place to eliminate financial and procedural barriers.
- Teachers, parents, children and the community at large shall be aware of the rights of the children.
- Teachers, parents and community should not only be aware of the children rights, but should be able to accept them as logical, human and essential.
- Each and every child is capable of learning and completing elementary education.

- The school curriculum shall be such as it enables the children to learn without fear and anxiety.
- There shall be effective mechanisms in place for the monitoring the enforcement of child rights and redressal of their grievances.

What does RTE Act provide for enforcement of the rights based approach?

Establishment of a school within such area or limits of neighbourhood as may be prescribed by the appropriate government or local authority within a period of three years from the commencement of this act. **(Section 6)**

1. The Central Government shall –
2. Develop a framework of national curriculum.
3. Develop and enforce standards for training of teachers.
4. Provide technical support and resources to the state government **[Section 7 (6)]**

The appropriate government and local authority shall be obliged to -

1. To provide free elementary education.
2. Ensure and monitor compulsory admission, attendance and completion.
3. Ensure that the child belonging to weaker section and disadvantaged group are discriminated against.
4. Provide infrastructure including school building, teaching staff and learning equipment.
5. Provide special training facility.
6. Ensure compliance with the standards and norms specified in the schedule.
7. Ensure timely prescribing of curriculum of courses.
8. Provide training facilities for teachers. **(Section 8)**

Every local authority shall also -

1. Maintain records of the children.

2. Ensure admission of children of migrant families.
3. Monitor functioning of schools within its jurisdictions.
4. Decide the academic calendar. **(Section 9)**
5. Every school shall provide such information as may be required by the appropriate government or the local authority. **[Section 12 (3)].**
6. A school or person receiving capitation fee shall be punishable with fine extending to 10 times the capitation fee charge. **[Section 13 (2) (a)]**

A school or person subjecting a child to screening procedure shall be punishable with fine extending to Rs 25,000 for the first contravention and Rs 50,000 for each subsequent contravention. **[Section 13 (2) (b)]**

Whoever subjects a child to physical punishment or mental harassment shall be liable to disciplinary action under the service rules. **(Section 17)**

No school can be established or function after the commencement of this act without obtaining a certificate of recognition to be granted only if the school fulfils norms and standards specified in the schedule and shall be liable to a fine of Rs 10,000 for each day during which violation of this provision continues. **(Section 18)**

A school established before the commencement of this Act shall fulfil all the norms and standards specified in the schedule at its own expenses within a period of three years from the date of commencement of this Act. **(Section 19)**

There shall be a School Management Committee for every school except the private un-aided school **(section 21)** and the SMC shall prepare a school development plan which shall be the basis for the plans to be made by the appropriate government or local authority. **(Section 22)**

Persons only with minimum qualifications laid down by the academic authority authorised by the central government shall be eligible for appointment as teacher. **(Section 23)**

PTR as laid down in the Act to be ensured in every school and the teacher posted in a school not to be made to serve in any other school or office or deployed for any non-educational purpose. **(Section 25)**

Vacancy of teacher in a school shall not exceed 10 per cent of the total sanctioned strength. **(Section 26)**

No teacher shall be deployed for any non-educational purposes other than the decennia population census, disaster-related duties or duties related to elections to the local authority, state legislature or parliament. **(Section 27)**

No teacher shall engage himself / herself in private tuition or private teaching activity. **(Section 28)**

A teacher shall perform the following duties –

- Maintain regularity and punctuality in attending school.
- Conduct and complete the curriculum in accordance with the provisions of **[Section 29 (2)].**
- Complete entire curriculum within the specified time.
- Assess the learning ability of each child.
- Hold regular meetings with parents and guardian and share with them the relevant information about the child.
- A teacher committing default in performance of these duties shall be liable to disciplinary action. **(Section 24)**

The academic authority while laying down the curriculum and evaluation procedure shall take into consideration the following:

- Conformity with the values enshrined in the constitution;
- All round development of the child,
- Building up child's knowledge, potentiality and talent;
- Development of physical and mental abilities to the fullest extent;
- Learning through activities, discovery and exploration in a child-friendly and child-centred manner;
- Medium of instructions shall, as far as practicable, be in child's mother tongue;

- Making the child free of fear, trauma and anxiety and helping the child to express views freely;
- Comprehensive and continuous evaluation of child's understanding of knowledge and his or her ability to apply the same. **(Section 29)**

The NCPCR and SCPCR / REPA shall perform following functions-

- Examine and review the safeguards for rights provided under this Act.
- Enquire into complaints relating to child's rights.
- Take necessary steps for protection of child rights. **(Section 31).**

Any person having any grievance relating to the right of a child make a written complaint to the local authority concerned which shall decide the matter within a period of three months and the person aggrieved by the decision of the local authority may prefer and appeal to the SCPCR / REPA. **(Section 32)**

Right to Education as a Right in the Global Context

The different national approaches to the right to education are reflected in varied constitutional provisions. As Table 15.1 illustrates, there are 43 countries where there is no explicit constitutional guarantee of the right to education, while such a guarantee does exist in 144 countries; that the vast majority of states constitutionally guarantee the right to education reflects the thrust of international human rights law. In 37 countries, however, the right to education is formally restricted to legal citizens.

Table 15.1: Countries which Guarantee Right to Education in their Constitution

Full Constitutional Guarantee	Albania, Algeria, Argentina, Australia, Austria, Azerbaijan, Barbados, Belgium, Belize, Bolivia and Herzegovina, Brazil, Bulgaria, Canada, Cape Verde, Chile, China, Columbia, Congo, Costa Rica, Croatia, Cuba, Denmark, Ecuador, Egypt, Estonia, Finland, France, Gambia, Georgia, Germany, Ghana, Haiti, Honduras, Iceland, **India**, Ireland, Italy, Japan, Latvia, Liechtenstein, Lithuania, Madagascar, Malta, Mauritius, Mexico, Netherlands, Norway, Palau, Panama, Paraguay, Peru, Poland,

	Portugal, Korea, Moldova, Romania, Russia, Rwanda, Saudi Arabia, South Africa, Spain, Sri Lanka, Suriname, Sweden, Switzerland, Tajikistan, Thailand, Trinidad and Tobago, Tunisia, Ukraine, UAE, UK, Uruguay, Venezuela, Former Yugoslavia.
Partial Constitutional Guarantee	Bangladesh, Belarus, Benin, Bhutan, Cameroon, Comoros, Guinea, Iran, Iraq, Israel, Micronesia, Maldives, Monaco, Mongolia, Myanmar, Namibia, Nepal, Nigeria, Pakistan, Sierra Leone, Sudan, Togo, Uganda, Tanzania, Uzbekistan, Zimbabwe.
Constitutional Guarantee only for citizens / residents	Armenia, Bahrain, Cambodia, Chad, Cyprus, Czech Republic, Korea, Dominican Republic, El Salvador, Equatorial Guinea, Greece, Grenada, Guatemala, Guyana, Hungary, Jordan, Kazakhstan, Kuwait, Kyrgyzstan, Libyan Arab Jamahiriya, Luxembourg, Malawi, Mali, Morocco, New Zealand, Nicaragua, Philippines, Qatar, Sao Tome and Principe, Seychelles, Slovakia, Slovenia, Syrian Arab Republic, Turkey, Turkmenistan, Vietnam, Yemen.
No Constitutional Guarantee	Angola, Antigua and Barbuda, Bahamas, Botswana, Brunei Darussalam, Burkina Faso, Burundi, Central African Republic, Côte d'lvoire, Djibouti, Dominica, Eritrea, Ethiopia, Fiji, Gabon, Indonesia, Jamaica, Kenya, Kirbati, Lao People's Democratic Republic, Lebanon, Lesotho, Liberia, Malaysia, Marshall Islands, Mauritania, Mozambique, Nauru, Niger, Oman, Papua New Guinea, Saint Lucia, Saint Vincent and the Grenadines, Samoa, San Marion, Senegal, Singapore, Solomon Islands, Swaziland, Tonga, Tuvalu, United States of America, Vanuatu, Zambia.

Source: Annual Report of Special Rapporteur on the Right to Education, Commission on Human Rights, 2001, 57th Session, E/CN 4/2001/42.

Table 15.1 has been modified by the author to include India in the list of countries that have full constitutional guarantees of the free and compulsory education after the Constitutional Amendment of 2002. The landmark passing of the Right of Children to Free and Compulsory Education (RTE) Act 2009 makes a historic movement for the children of India. For the first time in India's history, children are guaranteed their right to quality elementary education by the state. The RTE does not only remove the capitation fees, screening procedure for admission to schools but lays down norms and standards of working hours per week for the teachers. It also sets out duties and functions for appropriate authorities at different levels to monitor the progress of free and compulsory education in neighbourhood schools. For implementation of the Right to Education and for education to be a meaningful child right, government have to make education available, accessible, acceptable and adaptable. In the light of the above discussion, it can be inferred that the right to free and compulsory education for all children in present scenario seems to be a distant reality. Because, the prevailing harsh socio-cultural and economic ground realities pose daunting challenges for executing RTE. The factors of sex opportunity, cost of education and parents' attitude towards education considerably influence the decisions of children's enrollment. The spectrum of implementation issues covering finances, accountability, monitoring and schools managements need to be addressed forthwith. It is very necessary to involve the Panchayati Raj Institutions (RPIs) in rural areas for implementing the RTE Act. To achieve the objectives of the Right to Education, the RTE must be aligned with the Sarva Shiksha Abhiyan (SSA). The existing operational norms of the SSA must be revised to implement the right of children to free and compulsory education. Given the diversity and complexity of the situations of children, teachers need to have at their disposal a deep fund of empathy, commitment, conviction and ability and motivation to persevere; of knowledge and resources to respond and create meaningful educational experiences for all children. The RTE Act is the only single tool to usher all other child rights in India.

References

- Ghosh, Jayati (2011). Public Spending on Education in India, *Frontline* 28(24), 2–5 July 2011, pp. 10 -12.
- Gosai, M. R. (2009). The Recent Right to Education and the Present State of Primary Education, *University News*, 47 (47), Nov. 23 – 29, 2009, pp. 1-6, New Delhi.
- Jakhar, J. S. (2010). 'Right to Education Act, 2009: Salient Features of Major Problems of Implementation', *University News*, 48(47) : 06-12, New Delhi.
- Jha, P. and Parvati, P. (2010). Right to Education Act 2009 : Critical Gaps and Challenges, *Economic and Political Weekly*, Vol. XLV, No. 13, pp. 20-22.
- Juneja, Nalini (1997). Right of the child to Education and Issues in Implementation of Compulsory Education: Perceptions of Educational Administrators, *New Frontiers in Education* 27(1), pp. 1-12.
- MHRD (2009). The Right of the Children to Free and Compulsory Education, 2009, Department of Elementary Education and Literacy, MHRD, Government of India, New Delhi.
- Ministry of Statistics and Programme Implementation (2012). Children in India, 2012 – A Statistical Appraisal, New Delhi, MOSPI, GOI.
- Mondal, A. and Mete, J. (2011). *Common School System in the light of Right to Education Act, 2009*, Edusearch, Vol. 2, No. 2, pp. 45-55.

- Mondal, A. and Mete, J. (2011). Education for Minorities and SC / ST in the Context of SSA, *Educational Herald*, Vol. 14, No. 14, pp. 14-22.
- Mondal, A. and Mete, J. (2012). Continuous Comprehensive Evaluation and West Bengal Board of Secondary Education: An Overview, *Journal of Education and Culture*, Vol. 4, pp. 45-55.
- Mondal, A. and Mete, J. (2012). Right to Education – An Appraisal, *Kurukshetra*, Vol. 60, No. 11, Sept. 2012, pp. 11-14.
- NCERT (2005). National Curriculum Framework 2005, NCERT, New Delhi.
- Sadgopal, A. (2010). Right to Education vs. Right to Education Act, *Social Scientist*, Volume 38, No. 9/12 (Sept. – Dec., 2010), pp. 17-50.
- Sadgopal, A. (2011). 'Neoliberal Act', *Frontline*, India's National Magazine, 28(14) : 04-09, Chennai.
- Saiyidian, K. G., Naik, J. P. and Husai, S. A. (1966). *Compulsory Education in India,* Universal, Delhi.
- Sharma, R. and Saini, R. (2012). Implementation of RTE Act, 2009 in Rural India, *International Referred Research Journal,* Vol. III, Issue 29, pp. 60-62.
- Singh, J. (2012). Right to Education: An Assessment, *Indian Streams Research Journal*, Vol. 1, Issue XIII. Feb, 2012.
- Singh, R. (2012). Development of Right to Education in India: A Historical Appraisal, *University News*, 50 (30), July 23 – 29, 2012, pp. 16-25, New Delhi.
- Tomasevski, K. (1999). Children's rights, adult's duties. International Consultative Forum on Education for All. *Education – a right or a privilege? Student journalists report on the right to education worldwide*. 1999, p. 3.
- Tomasevski, K. (2001). *Right to Education Primers No. 3*, Swedish International Development Corporation Agency, Stockholm, Sweden.
- Tomasevski, K. (2003). *Education denied: costs and remedies.* London: Zed Books, 2003.
- Tomasevski, K. (2004). Manual on right-based education: global human rights requirements made simple, UNESCO, Bangkok.

Chapter - 16

Equity Issues in the Light of the RTE Act, 2009

Education is a basic human right and has been recognised since the adaptation of the Universal Declaration of Human Rights (1948, UNO). Since then numerous international treaties have reaffirmed this right and supported entitlement to free, compulsory and universal elementary education for all children. The right to education was finally made a fundamental right of Indian children in the 6–14 age groups to get free and compulsory education. It was enshrined in the Indian Constitution as a Directive Principle of State Policy in the Article 45 before the 86th Amendment, 2002. It was the visualisation of the Founding Fathers of the Indian Constitution that took almost 59 years to translate into reality. The Constitution (86th) Amendment Act introduced new Article 21A – "the State shall provide free and compulsory education to all children of the age of 6 – 14 years, in such a manner as the state may, by law determine". The Right of Children to Free and Compulsory Education Act, 2009, commonly known as RTE Act came in force with effect from 1st April, 2010.The enforcement of the Right to Education Act brings the country closer to achieving the objectives and mission of the EFA (Education for All) and MDGs (Millennium Development Goals), especially MDG_2 on (Universal Primary Education) and MDG_3 on (Gender Equality) by 2015 and hence is a historic step taken by the Government of India. Now in India, the Right to Education Act, 2009 has been implemented for all the children covering the age of 6-14 years. Therefore, education is now recognised as a birth right under the fundamental right of the Constitution.

But the problem of exclusion of children, especially from the "disadvantaged group" or from the "weaker section" still remains; and efforts are taken to find a way out to make elementary education, mandatory for all. However, the RTE Act, 2009 integrates gender and other social disadvantages under its ambit for equity and quality. This chapter intends to explore the provisions for equity issues related to the gender, the disadvantaged and weaker sections of India in the RTE Act, 2009.

Education is a human right and essential for realisation of all other human rights. It is a basic right which helps the individual to live with human dignity. It is for this reason, perhaps that framers of the constitution realised the importance of education and has thus imposed a duty on the state under Article 45 as one of the Directive Principles of State Policy to provide free and compulsory education to all children until they complete the age of 14 years within 10 years from the commencement of the constitution. The framers expected that the government would make effective and honest implementation of this directive and abolish illiteracy from the country but their expectation remained in vain. Later, the National Education Policy of 1968 talked of a free and compulsory education but the Right to Education Act came into effect only in April 2010. The government took more than six decades after independence to provide free and compulsory education as fundamental right for all children in the age group of 6-14 years. It is now a matter of satisfaction that the RTE Act is the first Central legislation in the landscape of Indian elementary education that puts the responsibility of ensuring enrollment, attendance and completion of elementary education by all children on the government. The title of the RTE Act incorporates the words 'free' and 'compulsory'. '**Free education**' means that no child, other than a child who has been admitted by his or her parents to a school which is not supported by the appropriate government, shall be liable to pay any kind of fee or charges or expenses which may prevent him or her from pursuing and completing elementary education. '**Compulsory education**' casts an obligation on the appropriate government and local authorities to provide and ensure admission, attendance and completion of elementary education by all children in the 6 – 14 age groups. With the Right to Education Act, 2009 coming into force, India has joined the league of over 130 countries which have legal guarantees to provide free and compulsory education to children. According to the UNESCO's Education for All Global Monitoring Report 2010, about 135 countries have constitutional provisions for free and non-discriminatory education for all.

Equity in School Education – A Concept

The concept of equity in school education is poorly defined. Equity means different things to different people. The OECD (2012) recognises two dimensions: **fairness and inclusion** to equity in education and sees them as intertwined. Equity as fairness implies that personal or socio-economic circumstances, such as gender, ethnic origin or family background are not obstacles to educational success. Equity as inclusion means ensuring that all students reach at least a basic minimum level of skills. Equitable education systems are fair and inclusive and support their students to reach their learning potential. Equity means equal opportunity for all children to complete elementary education irrespective of their gender, religion, caste, socio-economic, cultural or linguistic background and geographical location. Equity also means creation of conditions in which the disadvantaged sections and weaker sections girls, children of SC, ST, Muslim community, and children with disabilities etc. can avail of the opportunity (MHRD, 2011). Bronfen-brenner (1973) distinguishes between these two concepts by taking 'equity' to mean social justice or fairness. It refers to subjective and ethical judgment. 'Equality' refers to the pattern of distribution of something such as income or education. It is more objective and descriptive term and can be measured. But equity or fairness of a situation can be evaluated only by appealing to value judgment. Equity in education can be achieved by pursuing the policy protective discrimination in favour of the disadvantaged section of the society. The RTE Act integrates gender and other social disadvantages both explicitly and implicitly in its different sections for quality and equity. Equity has been seen as an integral part of the agenda on improving quality in the context of the RTE Act.

Equity Issues in the RTE Act, 2009

Education is the most potent tool for socio-economic and social mobility and a key instrument for building an equitable and just society.

That's why the RTE Act attempts to ensure that all children get the optimum opportunity to enrol in schools, acquire and complete elementary education, irrespective of their gender, caste, socio-economic, cultural or linguistic background and geographical location. The Act contains specific provisions for disadvantaged groups, such as child labours, migrant children, children with special needs (CWSN), or those who have a disadvantage owing to social, cultural, economical, geographical, linguistic, gender or any such factor. The RTE Act, 2009 under different sections makes reference to equity issues both explicitly and implicitly. They are -

Section 3(1) of the RTE Act 2009 Chapter II states: Every child of the age six to fourteen years shall have a right to free and compulsory education in a neighbourhood school till completion of elementary education. **Section 3(2)** states: For the purpose of sub-section (1), no child shall be liable to pay any kind of fee or charges or expenses which may prevent him or her from pursuing and completing the elementary education. It is worth mentioning here that in the first chapter of the Act **'child'** has been defined as "a male or female child of the age of six to fourteen years". The Act further points out that "child belonging to disadvantaged group" will include groups having disadvantage owing to social, cultural, economical, geographical, linguistic, **gender** or such other factors as specified by the government. A majority of out-of-school children belong to disadvantaged groups. Disadvantaged Groups are defined as those "belonging to the SC, ST, socially and educationally backward class or such other groups having disadvantage owing to social, cultural, economical, geographical, linguistic, gender, or such other factors as may be specified by the appropriate Government". Weaker Sections are defined as those "belonging to such parent or guardian whose annual income is lower than the minimum specified by the appropriate Government by notification". The Kolkata Gazette published on February 21, 2011 clarifies that "a child shall be deemed to belong to a weaker section, if either parent of the child duly recorded as a person belonging to Below Poverty Line (BPL) family as per list prepared by the appropriate local authority owing to his or her lower income".

Section 3(2) of the RTE Act qualifies that only a child suffering from disability as defined under clause (i) of section (2) of the Persons with Disabilities Act, 1995 shall have a right to pursue free and compulsory elementary education in accordance with provisions of Chapter V of the said Act. PWD Act excludes children suffering from certain disabilities such as cerebral palsy, autism etc. But later on The Right of Children to Free and Compulsory Education (Amendment) Bill, 2010 was introduced in the Rajya Sabha on 16th April, 2010 where the following amendments to the RTE Act were made relating to the CWSN:

(i) Inclusion of children with disabilities in the definition of 'child belonging to disadvantaged group' in clause (d) of section 2 of the RTE Act.

(ii) To provide that children with disabilities, including children with cerebral palsy, mental retardation, autism and multiple disabilities shall have the right to pursue free and compulsory education in accordance with Chapter V of the Persons with Disabilities (Equal Opportunities, Protection of Rights and Full Participation) Act, 1995."

Section 8(c) of RTE Act states while clarifying the duties of appropriate government: The appropriate government shall *"ensure that child belonging to weaker section and the child belonging to disadvantaged group are not discriminated against and prevented from pursuing and completing elementary education on any ground"*. In fact, articles like these are clear indication of the objective to do away with any kind of disparity on the ground of gender. The main objectives of the gender concern of RTE Act 2009 are not only to enable to keep pace with boys in education but to bring a basic change in the status of women in society.

However, RTE Act 2009 integrates gender and other social disadvantages in its concern for quality and equity. It is seen as a part of the quality agenda. Gender does not operate in isolation but in conjunction with other social categories. This results in girls' facing multiple forms of disadvantages. In order to address gender and equity issues in regard to RTE a strong conceptual understanding of the issue is really necessary. Gender should not be taken as a stand-alone category segregated from other issues of discrimination. The dimensions of location (rural, urban), caste, class, religion, ethnicity, disabilities etc.

intersect with gender to create a complex reality. Curriculum, textbooks, pedagogic practices need to capture the entire web of social and economic relations that determine an individual's location in the social reality and shape her life experiences. Developing such an understanding is necessary to reach all the children who are still out of school. Civil society interventions would be crucial here. Despite significant improvement in the enrollment of girls, girls from disadvantaged communities continue to form the bulk of out-of-school children. Therefore, access continues to be an equity issue in the case of girls which RTE tries to address.

Teachers are to play a very important role in implementing the mission of RTE Act, especially so in case of gender equity. If teacher is not sensitised to actively dispel traditional perceptions regarding gender or caste roles, she is unlikely to take measures to help girl students to pursue education which is equitable and free from anxiety. The teachers' own pattern of communication with children, seating arrangement in the classroom, allotment of works among the children may serve to reinforce or dispel societal perception about the appropriate role and place of girls. The RTE Act (2009) emphasises the importance of teachers' training which would enable teachers to promote inclusive classroom practices. The emphasis on professional training as a requisite qualification for recruitment of teachers in RTE Act 2009 **(Section 23 sub-Sections 1 and 2)** tries to ensure empathy of teachers towards every child. It clearly states (24[d]) that it is the duty of a teacher to *assess the learning ability of each child and accordingly supplement additional instructions, if any, as required* and [e] *hold regular meetings with parents and guardians and apprise them about the regularity in attendance, ability to learn, progress made in learning and any other relevant information about the child.*

Girls from SC, ST and minor communities and from families below poverty line usually face greater challenge in continuing education after the primary level. Localised context has to be analysed and a policy need be developed on the basis of such analysis to provide support to girl children to bring back girls who dropout of school without completing primary education. Community support and monitoring play an important role here. The RTE Act 2009 has provided scope for community to intervene in smooth running of the school. The act requires each school to constitute a School Management Committee consisting of the elected representatives of the local authority, parents or guardians of children admitted in such school and teachers. The act makes it mandatory that fifty per cent of members of such Management Committee shall be women **(Section 21[1]).** The School Management Committee shall monitor the work of the school, prepare development plan and thereby monitor use of allocation of grant and its use. The fifty per cent women member is expected to safeguard the interest of their girl children and protest against any kind of discrimination on the basis of gender **(Section 21[2]).**

RTE Act 2009 tries to involve all local stakeholders by making local authority responsible to ensure that the child belonging to any disadvantaged group may not be discriminated against and prevented from pursuing and completing elementary education. **Section 9** states that every local authority shall '*maintain records of children up to the age of fourteen years residing within its jurisdiction, in such manner as may be prescribed* **(sub-section-d)**; *ensure and monitor admission, attendance and completion of elementary education by every child residing within its jurisdiction* **(sub-section-e);** *provide infrastructure including school building, teaching staff and learning material* **(sub-section-f)**; *provide special training facility specified in Section 4* (sub-section-g); *provide training facility for teachers* **(sub-section-j);** *monitor functioning of the schools within its jurisdiction* **(sub-section-l)** and so on. **Section 10** makes it mandatory for the guardians to ensure admitting their children to school – *It shall be the duty of every parent or guardian to admit or cause to be admitted his or her child or ward, as the case may be, to an elementary education in the neighbouring school.* Other provisions of RTE Act 2009 to ensure girl child's right to education are provision of good quality education that includes equity issues, curriculum development in conformity with constitutional stipulations, training, and enrollment in age appropriated classes which will largely apply to girls, especially from disadvantaged communities.

However, mere sensitisation of teachers and involvement of local authority and community to safeguard the rights of girl child may not be enough and classroom practices would need to be monitored and grievance redressal mechanisms have to be established at the school and other levels. RTE Act (2009) provides for grievances too. **Section 31** under Chapter VI: ***(1)*** *The National Commission for Protection of Child Rights constituted under Section 3, or as the case may be, the State Commission for Protection of Child Rights constituted under section 17, of the Commission for Protection of Child Rights Act 2005, shall in addition to the functions assigned to them under that Act, also perform the following functions, namely : (a) examine and review the safeguards for rights provided by or under this Act and recommend measures for their effective implementation; (b) enquire into complaints relating to child's right to free and compulsory education ; (c) and take necessary steps as provided under sections 15 and 24 of the said Commissions for Protection of Child Right Act.* In addition to this **Section 32(1)** clearly states that *notwithstanding anything contained in section 31, any person having any grievance relating to the right of a child under this Act may make a written complaint to the local authority having jurisdiction* and **Section 32(2)** mandates that *after receiving the complaint the local authority shall decide the matter within a time period of three months.*

Besides the above mentioned anti-discrimination measures, the RTE Act, 2009 also made different remarkable provision for equity in education. Some of these are as follows:

Neighbourhood Schools: If schools are not located in or near the habitations where children reside, they may not complete schooling, even if they are formally enrolled in schools, on account of distance factor. The RTE Act mandates the appropriate governments and local authorities to provide for children's access to elementary schools within the defined area or limits of neighbourhood. A neighbourhood school is a school located within the defined limits (one kilometer for class I-V and three kilometers for class VI-VIII) or area of neighbourhood, which has been notified by the State Government under the State RTE Rules.

Special Training for out-of-school children: The RTE Act makes specific provision for Special Training for age-appropriate admission for out-of-school children. It also provides that such children shall continue to be provided free and compulsory elementary education even after they cross 14 years of age.

School Uniforms: SSA will provide two sets of uniform to all girls, SC, ST children and Below Poverty Line (BPL) children, wherever (i) State Governments have incorporated provision of school uniforms as a child entitlement in their State RTE Rules, and (ii) State Governments are not already providing uniforms from the State budgets.

Removal of financial barriers: The RTE Act provides that no child in a neighbourhood school, as notified by the State Government, shall be liable to pay any kind of fee, charge or expense that may prevent her/him from enrolling, participating and completing elementary education.

Removal of procedural barriers: The RTE Act also provides for removal of procedural barriers to school access. It provides that no child shall be denied admission in a school for want of a Birth or Transfer Certificate. Delay in issue of Transfer Certificate shall not be a ground for denial of admission to a child in the new school. Executive instructions may be issued to all Headmasters to issue Transfer Certificates on priority, whenever a child requires it.

Any-time admission in school: Ideally, all children should be enrolled in school at the beginning of the academic session. However, in the case of children in difficult circumstances, including children affected by migration, displacement or ill-health, etc schools may need to be flexible to allow admission at any time during the session.

The Sarva Siksha Abhiyan (SSA) has been implemented as a Centrally Sponsored Scheme in partnership with State Governments for universalising elementary education across the country. Its overall goals include universal access and retention, bridging of gender and social category gaps in education and enhancement of learning level. SSA provides for a variety of interventions, including opening of new schools and alternate schooling facilities, construction of schools and additional classrooms, toilets and drinking water, provisioning for teachers periodic teacher training and academic resource support, textbooks and support for learning achievement. These provision need to be aligned with the legally mandated norms and standards and free entitlement mandated by the RTE Act to enable our girl child, child with special needs, child from disadvantaged group and weaker section to enjoy the right to education and become empowered.

Limitations of the RTE Act, 2009 relating to Equity

In spite of having remarkable and pioneering contribution of RTE Act, 2009 to promote equity in education through its several provisions, some anomalies can be identified that may hinder the ultimate goal of equity, so far quality and quantity both are concerned in output. These are as follows:

Losing of right for Neighbourhood concept: Section 3(1) with Model Rule 6 and Section 10: By limiting neighbourhood to one or three kilometers geographical area affects the child belonging to the minority and tribal communities. The schools are few in States like Bihar, Jharkhand, Chhattisgarh, Odisha, West Bengal, Andhra Pradesh, Tamil Nadu etc. where substantial number of children are tribal or Scheduled Caste. The community has set up not only schools but also hostels for them at subsidised rates. The children from remote areas stay in these hostels and attend the schools. If the neighbourhood concept is accepted these children will have to lose their right to study in a school of his choice.

Establishment Neighbourhood school without norms: The Act specifies that it is the responsibility of the State Authority and Local Government to establish a school in a habitation (as per geographical norms) where there is none, within a period of three years. However, the Act does not specifically say whether the geographical norms or population norms or both need to be taken into consideration in this process. For instance, geographical limits that do not take into account the physical terrain, topography and availability of public transport system become meaningless. In densely populated urban areas, establishment of one school within a radius of one kilometer. (as the norm for establishing primary school) may be inadequate if the infrastructure cannot cater to the child population within the geographical limits. (Mehendele A. 2010: 10-11).

Improper definition of Neighbourhood school: With regard to the idea of inclusion of disadvantaged sections of children under the norm of 25 per cent reservation in the private unaided schools, there should be a separate definition of "neighbourhood", for two reasons. First, elite private schools are generally located in elite neighbourhoods where there may be few children from the disadvantaged sections filling the quota of 25 per cent. Second, smaller private un-aided schools in underprivileged areas may find excessive demand (Mehendele, A. 2010: 11).

Reservation of seats in unaided private schools: Section12: The fees for 25 per cent lesser privileged children will be borne by state government. There will be a wide gap between the cost of education per child and the reimbursement by the government. Who will bear this deficit portion? Obviously the remaining 75 per cent of the students will bear it. It's like providing benefit to one at the cost of other.

Age Verification: **Section 14(2)**: The managements' right to verify the age of a child is taken away by Section 14(2). It provides that no child shall be denied admission for lack of age proof and consequently keeps the door open to everyone without reference to age.

Late Comer: **Section 15(1) (2)**: A late comer is to be admitted even after the extended period and be permitted to complete his studies, – is nothing but interference in the academic calendar of the school thus interfering in administration.

Detaining of students in class: Section 16: This is totally unjust and arbitrary. This destroys the future of the children as the children are asked to move ahead without the necessary capacity to follow the class. Rather to stop drop-outs special study and coaching facilities and counselling incentives be introduced in schools with State funding.

No child can be expelled from school: Section 16: This takes away the right to take disciplinary action. This is almost the same as not to have prisons in the country.

No child is subject to punishment: **Section 17**: Physical punishment is understandable. Mental harassment can be interpreted according to each person's understanding. This will lead to unnecessary litigation.

Despite many gains under the RTE-SSA programme, education faces several challenges. A matter of particular concern is the steep dropout-rate after the elementary level. The increasing enrollment gap from elementary to secondary or higher secondary suggests that the gains at the elementary level have not yet impacted the school sector as a whole. Now is the time to turn from inputs and focus on the challenges related to retention, bridging of gender and social gaps in enrollment levels and enhancement of learning levels of all children. Some of the suggestions for minimising gender disparity and strengthening the RTE-SSA programme for Disadvantaged and Weaker Sections are as follows:

- It is necessary to involve the Panchayati Raj Institutions (PRIs) in rural areas for implementing the RTE Act, parents, teachers, professionals, social workers and NGOs should assist the government in this regard.
- Particularly in rural and poor areas, People's representatives – MPs, MLAs, PRI members should be made responsible for smooth functioning of the schools in their areas.
- The quality of teachers is the backbone of any teaching programme. Teachers need to have at their disposal a deep fund of empathy, commitment, conviction and ability and motivation to persevere; of knowledge and resources to respond and create meaningful educational experiences for all children.
- Seminars, Workshops, Conference, Orientation programmes should be organised for building awareness of all the stakeholders of education about the RTE Act, 2009.
- Although the RTE Act puts the applicable age-group at 6-14, the states should decide whether they want to widen this group, say from 0-18 as Kerala has done. States should think about including more children under the Act's ambit.
- The states must take steps to employ more teachers and not only to rely on Para-teachers to provide children with quality education.
- The government should ensure that all government schools are well-equipped to take in students, so that they are not left with the sole choice of going to private schools.
- School management committees should take it upon themselves to spread awareness about the Act at the community level, in panchayats, so that people are encouraged to send their children to school.

- School management committees should be provided the necessary financial and other support by the state to go about their duties.
- For effective implementation of the RTE Act, states should give some sort of judicial power to the education department.
- To effectively implement the RTE Act, the Human Resource Development Ministry, Labour Ministry, Women and Child Development Ministry, Panchayati Raj Ministry and Rural Development Ministry have to work together. There should be an umbrella body that brings all these agencies together to work towards a common goal.
- The government must make every effort to become self-sufficient by using the education cess and other taxes to effectively implement the RTE Act. It must not always beg from the private sector.
- Creative and sustained initiatives should be taken to train new and untrained teachers to reinforce the skills of in-service teachers to ensure child-friendly education.
- Families and communities also have a large role to play to ensure child-friendly education for each and every one of girls and boys in India who should be in elementary school today.
- Disparities must be eliminated to assure quality with equity. Investing in preschool is a key strategy in meeting goals.
- Bringing out-of-school children into classes at the age appropriate level with the support to stay in school through flexible, innovative approaches.
- A flexible and realistic view should be taken regarding age appropriateness of the children and after special training the actual admission should be in the class in which they would be able to be at par with other children.

The Right of Children to Free and Compulsory Education Act, 2009, (RTE Act) is path breaking in more ways than one. Not only does it make elementary education a fundamental right, but also for the first time in Indian legislative history 'discrimination' has been specifically acknowledged and prohibited in a universal social legislation that applies to all citizens. Inclusion in education has received renewed attention under the RTE Act. The Act attempts to analyse our social inequalities based on caste and other identities and bring children from all sections into our school system. Despite several problems associated with the strategies to implement inclusion policies in schools, there have been some remarkable achievements. Yet, access to basic schooling (even though it is free through the RTE) is not uniform across social groups. As a result of the boom in private-sector education and the attempts to universalise elementary education, there has been an unprecedented increase in school enrollment in India. Still, large numbers of children, especially from disadvantaged communities, are deprived of quality education, which has thwarted the equitable access to basic education (Govinda R., 2011). However, even if the more vulnerable children from lower socio-economic groups are brought into school system, it is unlikely that they will attend school regularly and will complete a cycle of education (Tilak, 2011). Here equitable access must amalgamate with equitable quality to institutionalise and sustain universal access. Such an understanding of access must percolate to the grassroots level for enriching the process of planning, implementation and monitoring, and moving away from the present practice of viewing access as a stand-alone intervention dealing merely with the physical availability of school and infrastructure. It is now incumbent upon us to seize the opportunities - to develop in India a comprehensive understanding of 'discrimination' and evolve mechanisms to end it, towards our stated goals of a truly inclusive modern democracy.

References

- Bordoloi, R. (2012). Accessibility and Equity: A Challenge for Higher Education in India. *Journal of Economics and Sustainable Development, 3*(4), 23-34.
- Govinda, R. (2011). *Who Goes to School? Exploring Exclusion in Indian Education*. New Delhi, India: Oxford University Press.
- Jakhar, J. S. (2010). Right to Education Act, 2009: Salient Features of Major Problems of Implementation. *University News*, 48(47): 06-12.
- Jha, P. and Parvati, P. (2010). Right to Education Act 2009: Critical Gaps and Challenges, *Economic and Political Weekly*, XLV (13), 20-22.

- Juneja, N. (2003). *Constitutional Amendment to make Education a Fundamental Right – Issues for a Follow-Up Legislation*. New Delhi: NIEPA.
- Kurhade, M.S.(2011). Education for All: But When? *University News*, 49(04): 6-8.
- Mehendele A. (2010, January 23). Model Rules for the Right to Education Act. *Economic and Political Weekly*, *45*(4), 16-17.
- MHRD (2011). Sarva Shiksha Abhiyan – Framework for Implementation Based on the Right of Children to Free and Compulsory Education Act, 2009, New Delhi: MHRD, Govt. of India.
- MHRD (2012). *The Right of Children to Free and Compulsory Education Act, 2009,* New Delhi: MHRD, Govt. of India.
- Mondal, A. and Mete, J. (2012). Right to Education – An Appraisal. *Kurukshetra*. 60 (11): 11 – 14.
- Mondal, A. and Mete, J. (2013). *Right to Education*. New Delhi: APH Publishing Corporation.
- NCPCR (2010). *Main Features of the Right of Children to Fee and Compulsory Education Act, 2009*. New Delhi: NCPCR.
- NCPCR (2010). *Right to Free and Compulsory Education – Frequently Asked Questions*. New Delhi: NCPCR.
- OECD (2012). *Equity and Quality in Education: Supporting Disadvantaged Students and Schools, Paris*: OECD.
- Raina, V. (2010). *FAQs on the Right to Free and Compulsory Education Act, 2009*. New Delhi: BGVS.
- Rao, D.B. (Ed.) (2011). *Right to Education*. Hyderabad: Neelkamal Publications Pvt. Ltd.
- Sharma, M. C. (Ed.). (2013). *Right to Education: Imperative for Progress*. New Delhi: Universal Law Publishing Co.
- Sharma, M. C. (Ed.). (2013). *Right to Education: Imperative for Progress*. New Delhi: Universal Law Publishing Co.
- Singh, R. (2012). Development of Right to Education in India: A Historical Appraisal. *University News*, 50 (30):16-25.

Chapter - 17

Responsibilities of Schools and Duties and Professional Ethics for Teachers under the RTE Act

The Right of Children to Free and Compulsory Education (RTE) Act, 2009 has been notified for enforcement from 1st April, 2010. Thereafter, it has become the state's, parent's, schools' and teacher's legal and moral duties and responsibilities to ensure that all children between the ages of 6–14 are entitled to free and compulsory admission, attendance and completion of elementary education (class I to VIII). Chapter-IV of the Act deals with the responsibilities of schools and teachers. Under the ambit of the RTE Act, schools and teachers play a crucial role in effective implementation of the Act. The extract of the Chapter – IV has been placed here for building awareness about the responsibilities of schools and teachers under RTE Act among the stakeholders of education.

Duties and Responsibilities of Schools

For the purposes section 12(1) of this Act stipulates a school –

(a) specified in the sub-section n (i) of section 2 shall provide free and compulsory elementary education to all children admitted therein;

(b) specified in the sub-section n(ii) of section 2 shall provide free and compulsory elementary education to such proportion of children admitted therein as its annual recurring aid or grants so received bears to its annual recurring expenses, subject to minimum of twenty-five per cent;

(c) specified in the sub-section n(iii) and (iv) of section 2 shall admit in class-I, to the extent of at least 25 per cent of the strength of class, children belonging to weaker section and disadvantaged group in the neighourhood and provide free and compulsory elementary education till its completion.

This Act further mandates that where a school specified in the sub-section n of section 2 imparts pre-school education, the provision of above mentioned clauses (a) to (c) shall apply for admission to such pre-school education.

Section 13(1) states that no school shall collect any capitation fee and subject the child or his or her parents or guardian to any screening procedure.

Section 14(2) says that school cannot deny admission to any child on the ground of lack of age proof.

Section 16 mandates that no child admitted in a school be held back in any class or expelled from school till the completion of elementary education.

Section 17(1) states that no child shall be subjected to physical punishment or mental harassment.

Section 18 declares that after the commencement any of the Act school other than a school established owned or controlled by the appropriate government or the local authority shall be established or function only after obtaining a certificate of recognition from the prescribed authority.

Section 19(1) stipulates that no school shall be established or recognised unless it fulfils the norms and standards specified in the schedule.

Sections 21 and 22 mandate that a school, other than a school specified in sub-section n(iv) of section 2, shall have a School Management Committee (SMC) comprising elected representatives of the local authority, parents or guardians of children admitted in such school and teachers who will monitor the progress of the school and drew up a school development plan.

Duties and Responsibilities of Teachers

Section 24(1) states that a teacher shall perform the following duties, namely:

(a) Maintain regularity and punctuality in attending school;

(b) Conduct and complete the curriculum in accordance with the provisions of section 29 of the RTE Act, within specified time;

(c) Assess the learning ability of each child;

(d) Hold regular meetings with parents and guardians and appraise them about the attendance of their children, the child's learning ability, progress and other relevant information.

Section 23 mandates that a person possessing minimum qualifications, as laid down by an academic authority (NCTE) shall have the eligibility for appointment as a teacher. Moreover, a teacher who, at the commencement of this Act, does not possess minimum qualifications as laid down by NCTE shall acquire such minimum qualifications within a period of five years.

Section 27 states that besides performing educational activities, each teacher must execute duties relating population census or disaster relief or elections to the local authority or the State Legislatures or Parliament.

Section 28 declares that no teacher shall engage himself or herself in private tuition or private teaching activity.

Code of Professional Ethics for Teachers in the Context of the RTE Act

The Right to Education (RTE) Act encompasses a gamut of educational issues. Its successful implementation begs attention towards many issues including the clarification of teaching standard, norms and ethics. In pursuance of the recommendations of the National Policy on Education (NPE), 1986, the National Council of Educational Research and Training (NCERT) in collaboration with the All India

Primary Teachers Federation (AIPTF), All India Secondary Teachers Federation (AISTF) and All India Federation of Educational Associations (AIFEA) had developed, for the first time, a Code of Professional Ethics for Teachers, in 1997. Recognising the need and importance of a Code of Professional Ethics for School Teachers, the National Council for Teacher Education (NCTE) appointed a Committee to review this code keeping in view the context of the relevant sections of the Right of Children to Free and Compulsory Education (RTE) Act 2009. In the light of the provisions under Section 24(1) of the RTE Act, 2009 regarding duties and functions of teachers and as per the directions of the Ministry of Human Resource Development, the National Council for Teacher Education (NCTE) has developed a draft document on "**Code of Professional Ethics for Teachers**" with a belief that –

> ...like all other professions, the teaching profession should also have its Code of Professional Ethics which is the prerequisite to ensure its dignity and integrity. It is also significant that the Right of Children to Free and Compulsory Act, 2009 entails on teachers some onerous professional responsibilities to be internalised by them in the performance of their duties. Accordingly, it is considered necessary that the Code of Professional Ethics be evolved and adopted by the teaching community.

For the purpose of this Code, the term "teacher" covers all school teachers, whether in government or private schools, on full time or part time basis, at the elementary and secondary levels and the teachers holding administrative and supervisory positions. The Code of Professional Ethics for teachers provides a framework of principles to guide them in discharging their obligations towards students, parents, colleagues and community. Increased awareness of the ethical principles governing the teaching profession is essential to ensure 'professionalism' among teachers.

1. Obligations towards Students

1.1 Treats all students with love and affection.

1.2 Respects the value of being just and impartial to all students irrespective of their caste, creed, religion, sex, economic status, language and place of birth.

1.3 Facilitates students' physical, social, intellectual, emotional, moral and spiritual development.

1.4 Respects basic human dignity of the child in all aspects of school life.

1.5 Makes planned and systematic efforts to facilitate the child to actualise his/her potential and talent.

1.6 Transacts the curriculum in conformity with the values enshrined in the Constitution.

1.7 Adapts his/her teaching to the individual needs of students.

1.8 Maintains the confidentiality of the information concerning students and dispenses such information only to those who are legitimately entitled to it.

1.9 Refrains from subjecting any child to fear, trauma, anxiety, physical punishment and mental and emotional harassment.

1.10 Refrains from any act involving sexual abuse of the child.

2. Obligations towards Parents, Community and Society

2.1 Establishment cordial relations with parents/guardians.

2.2 Desists from doing anything which is derogatory to the respect of the child or his/her parents/guardians.

2.3 Strives to develop respect for the composite culture of India among students.

2.4 Refrains from taking part in such activities as may spread feeling of hatred or enmity among different communities, religious or linguistic groups.

3. Obligation towards the Profession and Colleagues

3.1 Strives for his /her continuous professional development.

3.2 Creates a culture that encourages purposeful collaboration and dialogue among colleague and stakeholders.

3.3 Treats other members of the profession with respect and dignity.

3.4 Refrains from engaging himself/herself in private tuition or private teaching activity.

3.5 Refrains from accepting any gift, or favour that might impair or appear to influence professional decisions or actions.

3.6 Refrains from making unsubstantiated allegations against colleagues or higher authorities.

3.7 Avoids making derogatory statements about colleagues, especially in the presence of pupils, other teachers, officials or parents.

3.8 Respects the professional standing and opinions of his/her colleagues.

3.9 Maintains confidentiality of information concerning colleagues and dispenses such information only when authorised to do so.

Mechanism to deal with Violations

A possible mechanism to deal with non-observance of the Code is suggested here. A three-tier mechanism could be evolved to deal with the violations or reported, as outlined below :

(i) **School Level / Block Level Ethics Committee:** In the case of bigger secondary or higher secondary schools where the number of teachers is quite sizeable, an Ethics Committee at the school level comprising senior members of the staff including representatives of parents should be appointed. The Committee may deal with the complaints regarding punctuality, regularity, completion of curriculum, engagement in private tuitions, etc. and, in the first instance, should try to persuade the erring teachers to mend their ways. In case the Committee fells to persuade the concerned teachers, it may recommend to the concerned authorities that disciplinary proceedings should be initiated against such teachers. In the case of Primary / Elementary schools, keeping in view the fewer numbers of teachers, the Ethics Committee could be appointed at the Block or cluster level with members drawn from the teaching community and representatives of parents.

(ii) **State Level Ethics Committee:** The State Government in consultation with the organisation responsible for the registration of teachers may appoint an Ethics Committee comprising eminent educationists, representatives of teacher organisations and parents. The Committee should deal with complaints of serious nature such as violation of Constitutional provisions, cases of child abuse, spreading feelings of hatred or enmity among different communities, etc. The Committee may issue 'Advisories' to the erring teachers, if necessary. In case the Committee comes to the conclusion, that the case merits withdrawal of 'Eligibility', or cancellation of registration, it may refer it to the 'Ethics Committee' at the national level.

(iii) National Level Ethics Committee: At the national level, NCTE and All India Federations of school teachers may jointly appoint a National Ethics Committee comprising eminent educationists, representatives of Federations of Elementary and Secondary Teacher organisations. National Commission for the Protection of Child Rights (NCPCR) and parents. The cases forwarded by the State Ethics Committees should be taken up by the National Ethics Committee for appropriate decision. The NCTE may notify regulations relating to the composition, functions, powers and responsibility of Ethics Committees at the three levels mentioned above. The National Ethics Committee should have the powers to suspend / withdraw registration of the teacher concerned, once the mechanism of registration of teachers is put in place.

Awareness Generation

To begin with, the code should be translated into various Indian Languages and circulated widely amongst the teachers. The National Level and State Level Teachers' organisations and institutions responsible for teachers' in-service education should organise orientation programmes for teachers and discuss with them the implications of the code. The present code of Professional Ethics for school teachers has been evolved to provide direction and guidance to the teachers in enhancing the dignity of their professional work. But the code has still remained in draft form not in operation.

Chapter – 18

Curriculum and Evaluation Policy in the Light of the RTE Act

Education aims at making children capable of becoming responsible, productive and useful members of a society. Knowledge, skills and attitudes are built through learning experiences and opportunities created for learners in school. It is in the classroom that learners can analyse and evaluate their experiences, learn to doubt, to question, to investigate and to think independently. The aim of education simultaneously reflects the current needs and aspirations of a society as well as its lasting values and human ideals. As aspiration and expectations of each generation vary with time, constant review of curriculum and evaluation system becomes an essential exercise. The main purposes of evaluation is to help the learners improve their achievement in scholastic areas and to develop life skills and attitudes with reference to the larger context and canvas of life. In keeping with the above, reforms in the examination system are often recommended, sometimes discussed and rarely implemented. Introduction of Continuous and Comprehensive Evaluation (CCE) is one of such reforms which have undergone a long journey.

The Indian school education system has often been subjected to severe criticism, ranging from its inequitable and hierarchical nature to the poor quality educational experiences that children go through in its classrooms. Among the several limitations pointed out, the nature and manner in which students' learning is examined has also been a central and oft-repeated concern of educationists, policymakers, teachers and parents alike. At the moment, India is at a crucial juncture with education having been made a fundamental right for all children in the age group 6–14 years. Concerns are simultaneously being expressed about providing uniform good quality educational experiences to all children, irrespective of their socio-economic and cultural backgrounds. The need for meaningfully assessing children's growth in schools features in the recently enacted Right to Education Act (RTE) (Ministry of Human Resource Development or MHRD 2009) as well. It states that a "comprehensive and continuous evaluation of the child's understanding to knowledge and his or her ability to apply the same" will now be made. While the need for meaningful examination reforms can hardly be understated, it is important to exercise caution in proposing reforms and in understanding their potential, both in terms of addressing the malaise associated with the existing examination system and implications for facilitating enriching and equitable teaching-learning processes in classrooms.

Education is the training of the mind and assimilation of ideas leading to dynamism of character and creativity of personality. According to Indian education philosophy, education does not mean stuffing the brain which results into stagnation of personality. In fact, the primary function of education is to bring about all round development of a child with respect to body, mind and spirit. The western educationists also agree with this philosophy. They divide the human personality in three domains namely, cognitive, affective and psychomotor. These domains are related to head, heart and hand. When these domains are developed in a balanced way the purpose of education is achieved. In order to know the pace and direction of growth of individual through the process of education a system is required.

In school education system, the conduct of examination and evaluation for the promotion to next higher classes is an important activity. Conducting examinations in education system works like a regularity mechanism in improving quality in education. As child development is a continuous process, evaluation should be continuous. The progress of the learner will be evaluated quite often in continuous evaluation. Learner is subjected to schooling for scholastic and co-scholastic gains. In fact, comprehensive evaluation covers the whole range of student's experiences in the context of total school activities. It includes physical, intellectual, emotional and social growth comprising of social personal qualities, interest, attitude and values. Before going into our main discussion, we should have an understanding about education evaluation in the field of school education.

Defining Education Evaluation

The highest rung of the education-ladder is evaluation [aims and objectives of education – curriculum – syllabus – educational activities – methodology – evaluation] by which the extent of acquisition of learning competencies as well as changes in behavioural changes is measured. It is one of the cornerstones upon which the edifice of educational activities is built. After completing an instruction a teacher tries to evaluate the process by measuring students' academic achievement. This process is called educational evaluation.

Different authors have different notions of educational evaluation. These sometimes dissimilar views are due to the varied training and background of the writers in terms of their profession, concerned with different aspects of the education process. Perhaps the most extended definition of evaluation has been supplied by C. E. Beeby (1977), who described evaluation as "the systematic collection and interpretation of evidence leading as a part of process to a judgement of value with a view to action". Tyler (1951) defined educational evaluation as "Education evaluation is the judgment process for the educational goal (behavioural objectives) realised through education and class activities". Cronbach (1984) described educational evaluation as "Education evaluation is the process of information gathering and treatment necessary to make a decision for an education programme". By educational evaluation Stufflebeam (1971) meant "Process of information defining, acquiring and providing necessary for decision-making process". Thorpe (1980) described educational evaluation as "Evaluation is the collection, analysis and interpretation of information about any aspect of a programme of education, as a part of a recognised process of judging its effectiveness, its efficiency and any other outcomes it may have".

From the above definitions and if we go through some other definitions, we can find some characteristics of educational evaluation. Firstly, it collects data or evidence through a systematic and planned way with some degree of precision. Secondly, it interprets the data.

The information gathered for the evaluation of an educational programme must be carefully interpreted. Thirdly, it involves value judgement. Judgement of values far beyond the level of mere description of what is happening in an educational enterprise requires judgements about the worth of an educational endeavour. Thus, evaluation not only involves gathering and interpreting information about how well an educational programme is succeeding in reaching its goals but judgements about the goals themselves. It involves questions about how well a programme is helping to meet larger educational goals. Fourthly, it gives feedback to the process with a view to some actions to increase the effectiveness, efficiency etc. Educational evaluation is clearly decision-oriented and is undertaken with the intention that some action will take place as a result. It is intended to lead to better policies and practices in education.

Evaluation should ideally be valid, reliable, practicable, fair and useful. Evaluation therefore may be taken as a process of collecting evidences about learner's achievement or development in terms of educational objectives. Judgements are formed and decisions are taken on the basis of evidences. The components of evaluation are (WBBSE, 2009):

- Collection of information regarding learner's learning.
- Interpretation of the information.
- Formation of judgement.
- Decision making.

Information is gathered through different types of tests, assignments, project works etc. and by scoring it. Available information is then analysed for forming judgment regarding the pace of learning as well as level of learning of the pupils. For judgement we consider three points – his / her previous achievement, with respect to his / her peer group and a criteria determined by the teacher. So we consider – (1) whether the learner has improved or deteriorated in terms of his / her previous achievement. (2) What is his / her state of learning with respect to his / her peer-group. (3) Whether the learner could attempt all the questions or attempted only a part of them. The analysis leads us to decide whether the learning is improved or retarded and needs remediation. On the basis of the judgement, decision can be taken in the form of allotting marks or grades.

Function of Education Evaluation: Education evaluation has confirmation and judgement functions concerning how well the educational goal is realised based on the goal as originally defined. It also has information-gathering and application functions necessary for making decisions regarding learners, educational methods, and administrative assistance. In addition, it has formative functions for development, revision and supplementation, and alternatives research for new and better educational programmes, as well as the strategic functions of advertisement, attention, and motivation.

Types of Education Evaluation

Evaluation Types Based on Domain: Bloom (1956) suggested taxonomy of education objectives, setting standards on the content of education and behaviour dimensions, and dividing into goals of cognitive, affective, and psychomotor domains.

(i) **Evaluation of the Cognitive Domain:** This evaluation measures the achievement of cognitive education goals that can be achieved by conceptual process such as memorising, understanding, and reasoning on the educational contents specified in the educational goals.

(ii) **Evaluation of Affective Domain:** This evaluation looks at changes or improvements in interest, merit, confidence, and attitude, or characteristics such as a spirit of cooperation, responsibility, law-abiding nature, sociality, and self-consciousness.

(iii) **Evaluation of Psychomotor Domain:** This evaluation measures the achievement of education goals that can be achieved by using whole of parts of the body such as hands, feet, legs, and shoulders.

Evaluation Types Based on Methods: According to the education process or programme evaluation method, Scriven (1965) divided evaluation types into formative and summative evaluations.

(i) **Formative Evaluation:** This evaluation accumulates information to enhance methods and optimise education while the education is in progress.

(ii) **Summative Evaluation:** This final, total evaluation, which takes place after fixing and repairing by Formative Evaluation, gives a diversified decision about a completed education process or the total result or effectiveness of programme.

Evaluation may be external or internal. There are different activities learning process like teaching, setting questions, scoring. If all the mentioned activities are done by the same persons, then it is **internal evaluation**. Otherwise it is called as **external evaluation**. There are two approaches of evaluation according to the interpretation of scores obtained by the students — **criterion-referenced** and **norm-referenced evaluation**. Norm-referenced interpretation compares an examinee's performance to the performances of other examinees. On the other hand, criterion-referenced interpretation compares an examinee's performance to a specified level of performance.

Teacher generally uses different type of test items to evaluate the learner. We can classify test items as **selected-response item** and **constructed-response item**. If an item requires a student to select a response from available alternatives, it is called as a selected-response item, like-multiple choice, true false, matching etc. If it requires a student to create or construct a response, it is classified as a constructed response item, like-essay, short answer etc. Items can also be classified as objective and subjective item. When the personal characteristics of the scorer influence the scoring, then it is called subjectivity. If these factors are not influencing the scoring then it is called as objectivity. Generally it is concluded that objective item is good as it is free from any subjectivity. But there are some drawbacks of objective items. This type of items can not measure the higher order learning outcomes, like – organisation ability, writing ability, originality etc. A good evaluation programme is (WBBSE, 2009) – objective based, a continuous process, comprehensive, an integral part of instruction, cooperative, dynamic and a judgement-making process.

Evaluation is an integral part of any teaching and learning programme. The quality of education is directly linked with the quality of evaluation. Both teaching and evaluation are based on the instructional objectives which give the teachers direction. Instructional objectives are those desirable behaviours which are to be developed in students through the learning process. These are reflected in the form of syllabus, instructional material and information given by the teachers, and evaluation is done to see whether the instructional objectives have been achieved and to what extent. The three components of teaching, learning and evaluation constitute an integrated network. Through evaluation the teacher not only assesses as to how far the students have achieved the objectives, but also examines the effectiveness of the teaching strategy, teaching material as well as teaching methodology.

Phases of Education Evaluation

First Phase : Create the Evaluation Plan : Because the contents and methods of evaluation differ by evaluation plan, confirm the evaluation goals or necessity, and set up the evaluation plan and design by arranging for phases such as setting education goals, stating methods, selecting the evaluation design, producing the evaluation tools, collecting evaluation data, analysing evaluation results, and applying evaluation results.

Second Phase: State the Evaluation Goal: Decide on the evaluation goal, and select the best statement methods possible, based on the goals that the evaluation process is to achieve. Confirm the evaluation goal, state it, analyse and evaluate the stated goal, and create a dual classified table.

Third Phase: Select an Evaluation Design: Create a specific design, according to the evaluation goal, to collect, analyse, and compare the data expected to be received during the evaluation. Set up tests, composition of sample space, evaluation time, number of evaluations, and the relative standards for evaluation results.

Fourth Phase: Produce Evaluation Tools: Decide on the evaluation methods or measuring tools that will be used to collect data or information, and produce the best evaluation tool possible.

Fifth Phase: Collect the Evaluation Data: After selecting and producing the evaluation tools, collect the actual information and data by acquiring the necessary labour, facilities, and time; check and improve the given condition.

Sixth Phase: Analyse the Evaluation Results: Arrange and grade the information and data collected during the fifth phase to obtain the mean, variance, and standard deviation. Analyse the collected data qualitatively and quantitatively, according to the evaluation goal.

Seventh Phase: Report the evaluation results.

Eighth Phase: Apply the Evaluation Results: Based on the evaluation results, improve the education methods, induce motivation to learn, apply the various evaluation results according to the evaluation goals, and check the end result. The phases of education evaluation have been depicted in the following Figure 17.1 (Lee, 1999):

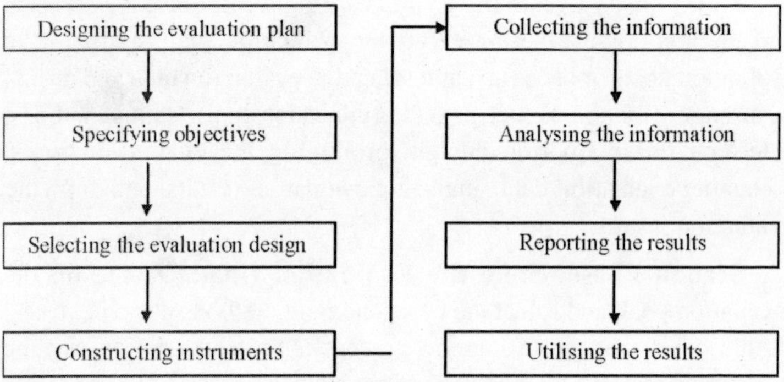

Figure 18.1: Phases of Education Evaluation.

Genesis of CCE - Historical Perspectives

Examination is an indispensable part of the educational process as some form of assessment is necessary to determine the effectiveness of teaching learning process and their internalisation by learners. Examinations today are not as effective as they ought to be. So they urgently need to be reformed in order to bring about a qualitative improvement in education. Various Commissions and Committees have felt the need for examination reforms. The Hunter Commission (1982), Calcutta University Commission or Sadler Commission (1917-1919), Hartog Committee Report (1929), the Report of Central Advisory Board / Sargent Plan (1944), Secondary Education Commission/Mudaliar Commission (1952-53) have all made recommendations regarding reducing emphasis on external examination and encouraging internal assessment through continuous and Comprehensive Evaluation.

This aspect has been strongly taken care of in the National Policy on Education–1986 which states that "Continuous and Comprehensive Evaluation that incorporates both scholastic and non-scholastic and non-scholastic aspects of evaluation, spread over the total span of instructional time" {8.24 (iii)}. Report on the Committee for Review of NPE–1986 – recommendation brought out by Government of India in 1991 lays down norms for "Continuous comprehensive internal evaluation and suggests safeguards against abuse of this evaluation system" {268 (iv)}. Report on the CABE Committee on Policy brought out by MHRD, Govt. of India in January, 1992 has also referred to the provisions of NPE with regard to evaluation process and examination reforms and also suggested 'continuous and comprehensive internal evaluation of the scholastic and non-scholastic achievement of the students' (16.8).

The need for Continuous and Comprehensive School-based Evaluation has been reiterated over the last few decades. The Kothari Commission report (1966) observed, 'on the completion of the course, at the end of the lower or higher secondary stage, the student should receive a certificate from the school also giving the record of his internal assessment as contained in his cumulative record. This certificate may be attached to that given by the Board in connection with the external examination...' (9.81). It further adds, 'This internal assessment or evaluation conducted by the schools is of greater significance and should be given increasing importance. It should be comprehensive, evaluating all those aspects of students' growth that are measured by the external examination and also those personality traits, interests and attitudes which cannot be assessed by it' (9.84).

The National Curriculum Framework–2005 (NCF–05) also proposed examination reforms. In its Position Paper on Examination Reforms 2.8 (1), NCERT mandates that School-based CCE system should be established to....

- reduce stress on children;
- make evaluation comprehensive and regular;
- provide space for the teacher for creative teaching; and
- provide a tool of diagnosis and for producing learners with greater skills.

The NCF - 2005 has also recommended several reforms regarding paper setting, examining and reporting (p. 114) : "The focus should shift to framing good questions rather than mere paper setting...we need to be able to increasingly shift towards school-based assessment, and devise ways in which to make such internal assessment more credible. Each school should evolve a flexible and implementable scheme of Continuous and Comprehensive Evaluation (CCE), primarily for diagnosis, remediation and enhancing of learning."

The RTE Act and CCE

On 27th August 2009, Govt. of India adopted a new act "Right of Children to Free and Compulsory Education Act, 2009 (RTE)." This law came into force for the entire country (except Kashmir) w.e.f. 1st April, 2010.

Section 29(2) mandates that the academic authority, while laying down the curriculum and the evaluation procedure under sub-section (1), shall take into consideration the following, namely –

(a) conformity with the values enshrined in the Constitution;

(b) all round development of the child;

(c) building up child's knowledge, potentiality and talent;

(d) development of physical and mental abilities to the fullest extent;

(e) learning through activities, discovery and exploration in a child-friendly and child-centred manner;

(f) Medium of instructions shall, as far as practicable, be in child's mother tongue;

(g) making the child free of fear, trauma and anxiety and helping the child to express views freely;

(h) Comprehensive and continuous evaluation of child understands of knowledge and his or her ability to apply the same;

(i) No child shall be required to pass any Board Examination till completion of elementary education.

The RTE Act mandates "No child admitted in a school till the completion of elementary" (Section – 16) and "Comprehensive and continuous evaluation of child understands of knowledge and his or her ability to apply the same" (Section – 29). The Section – 16 refers to No-detention policy and Section – 29 refers to evaluation policy. It must be clear at this juncture that implementing non-detention policy should not lead to absence of teaching-learning in schools. On the contrary, CCE can play as a powerful instrument in respecting the intent of RTE on the one hand and ensuring learning for all children on the other hand, as assessment during teaching-learning process would provide for necessary and timely feedback for further improvement. CCE in turn would encourage all to focus on child's progress with her/his own performance over time. MHRD in the notification dated 31st March, 2010 authorised the NCERT to lay down the curriculum and evaluation system of elementary education. Accordingly NCERT has developed exemplar material on continuous and comprehensive evaluation (CCE) for the elementary stage in all curricular areas.

Continuous and Comprehensive Evaluation: An Overview

The scheme of Continuous and Comprehensive Evaluation was recommended by many National Commissions and Committees like Radhakrishnan Commission (1948–49), Secondary Education Commission (1952–53), The Education Commission (1964–66), National Policy on Education (NPE 1986) etc. Thus, keeping these recommendations in the consideration the Ministry of Human Resource Development has recently brought in the scheme of Continuous and Comprehensive Evaluation as a part of Examination Reforms Programme with the aim of developing the holistic profile of the learner through CCE. The earlier over emphasis on cognitive domain has been replaced with a more holistic learning plan providing for development of affective and psychomotor domains of the learners personality such as human values, attitudes, life skills, physical and mental health. The scheme of CCE is an effective tool to enhance the quality of teaching learning processes in the school. The emphasis is now ensuring that every child not only acquire the knowledge and skills but also the ability to use these competencies in real life situations. Thus, the emphasis is now both on knowledge as well as on performance. The CCE or Continuous and Comprehensive Evaluation scheme refers to a school-based evaluation of students that covers all the aspects of a student's development.

With the broader aim of examination reforms in mind, the scheme of Continuous and Comprehensive Evaluation envisages that every learner is to be evaluated over the entire period of learning schedule rather than one-shot three hour external examination at the end of a course of learning. Besides, the process of evaluation should also include and reflect all components of personality of an individual. Such a scheme of CCE not only provides necessary feedback about the acquired levels of learning and areas of desired additional inputs of enhancement of learning in scholastic areas, it also lays equal emphasis on achievement in outdoor co-curricular activities including sports and games. It is hoped that due emphasis on development of necessary personality attributes and other co-scholastic areas along with desired levels of attainment in the scholastic domain will certainly help the young learners grow into better human beings and will enable them to contribute meaningfully towards societal requirements and national expectations.

In the scheme of Continuous and Comprehensive Evaluation the term "**Continuous**" is meant to emphasise that evaluation of identified aspects of students' growth and development is a continuous process rather than an event, built into the total teaching-learning process and spread over the entire span of academic session. It means regularity of assessment, frequency of unit testing, diagnosis of learning gaps, use of corrective measures, retesting and feedback of evidence to teachers and students for their self-evaluation. The second term "**Comprehensive**" means that the scheme attempts to cover both the scholastic and non-scholastic aspects of students' growth and development. Since abilities, attitudes and aptitudes can manifest themselves in forms other than written words, the term refers to the application of variety of tools and techniques (both testing and non-testing) and aims at assessing a learner's development in the various areas of learning (CBSE Manual, 2009, p. 5).

CCE encompasses the evaluation of both scholastic and co-scholastic aspects of pupil growth and is carried out on continuous basis spreading over the whole academic session. It not only counteracts the over emphasis on the development of intellectual abilities but also helps in removing the tension and fear from the minds of the students which they otherwise feel in examinations which are conducted on annual basis. Not only this it also helps in the removing of tension and fear in the minds of the students in examinations. Perhaps the greatest advantage of this reform is that it provides a more valid assessment of students as compare to one shot examination at the end of the year. Through CCE, the teacher knows the progress of the students and evaluates the process and product of learning. The scheme is thus a curricular initiative, attempting to shift emphasis from testing to holistic learning. It aims at creating good citizens possessing sound health, appropriate skills and desirable qualities besides academic excellence. It is hoped that this will equip the learners to meet the challenges of life with confidence and success.

The Objectives of the Scheme:

- To help develop cognitive, psychomotor and affective skills.
- To lay emphasis on thought process and de-emphasise memorisation.
- To make evaluation an integral part of teaching-learning process.
- To use evaluation for improvement of students achievement and teaching-learning strategies on the basis of regular diagnosis followed by remedial instruction.
- To use evaluation as a quality control devise to maintain desired standard of performance.
- To determine social utility, desirability or effectiveness of a programme and take appropriate decisions about the learner, the process of learning and the learning environment.
- To make the process of teaching and learning a learner-centred activity (CBSE, 2009:6).

Guiding Principles of CCE

Connecting knowledge to life outside the school, ensuring that learning is shifted away from rote methods, enriching the curriculum to provide for overall development of children rather than remain textbook centric, making examinations more flexible and integrated into classroom life and nurturing an over-riding identity informed by caring concerns within the democratic polity of the country are the main guiding principles of CCE (NCF 2005, p. 5).

What CCE is and what it isn't?

- The primary purpose of *assessment and evaluation is to improve children's learning to help them progress leading to their overall development.* Information about their learning gathered through assessment during teaching-learning, helps teachers to determine students' strengths and learning gaps in the concerned subjects which serves to guide teachers in adapting curriculum and teaching-learning approaches/ methods to suit children's needs. However, at the same time, it also serves the purpose to reflect how well a student has achieved the curricular expectations through the process of gathering information from a variety of sources.
- Assessment during teaching-learning process (i.e., continuous assessment) gives clues about children, which the teacher *can act upon timely* to enhance learning, especially where children are facing difficulties and special help is needed. Continuous assessment does not require the use of structured tests which are given to all children at the same time. In this process, they may not even know that they are being assessed. Thus, continuous should not mean *more frequent formal tests.*
- One major misconception is related to the words *formative assessment.* In report cards, in a large number of schools, currently teachers report formative assessment in every quarter including project work and other activities under that. Actually formative assessments are not meant to be reported in report cards. The word formative comes from 'formation', that is, formation of the learning process. These are assessments designed to monitor and improve students' progress during the teaching-learning process (also called assessment *for* learning).
- Any information on learning of a child, for example, by written work, oral responses or may be simply observing the child, can be used *formatively* by the teacher to help the learner further.
- The other 'C' in CCE is '*Comprehensive*' component of assessment. Comprehensive component means getting a sense of 'holistic' development of child's progress. Progress cannot

be made in a segregated manner, that is, cognitive aspects, personal-social qualities, etc. After completion of a chapter/ theme, teacher would like to know whether children have learnt (assessment of learning) as she/he expected based on lesson's objectives/learning points. For that she/he broadly identifies the objectives of the lesson and spells out learning indicators. The teacher designs activities based on expected learning indicators. These activities need to be of varied nature. Through these questions/activities she would assess the learners and that data would be one kind of summative data of a lesson/theme. *Such assessment data must be recorded by the teacher*. Likewise in one quarter, she/he would cover seven to eight lessons/topics and in this manner she/he would have substantial data covering varied aspects of child's behaviour. It would provide data on how the child was working in groups, doing paper-pencil test, drawing pictures, reading picture, expressing orally, composing a poem/song, etc. These data would give 'comprehensive' picture of child's learning and development. *This data would help to know to the assessment of learning among children.*

- Another misconception is related with assessment of personal-social qualities of children. These qualities such as empathy, cooperation, concern for others, etc., are generally assessed at five-point scale of grading. Assessment of personal-social qualities is neither confined to a specific subject nor requires assigning a specific time as it can be observed more effectively in various situations such as during teaching-learning, outdoor activities, other activities in the school and peer interaction, etc. These should not be assessed in terms of presence or absence. These must be described to state the extent the child displays these qualities.
- Assessment is a means to gather evidences to meet the requirements of evaluation. Assessment does not speak of final judgement but a process through which comparisons among various sets of observations are made. Evaluation is the process of finding out *as to what extent changes have taken place in the development and learning among children.*

It has to be based on reliable and valid evidences so as to arrive at precise formulations. *Good evaluation is one which provides a near complete picture of one's accomplishments and is based on multiple sources.*

- Most of the time the terms 'assessment' and 'evaluation' have been used interchangeably. There is a difference in what these imply. The purpose of assessment is judging the quality of performance of children *while learning is going on*. Evaluation focuses on the actual level attained after a certain period of teaching-learning with no interest in why and how that level was attained. It refers to judging the quality of students' work on the basis of established set of criteria, and assigning a value (e.g., marks or grades) to represent that quality. Formative assessment is process oriented while evaluation is product oriented.
- Educators think that the prime purpose of evaluation is labelling or comparing performance of children against each other. They also think that these processes are there to point out weaknesses of the child or what the child *does not* know, rather than focusing on improving child's learning. The spirit of CCE is to enhance student learning both through process of assessment and evaluation. It compares the performance of a child with her/his previous performance, instead of comparing her with her peers.
- One confusion is related with what will be treated as *curricular and co-curricular areas.* Arts Education, Health and Physical Education, and Work Education are often treated as co-curricular/ co-scholastic areas where as Language, Mathematics, EVS, Science, and Social Sciences are considered as curricular areas. National Curriculum Framework, 2005 places art education, health and physical education, work education also as curricular areas.
- Teachers think that in CCE they need to record each child's progress daily or the progress needs to be recorded on a large number of indicators continuously by them. This understanding

is totally contrary to the spirit of continuous assessment. Teachers *need not assess all the children all the time, nor do they need to make elaborate records of children's progress and report them to others*. Continuous assessment is only to help the teacher teach better, and she may record only that which would be genuinely useful for her to enhance teaching-learning in her diary/logbook in her own format, which need not be common for all.

- It is also mistakenly thought that in CCE, every child needs to be promoted whether he/she learns or not. The real spirit of CCE is that every child should *get an opportunity to learn all through the process and be helped whenever she/he needs feedback and support*. This means if the teacher regulates and monitors assessment throughout the year and devises strategies to help the child so that the child's learning improves, then the situation of the child 'failing' at the end of a term would not arise.
- CCE is also misunderstood as the sole responsibility of a teacher. This makes the task seem impossible and makes the teacher feel extremely burdened with unrealistic expectations. On the contrary, CCE aims at *reducing* the teacher's burden. Actually, it places the collective responsibility of implementing CCE by various stake-holders i.e. administrators, parents, children and teachers. Children need to take responsibility of assessing their own work, their peers' work and helping each other learn. Some children can be a good resource to help the teacher.

Differences between Conventional Assessment System and CCE

Continuous and Comprehensive Evaluation (CCE) is a term currently being used in the context of educational reforms, particularly reforms in assessment. If one were to differentiate between conventional systems of assessment and the CCE as articulated by CBSE (2010), one would perhaps come across the differences outlined in Table 18.1– both manifest and implied.

Table 18.1: Differences between Conventional Assessment System and CCE

Conventional Assessment	*CCE*
Assessment on a quarterly, half-yearly and annual basis, with disproportionate weightage to annual exams	Continuous and periodic (multiple ways and occasions of assessment) with even weightage across them
Scholastic abilities	Scholastic and non-scholastic
Limited tools of assessment	Multiple tools
Marks allotted	Grades awarded
Assessment of what has been achieved over A period of time (essentially summative)	Assessment of an ongoing process of growth (includes summative but is largely formative)
Stressful for students	Non-stressful
Assessment as an end in itself	Assessment used to both improve one's teaching and enhance support given to students – identification and classification of learners for requisite support.
Skewed development of scholastic abilities, limited to rote memorising	Overall growth and personality development

Source: Based on CBSE (2010).

Features of Continuous and Comprehensive Evaluation

In Appendix 17.2 of the Position Paper on Examination Reforms, NCF- 2005 mentions some features of CCE:

- Continuous and Comprehensive Evaluation (CCE) refers to a system of school-based evaluation of students that covers all aspects of students' development.
- The 'continuous' aspect of CCE takes care for 'continual' and 'periodicity' of evaluation.
- Continual means assessment of students in the beginning of instructions (placement evaluation) and assessment during the instructional process (formative evaluation), done informally using multiple techniques of evaluation.
- Periodicity means assessment of performance done frequently at the end of unit / term (summative) using criterion-referenced tests and employing multiple techniques of evaluation.
- The 'comprehensive' component of CCE takes care of assessment of all round development of the child's personality. It includes assessment in scholastic as well as co-scholastic aspects of the pupils' growth.

- Scholastic aspects include curricular areas or subject specific areas, whereas co-scholastic aspects include co-curricular and personal social qualities, interests, attitudes, and values.
- Assessment in scholastic areas is done informally and formally using multiple techniques of evaluation continually and periodically. The diagnostic evaluation takes place at the end of unit / term test. The causes of poor performance in some units are diagnosed using diagnostic tests. These are purposefully remediated by giving interventions followed by retesting.
- Assessment in co-scholastic areas is done using multiple techniques on the basis of identified criteria, while assessment in social personal qualities is done using behaviour indicators for various interests, values, attitudes, etc.

CCE – Major Emphasis on Scholastic and Co-scholastic Domain

The desirable behaviour related to the learner's knowledge, understanding, application, evaluation, analysis, and creating in subjects and the ability to apply it in an unfamiliar situation are some of the objectives in scholastic domains. The desirable behaviour related to learner's Life Skills, attitudes, interests, values, co-curricular activities and physical health are described as skills to be acquired in co-scholastic domain. The process of assessing the students' progress in achieving objectives related to scholastic and co-scholastic domain is called comprehensive evaluation (CBSE Manual, 2009).

In National Policy on Education (NPE) document, 1986 and as modified in 1992 also it is mentioned that the scheme of evaluation should cover all learning experiences of scholastic subjects and non-scholastic areas. It has been observed that usually the scholastic areas such as knowledge and understanding of the facts, concepts, principles etc. of a subject are assessed. The co-scholastic elements are either altogether excluded from the evaluation process or they are not given adequate attention. For making the evaluation comprehensive, the scholastic and co-scholastic both should be given importance. Simple and manageable means of assessment of co-scholastic aspects of growth must be included in a comprehensive evaluation scheme. The major emphasis of CCE is on the continuous growth of students ensuring their intellectual, emotional, physical, cultural and social development and therefore will not be merely limited to assessment of learner's scholastic attainments. It uses assessment as a means of motivating learners in further programmes to provide information for arranging feedback and follow up work to improve upon the learning in the classroom and to present a comprehensive picture of a learner's profile.

CCE Helps in Reducing Stress of Students by

- Identifying learning progress of students at regular time intervals on small portions of content.
- Employing a variety of remedial measures of teaching based on learning needs and potential of different students.
- Desisting from using negative comments on the learner's performance.
- Encouraging learning through employment of a variety of teaching aids and techniques.
- Involving learners actively in the learning process.
- Recognising and encouraging specific abilities of students, who do not excel in academics but perform well in other co-curricular areas.

How Does Continuous and Comprehensive Evaluation Help a Classroom Teacher?

In sum, the continuous and comprehensive evaluation helps a classroom teacher in the following ways:

- To identify learning difficulties in mastering certain competencies and the intensity of such learning difficulties.
- To improve students' learning through diagnosis of their performance.
- To plan appropriate remedial measures to enable the students who have learning difficulties in mastering the competency.
- To improve or alter instructional strategies to enhance the quality of teaching.
- To decide upon the selecting of various media and materials as a supportive system in mastering the competencies.
- To strengthen evaluation procedure itself.

Problems Associated with CCE

Singhal, P. (2012) conducted a study entitled "Continuous and Comprehensive Evaluation – A Study of Teachers' Perception". The results of the study revealed that the teachers faced the following problems while executing CCE at school level:

- **Large number of students in classes:** The results revealed that most of the teachers find it difficult to execute CCE in large classes as they are not able to give individual attention in such classes.
- **Lack of appropriate training:** Other constrain for the smooth execution of CCE was stated as lack of appropriate training among the school teachers.
- **Lack of seriousness amongst the students:** Further the teachers reported that there was lack of seriousness amongst the students regarding CCE as they were aware of the fact that they will pass without making enough efforts in academics.
- **Financial Constraints:** Likewise many teachers stated that CCE was time consuming and there were many financial constrains associated with it that does not suit the pocket of every student.
- **Lack of adequate infrastructural facilities and teaching materials:** Teachers felt that there was lack of adequate infrastructural facilities and teaching materials that made execution of CCE a difficult task in the classrooms.
- **Increased volume of work:** Teachers were over burdened with the increased volume of work that affected their teaching effectiveness in the classrooms.

Measures for the Smooth Execution of CCE

Some important points to be considered for implementing CCE smoothly are:

- Due to large number of students in classes teachers may find it difficult to execute CCE as they are not able to give individual attention in such large classes. That's why the number of students in classes should be limited to 30–40.

- Teachers may lack proper training. So the state should provide adequate training to conferences, meetings, workshops in the concerned area.
- Proper infrastructure facilities and teaching materials should also be provided to facilitate teaching learning process in government schools.
- Careful examination of the course, and specification of competencies to be attained by the learners in terms of knowledge, understanding, application (analysis, synthesis, evaluation for higher grades) and skill performance.
- Knowledge and ability to construct assessment tools that are criterion based appropriate for assessing the competencies.
- Careful planning of the competency-based teaching procedures. There should be congruence between teaching and assessment without which assessment would become distorted.
- Comprehensive evaluation of competencies as well as personality traits and attitudes.
- The maintenance of records.
- Requirement of knowledge and skills of evaluation, commitment, and assistance to provide remedial teaching on part of the teacher.
- Other issues that the teachers need for are financial support and detachment of extra duties other than teaching as it puts unnecessary burden on already busy teachers.

The scheme of CCE is an effective tool to enhance the quality of teaching learning processes in the school. The emphasis is now ensuring that every child not only acquire the knowledge and skills but also the ability to use these competencies in real life situations. CCE is an examination reform initiative which has the potential of removing almost all the ills of examinations improving learning through continuous feedback and brings in qualitative improvement in education at school level. The CCE model can be of immense significance in creating and institutionalising a learner centric education system in India. The operational and implementation challenges need to be taken care of by the provision of adequate teaching resources and training facilities. The new teaching-learning patterns envisaged by CCE will reap benefits in the long run by initiating Indian education into stress-free education. In concluding the discussion it can be said that the new concept comprehensive and continuous evaluation is a multidimensional one encompassing within its fold the act of identifying the weakness of a learner at every stage and thereby helping the process of remedial measures. It is also an indicator of lacuna / pitfall / shortcoming, if any, in planning the educational activity itself. It will reduce stress and anxiety which often builds up during and after the examination which could have an adverse impact on young students. It will also help the learners to develop holistically in terms of personality by also focusing on the co-scholastic aspects which will be assessed as part of the Continuous and Comprehensive Evaluation scheme. Indian schools need reasonable teacher-student ratios and changes in the nature of the teacher-student relationship, from an unequal, hierarchical relationship to that of co-participants in a joint process of knowledge construction. So also the creation of adequate resources and opportunities in schools for the development of the multiple facets of students' personalities, involving students and parents both in understanding the aims of assessments and ways of achieving it.

Curriculum Aspects and the RTE Act

The Central Government has also notified the National Council for Educational Research and Training (NCERT) as the academic authority for preparing the framework of national curriculum under section 7(6) of the RTE Act. The National Curriculum Framework (NCF), 2005 prepared by NCERT has been accepted as the curriculum framework till further directions in the matter. Therefore, in implementing the provisions of section 29, the academic authority notified by the appropriate governments shall ensure adherence to child centred principles of NCF 2005. In this context the Department of School Education and Literacy, Ministry of Human Resource Department (GOI) has issued an Advisory on implementation of the provisions of section 29 of the RTE Act, 2009 to State Governments on 31st January, 2012. The following guidelines are issued for the academic authority to implement the provision of section 29:

(a) **Formulate age-appropriate curricula and syllabi in keeping with NCF 2005:** The curriculum and syllabus document should be an explicit document indicating the goals and aims of education. This should address questions, such as, what is worth teaching, how much should be taught in a particular class, and in what sequence, with what methods and materials, the linkages across different aspects of knowledge, how teachers should be prepared and children's learning assessed, and how schools should be monitored.

There is a tendency to burden the curricula and syllabi with concepts which are not age appropriate. This often happens on account of a top-down approach to curriculum and syllabus formulation. Curricula and syllabi should be prepared from Class I upwards, based on what is age-appropriate for children, rather than by first fixing he curricula / syllabi for higher classes and working downwards. Educational research regarding the inter-relationship about age and concept needs to be kept in mind while formulating the curriculum.

(b) **Maintain subject balance:** While developing the curriculum and syllabus it will be important to rationalise the number of subjects and textbooks at the primary and upper primary levels such that there is no additional curriculum load on children. States that follow the seven – rather than the eight-year elementary education cycle, tend to introduce subjects of history, geography, science and social studies in Class V instead of Class VI. This adds to the curricular load on children. In transiting to an eight-year elementary education cycle these states should initiate a review of the subjects and textbooks currently taught in class V and VIII, and rationalise them according to the respective needs of the primary and upper primary stages. There is also need to integrate and align various learning materials like textbooks, workbooks, worksheets, supplementary materials etc. in order to reduce unnecessary burden on the teacher and child, bring in cohesiveness and reduce overlaps.

(c) **Initiate Textbook Contents Reform:** The academic authority notified by the appropriate Government under section 29(1) for developing curriculum and evaluation procedure is also responsible for textbook development. Textbooks must reflect the principles of child centred pedagogy as enunciated in :

(i) section 29(2) (e) learning through activities, discovery and exploration in a child-friendly and child-centred manner, and (ii) section 29(2) (g) making the child free of fear, trauma and anxiety and helping the child to express views freely. Textbooks developers should design books such that they provide interactive opportunities for group activities with continuous self and peer assessment. The textbooks should keep the principle of equity and inclusion at the forefront, proactively break extend stereotypes to reflect sensitivity to gender and caste, peace, health and the needs of differently-abled children.

(d) Textbook Language: Extensive research points to the fact that in a multilingual country like India, the child's 'home' language is often different from the 'standard' language in textbooks. This imposes enormous learning burden on the child, and is perhaps one of the chief reasons of low achievement in school subjects. The difference between the 'home' language and 'textbook' language not only affects the language learning in school, but also subjects like Mathematics, Environment Studies, etc. because these subjects also need a language for transaction. This is why the RTE Act stipulates that the mother tongue should be used as far as practicable. Thus, efforts to incorporate well known methods of bridging between the child's 'home' languages with the 'standard' classroom language need to be given utmost attention.

(e) Undertake Textbook Production Reform: Textbook production, encompassing the layout and design, text and cover, paper size and specifications, ink, printing and binding, etc. have significant implications for quality. There should be adequate focus on good quality printing and visual design of books alongside improvement in content.

SSA provides support for textbooks to all children in government, local body and government-aided schools, including Madrasas desirous of introducing the State curriculum, SSA provides support within an upper ceiling of Rs 150 per child at the primary stage and Rs 250 per child at the upper primary stage.

States that have been providing textbooks to children under State sector schemes and budgets since 2007-08 will continue to fund textbooks being provided from the State Plans. Wherever States have undertaken curricular reform in consonance with NCF-2005 and have taken steps to improve the development, production and printing quality of textbooks, support to improve the development, production and printing quality of textbooks, support under SSA will be available as 'top up' grants for children supported under the State sector schemes and budgets within the prescribed per child ceilings, subject however to evidence of such contents and production reform.

(f) **Ensure continuous and comprehensive assessment of learning:** There have been some misgivings on the provisions of 'no detention', which is wrongly interpreted to mean that children will not be assessed, but will be automatically promoted to the next class. RTE provides for Comprehensive and Continuous Evaluation (CCE). CCE implies continuous assessment, rather than no assessment. This means that assessment should be treated as an integral part of teaching and learning, as exemplified by the Activity Based Learning (ABL) methodology practiced in schools in Tamil Nadu, and piloted in several States, including Madhya Pradesh, Rajasthan, etc. Central to ABL is the "learning ladder" with a series of activity cards. Assessment is built into the "learning ladder" in the form of activity cards. When a child finishes with a set of activity cards, including the assessment cards, she completes a 'milestone' on the ladder, and can move to the next level. Every milestone involves completing several activities including games, rhymes, drawings and songs. There are no exams, but a student can move to the next level only after attaining proficiency in the previous one. Thus, assessment is inbuilt into the teaching learning process, and is recorded for each child at his / her own pace of learning, on an assessment chart.

Apart from the ABL methodology, there are other CCE techniques which provide for an appropriate assessment profile for each child, including five tools, namely (a) Engagement pattern of the child, (b) Observations in general, (c) Observations in classroom during group-work and individual activity (d) Understanding child's written work on work assigned by the teacher, and (e) an Anecdotal record. If CCE is implemented in this manner from the child's perspective, it will bring out the best in every child, rather than pressurizing the child to compete and out-perform in every aspect of learning, and show what progress the child has made with respect to her own performance over time.

This advisory issues with the approval of the competent authority and should be brought to the knowledge of all concerned. The Academic Authorities notified by the States under section 29(1) of the RTE Act need to undertake a comprehensive review of the curriculum and evaluation procedure. States are therefore requested to initiate steps to formulate age-appropriate curricula and syllabi in keeping with the principles of section 29 of the RTE Act and NCF-2005. In undertaking curricular renewal, the Academic Authorities may also ensure that the teacher training designs/modules and learner assessment systems conform to the principles in section 29(2) of the RTE Act.

References

- Aggarwal, J. C. (2005). *Essentials of Examination System.* New Delhi: Vikash Publishing House Pvt. Ltd.
- CBSE (2009). *Teacher's Manual on CCE.* New Delhi: CBSE.
- CBSE (2010). "Continuous and Comprehensive Evaluation Manual for Teacher, Classes VI-VIII", New Delhi: CBSE.
- Cronbach, L. J. (1984). *Essential of Psychology Testing*. New York: Harper & Row.
- Government of India (1986). *National Policy on Education*, New Delhi: MHRD, Department of Education.
- Lee, E. B. (1999). Evaluation of Patient Education. *Peritoneal Dialysis International*, Vol. 19, Supplement 2.
- MHRD (1986). *National Policy on Education*, Department of Education. New Delhi: Govt. of India.
- NCERT (1988). *National Curriculum for Elementary and Secondary Education – A Framework (Revised Version).* New Delhi: Publication Department, NCERT.
- NCERT (2000). *National Curriculum for School Education.* New Delhi: Publication Department, NCERT.

- NCERT (2000). National Curriculum Framework for School Education. New Delhi: NCERT.
- NCERT (2003). Continuous and Comprehensive Evaluation, Teachers Handbook for Primary Stage. New Delhi: NCERT.
- NCERT (2005). National Curriculum Framework – 2005. New Delhi: NCERT.
- NCERT (2006). Position Paper on Examination Reforms, NCF 2005. New Delhi: NCERT.
- NCERT (2006). Position Paper on Examination Reforms. New Delhi: NCERT.
- NCERT (2008). Executive Summary of National Focus Groups Position Papers, NCF 2005. New Delhi: NCERT.
- Patel, R. N. (1978). *Educational Evaluation – Theory and Practice*. New Delhi: Himalaya Publishing House.
- Prakash, V. et al. (2000). *Grading in Schools*. New Delhi : Publication Division, NCERT.
- Singhal, P. (2012). Continuous and Comprehensive Evaluation – A Study of Teachers' Perception. *Delhi Business Review*, Vol. 13, No. 1 (Jan. – June). pp. 81-99.
- Srivastava, K. S. (1989). *Comprehensive Evaluation in School*. New Delhi: NCERT.
- Stufflebeam, D. L. (1971). Educational Evaluation and Decision Making. *Ithaca*, IL: Peacock.
- Tyler, R. W. (1949). *Basic Principles of Curriculum and Instruction*. Chicago, IL: The University of Chicago Press.
- Tyler, R. W. (1951). The functions of measurement in improving instruction. In Lindquist EF, ed. *Educational Measurement*. Washington, D. C. : American Council for Education.
- Vadhel, H. B. and Patel, N. (2011). Continuous and Comprehensive Evaluation. *Sanshodhan : E-Journal*, Special Issue : On International Conference PRABUDDHAN, Dec. 2011.
- WBBSE (2009). Foundation Paper on C. C. C. E., Sarva Sikshya Abhiyan Cell. Kolkata: WBBSE.

Chapter - 19

Philosophy of Inclusion in the Context of the RTE Act, 2009

One of the most challenging issues in the global context is to provide free, compulsory and universal elementary education to all children irrespective of caste, creed, colour, religion and all other social stratifications across the globe. Education is a basic human right and has been recognised since the adaptation of the Universal Declaration of Human Rights (1948, UNO). Since then numerous international treaties have reaffirmed this right. 'Inclusive education' is an approach that implies the education for all the children with or without special needs as an "integral part" of the general mainstream education system. Though inclusive education may have initially started from a disability perspective, it hints at the Convention on the Rights of the Child (1989), the World Conference on Education for All (Jomtien, 1990), the World Conference on Special Needs Education (Salamanca, 1994), the E-9 Ministerial Conference on EFA (Brazil, 2000), the World Conference on Mental Retardation (New Delhi, 1994) and the World Education Forum (Dakar, 2000). The Right of Children to Free and Compulsory Education Act, 2009, commonly known as RTE Act in India has been designed to embrace all the children under the ambit of mainstream elementary education of eight years. The RTE Act for the first time targets to include all children who have been excluded from and within mainstream education. This chapter intends chiefly to explore the provisions for inclusion of all children of India in the RTE Act, 2009.

Education is a human right and essential for realisation of all other human rights. The framers of the Constitution realised the very importance of education and have thus imposed a duty on the state under Article 45 as one of the Directive Principles of State Policy to provide free and compulsory education to all children until they complete the age of 14 years within 10 years from the commencement of the constitution. The Government of India has taken more than six decades after independence to make free and compulsory education as fundamental right for all children in the age group of 6-14 years. The RTE Act is the first Central legislation in the landscape of Indian elementary education that puts the responsibility of ensuring enrollment, attendance and completion of elementary education by all children on the government.

RTE Act, 2009: A Brief Account

Ever since independence, India has undertaken several initiatives to achieve universalisation of elementary education. The Right to Education legislation in India has been a chequered history in evolving from a directive principle to a fundamental right. The Right to Education Act came to its present form after the concerted efforts of many groups and agencies in the country (Mondal and Mete, 2013). The first law on compulsory education was introduced by the State of Baroda, in 1906. This law provides education for boys and girls in the age group of 7-12 years and 7-10 years respectively. In 1911, Gopal Krishna Gokhle unsuccessfully moved a Bill for compulsory education in the Imperial Legislative Council. The Legislative Council of Bombay was first amongst the provinces to adopt a law on compulsory education. In spite of all these efforts universalisation of education in the country was poor due to lack of control over resources. Thereafter, National Policy on Education, 1968 was formed and implemented. It was the first official document evidencing Indian Government's commitment towards elementary education. Again, emphasis was given on universalisation of elementary education in 1990, when the policy was reviewed by the Acharya Ramamurthy Committee.The first official recommendation for inclusion of the right to education as a fundamental right was made by the committee (1990):

> "*Now time has come to recognise 'Right to Education' as one of the fundamental rights of the Indian citizens for which necessary amendments to the constitution may have to be made and more*

importantly, conditions be created in society such that this right would become available for all children" [**Towards an Enlightened and Humane Society (1990)**, *Para.* 6.1.3].

However, this recommendation was not implemented immediately. In 1992, in the case of *Mohini Jain* Vs *State of Karnataka*, the Supreme Court of India held that 'right to education is concomitant to fundamental rights enshrined under Part III of the constitution and that every citizen has a right to education under the constitution. Subsequently, in the case of *Unnikrishnana, J.P.* Vs *State of Andhra Pradesh*, the Supreme Court held that "though right to education is not stated expressively as a fundamental right, it is implicit in and flow from the right to life guaranteed under Article 21. The landmark judgments of the Hon'ble Supreme Court and initiatives from many other agencies had forced the government take initiatives in this direction. In 2002, the 86th Amendment Act of the Constitution states that the state shall provide free and compulsory education to all children of the age of six to fourteen years. The Right of Children to Free and Compulsory Education Act, 2009 received assent of the President of India on 26th August, 2009. With the Right to Education Act, 2009 coming into force, India has joined the league of over 130 countries which have legal guarantees to provide free and compulsory education to children (UNESCO's Education for All Global Monitoring Report, 2010).

The Salient Features of the RTE Act, 2009

The title of the RTE Act incorporates the words 'free and compulsory'. '**Free education**' means that no child, other than a child who has been admitted by his or her parents to a school which is not supported by the appropriate government, shall be liable to pay any kind of fee or charges or expenses which may prevent him or her from pursuing and completing elementary education. '**Compulsory education**' casts an obligation on the appropriate government and local authorities to provide and ensure admission, attendance and completion of elementary education by all children in the 6–14 age groups. The RTE Act is a detailed and comprehensive piece of legislation that includes provisions related to schools, teachers, curriculum, evaluation, access and specific division of duties and responsibilities of different stakeholders. The main features of the Act are overviewed as follows:

- Makes Elementary Education Free and Compulsory for the State to provide.
- Mandates education of children along their peer age group ("age-appropriate"); provides for "special training" to facilitate age appropriate education.
- Sets quality norms for all schools, and sets qualification and working norms for Teachers in all schools.
- Mandates curriculum in all schools to be in consonance with Constitutional Values.
- Mandates a system of comprehensive and continuous evaluation that is free of the oppression of annual examinations.
- Enhances role of PRIs in implementation as well as grievance redressal.
- Mandates participation of civil society in the management of schools; makes teachers accountable to parents and the community.
- Democratises education delivery in the country by mandating 25 per cent reservation for children from weaker sections in private schools.
- Protects children from labour, marriage, exploitation, discrimination, abuse, violence and neglect.
- Separates agency for implementation of Act (Education Department) from agency charged with monitoring the implementation of the Act (NCPCR).

Conceptualising Inclusive Education

'Inclusion' is such a concept that cannot be easily and clearly defined. 'Exclusion' is the opposite term of 'inclusion'. Exclusion from education is multi-dimensional in cause and effect. It concerns children prevented from attending school as well as those who attend but do not learn. It concerns national policies which sustain poverty and social marginalisation, and which undermine a family capacity to act on behalf of its child's development. It concerns education systems and schools that deny access to education. It is multi-dimensional because a child denied education is invariably also denied adequate healthcare and nutrition, shelter, protection and security (Nanda, 2008, p. 8). Inclusion is a philosophy which views diversity of strengths, abilities and needs as natural and desirable bringing to any community the opportunity to respond in ways which lead to learning and growth for the whole community, and giving each and every member a valued role. NCF 2005 reiterates inclusion is not confined to the disabled. It also means non-exclusion. Inclusive education is about embracing all (NCERT, 2005, pp. 84).

Inclusive education is a strategy for building inclusive society where everyone has right to access, participate and get complete success in education in the neighbouring regular school along with other age-mates without any discrimination. It has become the most effective approach to address the learning needs of all students in regular schools and classrooms (Alur, 2002). A working definition of inclusive education was given by Sebba and Ainscow (1996) in the following words: "An inclusive school works from the principle that all students in the community should learn together." They also defined inclusion on the basis of approach that "inclusion is the process and not a state". They reach in the following definition: "Inclusion describes the process by which a school attempts to respond to all pupils as individuals while by reconsidering its curricular organisation and provision. Through this process, the school builds its capacity to accept all pupils from the local community who wish to attend and, in so doing, reduces the need to exclude pupils".

If "Right to Life" is a "Human Rights Issue", then it is obvious that the persons denied or excluded from education surely denying that right, because without education, "Right to Life" has no meaning. Naturally, "Inclusion in Education" is also closely related to "Human Right Issue" (Mukhopadhyay, 2003). The inclusive education is on one hand, a human right issue and on the other, a strategy to develop a child into a balanced personality capable not only surviving in a society but also to compare with others without any fear of failure or a complex (Nanda, 2008, p. 7). The ideal system of inclusion is that the general education system itself should make education of special need children as its integral part. This implies that the general classroom teachers should be equipped with skills to address the educational needs of children with special needs with minimum or no assistance from special teachers (Mani, 2002). So, inclusive education refers to an education system that accommodates all children regardless of their physical, intellectual, social emotional, linguistic or other conditions. An inclusive class may have amongst others, children with disability or gifted children, street or working children, children from remote or nomadic populations, children belonging to ethnic, linguistic or cultural minorities or children from other disadvantaged or marginalised groups (The Salamanca Statement, 1994). The question of why Inclusive Education has also largely been addressed in the Salamanca Statement (1994) in the following ways:

- Every child has a fundamental right to education, and must be given the opportunity to achieve and maintain an acceptable level of learning.
- Every child has unique characteristics, interests, abilities and learning needs.
- Education systems should be designed and educational programmes implemented to take into account the wide diversity of these characteristics and needs.
- Those with special educational needs must have access to regular schools which should accommodate them with a child-centred pedagogy capable of meeting these needs.
- Regular schools with this inclusive orientation are the most effective means of combating discriminatory attitudes, creating welcoming communities, building an inclusive society and achieving education for all…(Article 2, The Salamanca Statement, 1994).

This framework stems from the messages of the Jomtien World Declaration on Education for All (1990) and was reaffirmed in the Dakar Framework for Action (2000): '…In order to attract and retain children from marginalised and excluded groups, education systems should respond flexibly… Education systems must be inclusive, actively seeking out children who are not enrolled, and responding flexibly to the circumstances and needs of all learners...'(Education for All: Meeting our Collective Commitments, Expanded Commentary on the Dakar Framework for Action, p. 16, Para 33).

Provisions in the RTE Act, 2009 for Inclusive Education

This RTE Act has given a new thrust to the inclusion of all children in the mainstream education, as without their inclusion, the objective of UEE cannot be achieved. The Act contains specific provisions for disadvantaged groups, such as child labours, migrant children, children with special needs (CWSN), or those who have a disadvantage owing to social, cultural, economical, geographical, linguistic, gender or any such factor. Different sections of the Act refer to inclusive education either explicitly or implicitly. They are as follows:

Section - 3(1) of the RTE Act 2009 Chapter - II states: Every child of the age six to fourteen years shall have a right to free and compulsory education in a neighbourhood school till completion of elementary education.

Section - 3(2) states: For the purpose of sub-section (1), no child shall be liable to pay any kind of fee or Charges or expenses which may prevent him or her from pursuing and completing the elementary education. It is worth mentioning here that in the chapter - I of the Act **'child'** has been defined as "a male or female child of the age of six to fourteen years". The Act further points out that "child belonging to disadvantaged group" will include groups having disadvantage owing to social, cultural, economical, geographical, linguistic, gender or such other factors as specified by the government. By the Amendment (2010) to the RTE Act, 2009 children with disabilities have been incorporated in the definition of 'child belonging to disadvantaged group' in clause (d) of section 2 of the RTE Act.

Section - 3(2) of the Act qualifies that a child suffering from disability as defined under clause (i) of section 2 of the PWD Act, 1995 shall have a right to purse free and compulsory elementary education in accordance with provisions of Chapter V of the said Act. The PWD Act, 1995 includes blindness, low vision, leprosy cured, hearing impairment, locomotor disability, mental retarded and mental illness and exclusive children suffering from certain other disabilities such as Creatable Palsy, Autism, Learning Disabilities and multiplex Disabilities.

Section - 8(c) of the RTE Act states while clarifying the duties of appropriate government: the appropriate government shall *"ensure that child belonging to weaker section and the child belonging to disadvantaged group are not discriminated against and prevented from pursuing and completing elementary education on any ground"*. In fact, articles like these are clear indication of the objective to do away with any kind of disparity on the ground of social, cultural, economical, geographical, linguistic, gender, disabilities or such other factors. The main objectives of the gender concern of RTE Act, 2009 are not only to enable to keep pace with boys in education but to bring a basic change in the status of women in society.

Teachers are to play a very important role in implementing the mission of RTE Act, especially so in case of inclusion. If teacher is not sensitised to actively dispel traditional perceptions regarding gender or caste or disability, he/she is unlikely to take measures to help children to pursue education which is equitable and free from anxiety. The RTE Act, 2009 emphasises the importance of teachers' training which would enable teachers to promote inclusive classroom practices. The emphasis on professional training as a requisite qualification for recruitment of teachers in RTE Act 2009 (Section 23 sub-sections - 1 and 2) tries to ensure empathy of teachers towards every child. It clearly states (24[d]) that it is the duty of a teacher to *assess the learning ability of each child and accordingly supplement additional instructions, if any, as required* and [e] *hold regular meetings with parents and guardians and apprise them about the regularity in attendance, ability to learn, progress made in learning and any other relevant information about the child.*

Children with disabilities and girls from SC, ST and minor communities and from families below poverty line usually face greater challenge in continuing education after the primary level. Community support and monitoring play an important role here. The RTE Act 2009 has also provided scope for community to intervene in smooth running of the school. The act requires each school to constitute a School Management Committee consisting of the elected representatives of the local authority, parents or guardians of children admitted in such school and teachers. The act makes it mandatory that fifty per cent of members of such Management Committee shall be women **(Section - 21[1])**. The School Management Committee shall monitor the work of the school, prepare development plan and thereby monitor use of allocation of grant and its use. The fifty per cent women member is expected to safeguard the interest of their girl children and protest against any kind of discrimination on the basis of gender **(Section - 21[2])**.

RTE Act 2009 tries to involve all local stakeholders by making local authority responsible to ensure that the child belonging to any disadvantaged group may not be discriminated against and prevented from pursuing and completing elementary education. **Section - 9** states that every local authority shall '*maintain records of children up to the age of fourteen years residing within its jurisdiction, in such manner as may be prescribed* **(sub-section-d)**; *ensure and monitor admission, attendance and completion of elementary education by every child residing within its jurisdiction* **(sub-section-e)**; *provide infrastructure including school building, teaching staff and learning material* **(sub-section-f)**; *provide special training facility specified in Section 4* **(sub-section-g)**; *provide training facility for teachers* **(sub-section-j)**; *monitor functioning of the schools within its jurisdiction* **(sub-section-l)** and so on. **Section - 10** makes it mandatory for the guardians to ensure admitting their children to school – *It shall be the duty of every parent or guardian to admit or cause to be admitted his or her child or ward, as the case may be, to en elementary education in the neighbouring school*.

However, mere sensitisation of teachers and involvement of local authority and community to safeguard the rights of every child may not be enough and hence classroom practices would need to be monitored and grievance redressal mechanisms have to be established at the school and other levels. The RTE Act (2009) provides for grievances too. **Section - 31** under Chapter VI: *(1) The National Commission for Protection of Child Rights constituted under Section 3, or as the case may be, the State Commission for Protection of Child Rights constituted under section 17, of the Commission for Protection of Child Rights Act 2005, shall in addition to the functions assigned to* *them under that Act, also perform the following functions, namely: (a) examine and review the safeguards for rights provided by or under this Act and recommend measures for their effective implementation; (b) enquire into complaints relating to child's right to free and compulsory education ; (c) and take necessary steps as provided under sections 15 and 24 of the said Commissions for Protection of Child Right Act.* In addition to this **Section - 32(1)** clearly states that *notwithstanding anything contained in section 31, any person having any grievance relating to the right of a child under this Act may make a written complaint to the local authority having jurisdiction* and **Section - 32(2)** mandates that *after receiving the complaint the local authority shall decide the matter within a time period of three months.*

Other provisions of the RTE Act, 2009 categorically says that schools have to be zones of non-discrimination. By prohibiting screening in admissions it creates an open door policy for admissions **[Section – 13(I)]**. By prohibiting corporal punishments or mental harassment it tries to create an environment free of fear, anxiety and stress for children **[Section – 17(I)]. Section – 16** mandates that no child can be expelled or held back in any class till the completion of elementary education. Mother tongue of the child as medium of instruction and Comprehensive and Continuous Evaluation (CCE) are expected to provide a facilitative environment for learning. Moreover, there are so many are provisions for inclusion in education that includes equity issues, curriculum development in conformity with constitutional stipulations, training, and enrollment in age appropriate classes.

Philosophy of Inclusion – the Task Ahead

Despite many gains under the impact of the RTE Act, elementary education faces several challenges. Now is the time to turn from inputs and focus on the challenges related to retention, bridging of gender and social gaps in enrollment levels and enhancement of learning levels of all children. Some of the suggestions for optimising non-discrimination environment, inclusiveness and strengthening implementation of the RTE Act for Disadvantaged and Weaker Sections are as follows:

- People's representatives – MPs, MLAs, Municipal Councillor, and members under the three-tier Panchayati Raj Institutions

(PRIs) should be made responsible for smooth functioning of the schools in their areas (Mondal and Mete, 2013, p. 265).

- Teachers need to have at their disposal a deep fund of empathy, commitment, conviction and ability and motivation to persevere; of knowledge and resources to respond and create meaningful educational experiences for all children.
- Seminars, Workshops, Conference, Orientation programmes should be organised for building awareness of all the stakeholders of education about the potentialities of the RTE Act, 2009.
- To implement the RTE Act, the Human Resource Development Ministry, Labour Ministry, Women and Child Development Ministry and Rural Development Ministry have to work together with a common goal.
- The quality of Mid Day Meal (MDM) needs to be improved, which will attract children of the weaker sections of the society.
- In the rural areas, the school hours and the duration will have to be adjusted according to the needs of the community.
- The school may put emphasis on providing some remedial education programmes. Adoption of instructional strategies, such as peer group learning, monitoring assistance, diagnostic testing and tutoring would help to improve the educational levels of the learners belonging to the weaker and disadvantaged sections of our society.

"Inclusion in Education" does not mean only inclusion of physically or mentally exceptional children in the mainstream education programme but it considers including each and every child who are excluded from the mainstream education setup. Thus, inclusive education is an approach to improve the education system by limiting and removing barriers to learning and acknowledging individual children's needs and potential. It is time to act, to share hands and efforts, to give information to everyone, to promote the right to education for everyone with dignity and respect as human being. Let us learn together, learn to live together for a future better world. The RTE Act has given a new thrust to inclusive education, as without inclusion of all children the objectives of UEE cannot be achieved. This piece of legislation holds a galaxy of clauses to promote effective inclusion in schools and classrooms and strengthen schools for the enrollment, retention and completion of elementary education by all the Indian children with or without special needs. We have to be hopeful for developing the required attitude and behaviour in inclusive education. The RTE Act, 2009 can create an inclusive society only when our political commitment is in favour of its proper implementation. The authors conclude the discussion by asserting the line "...to attract and retain children from marginalised and excluded groups, education systems should respond flexibly... Education systems must be inclusive, actively seeking out children who are not enrolled, and responding flexibly to the circumstances and needs of all learners..." (Dakar Framework for Action, Para 33).

References

- Alur, Mithu (2002). Introduction. In Seamus Hegarty and Mithu Alur (ed.), *Education and Children with Special Needs: From Segregation to Inclusion.* New Delhi: Sage Publications.
- Govt. of India (1968). *National Policy on Education, 1968.* New Delhi: Ministry of Education, Government of India.
- Govt. of India (1990). *Report of the Committee for Review of National Policy on Education 1986.* New Delhi: Ministry of Human Resource Department, Government of India.
- Govt. of India (1998). *National Policy on Education 1986* (As modified in 1992) with National Policy on Education, 1986. New Delhi: Ministry of Human Resource Development, Department of Education, Government of India.
- Govt. of India (1966). *Report of the Education Commission, 1964-66,* New Delhi: Ministry of Education, Government of India.
- Juneja, N. (2003). *Constitutional Amendment to make Education a Fundamental Right – Issues for a Follow-Up Legislation.* New Delhi: NIEPA.
- Mani, M.N.G (2002). Integrated Education for Disabled Children: Cost Effective Approaches In Hegarty, S. and Alur,

M. (Eds.), *Education and Children with Special Needs.* New Delhi: Sage Publications.

- MHRD (2012). *The Right of Children to Free and Compulsory Education Act, 2009,* New Delhi: Ministry of Human Resource Development, Govt. of India.
- Mondal, A. and Mete, J. (2012). Right to Education – An Appraisal. *Kurukshetra.* 60 (11), pp. 11-14.
- NCERT (2006). *National Framework of Curriculum 2005.* New Delhi: National Council of Educational Research and Training.
- Mondal, A. and Mete, J. (2013). *Right to Education.* New Delhi: APH Publishing Corporation.
- Mukhopadhyay, D. (2003). Inclusion in Education: Protection of Human Rights and Sustainable Livelihood. Paper presented in National Seminar "Inclusion in Education: A Matter of Right to Education For All". University of Kalyani, West Bengal.
- Nanda, B.P. (2008). *School Without Walls in 21st Century,* New Delhi: Mittal Publication.
- Sebba, J. and Ainscow, M. (1996). International Development in Inclusive Schooling: Mapping the Issues. *Cambridge Journal of Education,* 26(1), 5-18.
- UNESCO (1990). World Conference on Education for All Meeting Basic Learning Needs, Paris: UNESCO.
- UNESCO (1994). The Salamanca Statement and Framework for Action on Special Needs Education, Paris: UNESCO.
- UNESCO (2000). Dakar Framework for Action, Education for All: Meeting our Collective Commitments, Paris: UNESCO.

Chapter - 20

Monitoring Issues of the RTE Act, 2009

The Right of Children to Free and Compulsory Education Act, 2009 (henceforth, referred to as RTE Act) passed by the Parliament of India makes education a fundamental right for all children between the ages of six and fourteen. The Act was notified on 1st April 2010 and is a landmark development in ensuring universal primary education and making it accessible as well as affordable. The RTE Act as well as the accompanying Model Rules provide a detailed framework for the inputs required in primary education and have provisions related to almost every aspect of education such as accessibility, infrastructure, curriculum, teachers, school management committees and guarantees free and compulsory primary education as a responsibility of the state government.

The RTE Act has introduced many new safeguards to ensure that every child between the ages six to fourteen has access to education. The Act guarantees free primary education in state government and local authority schools, and outlaws charging of capitation fees, corporal punishment, screening procedures for admissions and holding back or expulsion of students. The Act also provides for reservation of 25 per cent seats in private unaided schools for children belonging to the economically weaker sections (EWS) and socially discriminated sections of society. In this context, this Act for the first time has given the role of monitoring the provisions to a statutory body, the National Commission for Protection of Child Rights (NCPCR) which is independent of the implementing agency i.e. the Ministry of Human Resources Development.

The National Commission for Protection of Child Rights (NCPCR) has been assigned with the following additional responsibilities for monitoring of child's right to education under Section 31 of the Right of Children to Free and Compulsory Education Act, 2009.

(i) To examine and review the safeguards for rights provided by or under the Act and recommend measures for their effective implementation;

(ii) To inquire into complaints relating to child's right to free and compulsory education; and

(iii) To take necessary steps as provided under sections 15 and 24 of the Commissions for Protection of Child Rights (CPCR) Act, 2005.

The role of other stakeholders, apart from the NCPCR in monitoring the implementation of the Act such as State Commissions, Right to Education Protection Authorities, Local Authorities and school management committees are also covered. The Table 20.1 below mentions the various stakeholders in monitoring the RTE and where they are mentioned in the Act.

Table 20.1: Stakeholders in Monitoring the RTE Act

Stakeholders	*Mentioned in the Act*
National Commission for Protection of Child Rights (NCPCR)	Chapter VI, Section 31
State Commission for Protection of Child Rights (SCPCR)	Chapter VI, Section 31
Right to Education Protection Authority (REPA)	PART–VIII (Model Rule), Section 24
Local Authority	Chapter – III, Sections 8 and 9
School Management Committee (SMC)	Chapter–IV, Sections 21 and 22

In states that do not have an SCPCR, the state government has to assist in setting up of a Right to Education Protection Authority (REPA). The NCPCR, SCPCR and the REPA are the main instruments for monitoring the Act. However, the Act does not mention other stakeholders who will play a role in implementing the provisions of the Act. The Central Government and the State Government also have to constitute a National Advisory Council and a State Advisory Council whose function is to advise the Central Government and the State Governments respectively on implementation of the provisions of the Act in an effective manner.

National Commission for Protection of Child Rights (NCPCR)

National Commission for Protection of Child Rights has been set up under the Commissions for Protection of Child Rights Act, 2005 by the Ministry of Women and Child Development, Government of India, for protection of child rights in the country (National Commission for Protection of Child Rights, 2009). As previously mentioned the NCPCR has been assigned the primary role in monitoring of the Right to Education. Here, the Table 20.2 includes details about the structure of NCPCR and its functions and quasi-judicial authority.

Table 20.2: Structure of NCPCR

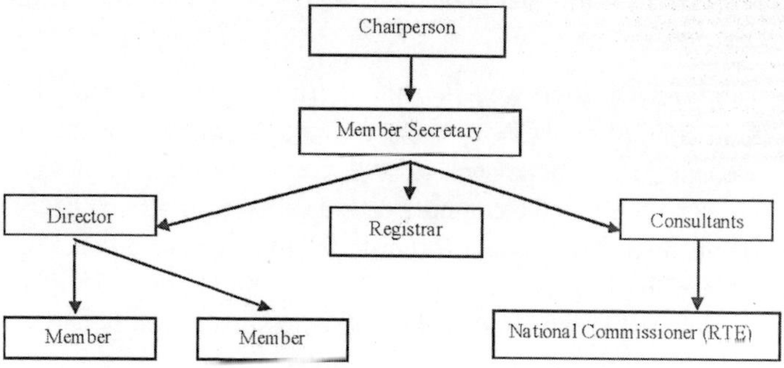

Source: National Commission for Protection of Child Rights 2009.
Note: This table only includes the relevant details for monitoring RTE.

Functions and quasi-judicial authority of NCPCR

NCPCR was established in 2005 to ensure that –

All Laws, Policies, Programmes and Administrative Mechanisms are in consonance with the Child Rights perspective as enshrined in the Constitution of India and also the UN Convention on the Rights of the Child. (National Commission for Protection of Child Rights). Currently, the commission focuses on building public awareness on issues related to the rights of children suggesting policy as well as legal measures and looking into complaints received or *suo moto* on violation of child rights. The Commission is governed by the National Commission for Protection of Child Rights (NCPCR) Act, 2005. The Commission, while enquiring into any matter, has all the powers of a Civil Court trying a suit under the Code of Civil Procedures, 1908.

Measures Taken by NCPCR with respect to Monitoring the RTE

Since the role of monitoring has been assigned to NCPCR, it has taken some measures to fulfil its responsibilities. Some of the measures taken by NCPCR include –

- Establishment of an RTE Division within NCPCR.
- Appointment of state representatives to assist NCPCR.
- Maintaining a web-based portal for registering and tracking complaints online.
- Social Audits and public hearings to be conducted at regular intervals.

The RTE Division website (http://rtemonitoringcell.info/) is an excellent attempt by NCPCR to disseminate information about RTE. The website has sections such as RTE primers, facility to initiate a petition, details about the committees and sub-groups set up under the RTE Division and discussion forum to facilitate debate and dialogue about the RTE. The website also has the facility to post RTE related information and events. It also plans to maintain a directory and send out newsletters to provide regular updates.

Besides this, there are some measures that need to be taken by NCPCR to facilitate their monitoring procedures such as publicising the role of NCPCR in the RTE Act via information campaigns and media outreach, making the RTE Division more accessible to the general public and initiating online complaint registration and follow-up mechanism. NCPCR also needs to work out modalities of interaction with MHRD at the earliest and ensure that NCPCR's autonomy is not hindered despite the financial support from MHRD.

NCPCR or SCPCR or REPA may have received complaints relating to children regarding violations ranging from denial of admission, corporal punishment and admission under freeship quota and cases of dropouts. That's why the monitoring agencies need to strengthen the monitoring mechanisms and work on specific issues such as setting up a website at the earliest to ensure that complaints can be received and tracked online and recruiting more consultants and staff for the RTE Division to deal with the large volumes of complaints. Measures also need to be taken to make the list of complaints public without disclosing the identity of the complaint to ensure accountability and transparency. Moreover, there is need to create a computerised database of complaints received and their follow-up to reduce unnecessary secretarial work and speed up processes. There is also need to publicise the role of NCPCR for RTE monitoring and build awareness about the proposed grievance redressal mechanism. It is evident that the NCPCR is doing good work to fulfil their responsibility. However, to ensure proper implementation and monitoring, the setting up of other state commissions and the Right to Education protection authorities must be accorded the highest priority.

Another issue that arises is the bringing together of the *Sarva Shiksha Abhiyan* and the RTE Act. Both RTE and SSA have the same goal in mind – ensuring access to quality education for all children. However, while SSA is implemented and monitored by the MHRD, RTE is to be implemented through SSA and monitored by NCPCR. This is a welcome step as differentiated responsibility can result in higher accountability. Going forward there is a need to ensure that the monitoring failures and successes of SSA are successfully applied to RTE.

Grievance Redressal under RTE Act

The Right of Children to Free and Compulsory Education (RTE) Act, 2009 provides for monitoring and protection of child's rights under the Act. Under Section 31, the National/State Commission(s) for the Protection of Child Rights (NCPCR/SCPCR), or Right to Education Protection Authority (REPA) in respect of a State which has not constituted the SCPCR have been empowered to (a) monitor and review the safeguards for rights provided under the RTE Act; (b) inquire into complaints relating to child's rights to free and compulsory education; and (c) take necessary steps as provide under sections 15 and 24 of the Commissions for Protection of Child Rights Act, 2005. Section 32 provides for redressal of grievances relating to rights of a child under the RTE Act by the jurisdictional local authority within a period of three months, and appeal against the decision of the local authority before the SCPCR / REPA.

Wherever the State Commissions for Protection of Child Rights have not been constituted, the Model Rules suggest the setting up the Right to Education Protection Authority (REPA) on interim basis. To-date 19 states have constituted SCPCR / REPA. These States are requested to ensure that the SCPCR / REPA have the necessary structures and staff to enable it to function effectively. The States which have not constituted SCPCR / REPA are: Andaman and Nicobar Island, Andhra Pradesh, Chandigarh, Dadra and Nagar Haveli, Daman and Diu, Jharkhand, Lakshwadweep, Manipur, Meghalaya, Nagaland, Puducherry, Tamil Nadu, Tripura, Uttar Pradesh, Uttarakhand. These States are requested to expedite the constitution of SCPCR / REPA (*Source*: Conference of State Education Ministers – Agenda Items and Background Notes, MHRD, 22 Feb. 2012).

Responsibilities of State Government

For the implementation of the provisions of Section 32 of the RTE Act, the State Governments have to notify the local authorities for the purposes of receiving grievances and formulate guidelines and procedures for the functioning of local authorities, including the mechanism for appeal before the SCPCR / REPA. In this regard, the State Government may undertake the following measures:

(i) Identify the local authority (ies), within the meaning of Section 2(h) of the RTE Act, for performing the functions envisaged in Section 32(1) and (2) of the Act.

(ii) Notify the local authority at the village, block/mandal and district level having jurisdiction in respect of the responsibilities specified for local authorities under Section 9, who would perform the functions envisaged in Section 32 (1) and (2) of the RTE Act. The Notifications should be placed in public domain and given wide publicity.

(iii) Prepare a list of legal entitlements of a child guaranteed under the RTE Act and State RTE Rules and make this information widely available.

(iv) Prescribe the manner in which grievance would be filed u/s 32(1) of the RTE Act and the manner in which the decision is to be taken by the notified local authority under Section 32(2) of the Act.

Processing Grievances / Complaints

Grievances may relate to violation of any of the provisions under the RTE Act and may be against any public office, public servant, private institution, private person or any other agency responsible directly or indirectly for the effective implementation of provisions of the RTE Act. The notified local authority shall take into consideration the following factors while developing a procedure for filing and processing of such grievances:

(i) The local authority can accept written complaint made by any person on behalf of the child. Complaints could be sent by post, fax, e-mail, or in person. The authority prescribed to address grievances at various levels will prescribe relevant formats which are simple and easy to understand, comprehend and furnish.

(ii) The notified local authority will develop a system of registration of grievances, and a receipt of registration of the grievance should be provided to the complainant instantly.

(iii) For the purpose of deciding a matter arising out of a grievance / complaint, the notified local authority may cause such verification and call for such information as it considers necessary.

(iv) The grievance should be decided by the notified local authority within three months of its filing, after affording adequate opportunity to both parties. The decision of the notified authority under section 32(2) shall be a reasoned order, and should contain the details of the Appellate Authority (SCPCR / REPA) before whom an appeal can be preferred under section 32(3) of the RTE Act.

(v) In respect of grievances relating to matters of urgency, such as denial of admission, etc. the notified local authority shall endeavour to decide the matter in a shorter time. Further, in respect of grievances relating to violation of Indian Penal Code, such as violence, child abuse, corporal punishment, etc., the notified local authority may facilitate filing of FIR before the police authorities.

(vi) In respect of a grievance registered before the notified local authority which requires to be decided by an authority other than the notified authority, such grievances be sent to that authority which is competent and empowered to decide the matter, and on receipt of such grievance, the other authority shall take steps to decide the matter expeditiously.

(vii) Every notified local authority shall maintain a record of grievances filed and decisions taken by it and submit a periodic report to the State Government.

(viii) The notified local authority shall keep aside fixed days / timings for hearing grievances and for personal meetings with aggrieved parties.

Role of SCPCR / REPA and Process of Appeal

Section 32(3) of the RTE Act provides for appeals against the decision of the notified local authority. In order to develop a transparent procedure for furnishing and disposal of appeals by the SCPCRs / REPA, the following measures should be taken by the State Government and the SCPCR / REPA. They are -

(i) The State Government shall provide adequate resource support to the SCPCR / REPA to enable it to perform its functions under the RTE Act.

(ii) The SCPCR would follow the procedures of an appellate body to hear grievances. For this purpose, the SCPCR shall prepare a Memorandum of Appeal in which appeals can be furnished before it. This Memorandum may be placed on the website of the SCPCR, the State Education Department and made available to the public by the notified local authorities.

(iii) Any person aggrieved by a decision or direction of the notified local authority may file an appeal to the State

Commission for Protection of Child Rights. The SCPCR / REPA may prescribe the time limit within which an appeal can be furnished, which can also be extended by it if it is satisfied that the appellant was prevented by sufficient cause from the filing the appeal within the prescribed period. The Memorandum can be filed by post or in person.

(iv) Upon consideration of the appeal, and after affording opportunity to both parties, the SCPCR may pass an order upholding the decision of the local authority, or modify or set aside the decision of the local authority, or make such recommendations as it deems fit in accordance with the provisions of section 15 of Commission for Protection of Child Rights Act, 2005. A copy of the order shall be sent to the applicant, the State Government and the local authority against whose decision the appeal was filed.

(v) Every order of the SCPCR / REPA shall be taken into account by the State.

Government or the local authority, as the case may be, for expeditious action, under intimation to the SCPCR / REPA.

(vi) The SCPCR / REPA shall maintain a record of all appeals filed and decided by it.

The State Government and the SCPCR / REPA may take steps put in place the grievance redressal and appellate mechanism taking into account the aforementioned guidelines.

Chapter - 21

Common School System (CSS) in the Light of the RTE Act

It is well known fact that knowledge is power and the main gateway to knowledge is education. India has the second largest education system in the world after China. Since independence India has viewed education as the best way of bringing social change. The Education Commission (1964-66) had recommended a Common School System (CSS) of public education as the basis of building up the National System of Education with a view to bring the different social classes and groups together and thus promote the emergence of an egalitarian and integrated society. For several reasons, CSS remained only a recommendation and has never turned into reality. Now education is Fundamental Right of every Indian. Under Right to Education Act (2009) it is mandatory to all children who reside in Indian Territory. The existing operational norms of the Sarva Shiksha Abhiyan (SSA) have also been revised to implement the right of children to free and compulsory education which has came into effect from 1st April 2010. In this present chapter, there is an attempt to discuss about the various aspects of common school system in the context of RTE Act (2009).

The Common School System (CCS) is a much talked system as one of the most possible solution to the social evils of Indian society. The Education Commission (1964-66) aimed at providing quality education to all children irrespective of caste, creed, sex or class. Under the ambit of the Common School System all schools act as common government funded schools where all children will have the right to good quality education. Some components of the CCS have been incorporated in other forms and context to some extent in the Right to Education Act, 2009. Now let us have a clear idea about Common School System in this regard.

Understanding Common School System

The concept of Common School System (CSS), also called a neighbourhood school, was advocated in post civil war as a 'right' and institionalised in the early 1900s. CSS may be a new concept for India, but it is not a new over the world. It has been successfully operating in Cuba, USA, UK, China and Russia. The CSS was introduced in India by the Kothari Commission constituted in 1964. The Kothari Commission dreamed of a society which will be free of all discriminations and education having the role of bringing the social change which creates a socially just and equal society for all. The Commission also mentioned the CSS is a tool for social transformation. It will weaken the disparity and inequality in Education as well as destroy all the discriminatory walls created by caste, class and socio-economic status or gender bias prevalent in our educational system. For fulfilment of this dream, the commission recommended a school system commonly known as CSS which will provide equal opportunities to all to gain quality education and equal schooling opportunities. The system recommended by the commission is not supposed to be uniform but of equitable quality such that it serves the local needs, however there will be certain uniform norms and standards of quality which needs to be fulfilled by all the schools.

Why Common School System?

The commission observed, "In a situation of the type we have in India, it is the responsibility of the educational system to bring the different social classes and groups together and this promote the emergence of an egalitarian and integrated society." The commission stated that if these evils are to be eliminated and the educational system is to become a powerful instrument of traditional development in general and social and national integration in particular, we must move towards the goal of a common school system of public education.

Characteristics of the Common School System

Some of the salient features of the Common School System recommended by the Kothari Commission are (Chand, 2007):

- It will be opened to all the children irrespective of caste, creed, community, religion, economic sanctions or social status.
- In this system access to good education will depend, not on wealth or class, but on talent.
- It will maintain adequate standards in all schools and provide at least a reasonable proportion of quality institutions.
- In this system no tuition fee will be charged.
- It would meet the needs of the average parent so that he would not ordinary feel the need to send his children to expensive school outside the system.
- Minimum level of infrastructure facilities like building, drinking water, toilet facilities, libraries etc.
- Well-trained teachers, optimum student-teacher ratio, decentralisation at the level of school management etc.
- Mother tongue as the medium of instruction at primary level.
- Each community will have a neighbourhood school which can be attended by all the children in the neighbourhood.

Kothari Commission Formulations about CSS

The concept of Common Schools can be found at a number of places in the Report of the Kothari Commission (KCR). The vision of the national system of education that incorporates Common Schools is eloquently elaborated in the well-known section 1.36 of the report, too long to produce here is in full. A summary can however be found at section 1.38: "If ……..the educational system is to become a powerful instrument of national development in general, and social and national integration in particular, we must move towards the goal of a common school system of public education.

- Which will be open to all children, irrespective of caste, community, religion, economic conditions or social status;

- Where access to good education will depend not on wealth or class but on talent;
- Which will maintain adequate standards in all schools and provide at least a reasonable proportion of quality institutions;
- In which no tuition fees will be charged ; and
- Which would meet the needs of the average parents so that he would not ordinarily feel the need to send his children to expensive schools outside the system".

The invocation of the term 'talent' instead of 'right', and the uninhibited reference to the provision of a 'reasonable proportion of quality institutions' demand particular attention. Such a provision of quality institutions in quantified further in section 10.02 "A nation-wide programme of school improvement should be organised with three objectives: (a) to raise all schools to at least to a minimum prescribed level; (b) to assist every school to rise to the highest level of which it is capable ; and (c) during the next ten years, to raise at least ten per cent of the institutions to an optimum standard".

Clearly, the KCR foresees that only a small proportion of schools ten per cent, could be raised to 'optimum standards', implying that there would exist a difference in the quality of the bulk of the schools (to be raised to a minimum prescribed level and a small proportion of quality schools, at least for a decade or more. In section 10.31, the Report clearly suggests a classification of schools into three categories, A, B and C based on their quality; something that would seem to dilute, or even negate, the concept of a common school. The differentiation of schools is however made unambiguously explicit in section 10.31 thus:

> It will not be possible for lack of resources to raise all schools to a high level within a short period. The strategy to be adopted for development should therefore be on the following lines: "Highest priority in the programme should be given to the minimum proportion of 'quality' schools at every stage which would serve as pace setting institutions....... It is necessary to concentrate available resources in a few centres for primary schools 10 per cent quality schools for secondary – one in each block".

The lack of urgency in implementing the common school system and tentativeness in the proposal asking for a pilot phase contingent on the approval of the concerned people can be found at section 10.19.

We are of the view that the neighbourhood school concept should be adopted as a long-term goal, to be reached in a well planned programme spread over two years. The strategy for its adoption should be as follows:

- During the next ten years, two programmes should be pursued side by side. The first is to improve all primary schools to a minimum level prescribed and to raise about ten per cent of them to a higher standard of quality.
- Simultaneously, the neighbourhood school system should be introduced at the lower primary stage, as a pilot project, in a few areas where public opinion is favourable to the acceptance of the proposal.

The exclusion private schools from common schooling and the national system of public education in further reiterated in the following explicit insertion in the Summary of Chapter 10 of the Report: The Common School System of Public Education would include all government schools, all local authority schools and all aided private schools. Only two types of schools will remain outside it - independent (private) schools and unrecognised schools.

No wonder that the Government of India accepted the recommendations with the following summary of this portion of the Report:

"To promote social cohesion and national integration the Common School system as recommended by the Education Commission should be adopted. Efforts should be made to improve the standard of education in general schools. All special schools like Public Schools should be required to admit students on the basis of merit and also to provide a prescribed proportion of free-studentships to prevent segregation of social classes. This will not however affect the rights of minorities under Article 30 of the Constitution."

(4b, "The Resolution issued by the Government of India on the Report of the Education Commission")

Right to Education Act, 2009

Right to Education Act (2009) is a landmark initiative of the government to strengthen the education system in India. The RTE Act (2009) came into force in the entire country from April 1, 2010. It is now legally enforceable for every child between the age of six and fourteen years to demand free and compulsory elementary education. The RTE Act is the first legislation in the world that puts the responsibility of ensuring enrollment, attendance and completion on the government. The Act makes education a fundamental right of every child between the ages of 6 and 14 and specifies minimum norms in elementary schools. The existing norms of Sarva Shiksha Abhiyan (SSA) have also been revised to implement the right children to free and compulsory education. Briefly speaking, SSA is the vehicle for implementation of RTE Act (2009). Some of the salient features of the act are:

- Free and compulsory education in a neighbourhood school till elementary education to all children of India in 6-14 age groups.
- No child shall be held back, expelled or required to pass board examination till completion of elementary education.
- A child who completes elementary education shall be awarded a certificate.
- Calls for a fixed student-teacher ratio.
- RTE Act will apply to the whole of India except Jammu and Kashmir.
- Provides for 25 per cent reservation for weaker section and disadvantaged section in admission to class 1 to in all private schools.
- Ensures good quality of elementary education.
- School teachers will need adequate professional degree within five years.
- No child shall be subjected to physical punishment or mental harassment.
- Screening procedure shall be punishable with fine. No donation and / or capitation fee.

- No teacher shall be deployed for any non-educational purposes other than Census, disaster relief duties and election duties.
- To constitute a School Management Committee consisting of the elected representatives of the local authority, parents or guardians of the children.
- No teacher shall engage himself or herself in private tuition.
- School infrastructure to be improved in the three years, else recognition cancelled.
- Financial burden will be shared between stated cultural governments.
- Child's mother tongue as medium of instruction and, comprehensive and continuous evaluation system of child's performance will be used.

CSS and RTE Act, 2009: A Comparative Study

Right to Education is considered as major step towards the implementation of a common school system first proposed by Kothari Commission (1966), where every child gets an equal right to equitable education and quality schooling. We may now compare some of the key provisions of the Right to Education Act with the recommendations of the Kothari Commission Report regarding common school system to arrive at somewhat national conclusions regarding the supposed derivations of the Act from the Report.

As recommended by the Kothari Commission, the RTE Act also states that it will ensure that good quality elementary education is available to all the children in their respective neighbourhood schools. Like the Kothari Commission Report, the RTE Act recognises four categories of schools – governmental (either under departments of education or local authorities, private but aided by the government, private unaided, and special category schools of the government – the Kendriya, Navodaya etc. (called 'quality' schools in the KCR).

The Act asks for the establishment of a neighbourhood government school within three years from the time of enactment of the Act; for free education to every 6 to 14 years old in the entire country. The Kothari Commission Report recommended experimenting with it in a few places, with the consent of the local people.

The RTE Act obliges aided-private schools to admit children for free admission proportional to the aid they receive, the minimum being 25 per cent. This means if a school receives 70 per cent of its funds from the government, it will have to admit 70 per cent children from its neighbourhood for free education, and will receive no further grants for these children from the state. As for private schools, minority schools and special category schools, instead of scholarships and freeships from government funds to meritorious students, the Bill obliges the schools to admit 25 per cent children from the neighbourhood from disadvantaged sections, without assessing their merit or submitting them to admission tests; with the provision that the school shall be reimbursed for this proportion of children by the state at the states per child cost, or the school cost, whichever is less.

Unlike the KCR, the RTE Act does not exclude the independent, minority and special category schools but brings them into the ambit of neighbourhood schools, at a proportionate responsibility; completely doing away with the mention of 'merit', 'talent' scholarships, freeships and the consequent screening procedures. Regarding the overall improvement of quality, the KCR mentions 'the first is to improve all primary schools to a minimum level prescribed.' The Act through a mandatory infrastructural and Pupil-Teacher Ratio Schedule prescribes the minimum standards without which no school, government-aided or private shall be allowed to operate.

Looking at some of the salient features of the RTE Act, one feels that common school system has been rather delayed than focused in the Act. It is now imperative to overcome the feasible hurdles in the implementation of the RTE. Though the CSS has been well recognised decades ago that CSS is an essential step for attaining equality, social justice and social change but no concrete and effective steps have been taken for its implementation. Even its inclusion in policies has been more name sake kind than for real purpose of implementation. The CSS has remained only a recommendation and has never turned into reality. Like the CSS, the RTE Act may meet the same fate if concurrent responsibilities of the central and the state governments are not in full swing for implementation. It is very necessary to involve the Panchayati Raj Institution in rural area for implementing RTE Act, 2009.

Chapter - 22

Disadvantaged Groups and Weaker Sections under the RTE Act

Among the 67 million children who are currently not enrolled in school worldwide, 26 million of them live in the Asia-Pacific Region (UNICEF-EAPRO, 'School for Asia' Bangkok, 2012). There are 81,50,619 children in the age group of 6–14 out of school in India (RTE Act: First Anniversary Status Report, MHRD, 2011) and many of them are children belonging to disadvantaged groups and weaker sections and children with disabilities. In the last decade, the Sarva Shiksha Abhiyan has played a key role providing elementary education to all children without discrimination. However, inclusion of all children in the periphery of education still remains an exclusive goal. The Right to Free and Compulsory Education Act, 2009 tries to safeguard the rights of the children belonging to the disadvantaged groups and the weaker sections, protect them from any kind of discrimination and ensure their completion of elementary education.

Disadvantaged Group under the RTE Act: According to the RTE Act, "child belonging to disadvantaged group" means a child belonging to the Scheduled Caste, the Scheduled Tribe, the socially and educationally backward class or such other group having disadvantage owing to social, cultural, economical, geographical, linguistic, gender or such other factor, as may be specified by the appropriate Government by notification". By the Amendment (2010) to the RTE Act, 2009 children with disabilities have been incorporated in the definition of 'child belonging to disadvantaged group' in clause (d) of section 2 of the RTE Act.

Weaker Section under the RTE Act: "A child belonging to weaker section means a child belonging to such parent or guardian whose annual income is lower than the minimum limit specified by the appropriate government, by notification". For example, in West Bengal, the Kolkata Gazette published on February 21, 2011 clarifies that "a child shall be deemed to belong to a weaker section, if either parent of the child has been duly recorded as a person belonging to Below Poverty Line (BPL) family as per the list prepared by the appropriate local authority owing to his or her lower income".

Need for Categorising the "Disadvantaged Group" and "Weaker Section": While 'education for all' is still to be achieved, the under-privileged groups have been considerably subjected to exclusion from educational institutions. Some of the problems faced by the children of these groups are given below:

- Segregated seating arrangements.
- Making derogatory remarks about the communities, names and cultural practices.
- Lack of understanding of the diverse background, mainly in case of children belonging to the Scheduled Tribe Category.
- Tribal population being chiefly concentrated in remote areas, access to school becomes difficult.
- Language barrier, especially in case of tribal children.
- Children serving as child labour, domestic help or suffering from extreme economic deprivation do not get the appropriate learning situation.
- Civil strife often prevents children from attending schools.

Keeping in mind all these and many more problems faced by the children of the "disadvantaged group" and the "weaker section", the RTE attempts to ensure that all these children get the optimum opportunity to enrol in schools, acquire and complete elementary education. Thus, while it is the duty of the parents to send their children to schools, the RTE Act explicates that "compulsory education" is an "obligation of the appropriate Government" to ensure compulsory admission, attendance and completion of elementary education by every child of the age of six to fourteen years". Moreover, the government has to "ensure that the child belonging to weaker section and the child belonging to disadvantaged group are not discriminated against and prevented from pursuing and completing elementary education on any grounds". In this way, the RTE Act tries to solve all the problems faced by the under-privileged children.

Another pioneering step mentioned in this Act is that Clause 12(1) (c) mandates for private unaided and specified category schools to admit in class I, to the extent of at least twenty five per cent of the strength of that class, children belonging to weaker section and disadvantaged group in the neighbourhood and provide free ad compulsory elementary education till its completion. For this category of students the state government shall reimburse schools an amount equal to either the fees charged by the school or the per child expenditure in state schools, whichever is lower. The constitutional validity of this clause was challenged in the apex court of the country. In a recent Supreme Court of India's verdict dated, 13 April, 2012, a bench comprising Chief Justice S. H. Kapadia, Justice K. S. Radhakrishan and Swantanter Kumar, upheld the constitutional validity of the section 12. The bench said that 25 per cent reservation for students, from 'weaker and disadvantaged sections' of society would apply uniformly to all government and unaided private schools except unaided private minority schools and boarding schools. The decision has wiped away many apprehensions regarding the future of the Act. It has been welcomed by academicians, politicians, journalists and others.

Popularising RTE-SSA among the Children of Disadvantaged and Weaker Sections

Some pragmatic steps are stated in promoting education among the children of disadvantaged and weaker sections:

Introduction of Tribal Dialects and Medium of Instruction: In tribal areas, having a large population where people do not understand the regional language, tribal dialects may be introduced as the medium of instruction wherever possible in the initial stages and then they should be integrated with the general educational system and may be taught regional languages. But in the tribal areas where the children understand the regional language, it can be used as medium of instruction. Such practice will reduce the rate of wastage and stagnation and also create interest among the children.

Suitable Curriculum for the Schools: There is a need for evolving a suitable curriculum for the schools functioning in tribal or minority areas. This curriculum may be science-oriented but culture-based. The curriculum should include the various aspects of life and culture of the tribal or minority communities.

Encouragement of Participation of the Parents of the Marginalised Children: Participation of parents of the children belonging to disadvantaged and weaker sections in the educational programmes may also be encouraged. The awareness and interest regarding the utility of education for the children should be created among the parents.

Flexibility in Schools Hours: In the tribal and minority areas, the school hours and the duration will have to be adjusted according to the needs of the community.

Incentives for Students: The children of disadvantaged and weaker sections should be provided with various incentives like tuition free education, free books, free stationery, free uniform, free mid-day meals and scholarships.

Facilities for Teachers: It may be made obligatory for teachers to stay in the vicinity of the school as far as possible. As an incentive, payment of backward area accommodation allowance to teachers who live within the vicinity of the school may be considered.

Remedial Instruction: Students coming from Scheduled Castes and Scheduled Tribes are also likely to be deficient in the scholastic areas. The school may provide some remedial education programmes. Adoption of instructional strategies, such as peer group learning, monitoring assistance, diagnostic testing and tutoring would help to improve the educational levels of these learners.

Profile of Teacher's Role in Implementing RTE-SSA among Disadvantaged and Weaker Sections

Following are the important points which a teacher should take into account while teaching the students belonging to disadvantaged and weaker sections:

- The teacher should take interest in meeting the needs of every type of child.
- The teacher should ensure that his own behaviour and behaviour of students is free from bias.
- The teacher should understand the learning process in the context of characteristics of learners.
- The learner should be given importance as an individual rather than as a disabled or as a scheduled caste or scheduled tribe or a girl or a Muslim or a Christian.
- A teacher should be sensitive to the needs of socially disadvantaged learners.
- The teacher should have a close link with parents to ensure regular attendance.
- The teacher should make the parents aware of the special educational and other facilities in the school and the neighbourhood and impress upon them to make use of them.
- The teacher's own example in his behaviour towards students belonging to these castes is the most effective and powerful way to build up a congenial climate.
- The school staff should ensure non-discrimination between the children of Scheduled Castes, Scheduled Tribes, socially and educationally backward class and weaker sections.
- The school staff should avoid the use of the caste names or derogatory words while calling roll calls or naming children.
- Frequent meetings between the staff, school teachers and parents of disadvantaged groups and weaker section children should be arranged. The details of the schemes for promoting education amongst such students should be explained to the parents at these meetings. It should be impressed upon them that they must continue the education of their children.

Chapter - 23

The RTE Act, 2009 : Anomalies and Challenges

Although enforcement of this right had a very symbolic and historic value, because it was a step ahead in the more than one and half a century long struggle for universalising the elementary education, yet the intellectuals in general and the educationists in particular criticised various provisions made under the Act. There are some loopholes which pose daunting challenges for effective implementation. These are discussed below :

This Act entitles every targeted child the right to free and compulsory education. The appropriate governments shall also make necessary arrangement for providing free pre-school education to child or ward above the age of three years. Thus, the Act specifically mentions the age of three years to fourteen years in the definition of children. The RTE Act should have extended the benefit of free and compulsory education to children upto the age of 18 years as the United Nations Convention on Rights of the Children (UNCRC) defines any individual below 18 years of age as a child, when India is a signatory to that convention (Jakhar, 2010).

The RTE Act provides for free and compulsory education only upto class – VIII. There is no reference in the Act at all either to secondary education or to the children in the relevant age group of 14–18 (Sadgopal, 2011). The Act is unconcerned thoroughly about the most important formative years in the child's upbringing. It denies to children the right to secondary education (class IX–XII) because this right is restricted to elementary education only (Gosai, 2009).

The RTE Act, 2009 puts the imposition of an age bar which excludes the age groups of 0-6 and 14-18 years from the guarantee of right to education provided by the Constitution under Article 21-A which was introduced by the Constitution (Eighty Sixth) Amendment Act, 2002. Often, rescued child labourers are of the twilight age of 12-15, as a result of which they are excluded from the purview of the public education system, leading to the creation of another generation of educationally and economically deprived individuals, which further perpetuates the necessity for the existence of child labour. However, this Act is more exclusionary in its approach and introduces an age bracket of 6 -14 years in identifying the beneficiaries of this right.

The ban in section 13 on charging capitation fees is a smoke screen (Sadgopal, 2011). According to Section 2(b), "Capitation fee" means any kind of donation or contribution or payment other than the fee notified by the school. The definition of capitation fee indeed permits the private schools to charge capitation fee as long as it is included in the fee being notified at the time of admission.

Section 12 is perhaps the most retrogressive provision in the Act. It fixes 25 per cent compullsory enrollment for children belonging to weaker sections and disadvantaged groups in the private schools. The Act provides only for reimbursement of tuition fees of poor children enrolled in private schools but not other fees (e.g. art and craft, sport, excursion etc.), which are levied by most private schools (Gosai, 2009). Unjustifiably, this burden may be passed on to the rest of their pupils. This Act indicates that private schools shall be free to raise fees for the 75 per cent of the fee-paying students and under-pay the teachers since the Act has no provision to regulate fees / salaries.

The Act does not provide for the exclusion of teachers from population census, elections and disaster relief duties. Moreover, there is no provision in the Act for decent salaries, professional development, promotional avenues and social security for teachers (Gosai, 2009).

The Act prohibits not only corporal punishment but also mental harassment of pupils. But mental harassment is left without a clear definition. This ambiguous part of prohibitory provision may be misused against teachers by parents or school managements.

The RTE Act is quite silent on the rights of children with disability. It does not facilitate the education for children with disability since as per the Persons with Disability Act, 1995, 26(a), the appropriate governments and the local authorities shall "Ensure that every child with a disability has access to free education in an appropriate environmental till he attains the age of eighteen years" and not just up to 14 years as provided under the RTE Act.

The coverage of school system under RTE by ignoring the identity of religions and minority community also attracts the criticism (Jakhar, 2010). This Act encourages implementation of its provisions through Public-Private Partnership, which therefore would lead to privitisation and commercialisation of education.

After getting admission to the age-appropriate class a learner is entitled to get special training to be cognitively at par with his peers. But how? The solution is a bureaucratic clause: "...in such manner, and with such time-limit, as may be prescribed" (Section 4). Learning gap of several years cannot be alleviated in regular teaching-learning procedure. Additional teachers are required beyond 30 : 1 ratio. Besides, learners admitted in this way will be kept in the school even when they would cross 14. Psychosomatic difference between the learners of 14 years old and those of 17 or 18 years old shall create disciplinary problem, especially in the co-educational school.

Disciplinary action will be taken against heads of the institutions, if issuance of transfer certificate is delayed but there is no direction to harness a well-to-do parent if he wants to remove his ward without paying the dues.

To execute the Act, Central Government will make a profile of expenditure and give some aids after discussion with the respective state government. If political philosophy of the two does not conform, may it cast any negative impact upon the aid? Directive authority will be in the hand of central government but the onus of comprehensive infrastructural development has to be shouldered by the state governments. In the name of involvement of "Panchayati Raj" institutions, as envisaged by NCF-2005, local authority has been empowered even in framing of academic calendar but no minimum academic standard of the members of the school management committee (SMC) has been defined. It is alarming when number of teacher representative in SMC has been reduced next to nothing leaving no room for non-teaching staff representative in the same.

It is a strange irony that while on the one hand the government wants to provide quality education to all children, across all barriers, on the other hand it recognises four kinds of schools under the Right to Education Act. With such a variety of schools, it is only natural that quality of education varies. Once again it boils down to the rich being able to afford better quality education and the poor having to compromise with something inferior.

The RTE Act overlooks guarantee of dignified salaries, professional development, promotional avenues and social security for teachers and prevention of fragmentation of teacher's cadre.

The Act and the Rules require all private schools (whether aided or not) to reserve at least 25 per cent of their seats for economically weaker and socially disadvantaged sections in the entry level class. These students will not pay tuition fees. Private schools will receive reimbursements from the government calculated on the basis of per-child expenditure in government schools. Greater clarity for successful implementation is needed on:

- How will 'weaker and disadvantaged sections' be defined and verified?
- How will the government select these students for entry level class?
- Would the admission lottery be conducted by neighbourhood or by entire village / town / city? How would the supply-demand gaps in each neighbourhood be addressed?
- What will be the mechanism for reimbursement to private schools?
- What would happen if some of these students need to change school in higher classes?

- There may be more than one private school in a neighbourhood, so how will they decide who will go where?

The RTE Act, 2009 clause, 12(1)(c) mandates for private schools to admit quarter of their class strength from weaker section and disadvantaged groups. The constitutional validity of this clause was challenged in the apex court of the country. However, on 12 April, 2012, a bench of Chief Justice S. H. Kapadia, Justice K. S. Radhakrishnan and Swatanter Kumar upheld the constitutional validity of the Act. The judgment makes it mandatory for the government, local authorities and private schools to reserve 25 per cent of their seats for 'weaker and disadvantaged sections' of society. The decision has wiped away many apprehensions regarding the future of the Act. It has been welcomed by academicians, politicians, journalists and others. The Union Minister for human resources development Mr Kapil Sibal, articulated, "RTE can be a model for the world". While there has been enthusiastic praise of the judgment, concerns related to quality, finance, ensuring of 25 per cent reservation in private schools and change in classroom structure cannot be thrown into the winds.

The amount put aside by Finance Minister Pranab Mukherjee, for the RTE-SSA Programme is only Rs 25,555 crores for 2012–13, which falls short of the recommended financial requirement of Rs 1.82 lakh crore. From where will the rest of amount come?

The 25 per cent reservation in private schools will dramatically change the structure of classrooms in schools. Whether diversity of classroom will create democratic learning environment and enhance teaching learning process or will it put children from 'weaker and disadvantaged sections' in discomfited position?

Reacting to the 25 per cent reservation Kumar (2012) penned down "most ambitious among its objectives is the social engineering it proposes by guaranteeing at least 25 per cent share of enrollment in unaided fee-charging schools to children whose parents cannot afford the fee". Both Krishna Kumar and Kapil Sibal did not give in-depth critical insight to the provision. The questions like, what will be the mechanism of selection process of 25 per cent children from 'weaker and disadvantaged sections'. Some private schools are very reputed and provide very high quality of education and some are either at part with government schools or little ahead. There is a hierarchy of private schools which are stratified in quality education. Who will go where what will be the criteria for that? Furthermore Indian society is patriarchal in nature; boys are even served good food in comparison to girls how one can expect parents or guardians will send a girl child to these private schools. The reservation benefits will go to a particular gender of society. This will further reinforce and reproduce gender bias and social inequality in society. Thus, RTE itself creates a vacuum for 'reproduction of culture". Ahmad (2009) underlines, parents prefer schooling for their girl child but prefer government schools for them in comparison to a male child.

Moreover, school education cannot be separated from its social context, those who teach and learn carry with them attitudes, beliefs, habits, customs, orientations which differ from class to class. The elite schools have their own culture which suits to children of upper class. The teaching-learning environment at these schools suits children of upper class while children from weaker sections may find themselves alienated from the schools. There are also concerns whether those enrolled in private schools will cope and adjust with education system and culture of elite schools.

The right to education act guarantees education of "equitable quality" to children in schools but this guarantee has no meaning unless the term "equitable quality" is defined (Nehru and Raghupathi, 2008).

That the children once admitted cannot be held back in class or expelled might result into unhealthy practices among children or their parents who would like to take protection under the provision.

Government has already shown its inability to provide adequate funds of 2,31,233 crores as it does not have sufficient resources and is keen to involve private sector in the name of Public Private Partnership (PPP) which will be diluting the rights-based concept of elementary education. The RTE Act does not include its regularity mechanism to private unaided schools.

The child rights under the RTE Act will be monitored through National Commission for Protection of Child Rights (NCPCR) and SCPCR or REPA. NCPCR / SCPCR fall under the Ministry of Women and Child Development whereas the RTE Act 2009 is a matter of Ministry of Human Resource Development. The NCPCR / SCPCR are set for taking care of children. This body does not have pedagogical expertise to deal with educational matters. We fail to understand how this body will be redressing the grievances of children and teachers without pedagogical expertise.

According to the Act, the Central Government and the State Governments would make available the funds and administrative machinery for the implementation of various provisions of the Act. But, the Centre cannot prescribe a uniform formula for all the States regarding financing aspect of the Act. Since many States are not in a comfortable position financially and administratively. This has been accepted even by the Government of India in its approach paper to 12th Five Year Plan (GOI, 2011: 96).

Further, the Act did not address the issue of Vagrant Street Children and the child labourers. India harbours the world's largest child workforce despite the Child Labour (Prohibition and Regulation) Act, 1986 in force. In addition, there are huge numbers of vagrant street children who leave their homes to find escape from unhappy family. Thus, the Right to Education Act is of no use for the child labourers and vagrant street children unless it addresses their problems. (Gosai, 2009: 6). Just stating about the prohibition of child labour is not enough.

In spite of inclusion of the disabled children in the category of 'disadvantaged group' through an amendment as an afterthought, there is hardly any provision in the schedule of norms and standards, except for barrier-free access in the case of locomotor disability, to ensure that the rest of the disabled children would be able to study in a regular school (Sadgopal, 2010: 41).

There are many other loopholes which are pressing and challenging in the way of RTE. Quality education, funding, teacher skills, harmonisation of rules and provisions in place in different states with the RTE Act, 2009 and enhancement of reservation policy are some major concerns. We can only conclude that various lacunae and problems of implementation of this Act should be addressed well in time otherwise the target of Universalisation of Elementary Education (UEE) in India would remain a distant reality.

Chapter - 24

Recommendations on Implementation Issues

For implementation of the Right to Education and for education to be a meaningful right it must be available, accessible, acceptable and adaptable. There could be no right to education without corresponding obligations for governments. The basic framework of governmental obligations is outlined through a series of explicit guarantees of the right to education in international human rights treaties, national constitutions and domestic laws. These obligations are structured into the 4-As Scheme, as sketched in Box 24.1: governments have to make education available, accessible, acceptable and adaptable. The concept of 4-As Scheme was developed by the former UN Special Rapporteur on the Right to Education, Katarina Tomasevski.

The 4-As are to be respected, protected and fulfilled by the government, as the prime duty-bearer, but there are also duties on other actors in the education process: the child as the privileged subject of the right to education and the bearer of the duty to comply with compulsory-education requirements; the child's parents who are the 'first educators'; and professional educators, namely, teachers. Tomasevski (1999) carved governmental obligations into the 4-As scheme establishing parameters for the analysis of the implementation of the right to education. The 4-As relate to availability, accessibility, acceptability and adaptability. They refer to obligations which should be undertaken by the government in order to fulfil its commitments.

Availability is the first component of the right to education in Tomasevski's (1999) framework. It relates to the possibility of education being obtained by all without any discrimination. It refers to existence of educational institutions within reasonable distance for pupils' attendance. It refers to security within the educational system, as well as to making entry into the educational system available to all regardless of age or social condition. As far as infrastructure for schooling is concerned, it requires active employment of resources from the nation-states that can be a constraint to the realisation of rights but, as Tomasevski (1999: 18) highlights, others actors, like private investors, can assist on the realisation of this aspect of the right to education. In terms of ideological freedom, the availability of the right to education aims to assure that no indoctrination occurs in the educational system. There is no discrimination for the entry into the schooling system due to cultural characteristics.

However, even if all those aspects of the right to education are assured in practice, the right to education would not be complete. It requires other components to make it holistic to all. Therefore, white availability of education refers to the existence of the schooling system; accessibility refers to the possibility of entering it and remaining in it.

Accessibility means governments must strive for the practical elimination of gender and racial discrimination and ensure the equal enjoyment of all human rights, and must not be satisfied with merely formally prohibiting discrimination. In addition, accessibility relates to the primary, secondary and tertiary levels of education in different ways; governments are only obliged to provide access to free and compulsory education for all children in the compulsory age range. The right to education should be realised progressively, ensuring all encompassing, free and compulsory education for all children in the compulsory age range. The right to education should be realised progressively, ensuring all encompassing, free and compulsory education is available as soon as possible, and facilitating access to post-compulsory education as circumstances permit (Tomasevski, 2004). Accessibility also relates to gender and racial discrimination, complementing the cultural and ethnic discrimination variable described in availability. Measures for preventing such discrimination should be in place to insure that all have access to the educational system. The degree to which accessibility of education should be made available, however, changes as the schooling cycle progresses. Special importance is given to primary education in all of the international legislation concerning the right to education. All treaties establish that primary education shall be compulsory and available free to all.

Acceptability requires minimum guarantees regarding the quality of education, for example, in terms of health and safety or professional requirements for teachers, but it is much wider in scope than this. These guarantees have to be set, monitored and enforced by the government throughout the education system, whether the institutions are public or private. Acceptability has been considerably broadened through the development of international human rights law: indigenous and minority rights have prioritised the language of instruction, while the prohibition of corporal punishment has transformed methods of instruction and school discipline. The emerging perception of children as subjects with the right *to* education and with rights *in* education has further extended the boundaries of acceptability to include the contents of educational curricula and textbooks, which are increasingly considered from the perspective of human rights (Tomasevski, 2004).

Acceptability is one of the very important themes that guide discussions regarding the right to education for the people that might have education available and accessible but with poor quality which does not lead to the desired outcomes. It involves curricula setting and respect for parent's views on the education of their children, the language of education and the culture of education, for example. As Tomasevski says, there are very few guidelines given by international treaties and national legislations on this matter. In theory, however, international organisations such as UNESCO should be available to assist states in the formulation of technical expertise to develop a coherent curriculum which would enable students to learn skills to match the goals of education. It would also be part of the same groups of institutions to assist countries on the formulation of indicators to measure the quality of the educational system.

Another aspect of acceptable education lies in the bridge between the educational system and the labour market. Achieving an acceptable level of quality education also demands that attention be paid to the opportunities school-leavers can expect to enjoy when finishing education and entering the job market. One important aspect of this involves close participation between education and the labour sectors, and this is another example of how education must develop a balanced, mutual relationship with all other areas of society to maximise its effectiveness (Tomasevski, 2004). Making education acceptable also means attending to other actors, such as teachers and parents for instance, who become plaintiffs of better educational policies as well as demand for collective rights. The International Labour Organisation (ILO) conventions have been instrumental in assuring this aspect of the right to education as they handle issues such as the right of teacher to organise for better working conditions, training and salaries. Concern regarding discrimination also figures within ILO rulings.

Adaptability requires that schools respond to the needs of each individual child, in keeping with the Convention on the Rights of the Child. This reverses the traditional approach in which schools expected the children to adapt to whatever form of education the school provided. As human rights do not exist in isolation, adaptability involves safeguarding all human rights *within* education as well as enhancing human rights *through* education. This necessitates cross-sectoral analysis of the impact of education on the whole range of human rights, to monitor, for example, graduate employment by ensuring integrated planning between the relevant sectors (Tomasevski, 2004).

However, none of the above aspects of the right to education would be complete without the adaptability of education to the best interest of each student. The ideal that education only regards children permeates the literature regarding this aspect of the right to education but adaptability should concern every student, regardless of age, sex, ethnic origin or whichever other circumstances. The characteristic of adaptability directly deals with methods of teaching and with "[m]aking education responsive to the immediate reality facing children in their own community" (Tomasevski, 1999:23). Participation becomes a valuable resource in this context as it enables the children to voice their experiences and demand for responsiveness of the schooling institutions towards their individual education process.

Box 24.1: 4-As Scheme : Governmental Obligations for Implementation of RTE

Availability	Schools	• Establishment / closure of schools. • Freedom to establish schools • Funding for public schools • Public funding for private schools
	Teachers	• Criteria for recruitment • Fitness for teaching • Labour rights • Trade union freedoms • Professional responsibilities • Academic freedom
Accessibility	Compulsory	• All-encompassing • Free-of-charge • Assured attendance • Parental freedom of choice
	Post-Compulsory	• Discriminatory denials of access • Preferential access • Criteria for admission • Recognition of foreign diplomas
Acceptability	Regulation and Supervision	• Minimum standards • Respect of diversity • Language of instruction • Orientation and contents • School discipline • Rights of learners
Adaptability	Special needs Out-of-school Education	• Children with disabilities • Working children • Refugee children • Children deprived of their liberty

Source: Cited from K. Tomasevski, 2001, Right to Education Primers No. 3, p. 14.

RTE Act is a historic move and a major achievement by Indian government. But the Act will serve its purpose only if the hurdles that keep away from the school are removed.

Other Useful Suggestions for Effective Implementation

- Seminars and workshops should be organised for building awareness of all the stakeholders of education about the RTE Act, 2009.
- The RTE Act, 2009 puts the imposition of an age bar which excludes the age groups of 0-6 and 14-18 years from the guarantee of right to education provided by the Constitution

under Article 21-A which was introduced by the Constitution (Eighty Sixth) Amendment Act, 2002. Often, rescued child labourers are of the twilight age of 12- 15, as a result of which they are excluded from the purview of the public education system, leading to the creation of another generation of educationally and economically deprived individuals, which further perpetuates the necessity for the existence of child labour. However, this Act is more exclusionary in its approach and introduces an age bracket of 6 -14 years in identifying the beneficiaries of this right. In order to effectively tackle child labour, the age-restrictive approach towards education must be replaced by one which is more inclusive, thereby enabling effective rehabilitation and empowering the victims of child labour.

- Parents, teachers, professionals, social workers and NGOs should assist the government for the successful implementation of this Act.
- The academicians and people belonging to educational fraternity have an immense role to play through :
- Creating awareness about the Act and its benefits as well as hurdles.
- Helping the governments at various levels in developing curriculum as well as training teachers for elementary sector.
- Conducting research and providing inputs to the governments / relevant authorities about the effectiveness of the Act at the ground level.
- It is necessary to involve the Panchayati Raj Institutions (PRIs) in rural areas for implementing the RTE Act.
- According to Jakhar (2010), teachers need to have at their disposal a deep fund of empathy, commitment, conviction and ability and motivation to preserve; of knowledge and resources to respond and create meaningful educational experiences for all children.
- There should be provision to provide scholarships to those students who will get admission in private schools under 25 per cent reserved seats, as all state governments have in

government schools students under various scholarship schemes.

- Particularly in the rural and poor areas, people's representatives – MPs, MLAs, and Ministers – should be made responsible for smooth functioning of the schools in their areas. Local relevant NGOs and other organisations may also be involved. They can provide support through the School Management Committees.
- The quality of teachers is the backbone of any teaching programme. Untrained or unmotivated teachers can mar any programme, no matter how ambitious it is. That is why creating a standard training programme to train and generate quality teachers is crucial for the RTE Act to produce meaningful results.
- Create mobile units that pay visits to different schooling centres, particularly in remote areas. This will help sustain interest and arouse curiosity. Even visiting once in a fortnight or month would serve the purpose.
- The responsibility of bringing children to schools and providing them quality education is the work of the child rights commissions in each state, which are under the Women and Child Development Department. It is crucial therefore that the efforts of all these agencies should be coordinated for the larger goal of providing education to all children to become a reality.
- Each state should prepare a set of model rules for implementation of the right to education, with the participation of the community and other stakeholders.
- Although the RTE Act puts the application age-group at 6–14, it has been left to the states to decide whether they want to widen this group, say 0–16 as Kerala has done. States should think about including more children under the Act's ambit.
- With the Act coming into effect, it has been found that there is a shortage of 12–13 lakh teachers in schools. The states must take steps to employ more teachers and not rely on para-teachers to provide children with quality education.

- The government should ensure that all government schools are well-equipped to take in students, so that they are not left with the sole choice of going to private schools.
- School management committees should take it upon themselves to spread awareness about the Act at the community level, in panchayats, so that people are encouraged to send their children to school.
- School management committees should be provided the necessary financial and other support by the state to go about their duties.
- For effective implementation of the RTE Act, states should give some sort of judicial power to the education department.
- The public private partnership (PPP) model in primary education should be avoided at all costs so that there is no commercialisation of education.
- There is a conflict between the child labour law and the Right to Education Act, although both deal with related issues and promote the overall development of children. It is important to bring them in step, to avoid confusion.
- To effectively implement the RTE Act, the Human Resource Development Ministry, Labour Ministry, Women and Child Development Ministry, Panchayati Raj Ministry and Rural Development Ministry have to work together. There should be an umbrella body that brings all these agencies to work towards a common goal.
- The government must make every effort to become self-sufficient case and other taxes to effectively implement the RTE Act, it must not always beg from the private sector.
- In villages the Panchayat members can play role in promoting education. The village committee should not be an ad hoc project arrangement and should be permanent.
- There should be a teacher and parent interaction because a frequent parent and teacher interaction will enhance student enrollment and attendance rate.
- The incentives like books, uniforms etc. available to the students must be made at the beginning of session.

- The quality of MDM needs to be improved, which will attract children of the weaker sections of the society.
- Village monitoring committees must be formulated so that they will monitor the enrollment and student absenteeism.
- More Acts like Mahatma Gandhi National Rural Employment Guarantee Act should be started because only those parents who employed think about not to employ their children in any labour work.
- The goal of 100 per cent female education can be achieved by creating community awareness for girls education at all levels.
- Improvement in the infrastructure like availability of water, sanitation and toilets in schools should be done on priority basis.
- Proper training for teachers and staff should be provided.
    - six per cent of GDP or 20 per cent of government expenditure should be provisioned for education, and half of this public spending on education needs to be targeted towards elementary education.
    - To ensure quality of education, regular and trained teachers should be recruited in place of untrained and para-teachers. Para-teachers recruited so far should be trained and regularised.
    - The existing laws for protection of child rights should be enforced suitably and implemented strictly for total eradication of the menace of child labour, child servitude and child trafficking, and all the children of age group 0–18 years are enrolled in schools.
    - Provisions should be made in the said legislation for quality education system with measurable indicators so that parents and community can monitor the quality of education.
    - All efforts should be geared to ensure the common schooling system for all the children irrespective of their parent's socio-economic status.

- All forms of privatisations including the Public-Private Partnership or franchise to corporate bodies that leads to profiteering, commoditisation and weakening the public education system should be dropped.
- Article 24 mandates that prohibition of employment of children in factories, etc. —No child below the age of fourteen years shall be employed to work in any factory or mine or engaged in any other hazardous employment. An examination of the Constituent Assembly Debates Article 45 reveals that fourteen was set as the upper age limit for compulsory education in order to bring it in agreement with the minimum age for employment as laid down in Article 24. In order to effectively tackle child labour, the age-restrictive approach towards education must be replaced by one which is more inclusive, thereby enabling effective rehabilitation and empowering the victims of child labour.

Finally, how far the Act succeeds in creating an inclusive society in the long-run will be the acid test of its effective implementation. Free and compulsory elementary education for all children in the age group of 6 – 14 at long last has become a 'so called' legal reality with the implementation of Right of Children to Free and Compulsory Education Act, 2009 being made enforceable from April, 2010. What could have been easily done 60 years ago with massive support from a newly liberated and brand new Constitution has been enacted without implementing the Common School System. Moreover, big claims were made while implementing the Act, but even after two years of its implementation the Act, but even after two years of its implementation we have not started receiving the desired results in the area of elementary education. If the government really wishes to achieve the goal of Universalisation of Elementary Education, Right to Education must be provided to all the children through a common school system as recommended by Education Commission (1964–66) and committed by Government of India in NPE (1968), NPE (1986) and NPE (1992). Education being a concurrent subject, Centre and States will have to collaborate to implement the Act in its true spirit. It is further suggested that the HRD ministry should constitute a high-level group comprising members from the government: centre, states and key stakeholders from the society to act towards addressing the various lacunae and arrive at an implementable programme. A statutory body should monitor the progress of the implementation of the Act continuously. Furthermore, we also need a national awareness campaign to drive home the nuances of this law, whose provisions resonate with the aspirations of the poorest. The Centre shall also evolve an actionable scheme for nationwide advocacy of the Act: A message must go out that we want to implement the Act in its true spirit. The last person in the street must know what the law provides. Thus, at this stage, we can only conclude that various lacunae and problems of implementation of this Act should be addressed well in time otherwise the target of Universalisation of Elementary Education (UEE) in India would remain a distant reality.

Bibliography

Journals

- Acharya, P. (1994). Problems of Universal Elementary Education. *Economic and Political Weekly.* 29(49): 3098-3105.
- B. G. Tilak, Jandhyala (6 July 2010). RTE Act 2009 — illusory promises. Retrieved from http://educationworldonline.net/index.php/page-article-choice-more-id-2288
- Bharambe, V.S. and Sharma, S.D.(2013). Education for All: Issues, Challenges and Opportunities. *Educationia Confab*, 2(4), 214-116.
- Bordoloi, R. (2011). Challenges in Elementary Education in India: Various Approaches. *Journal of Education and Practice*, 2(7), 39-45.
- Chaudhary, L. (2009). Determinants of Primary Schooling in British India. *Journal of Economic History*, 69(1), 269-302.
- Chowdhury, R. (2010). "The Road Less Travelled": Article 21a and the Fundamental Right to Primary Education in India, *INJlConLaw 2; (2010) 4 Indian Journal of Constitutional Law 24,* pp. 24-46. Retrieved fromhttp://www.commonlii.org/in/journals/INJlConLaw/2010/2.html.
- Desai, F. P. (2010). Tagore's Educational Experiments and Right to Education Bill: A Comparison, *Rupkatha Journal on Interdisciplinary Studies in Humanities*, 2(2): 628-640.
- Devan, K. (2011). Development of the Right to Education in India. *Indian Journal of Adult Education*, 72(2), 93-98.
- Dinda, M. (2010). Literacy: Is It A Human Right? *Anwesa*, Vol. 5, 120-127.
- Gandhi, V. and Yadav, N. (2013). A Study of Awareness among Primary School Teacher's Towards "Right to Education Act, 2009", *Shodh, Samiksha Aur Mulyankan*, IV(48):48-49.
- Garg, P.K. (2013). Fundamental Right of Children to Free and Compulsory Education – Its Implementation and Future Strategies. *International Journal of Basic and Advanced Science,* 2(1), 4-7.

- Ghosh, J. (2011). Public Spending on Education in India, *Frontline* 28(24), 10-12.
- Godbole, M. (2001). Elementary Education as a Fundamental Right – The Issues. *Economic and Political Weekly*, XXXVI(50).
- Gosai, M.R. (2009). The Recent Right to Education and Present State of Primary Education. *University News*, 47(47), 1-6.
- Islam, N. and Chakraborty (2013). A Study on the Awareness of Equitable Quality in the Light of RTE Act' 09 among In-Service School Teachers, *Indian Journal of Applied Research*, 3(6):142-143.
- Jain, P.S. and Dholakia, R.H. (2009). Feasibility of Implementation of Right to Education Act. *Economic and Political Weekly,* XLIV (25), 38-43.
- Jain, P.S. and Dholakia, R.H. (2010). Right to Education Act and Public-Private Partnership. *Economic and Political Weekly,* XLV (8), 78-80.
- Jakhar, J. S. (2010). Right to Education Act, 2009: Salient Features of Major Problems of Implementation. *University News*, 48(47), 06-12.
- Jha, P. and Parvati, P. (2010). Right to Education Act 2009: Critical Gaps and Challenges, *Economic and Political Weekly,* XLV (13), 20-23.
- Juneja, N. (1997). Right of the child to Education and Issues in Implementation of Compulsory Education: Perceptions of Educational Administrators. *New Frontiers in Education*, 27(1), 1-12.
- Kamalakar, G. and Bhojanna, N. (2012). Reservation in Private Schools under the Right to Education Act: Model for Implementation. *International Journal of Management Research and Review,* 2(6), 958-966.
- Kamath, A.K.V.D. (2013). Awareness on Right to Education Act – 2009 among Elementary School Teachers, *Indian Journal of Education Experimentation and Innovation,* 3(5).
- Karande, K. and Gogtay, N. J.(2010). Specific Learning Disability and the Right to Education 2009 Act: Call for Action. *J Postgrad Med*, 56(3), 171-172.
- Kaur, B. (2013). The Right to Children to Free and Compulsory Education Act. *Educationia Confab*, 2(4), 177-181.
- Kaur, R. (2013). Universalisation of Elementary Education in India: The Policy Perspective. *Educationia Confab*, 2(4), 205-213.
- Kothari, V.N. 2004. Challenges of Universalisation of elementary education in India, *Journal of Education Planning and Administration* XVIII (3) 363-378.

- Kumar, J. (2012). Right to Education: Its Problems and Suggestions. *Educationia Confab*, 1(2), 14-19.
- Kumar, N. (2007). British rule and problems of the present education system. *Ghadar Jari Hari.* 1(2): 30-32.
- Kumar, R. Ravi (2012). Primary Educational System in Rural India. A Sociological View. *Indian Journal of Innovations and Developments*, 1(10), 430-432.
- Kurhade, M.S. (2011). Education for All: But When? *University News*, 49(04), 6-8.
- Meenakshi, C. (2012). Universalisation of Education: A Challenging Issue. *Research Journal of Social and Life Science*, 12 – 1 (Year 06), 236-243.
- Mehrotra, S. 2006. Reforming Elementary Education in India. A Menu of options. *International Journal of Educational Development* 26(3).
- Mohanty, T. (2011). Constitutional Provisions and Amendments on Fundamental Duties, Right to Education Act and on Secularism. *Orissa Review*, LXVII (6), 39-41.
- Mondal, A. and Mete, J. (2011). Common School System in the light of Right to Education Act, 2009. *Edusearch*, 2(2), 45-55.
- Mondal, A. and Mete, J. (2011). Education for Minorities and SC / ST in the Context of SSA. *Educational Herald*, 14(14), 14-22.
- Mondal, A. and Mete, J. (2012). Right to Education – An Appraisal. *Kurukshetra*. 60(11). 11-14.
- Nawani, D. (2013). Corporal Punishment in Schools. *Economic and Political Weekly,* XLVII (24), 23-26.
- Nehru, A. and Raghupathi, H. (2008). Massive Funding of Right to Education Bill, *Education World,* October, pp. 76-79.
- Paur, S.S. (2012). Right to Education Act: A Critical Analysis. *International Journal of Educational and Psychological Research*, 1(2), 27-30.
- Ramachandran, V. (2009). Right to Education Act: A Comment. *Economic and Political Weekly,* XLIV (28), 155-157.
- Rana, K.M. (2013). Education for All – Challenges and Opportunities. *Educationia Confab*, 2(4), 241-247.
- Rani, N. (2012). Mid-Day Meals Scheme: Achieving Right to Education and Right to Food Simultaneously. *e – Reflection,* I(III), 122-130.
- Rathee, Indu and Rana, S.S. (2012). Education as Human Right: Provisions and Implementation. *Journal of Educational and Psychological Research*, 2(2), 124-129.

- S Ojha, Seema (2013). Implementing Right to Education: Issues and Challenges. *Research Journal Educational Sciences*, 1(2), 1-7.
- Sadgopal, A. (2003). Education for too few. *Frontline*, Vol. 20, Issue 24, November 22 - December 05.
- Sadgopal, A. (2010). Right to Education vs. Right to Education Act. *Social Scientist*, Vol. 38, No. 9-12 September–December 2010, pp. 17-50.
- Sadgopal, A. (2011). Neoliberal Act. *Frontline*, 28(14), 04-09.
- Sarkar, B. (2011). Education – A Basic Human Right: An Analysis in Indian Perspective, *Indian Journal of Human Rights Studies*, 1 (Jan. – Feb. 2011):1-10.
- Savagaon, G. (2012). Elementary Education and Inclusive Development in India. *Abhinav*, 1 (6), 16-23.
- Sharma, H. I. (2013). Universalisation of Elementary Education under Sarva Shiksha Abhiyan in Manipur. *Voice of Research*. L (4): 14-17.
- Sharma, M. K. and Jain, J.L. (2013). Qualitative Education for All: Challenges and Strategies. *Educationia Confab*, 2(4), 187-195.
- Sharma, R. and Saini, R. (2012). Implementation of RTE Act, 2009 in Rural India. *Research Analysis and Evaluation*, III (29), 60-62.
- Sharma, S. and Kumawat, S. R.(2013). Inclusive Education in Right To Education Act 2009. *Research Analysis and Evaluation*, IV (42), 103-104.
- Shukla, P.D. 2000. Non Enforcement of Compulsion in Education in India. *Journal of Indian Education* XXVI (1).
- Siddiqui, S. (2008). Universalisation of Elementary Education in India. *Journal of Educational Research*. 11(1): 4-12.
- Singh, J. (2012). Right to Education: An Assessment. *Indian Streams Research Journal*. 1(XIII), 60-62.
- Singh, R. (2012). Development of Right to Education in India: A Historical Appraisal. *University News*, 50 (30), 16-25.
- Singh, V. P. (2013). The Right of Children to Free and Compulsory Education Act, 2009: An Exploratory Study. *Journal of Indian Research*, 1(1), 118-135.
- Sonia (2012). The Right to Education Act: An Overview. *Indian Stream Research Journal*, 2(11), 1-6.
- Sunita, M. (2010). Teachers Literacy towards the Child Rights. *Edusearch- Journal of Educational Research*: 1(2).

- Tarafdar, M. (2007). Universalisation of Education: A Study in the Indian Context. *Our Education – Journal of Educational Ideas and Research*, Volume-8, pp. 61-62.
- Teltumbde, A. (2012). A Symbolic Gesture, *Economic and Political Weekly*, XLVII (19).
- Thote, P., Mathew, L. and S Rathoure, D.P. (2013). Right to Education Act: An Analysis of Teachers Awareness in Central India. *International Journal of Advanced Research*, I (3), 184-187.
- Tilak, Jandhyala B. G. (2012). Right to Homeschooling vs Right to Education. *Economic and Political Weekly*, XLVII (41).
- Uma (2013). Right to Education (RTE): A Critical Appraisal. *IOSR Journal of Humanities and Social Science,* 6(4), 55-60.
- Usmani, M. (2012). Right To Education Act 2009: A Dream in the Sunlight or A Divine. *International Journal of Research in Social Sciences and Humanities*, 1(VI), 1-11.
- Vithalrao, M. S. (2011). Child Rights as a Part of Human Rights – A Comparative Study, *International Education E-Journal (Quarterly)*.1(1):13-17.
- Yadav, Raj Kumar (2012). Right To Education in India: A Study. Accessed from http:// ssrn.com/abstract = 2014933 on 12.06.2013.

Books

- Aggarwal, D. D. (2002). *History and Development of Elementary Education in India.* New Delhi: Sarup & Sons.
- Aggarwal, J. C. (2008). *Development and Planning of Modern Education.* New Delhi: Vikas Publishing House Pvt. Ltd.
- Aggarwl, J. C. and Gupta, S. (2010). *Right to Education and Revitalizing Education.* New Delhi: Shipra Publication.
- Aradhya, N. and Kashyap, A. (2006). *The 'Fundamentals' – Right to Education in India*. Bangalore: Books for Change.
- B. C. Rai (1997). *History of Education in India and Problems.* Lucknow: Prakashan Kendra.
- Babu, J. R. (2009). *Universalisation of Elementary Education: A Study of District Primary Education Programme from South India.* UK: Cambridge Scholars Publishing.
- Baneerjee, J.P. (1985). *Education in India – Past Present, Future*, Kolkata: Central Library.
- Bapat, S. and Karandikar, S. (1998). Rural Context of Primary Education Searching for the Roots. In Saraswati, Baidyanath (1998). *The Cultural Dimension of Education.* New Delhi: Indira Gandhi National Centre for the Arts.

- Basu, A. (1982). *Essays in the History of Indian Education*. New Delhi: Concept Publishing Company.
- Basu, A.N. (1941). (Ed.). *Adam's Reports of the State of Education in Bengal and Bihar*. Calcutta: University of Calcutta Press.
- Basu, B. B. (1994). *Human Rights in Constitutional Law*. New Delhi: Prentice Hall of India Pvt. Ltd.
- Basu, B.D. (1935). *History of Education in India under Rule of East India Company*. Calcutta: The Modern Review Office.
- Bhattacharya, S. (2000). *National Education Movement – Analysis of the Role of Bengali Intelligentsia and its Impact on Indian Education*. Ph. D. Thesis (Unpublished), Department of Education, University of Kalyani.
- Biswas, A. and Agarwal, S. P. (1994). *Development of Education in India – A Historical Survey of Educational Documents before and after Independence*. New Delhi: Concept Publishing Company.
- Biswas, A. and Agrwal, S.P. (1986). *Development of Education in India -A historical Survey of Educational Documents Before and After Independence*. New Delhi: Concept Publishing House.
- Chand, J. (2007). *Education in India during British Period*. New Delhi: Anshah Publishing House.
- Chatterjee, S. (2010). Inaugural Address. In Habib, S. Irfan (Ed.). *Maulana Abul Kalam Azad and the National Education System*. New Delhi: NUEPA.
- Chauhan, C.P.S. (2004). *Modern Indian Education - Policies, Progress and Problems.* New Delhi: Kanishka Publishers, Distributors.
- Deogirikar, T. R. (1992). *Gopal Krishna Gokhale*, New Delhi: Ministry of Information and Broadcasting, Government of India.
- Desai, D. M. (1993). *Universal Compulsory and Free Primary Education in India.* Bombay: Indian Institution of Education.
- Ghosh, S.C. (1989). *Education Policy in India since Warren Hastings*. Calcutta: Naya Prokash.
- Ghosh, S.C. (2013). *The History of Education in Modern India, 1757-2012*. New Delhi: Orient Black Swan Private Limited.
- Gopalan, K. (1998). Indian Strategies to Achieve Universalisation of Elementary Education. In Saraswati, Baidyanath (1998). *The Cultural Dimension of Education.* New Delhi: Indira Gandhi National Centre for the Arts.
- Grover, B.L. and Mehta, Alka (2014). *A New Look at Modern India History*. New Delhi: S. Chand Publishing.

- Gupta, S. (2009). *What are the different strategies and approaches to realize Right to Education (RTE) in India?* Institute of Development Studies (IDS), University of Sussex.
- Hayre, S.K. (1966). *The Development of Elementary Education in India.* Manhattan, Kansas: School of Education, Kanasas State University.
- Hodgson, D. (1998). *The Human Right to Education.* Aldershot: Dart-mouth Publishing Company Limited.
- Howell, Arthur (1872). *Education in British India Prior to 1854 and in 1870-71.* Calcutta: Superintendent of Government Printing.
- Jayapalan, N. (2000). *History of Education in India.* New Delhi: Atlantic Publishers and Distributors.
- Juneja, N. (2003). *Constitutional Amendment to make Education a Fundamental Right – Issues for a Follow-Up Legislation.* New Delhi: NIEPA.
- Kochhar, S. K. (1982). *Pivotal Issues in Indian Education.* New Delhi: Sterling Publishers Private Limited.
- Lall, M. (2005). *The Challenges for India's Education System.* London: Chatham House, the Royal Institute of International Affairs, Retrieved on 12.09.2013 from http://marielall.com/wp/wp-content/uploads/Chatham-house-indiaeducation.pdf
- Latika C. (2007). *An Economic History of Education in Colonial India*, Hoover Institution. April 28, 2007 Retrieved on 10.03. 2014 fromhttp://economics.ucr.edu/seminars_colloquia/2007/political_economy_development/LatikaChaudhary5-6-07.pdf
- Latika C. (2007). *Determinants of Primary Schooling in British India*, Hoover Institution, August 2, 2007. Retrieved on 23.04.2013 fromhttp://eml.berkeley.edu/~webfac/cromer/e211_f07/chaudhary.pdf
- Mayhew, Arthur (1928). *The History of India.* London: Faber and Gwyer Limited.
- Misra, B.D. (1089). *A History of the Secondary Education in Uttar Pradesh 1843-1900.* Delhi: Anamika Prakashan.
- Mohanty, S. B. (1985). *Universalisation of Elementary Education in India: Lessons of Experience and Pointers for Action*, New Delhi: New Delhi Publication.
- Mukerji, S. N. (1974). *History of education in India.* Baroda, India: Acharya Book Depot.
- Mukherji, S. N. (1964). *Education in India – Today and Tomorrow.* Baroda: Acharya Book Depot.

- Naik, J. P. (1942). *History of the Local Fund Cess (Appropriated to Education) in the Province of Bombay*. Bombay: The Local Self-Government Institute.
- Naik, J. P. (1942). *Studies in Primary Education*, First Series. Bombay: The Local Self-Government Institute (Bombay Presidency).
- Naik, J. P. (1965). Elementary *Education in India – The Unfinished Business*. Bombay: Asia Publishing House.
- Naik, J. P. (1975). *Elementary Education in India – A Promise to Keep*. Bombay: Allied Publishers.
- Naik, J. P. (1978). Educational Reform in India: A Historical Review. Bombay: Orient Longman Limited.
- Naik, J.P. (1943). *A Review of Modern Education in India (1813-1942)*. Tilak College of Education, Poona: The Aryabhushan Press.
- Nanda, N. (1998). The School System in India - A critique In Saraswati, Baidyanath (1998). *The Cultural Dimension of Education*. New Delhi: Indira Gandhi National Centre for the Arts.
- Narulla, S. and Naik, J.P. (1943). History of Education in India. Bombay: Macmillan.
- Natesan, G. A. (1916). *Speeches of Gopal Krishna Gokhale*. Second Edition. Madras: G. A. Natesan & Co.
- Niranjanaradhya, V. P. and Kashyap, A. (2006). *The Fundamentals of the Fundamental Right to Education in India*. Bangalore: Books for Change.
- Niranjanaradhya, V. P. (2004). *Universalisation of School Education — the Road Ahead*. Bangalore: Books for Change.
- Nurullah, S. and Naik, J. P. (1964). *A Students' History of Education in India*. London: Macmillan and Company Limited.
- Nururllah, S. and Naik, J. P. (1943). *History of Education in India during the British Period*. New York: The MacMillan Company.
- Pathania, A. and Pathania, K. (2006). *Primary Education and Mid-Day Meal Scheme – Results, Challenges and Recommendations*. New Delhi: Deep and Deep Publications Private Limited.
- Planning Commission, GOI. (2008). *Eleventh Five Year Plan (2007-2012), Social Sector, Volume II*. New Delhi: Oxford University Press.
- Purkait, B. R. (1992). *Milestones in Modern Indian Education*. Kolkata: New Central Book Agency.
- R. P. Paranjpye (1915). *Gopal Krishna Gokhal*. Reprinted from Fergusson College Magazine, Poona. Published by Natesh Appaji Dravid, the Aryabhushan Press.

- Rai, Vinay and Kumar, Narendra (2010). *Right to Education: The Way Forward*. New Delhi: Perfect Publications.
- Raina, V. (2010). *Education and Knowledge in the Time of Globalisation Inclusion, Quality and Agency*. B.M. PUGH Fourth Memorial Lecture, 2010, NERIE, NCERT, Shillong.
- Raina, V. (2010). *Education and Knowledge in the Time of Globalisation Inclusion, Quality and Agency*. Shillong: B. M. PUGH Fourth Memorial Lecture, 2010, NERIE, NCERT. Retrieved from http://nerie.nic.in/pdf/txtVinod-Raina-during-IVth-BM-Pugh.pdf. on 10.4.2013.
- Raina, V. (2010). Maulana Azad and Right to Education. In Habib, S. Infan (2010). *Maulana Abul Kalam Azad and the National Education System*. New Delhi: NUEPA.
- Rajkhowa, S. C. (1964). Towards Universal Elementary Education (1921-61). In NCERT (Eds.), *The Indian Year Book of Education 1964 Second Year Book Elementary Education* (pp. 21-40). New Delhi: NCERT.
- Ramachandran, P. and Ramkumar, V. (2005). *Education in India*. New Delhi: National Book Trust.
- Ramana, M.V. (2012). *Right to Education – the Parameters and the Paradoxes*. Unpublished Ph.D. Thesis. Guntur: P.G. Department of Legal Studues and Research, Acharya Nargarjuna University.
- *Rani, S.* (2012). *An Objective Based Evaluation of Rehbar-E-Taleem Scheme in Kashmir Division* (Unpublished Doctoral Thesis). University of Kashmir, Faculty of Education, Srinaga, Kashmir.
- Rao, D.B. (Ed.) (2011). *Right to Education*. Hyderabad: Neelkamal Publications Pvt. Ltd.
- Rastogi, K.G. and Sharma, H.L. (1981). *Universalisation of Elementary Education Brochure – V*, New Delhi; NCERT.
- Saiyidian, K. G., Naik, J. P. and Husain, S. A. (1966). *Compulsory Education in India*. Delhi: Universal.
- Sen, J. M. (1925). *Primary Education Acts in India – A Study*. Calcutta: Calcutta Young Men's Christian Association (CYMCA).
- Sen, J. M. (2010). *History of Elementary Education in India*. New Delhi: Pacific Publication.
- Sharma, M. C. (Ed.).(2013). *Right to Education: Imperative for Progress*. New Delhi: Universal Law Publishing Co.
- Sharma, N. (2011). *Universalisation of Elementary Education among Tea-Tribe of Assam with special reference to Jorhat District. Assam: Assam State Commission for Protection of Child Right Guwahati.*

Retrieved on 12.04.2012 fromhttp://righttoeducation.in/sites/default/files/elementary_education_research.pdf

- Sharma, R.N. and Sharma, S.K. (2012). *History of Education in India*, New Delhi: Atlantic Publishers & Distributors (P) Ltd.
- Shiva Kumar, A. K. and Rustagi, Preet (2010). *Elementary Education in India: Progress, Setbacks and Challenges.* New Delhi: Oxfam India.
- Thakur, A.S. and Berwal, S. (2008). *Development of Education System in India (A Source Book for Teacher Educators and Teachers-in-Training).* New Delhi: Shipra Publications.
- The Servants of India Society (1917). *A Brief Account of the Work of the Servants of India Society, Poona (from June 1905 to December 1916).* Poona: The Aryabhushan Press.
- Thomas, F. W. (1891). *The History and Prospects of British Education in India.* Cambridge: Deighton Bell and Co.
- Tomasevshki, Katerina (2003). *Education Denied: Costs and Remedies.* New York: Zed Books Ltd.
- Tomasevski, K. (2001). *Right to Education Primers No. 3.* Stockholm: Swedish International Development Corporation Agency.
- Trevenlyan, C. E. (1838). *On the Education of the People of India.* London: Longman, Orme, Brown, Green, & Longmans.
- UNESCO (1984). *Towards Universalisation of Primary Education in Asia and the Pacific Country Studies India.* UNESCO Regional Office for Education in Asia and the Pacific: Bangkok.
- Weiner, Myron (1991). *The Child and the State in India; Child Labour and Education Policy in Comparative Perspective.* Princeton, NJ: Princeton University Press.
- Yadav, S.K. (2011).*National Study on Ten Year School Curriculum Implementation.* New Delhi: Department of Teacher Education and Extension, National Council of Educational Research and Training (NCERT).

Reports and Documents

- CABE (2005). *Report of the Central Advisory Board of Education (CABE) Committee on Free and Compulsory Education Bill And Other Issues Related to Elementary Education (Right to Education Bill 2005).* New Delhi: CABE, GOI.
- Government of Bihar (2007). *Report of the Bihar Common School System Commission.* Patna: Common School System Commission, Govt. of Bihar.

- Government of Bombay (1859). *Report of the Director of Public Instruction, Bombay, for the Year 1857-58*. Bombay: The Education Society's Press.
- Government of India (1868). *Adam's Reports on Vernacular Education in Bengal and Behar with a Brief View of its Past and Present Condition by Rev. J. Long.* Calcutta: The Home Secretariat Press.
- Government of India (1881). *Education Commission Bombay Vol. II Evidence taken before The Bombay Provincial Committee, and Memorials addressed to The Education Commission.* Calcutta: The Superintendent of Government Printing, India. Government of India.
- Government of India (1883). *Report of the Indian Education Commission, 1882.* Calcutta: Superintendent of Government Printing India.
- Government of India (1915). *Indian Educational Policy, 1913.* Calcutta: Superintendent Government Printing, India.
- Government of India (1929). *Indian Statutory Commission. Interim Report of the Indian Statutory Commission. (Review of Growth of Education in British India by the Auxiliary Committee appointed by the Commission).* Calcutta: Government of India.
- Government of India (1929). *Review of the Growth of Education in British India by the Auxiliary Committee of the Indian Statutory Commission*, Delhi: the Manager Government of India Press.
- Government of India (1947). *Post-War Educational Development in India, Report by the Central Advisory Board of Education, January 1944.* Delhi: The Manager of Publications, Government of India.
- Government of India (1948). *Committee on the Ways And Means of Financing Education Development in India, 1948*, Delhi: Manager of Publications, 1950, Bureau of Education, Pamphlet No. 64.
- Government of India (1948). *Education in Free India (August 1947 – August 1948).* New Delhi: The Ministry of Education, Government of India.
- Government of India (1948). *Education in Free India (August 1947 – August 1948).* New Delhi: The Ministry of Education, Government of India.
- Government of India (1950). *Committee on the Ways and Means of Financing Education Development in India, 1948.* Delhi: Pamphlet No. 64, Manager of Publications, Bureau of Education.
- Government of India (1965). *Education in Eighteen Years of Freedom.* New Delhi: Ministry of Education, Government of India

- Government of India (1966). *Education and National Development: Report of the Education Commission 1964 - 66*, New Delhi: Ministry Of Education, Govt. of India.
- Government of India (1974). *National Policy for Children*. New Delhi: Department of Social Welfare, Government of India.

- Government of India (1974). *National Policy for Children*. New Delhi: Department of Social Welfare, Government of India.

- Government of India (1979). *Draft National Policy on Education*, 1979. New Delhi: Ministry of Education and Social Welfare, GOI.

- Government of India (1979). *Draft National Policy on Education*, 1979. New Delhi: Ministry of Education and Social Welfare, GOI.

- Government of India (1985). *Challenge of Education – A Policy Perspective*. New Delhi: Ministry of Education, Government of India.
- Government of India (1986). *National Policy on Education*, New Delhi: Department of Education, Govt. of India.
- Government of India (1993). Report of National Development Council Committee on Literacy, Planning Commission 1993. New Delhi: MHRD. Retrieved on 12.09.2012 from http://www.teindia.nic.in/mhrd/50yrsedu/y/3P/45/toc.htm
- Government of India (1998). *Report of the Steering Committee for Formulation of Ninth Plan (1997-2002) on Early Childhood Education Elementary Education (Formal) Non – Formal Education Secondary Education Vocational Education Distance Education Adult Education*. New Delhi: Education Division, Planning Commission, Government of India.
- Government of India (1999). *Expert Group on Financial Requirements for Making Elementary Education A Fundamental Right, (Chairman: Prof. Tapas Majumdar)*. New Delhi; Ministry of Human Resources Development, Government of India.
- Government of India (1999). *Expert Group Report on Financial Requirements for Making Elementary Education a Fundamental Right (also known as Tapas Majumdar Committee Report of 1999)*.New Delhi: Department of Education Ministry of Human Resource Development, GOI.
- Government of India (2000). Report on a Policy Framework for Reforms in Education. New Delhi: Prime Minister's Council on Trade and Industry, Government of India.
- Government of India (2002). *Report of the National Commission to Review the Working of the Constitution*. New Delhi: Ministry of Law, Justice and Company Affairs, Department of Legal Affairs, GOI.

- Government of India (2004). *National Common Minimum Programme of the Government of India May 2004.* New Delhi: GOI. Retrieved from http://architexturez.net/system/files/pdf/cmp_0.pdf
- Government of India (2005). *Government of the United Progressive Alliance Report to People - 1, Implementation of National Common Minimum Programme and Other Initiatives May 2004 – February 2005. New Delhi: GOI.*
- Government of India (2005). *Report of the Committee of CABE on "Universalisation of Secondary Education.* New Delhi: Ministry of Human Resource Development, Government of India.
- Government of India (2005a). *Report of the CABE Committee on Free and Compulsory Education Bill and Other Issues Related to Elementary Education*, June 2005. Available at www.education.nic.
- Government of India (2005b). *Report of Committee on National Common Minimum Programmes Commitment of Six Per cent of GDP to Education, (Chairman: Prof. Tapas Majumdar).* New Delhi: National Institute of Educational Planning and Administration. Available at www.niepa.org.
- Government of India (2006). *Report on the Social, Economic and Educational Status of the Muslim Community of India.* New Delhi: Ministry of Minority Affairs, Government of India.
- Government of India (2006). *Report on the Social, Economic and Educational Status of the Muslim Community of India.* New Delhi: Ministry of Minority Affairs, Government of India.
- Government of India (2007). *National Knowledge Commission – Recommendations on School Education.* New Delhi: National Knowledge Commission, Government of India.
- Government of India (2008). *Department – Related Parliamentary Standing Committee on HRD: Two Hundred Thirteenth Report on the Right to Free and Compulsory Education Bill, 2008.* New Delhi: Parliament of India, Rajya Sabha Secretariat.
- Government of India (2010). *Prime Minister's Address to the Nation on Fundamental Right of Children to Elementary Education* New Delhi: Prime Minister's Office, Press Information Bureau, Government of India.
- Law Commission of India (1998). *One Hundred Sixty Fifth Report on Free and Compulsory Education for Children.* New Delhi: Law Commission of India.
- Law Commission of India (1998). *One Hundred Sixty Fifth Report on Free and Compulsory Education for Children.* New Delhi: Law Commission of India.

- MHRD (1997). *Convention on the Rights of the Child – Country Report, 1997.* New Delhi: Department of Women and Child Department, MHRD. Retrieved from http://wcd.nic.in/crcfebmr.htm
- MHRD (1997). Report of the Committee of State Education Ministers on Implications of the Proposal to Make Elementary Education a Fundamental Right, (chairman: Muhi Ram Saikia), Ministry of Human Resource Development, Department of Education, New Delhi.
- MHRD (1998). *National Policy on Education 1986 (as modified in 1992)*. New Delhi: Department of Education, Ministry of Human Resource Development, GOI.
- MHRD (2003). *Education for All – National Plan of Action*. New Delhi: Department of Elementary Education and Literacy, MHRD. GOI.
- MHRD (2005). *Annual Report 2004-05*. New Delhi: Department of School Education and Literacy, Department of Higher Education, Ministry of Human Resource Development (MHRD), Government of India.
- MHRD (2005). *Annual Report 2004-05*. New Delhi: Department of School Education and Literacy, Department of Higher Education, Ministry of Human Resource Development (MHRD), Government of India.
- MHRD (2009). *Fifty Fifth Meeting of the Central Advisory Board of Education Agenda Items & Background Notes*, Dated Tuesday, The 10th February, 2009. New Delhi: Ministry of Human Resource Development, Government of India.
- MHRD (2009). *Fifty Fifth Meeting of the Central Advisory Board of Education Agenda Items & Background Notes*, Dated Tuesday, The 10th February, 2009. New Delhi: Ministry of Human Resource Development, Government of India.
- MHRD (2009). *The Right of the Children to Free and Compulsory Education Act, 2009*. New Delhi: Department of Elementary Education and Literacy, MHRD, Government of India.
- MHRD (2011). *Framework of Implementation Based on the Right of Children to Free and Compulsory Act, 2009*. New Delhi: Department of School Education and Literacy, MHRD, Govt. of India.
- MHRD (2012). *Conference of State Education Ministers – Agenda Items and Background Notes.* New Delhi: MHRD, Govt. of India.
- MHRD (2012). *The 2nd Year – The Right of Children to Free and Compulsory Education Act, 2009.* New Delhi: Department of School Education and Literacy, MHRD, Govt. of India.

- MHRD. (2005). *Report of the Central Advisory Board of Education (CABE) Committee on Free and Compulsory Education Bill and Other Issues Related to Elementary Education, June 2005*. New Delhi: MHRD, GOI.
- NCERT (1970). *Education and National Development Report of the Education Commission, 1964-66 (Reprinted)*. New Delhi: National Council of Educational Research and Training.
- Planning Commission, GOI. (2008). *Eleventh Five Year Plan (2007-2012), Social Sector, Volume II*. New Delhi: Oxford University Press.
- Rajya Sabha Secretariat (2009). *213th Report of the Department – Related Parliamentary Standing Committee on Human Resource Development on the Right of Children to Free and Compulsory Education Bill, 2008*. New Delhi: Rajya Sabha, Parliament of India.
- Sharp, H. and Richey, J.A. (eds.) 1920. *Selections from Educational Records*. Vol. I, Calcutta: Superintendent of Government Printing.
- Sharp, H. (1914). *Progress of Education in India 1907-1912. Volume 1*. Calcutta: Superintendent of Government Printing, India.
- Sharp, H. (1920) (Ed.). *Selections from Educational Records, Part I (1781-1839)*. Calcutta: Bureau of Education, Superintendent Government Printing, 1920. (Reprint) Delhi: National Archives of India, 1965.
- UNESCO (1984). *Towards Universalisation of Primary Education in Asia and the Pacific Country Studies India*. UNESCO Regional Office for Education in Asia and the Pacific: Bangkok.
- University of Delhi (1997). *Convention on Education as a Fundamental Right, Golden Jubilee Celebrations*, Delhi: Central Institute of Education, Department of Education, University of Delhi.

Newspapers

- Bhaumik, P.K. and Banik, A. (2006, April 8). Making the education cess work, The Economic Times. Retrieved from http://articles.economictimes.indiatimes.com/2006-04-08/news/27454253_1_education-cess-duties-and-service-tax-elementary-education
- Malani, Gaurav (2004, Sep 23). Fund for education cess gets finance ministry nod. The Economic Times. Retrieved from http://articles.economictimes.indiatimes.com/2004-09-23/news/27370798_1_education-cess-mid-day-meal-scheme-elementary-education
- Seetharamu, A.S. (2002, February 9). Fundamental Right Status for Education: Opportunity or eyewash? Retrieved from http://www.deccanherald.com.

Websites

(1) http://righttoeducation.in
(2) http://www.isrj.net
(3) http://mhrd.gov.in
(4) http://www.jamiajournal.com
(5) http://www.teacherplus.org
(6) http://www.booksforchange.net
(7) http://www.educationforallindia.com
(8) http://www.right_to_education.org
(9) http://www.unmid.com
(10) http://educationworldonline.net
(11) http://indiacode.nic.in
(12) http://socialissuesindia.worldpress.com
(13) http://indiabudget.nic.in
(14) http://lawmin.nic.in
(15) http://www.education.nic.in
(16) http://nuepa.org.in
(17) http://www.ncte_india.org
(18) http://ncert.nic.in
(19) http://www.azimpremjifoundation.org
(20) http://www.rteindia.com
(21) http://india.gov.in
(22) http://parisar.worldpress.com
(23) http://schoolofeducators.com
(24) http://www.censusindia.gov.in
(25) http://www.indg.org
(26) http://www.un.org
(27) http://undp.org
(28) http://ssa.nic.in
(29) http://asercentre.org
(30) http://rtemonitorcell.info

Primary Sources

(1) National Library of India, Kolkata,
(2) Digital Repository of West Bengal Public Library Network,
(3) Digital Library of Gokhale Institute of Politics and Economics (Pune),

(4) Digital Library of India at Osmania University, Hyderabad,

(5) Shodhganga@INFLIBNET Centre,

(6) Digital Archives of Education Documents (NUEPA),

(7) West Bengal State Archives, Kolkata,

(8) Indira Gandhi National Centre for the Arts (IGNCA),

(9) Archaeological Survey of India, New Delhi,

(10) Digital Library of India hosted by: IISC, Bangalore.

Appendixes

- The Constitution (Eighty – Sixth Amendment) Act, 2002, The Gazette of India, Ministry of Law and Justice, GOI, New Delhi.
- Notification dated 16th February, 2010 enforcement of regarding Constitution (Eighty-Sixth Amendment) Act, 2002 and Right of Children to Free and Compulsory Education Act, 2009, The Gazette of India, MHRD, GOI, New Delhi.
- The Right of Children to Free and Compulsory Education (Amendment) Act, 2012, The Gazette of India, Ministry of Law and Justice, GOI, New Delhi.
- The 4th Year of the RTE Act, 2009 – Status Report, MHRD, New Delhi, 2014.

Index

D

T

U

V

W